Experiments With People

D0860927

This book showcases 28 intriguing social psychological experiments that have significantly advanced our understanding of human social thinking and behavior. Each chapter focuses on the details and implications of a single study, while citing related research and real-life examples along the way. All the chapters are fully self-contained, allowing them to be read in any order without loss of coherence. This second edition contains a number of new studies and, together with its lively, conversational tone, it makes an ideal text for courses in social psychology, introductory psychology, or research design.

Kurt P. Frey is Adjunct Professor of Psychology at the College of New Rochelle, having received his Ph.D. in Social/Personality Psychology at Purdue University in 1993. He has had an extensive teaching career, in addition to publishing articles in scholarly journals.

Aiden P. Gregg is Associate Professor of Psychology at the University of Southampton, having received his Ph.D. in Psychology from Yale University in 2000. He has published extensively in scholarly journals.

Experiments With People

Revelations From Social Psychology

Second Edition

Kurt P. Frey and Aiden P. Gregg

NEW YORK AND LONDON

Second edition published 2018
by Routledge
711 Third Avenue, New York, NY 10017

and by Routledge
2 Park Square, Milton Park, Abingdon, Oxon, OX14 4RN

Routledge is an imprint of the Taylor & Francis Group, an informa business

First edition published by Lawrence Erlbaum Associates 2003

Library of Congress Cataloging-in-Publication Data
Names: Frey, Kurt P., author. | Gregg, Aiden P., author. |
   Abelson, Robert P. Experiments with people.
Title: Experiments with people : revelations from social psychology /
   Kurt P. Frey and Aiden P. Gregg.
Description: Second edition. | New York, NY : Routledge, 2018. |
   Earlier edition authored by Robert P. Abelson.
Identifiers: LCCN 2017017285 | ISBN 9781138282100
   (hbk : alk. paper) | ISBN 9781138282117 (pbk : alk. paper) |
   ISBN 9781315101347 (ebook)
Subjects: LCSH: Social psychology—Experiments.
Classification: LCC HM1011 .A24 2018 | DDC 302.072—dc23
LC record available at https://lccn.loc.gov/2017017285

ISBN: 978-1-138-28210-0 (hbk)
ISBN: 978-1-138-28211-7 (pbk)
ISBN: 978-1-315-10134-7 (ebk)

Typeset in Times New Roman
by Apex CoVantage, LLC
Printed and bound by CPI Group (UK) Ltd, Croydon, CR0 4YY

Contents

Acknowledgments

We wish to acknowledge the late Robert Abelson, one of the authors of the first edition, for his past leadership and contributions. Bob is warmly missed. (His chapter, "The Eye Is Quicker Than the Mind: Believing Precedes Unbelieving," has been retained in this second edition.)

To my awesome sons, Kyle and Luke.

—KPF

To my family, for its constant support and love.

—APG

Introduction

Welcome! This book is about the fascinating—and yet often misunderstood—subject of social psychology. It features 28 intriguing studies that shed light on human social thinking and behavior. The studies, mostly laboratory experiments, address such topics as conformity to group norms, unrestrained mob behavior, coping with the prospect of death, the functions of gossip, and the shortcomings of introspection. The studies will help you understand many social phenomena that would otherwise remain deeply puzzling, such as intense loyalty to questionable groups, the operation of unconscious prejudice, the failure of bystanders to help in emergencies, the tragic consequences of social ostracism, and the nature of love. We chose each study because it raised a question of theoretical significance or addressed an issue of practical importance, and because it was ingeniously designed and carefully executed.

Note that this book is not a *reader*. We do not reproduce (lawyers take note!) any of the original journal articles. Rather, each chapter offers a detailed account of a single study, along with relevant commentary. We first introduce the problem that the researchers addressed: "Background." We then describe how the study was conducted—"What They Did"—and delve into its findings—"What They Found." Next comes a "So What?" section, the purpose of which is to emphasize the profound and counterintuitive nature of the study. We continue with an "Afterthoughts" section in which we connect to some broader issues of a conceptual, practical, or ethical nature. This is followed by an explicit "Revelation"—a vital truth that will add to your social wisdom. We conclude each chapter with one or more "What Do You Think?" questions to elicit further reflection.

One of our goals in writing this book is to make a convincing case for the use of *experiments* in social psychological research. Colloquially, the word *experiment* means to try out some new idea or technique. Our usage is more technical. It refers to the random assignment of many subjects—here human participants—to different groups. These groups are treated identically except in one or a few crucial respects (the *independent variables*). The impact of these independent variables on how participants think or act (the *dependent variables*) is then assessed to determine if the manipulations had an effect. Experiments have the unique advantage of allowing confident *causal* inferences (X causes Y). They also permit alternative explanations to be efficiently ruled out.

That's a bit abstract, so let's make it more concrete. Being in a good mood and being sociable often go together. That is, the two are *correlated*. Now, is this because being in a good mood *makes* people more sociable? Or is it because being sociable *puts* people in a good mood? Or is it because any number of other factors—such as being an extravert (an outgoing person)—makes people more sociable *and* puts them in a good mood? Clearly, observing a bare correlation between positive mood and sociability leaves all these possibilities open and unresolved.

So how does one proceed? Well, to test whether mood is definitely a cause of sociability, one can run an experiment. In it, mood is made the independent variable—which the researcher manipulates. For example, in one condition, research participants are made happier, and in another condition, sadder. However, everything else, more or less, is held *constant* (e.g., participants listen to music in both conditions, just either upbeat or downbeat). Research participants themselves, in each condition, can be assumed to be *equivalent*, there having been no reason why participants of one type would have ended up in one condition rather than the other. Sociability, in turn, is made the dependent variable—which the researcher measures. Now, any observed differences in sociability between conditions can be confidently attributed to the manipulation of mood, and to nothing else—short of a fluke.

Although we do not claim that experimentation, as illustrated above, provides absolute knowledge, we do claim that it enables researchers to better distinguish between correct and faulty theories about social dynamics. Indeed, when the findings of social psychology come in, the pitfalls of commonsense are often shockingly exposed. Not all findings are as expected as the plausible link between mood and sociability.

Still, two troublesome issues seem to cling to any discussion of psychological experimentation: *ethics* and *artificiality*. First, ethics. Social psychologists are often depicted as monsters in lab coats who do not scruple to take advantage of unsuspecting participants. (Indeed, the very title of this book, *Experiments With People*, may send a shiver down your spine!) This depiction is a perversion of the truth. Social psychologists are, in fact, acutely sensitive to the impact of their procedures on participants. It is standard practice, for example, to tell participants in advance what will happen in a study, and to obtain their *informed consent* (expressed willingness to undergo described procedures). Moreover, before any study can be carried out, an independent ethics committee must approve it. Such precautions are all to the good, but it should be noted that the majority of social psychological studies—even those that involve deception—rarely raise ethical concerns. Most participants regard such studies as interesting and informative ways to spend half an hour, and are often found afterward chatting amiably with the experimenter. This gives the experimenter the chance to *debrief* participants (let them in on the purpose of the study) and to obtain feedback from them. Human participants are the lifeblood of social psychology, so researchers are understandably eager to make their experiences as rewarding as possible.

Second, artificiality. Much criticism of the experimental method has centered on the claim that, because laboratory settings do not, for the most part, resemble the real world, they do not tell us much about it. For several reasons, this criticism is *specious* (apparently convincing, but actually unsound; see Mook, 1980). Primary among these reasons is that artificiality is necessary if ever one is to clarify what *causes* what. The best way to get rid of *confounds* (other factors that might explain a link between two variables) is to strip phenomena down to their bare essentials. To take an example from "hard science," suppose you wish to test whether the metallic element potassium burns brightly (as it does). Unfortunately, because of potassium's chemical reactivity, it is always found in nature as a salt, namely potash. Consequently, to test the hypothesis that potassium per se burns brightly, you must first artificially purify potash, lest the other elements with which potassium is naturally combined obscure its incandescence, or turn out to be misleadingly incandescent themselves. In a similar manner, to test any hypothesis about social thinking or behavior, you must first purify the phenomenon of interest in the laboratory, in case the ebb and flow of everyday life obscures its true nature, or misleadingly creates the impression that its true nature is other than what it actually is.

Artificiality is only a drawback if researchers are seeking to generalize their findings immediately to a specific setting or group of people. However, researchers spend much of their time testing general theories or demonstrating classes of effects. This is a worthwhile enterprise, because theoretical knowledge enriches our understanding of specific problems, and suggests solutions to them based on *underlying principles*. Thus, *basic research* informs practical interventions, and in a systematic way. Moreover, social psychological experiments are not always "artificial," and everyday life is not always "real." The studies featured in this book, for example, have participants doing a variety of interesting things: They lie to others, submerge their hands in ice water, recall their menstrual symptoms, offer assistance to epileptics, prepare to deliver a sermon, and send gossip notes. We daresay that such activities are no less real than many everyday activities, such as watching television, driving a car, or flipping hamburgers (Aronson, Wilson, & Brewer, 1998).

The foregoing examples are referred to as *operationalizations*. They are manipulations and measures that map on to the elements of a theory. If a social psychologist has a theory, and that theory states that some X should cause some Y, then she could, in any given experiment, pick one example of X to manipulate, and one example of Y to measure, and observe what happens. Across many studies, she could also pick different Xs and Ys—to ensure that her findings were not an artifact of a single method. So, suppose that a social psychologist theorizes that a positive mood makes people more sociable, whereas a negative mood makes them less so. She could manipulate mood by having participants listen to happy or sad music, speak to a jolly or gloomy person, or recall a pleasant or unpleasant experience. Equally, she could measure sociability by having participants rate their interest in socializing, quantifying how much they talk to a confederate (i.e., an accomplice of the experimenter, posing as a participant), or having the confederate rate how friendly participants are when interacting. If the predicted finding emerged across all or most of the operationalizations, then the "positive-mood-causes-sociability" theory would enjoy good experimental support.

Now, what would happen if social psychologists were to abandon experimentation altogether, and study only everyday experiences in people's lives? Years ago, Barker (1965) pioneered what he called the ecological approach to human behavior. He and his colleagues had the goal of recording the activities of people in a small Kansas town using large numbers of observers stationed in various strategic locations. Much data were collected in grocery stores, on park benches, near soda fountains, and so on. Although the observations collected added up to a number of curious factoids about what really happened in this small town, almost none of them contributed significantly to our deeper understanding of social phenomena. The laboratory is the place to create conditions that put theories—about social thinking and behavior—to the test.

In this book, as we have said, we make the case for the unique merits of experimentation as a method of gaining knowledge about people in their social world. Without experimentation, researchers could not establish, with a fair degree of precision or assurance, whether some causal link was present or not, and so, whether the theory predicting that link was supported or not. However, we must also point out that, although experimentation may be a *necessary* condition for gaining knowledge, it is not always a *sufficient* one. That is, although experimentation is the best method available for determining what the facts ultimately are, it may not always be enough, especially in the short-term. A single experiment, or even a succession of experiments, may not sort matters out once and for all, and may even lead researchers down a temporary false path. Such pitfalls have recently been brought home by the so-called *replication crisis* (Ioannidis, 2005)—not only in social psychology, but also in biology and medicine—which has arisen since the first edition of this book was published. Hence, we should say a few words about it.

What has essentially happened is that researchers, in their ongoing quest for truth, have been increasingly scrutinizing the cumulative results of many experiments over time—experiments conducted by many different researchers employing a variety of operationalizations. The results of such *meta-analyses* typically find a mixed picture of hits and misses, from which robust overall conclusions can nonetheless be drawn (e.g., a statistical preponderance of hits supports a particular theory). However, the fact that a mixed picture often emerges has prompted further reflection about the reasons *why* results might vary across studies. One answer is that effects typically require various preconditions to be met before they emerge (so-called *moderators*). Another is that, for statistical reasons, even effects that actually exist may not be detected (a so-called *Type II error*), or effects that do not exist may be falsely obtained (*Type I error*). To investigate the matter, empirically minded researchers have recently attempted, more than they ever did before, to systematically *replicate* earlier findings (i.e., to repeat studies, to verify that the new results match the old). Unfortunately, replication has sometimes turned out to be an unexpectedly tricky business. In social psychology, some findings (although not those we focus on in this book, which have generally stood the test of time) emerge only weakly, or do not emerge at all (Open Science Collaboration, 2015).

Interpretations of this situation differ. For some pessimistic commentators, it sounds a death knell for experimental science. Experimental findings are fundamentally untrustworthy, they declare, and the whole process is an exercise in self-delusion. But for more optimistic commentators—and we count ourselves among them—it is just a sobering reminder that the enterprise of science never ends, and that establishing the truth may take longer than anticipated.

In principle, the logic of experimentation, as we have outlined it, is perfectly sound. In practice, a variety of biases and flaws creep in, due to the broader context in which experimental research is conducted. Several factors may, for example, innocently bias researchers toward emphasizing positive findings. First, the failure to obtain a predicted effect is always ambiguous. Does it mean the effect is not there, or that some feature of the study was faulty? If a study fails, a researcher may reasonably assume that he or she was at fault, and then try to run an improved study. However, if an initial study succeeds, then a researcher may leave it at that. "Misses" may therefore get a second chance to be "hits," whereas "hits" may rarely get a second chance to be "misses." This tendency pulls for the confirmation of a theory. Second, incentives have traditionally not rewarded researchers who pursue replications, but rather researchers who pursue novel avenues of research. The business of replication has been generally regarded as boring and backward-looking—revisiting old issues that may be settled anyway. In a "publish-or-perish" environment, replications did not advance one's career. Finally, the wish to tell a constructive and compelling story may lead researchers to underemphasize less "cooperative" findings, and to focus instead on those manipulations and measures where the predicted effect emerged clearly and cleanly.

The good news is that social psychologists, and scientists in other fields, are now squarely tackling these important issues. For example, leading academic journals are now increasingly requiring researchers to report all of their findings, as well as the nitty-gritty details of their manipulations and measures. In addition, a burgeoning movement has now emerged toward *open science*, which emphasizes the free sharing of research materials and raw data among researchers. Finally, a new methodology, designed to eliminate publication bias, has been devised: the *preregistered report*. Here, one or more research teams submit a detailed description of their experimental protocol in advance; and if this survives *peer review* (scrutiny by randomly selected colleagues in the same field), then the research is conducted in strict accordance with that protocol, with its results being guaranteed publication regardless. Note that social psychologists themselves have been the ones spearheading these precautionary innovations. One way science progresses is by being critical of its prior methods.

Thus, we believe that it can be confidently claimed that social psychology, as a scientific discipline, is alive and well! This brings us to the book you are now holding. This second edition of *Experiments With People* features revised and updated chapters. Four chapters from the first edition have been deleted, and four new chapters (based on research published in 1971, 2012, 2012, and 2014, respectively) have been added. As with the first edition, the second edition may well have featured different or additional studies. We preemptively apologize to any researchers who feel unjustly sidelined. We nonetheless believe that the studies we do showcase make a prize package. Enjoy!

References

Aronson, E., Wilson, T. D., & Brewer, M. B. (1998). Experimentation in social psychology. In D. Gilbert, S. Fiske, & G. Lindzey (Eds.), *The handbook of social psychology* (4th ed., Vol. 1, pp. 99–142). New York: Random House.

Barker, R. G. (1965). Explorations in ecological psychology. *American Psychologist, 20*, 1–14.

Ioannidis, J. P. A. (2005). Why most published research findings are false. *PLoS Medicine, 2*(8), e124. doi:10.1371/journal.pmed.002012

Mook, D. G. (1980). In defense of external invalidity. *American Psychologist, 38*, 379–388.

Open Science Collaboration. (2015). Estimating the reproducibility of psychological science. *Science, 349*(6251), aac4716. doi:10.1126/science.acc4716

1 Going Along to Get Along

Conforming to Group Norms

"Social man is a somnambulist."

—Gabriel de Tarde (1843–1904), French sociologist and criminologist

Background

Social life is structured by *norms*: rules, shared by a group of people, about what behaviors are appropriate. Norms prescribe certain practices ("do this") and proscribe others ("don't do that"). Norms govern most social situations: job interview, first date, classy restaurant, funeral service, even a crowded elevator. Crammed into one recently, I announced, "seven please," and someone in the opposite corner (whom I could not see) pushed seven. In my mind I counted three or four other elevator norms. (Another might be: Don't stand facing a stranger.) Norms grease the wheels of social interaction.

Norms can exist at the level of entire nations or cultures, and some are almost universal. The norm of *social responsibility* stresses one's duty to help nearby people in desperate need: A crying child, apparently lost or hurt, is everyone's responsibility. The norm of *reciprocity* requires one to repay gifts or favors: After someone attends your wedding, it would be awkward to turn down an invitation to attend theirs. Although there are some universal norms (such as prohibitions against murder, theft, kidnapping, and rape), cultures differ, often greatly, in what they expect or accept from their members. One culture values promptness ("come on time or don't come at all"), whereas another values spontaneity ("come when you get here"). One encourages premarital sex, whereas another places a premium on virginal brides. Romantic love is a norm here, arranged marriages there. In one culture women cover themselves from head to toe, whereas in another they wear hardly anything (in *National Geographic* fashion). Here you eat with silverware, there with chopsticks, and somewhere else with fingers. In one culture a firm handshake is respected, whereas in another a gentle handshake is preferred. In some countries it is an insult to face the soles of one's feet or shoes toward another person; in another, who cares? People in different corners of the world have different personal spaces and conversational distances. Without knowing these, a foreigner might be perceived as cold and unfriendly, or too intimate or pushy. Thus, norms define social *sins of commission* (doing what one should not be doing) and *sins of omission* (failing to do what one should be doing).

Even what we eat is normatively influenced. It has been said: "Americans eat oysters but not snails. The French eat snails but not locusts. The Zulus eat locusts but not fish. The Jews eat fish but not pork. The Hindus eat pork but not beef. The Russians eat beef but not snakes. The Chinese eat snakes but not people. The Jale of New Guinea find people delicious" (Robertson, 1987, p. 67). This lengthy saying, though it indulges stereotypical exaggeration, highlights cultural differences with respect to diet.

Differences in sexual norms have often fascinated, if not titillated, anthropologists and other social scientists. It was once normative among the Tiwi people of Melville Island (off the northern coast of Australia) for young girls to have sexual intercourse with their much older future husbands, because doing so was believed to stimulate the onset of puberty (Goodall, 1971). The Sambia of New Guinea believed that young boys also needed sexual stimulation. The boys swallowed semen (supplied by local men) in order to achieve manhood (Herdt, 1981). Operating under a different set of norms, the Mehinaku of central Brazil refrained from sexual contact with children. However, they believed that fathering a child was a group project. Multiple men ejaculated into a woman's vagina, thus contributing collectively (they believed) to conception (Gregor, 1985). One wonders if these norms continue to exist.

Norms can occur in groups of all sizes and shapes: a religion, profession, gang, audience, or family. Norms are even found in personal relationships. A close relationship is said to represent a *reich der zwei* (country of two), replete with its own dyadic norms. Each friendship or love relationship develops its own modus operandi. She cooks; he clears the table and washes the dishes. She says, "I'm going up for a nap." He says, "Me too!"

Observing norms in everyday life reveals how ubiquitous and consequential they are. We usually abide by them automatically and without question. Group members tend to conform to the norms of their collectives. In many ways, we are all somnambulists, sleepwalking our way through the normative influences of our social world.

An experiment by Langer, Blank, and Chanowitz (1978) illustrated just how mindless people can be in everyday social situations. A research assistant asked unsuspecting participants whether she could skip to the front of the line at a photocopier in order to copy five pages. She made her request in one of three ways. She either gave a legitimate reason for the request (she needed to make copies for a looming deadline), a pseudo-reason (she asked to use the photocopier because she wanted to make copies), or no reason at all (she simply asked to use the photocopier). As you might expect, compliance was higher when the assistant gave a legitimate reason (94%), and relatively lower when she gave no reason at all (60%). However, the surprise was that compliance was as high in the pseudo-reason condition (93%) as in the legitimate reason condition. Merely hearing someone going through the motions of supplying a reason was enough to activate the social norm that one should defer to others who make a request with a justification attached. Importantly, however, when the assistant asked to be able to jump to the front of the line to make *20* copies, compliance was lower, especially in the pseudo-reason and no reason conditions (in both cases it was only 24%, whereas it was 42% in the legitimate reason condition). Evidently, when confronted with larger demands on our time or energy, we go off automatic pilot.

Muzafir Sherif (1936) was one of the first social psychologists to investigate the emergence and perpetuation of norms—in this case, *perceptual* norms—in the laboratory. He presented participants with a stationary dot of light for two seconds in an otherwise dark room. This created an optical illusion known as the *autokinetic effect*: The stationary dot appeared to jump about (due to natural twitching movements of the eyeballs). When participants were asked to judge how much the light had moved, they typically gave an estimate of between 1 and 10 inches (although one participant claimed that the dot had moved 80 feet!). When groups of participants were asked to announce their estimates out loud on consecutive days, a norm spontaneously emerged. Their estimates gradually converged. Once such a norm was established, and some group members were replaced with new members, their estimates quickly fell into line with the previously established norm. Research by Jacobs and Campbell (1961) found that, when a *confederate* (someone posing as a research participant) gave an extreme estimate, this too affected the perceptual norm of the group. When the confederate was then replaced with an actual participant, and that participant replaced with another participant, and so on, the inflated norm persisted through as many as five generations of changing group members.

In Sherif's study, participants could not be sure how much the light moved. The estimates of others therefore provided valuable information, which it was rational to incorporate into their own judgments. The emerging norm was most likely the result of participants *internalizing* (agreeing with) others' estimates. Jacobs and Campbell (1961) demonstrated that participants did, indeed, internalize the norms and abide by them when tested alone several months later.

Two decades after Sheriff's study, Solomon Asch (1955) revisited the issue. What would happen if stimuli were less ambiguous?, he wondered. What if others disagreed with one's judgment of something *obvious*? To what extent might one conform to their erroneous judgments, and what factors might influence their degree of conformity?

What He Did

Asch (1955) presented a group of seven college students, sitting around a large table, with a series of pairs of large white cards. On one card was a single vertical black line (a *standard*). On the other card, there were three vertical black lines of different lengths (*comparisons*). One comparison line was exactly the same length as the standard line; the other two were of different lengths. One by one, the participants announced which of the three lines (*a*, *b*, or *c*) was the same length as the standard. This process was repeated over 18 trials, with the standard and comparison lines varying on each trial. Simple question: How often did participants choose the correct comparison line?

Under normal circumstances, individuals would state the correct line over 99% of the time; the correct match was always obvious. Yet there was something unusual about this situation: Only one of the group members was a true participant! This lone participant was blissfully unaware that the other group members were *confederates* (research assistants posing as participants) coached beforehand to give unanimously wrong answers on prearranged trials.

On the first trial, everyone, including the true participant who sat in the sixth position around the table, chose the correct matching line. The same thing occurred on the second trial after a new pair of cards was displayed. On the third trial, however, each of the first five confederates (whom, again, the participant had every reason to believe was also an actual participant in the study) casually, but confidently, stated the wrong answer. Surprised and a bit unnerved, the participant then gave his answer. Finally, the sixth confederate gave the same wrong answer, as did the five others. On 10 of the next 15 trials, the other group members again all gave wrong answers. Asch subjected each participant (one per group) to the same procedure.

Pause for a moment. What goes through the mind of someone who is a lone minority? What would you have done in this situation? Perhaps you would have ignored the majority and have stated the obviously correct answers. Maybe you would have had steadfast confidence in your own judgments, thinking that the other group members were docile sheep following a myopic first responder, or that they were all victims of some optical illusion. Maybe you would have viewed the majority as probably correct but still felt obliged to give your own dissenting answer. Or perhaps you would have ignored the evidence of your senses and gone along with the majority, even interpreting your dissimilar perceptions as embarrassing, something to hide. Asch's participants reported such varied reactions in follow-up interviews.

Asch took his basic paradigm in several directions. For example, he sought to determine which mattered more in producing conformity, the *size* of the majority or its *unanimity*. So, to begin with, he varied the number of group members present. Sometimes there was only one other group member (a confederate), sometimes there were as many as 15 (all confederates). Would the number of others determine a participant's inclination to conform? In addition, Asch sometimes planted a dissenter in the group, to break the majority's unanimity. This person was either another actual participant or a confederate instructed to always give correct answers. What effect would this *ally* have on the participant's degree of compliance with the majority? Would his presence undermine the group's influence? Asch also wondered if any effect of an ally would be due to his dissenting from the majority or to his being correct, so in some conditions he arranged for the ally to give a dissenting but also wrong answer. Furthermore, Asch examined the effect of having an ally cross over to the side of the majority or leave the group altogether (because of a supposed appointment with the dean) midway through the experiment. Finally, Asch systematically manipulated the discrepancy between the standard line and the other lines to see if there was a point at which the majority would be perceived as being so flagrantly wrong that the participant would in no way parrot their answers. Whew! Don't experimental social psychologists ever get tired?

What He Found

Asch's (1955) astonishing finding was that, even though the correct answer on each trial was perceptually obvious, participants still often went along with the majority. On critical trials, those where the majority gave a wrong answer, the lone participants echoed the majority's verdict over a *third* of the time (37% of the time to be exact). Who would have guessed that so much unprovoked compliance would occur? Why did participants so often fail to announce the obviously right answer?

Importantly, there were differences among participants in levels of compliance. On the one hand, about a quarter of them (the mavericks) never agreed with the erroneous perceptions of the majority. On the other hand, a smaller number (the sheep) sided with the majority almost unwaveringly (8% conformed on 10 or more of the 12 critical trials). Most participants fell between the two extremes.

Did the size of the group matter? It did. Participants opposed by only a single group member chose the wrong comparison line only about 4% of the time. With two opposing group members, participants' errors jumped to about 14%. When there were between 3 and 15 opposing group members, error rates ranged between 31% and 37%. Any variation within this range was not statistically significant. In other words, group influence appeared to max out after group size reached about three or four members, with no increase in compliance observed thereafter (Figure 1).

Did having an *ally*—someone who did not side with the majority—make a difference? It did. Asch (1955) found: "Disturbing the majority's unanimity had a striking effect" (p. 34). The

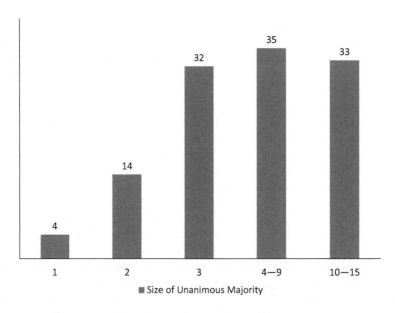

Figure 1 Percentage of trials on which participants went along with unanimous majorities of various sizes, by saying that lines of obviously different length were equal

presence of a supportive partner—an individual who was not aware of the prearranged agreement among the other group members, or a confederate who was instructed to always answer truthfully—drained the majority of much of its power. Participants with an ally answered incorrectly only about a quarter as often as they did when the rest of the group was unanimous in its opposition. An ally who announced a less incorrect answer than other group members decreased the participants' conformity by about a third, whereas an ally who announced a more incorrect answer decreased the participants' conformity by about two-thirds. In the latter case, the participants reported incorrect answers only 9% of the time.

When an ally, after six trials, joined the ranks of the majority, errors by participants jumped to about what was found in conditions where there had never been an ally (participants yielded to the group on over a third of the remaining trials). In other words, the independence shown by participants disappeared once the ally's support waned. However, when the ally left the group altogether, his emboldening influence on the participant persisted. Participants' errors increased slightly upon his leaving, but not nearly as much as when he defected to the majority.

Finally, what happened when the difference between the standard and the comparison line chosen by the majority was as great as 7 inches? Asch found that, even then, a substantial number of the participants went along with the group's grossly inaccurate judgments.

So What?

Asch's (1955) study makes vivid the human tendency to go along with the group. It is unlikely that his participants *internalized* (were actually persuaded by) the majority's position on each trial. The correct matches between standard and comparison lines were too apparent for that to happen. Even so, many announced the same erroneous answers as other supposed participants, even though they knew them to be incorrect. They complied with the majority but were not persuaded by it. They went along, presumably to get along.

Evidently, it doesn't take much to make a powerful majority. Asch (1955) found maximum adherence to the majority as soon as its size reached about three or four. Other studies have yielded similar results (although see Bond, 2005). For example, Milgram, Bickman, and Berkowitz (1969) had 1, 2, 3, 5, 10, or 15 people pause on a crowded New York City street to look up at a sixth floor window. The number of others who followed suit increased as group size increased from 1 to 5, but there were no significant increases with larger groups. Just a small group of apparently distracted people provoked as many as 80% of the others present to mimic their upward gaze. Again, small groups can have great impact, and increasingly larger groups seem to have no additional effect (see Gerard, Wilhelmy, & Conolley, 1968).

Also evident in Asch's study was the difference the presence of an ally made. Apparently, a unanimous majority frequently has an irresistible impact on a lone individual. But given just one fellow dissenter, an individual finds the courage to resist social pressure. Other studies bear this out. For example, Nemeth and Chiles (1988) had participants publicly judge the color of an obviously red slide that others were claiming was orange. The participants correctly claimed it to be red only 30% of the time (and incorrectly claimed it to be orange 70% of the time). However, if they observed just one lone individual misjudge to be blue a stimulus that the majority had correctly judged to be green, they then correctly claimed to see a red slide 80% of the time (they claimed to see an orange slide only 20% of the time). Thus, observing even mistaken defiance can increase one's independence.

Why do people conform? Deutsch and Gerard (1955) distinguished between *informational* influence and *normative* influence. In the first case, others influence us because we recognize that their opinions often reflect reality. We accept their influence and conform out of a desire to be right. The participants in Sherif's (1936) study were not sure how much the light was actually moving (they were in the dark, literally), so they let themselves be swayed by the estimates of others. They partly accepted the validity of those estimates and adjusted their own estimates accordingly (often settling on a compromise). However, in the case of normative influence, we fall in line because we feel, at some level, pressure to do so. We sense that the group is seeking our compliance. We want to live by its norms and not appear atypical or conspicuous, deviant or strange. The participants in Asch's (1955) study knew which one of the comparison lines was equal to the standard lines. They echoed the judgments of the majority, not because they lacked information, but because they did not wish to stand out. They wanted to be accepted and liked (see Chapter 25 for what can happen when people find themselves chronically rejected). Asch's participants were caught between the desire to be right and the desire to be liked, but the latter desire often proved stronger (see Insko, Smith, Alicke, Wade, & Taylor, 1985). More fundamentally, people comply with the practices, perceptions, or beliefs of others out of a desire to feel better about themselves. It has been suggested that self-esteem primarily reflects how well one feels he or she is fitting in socially (Leary, Tambor, Terdel, & Downs, 1995). Fitting in socially, of course, requires meeting approved norms of conduct.

Just as individuals readily submit to group norms, groups readily demand conformity. Deviance threatens the group and its agenda. A group is like a train moving down a track: Deviance derails it. Nonconformity undermines a group's *raison d'etre* and so is seldom welcome. Groups insisting on compliance are found throughout history and in every part of the world. The Catholic Church resorted to torturing and murdering heretics during the Spanish Inquisition. The Soviet empire reserved the Gulag for political dissenters. The Mafia had a pair of cement shoes for any of its wayward members. The Chinese government attempted to suppress the hugely popular religious practice of Falun Gong. The Taliban regime in Afghanistan dealt brutally with even trivial violations of their fundamentalist Islamic code: Women not wearing burkas, or men not wearing beards, were systematically beaten. Presently, the Islamic State of Iraq and Syria (ISIS) has a code of conduct, violations of which result in floggings, amputations, and crucifixions. What forms of conformity does the United States or other relatively progressive societies require?

The more *cohesive* (tight-knit) a group is, the more it demands conformity. A study by Schachter over 60 years ago (1951) had high cohesive groups and low cohesive groups discuss ways to handle a particular wayward teenager, Johnny Rocco (whose very name suggests delinquency!). Three confederates were planted in the group: *deviate*, *slider*, and *mode*. The first consistently deviated from the majority; the second started out in the same way, but then slid to the side of the majority; the third always sided with the majority. The groups, especially the high cohesive group, applied great pressure to the deviate, trying to get him to conform to the group. Group members eventually gave up on him, ceasing to talk with him at all. Needless to say, when jobs in the group were divided up, the deviate got the least desirable ones. No wonder people fear standing apart from their peers. (Even Supreme Court justices avoid being lone dissenters; see Granberg & Bartels, 2005.)

Afterthoughts

Two final thoughts: First, notice how labor-intensive Asch's (1955) the procedure was. In each group, everyone but one actual participant was part of Asch's conspiracy. Crutchfield (1955) developed a more economical procedure for studying conformity. Participants each sit alone in a booth facing a box with a panel of switches for indicating their responses and lights registering others' responses. Each participant is told that he or she is the last to respond in a preordained sequence. A cover story justifies this setup. What the participants do not know, however, is that the experimenter manipulates the responses of the other supposed participants. Each real participant therefore responds according to what he or she falsely believes are the responses of the other participants. With this system, there is no need to train and pay a team of warm-blooded research assistants. Necessity, or perhaps economy, is the mother of invention! Research using this Crutchfield technique does not find as much conformity as did Asch's research. Apparently, normative pressure is more powerful when it occurs face-to-face, as it did in Asch's study.

The second afterthought has to do with *deviance*. As history attests, just as groups can influence their members, so too certain individuals and subgroups can influence their groups or the prevailing social order (Maass & Clark, 1984). Indeed, minorities sometimes sway majorities, and thereby act as potent agents of social change. This echoes what Asch found: The lone dissenting ally had a powerful impact.

Think of Galileo. With the help of a low-power telescope, he spied four moons circling Jupiter and mountains and craters on the moon. This led him to claim, as had Copernicus before him, that the geocentric worldview was mistaken and that the celestial bodies are pocked, not perfect. Though he lived the later part of his life under house arrest, his evidence was not lost on the outside world. Think of Mohandas Gandhi. He led a series of peaceful protests and marches that defied India's salt laws, a symbol of hated British rule in India. Despite encountering brutal police violence, notably at the Dharsana salt factory, Gandhi and his followers courageously persisted, paving the way for Indian independence 17 years later. Think of Rosa Parks. She refused to sit in the back of a city bus in Birmingham, Alabama, in 1958. Her bold act was a catalyst for a nationwide civil rights movement, which ultimately led to the abolition of racial segregation. Think of the 9/11 terrorist attacks on the World Trade Center and Pentagon in the United States. These actions were undertaken in an effort to disrupt American financial and military centers and incite a *jihad*, or holy war. Only time will tell its ultimate impact. Even in smaller circles—an atheist among believers, a vegan among meat eaters, someone who chooses to "just say no" among pressuring peers—numerical minorities often have a remarkable effect.

One of the most dramatic depictions of such *minority influence* is the vintage film, *12 Angry Men*. A teenager is on trial for murder and a jury must decide the case. In a show-of-hands vote, Henry Fonda is the only holdout against a quick conviction. The film shows his slow but inexorable progress in turning an 11–1 guilty vote into a 0–12 not guilty vote. Although research finds that the initial positions of jurors are typically strongly predictive of their final verdict, and that group discussion only tends to polarize opinions, this film about minority influence is still a classic.

Deviant individuals or minorities may not always achieve this kind of dramatic success, but they can still have considerable impact. Research finds that, whereas majorities inspire heuristic judgments (their sheer number suggests they must be right) and often compliance ("I'd better go along with them"), minorities provoke a more systematic consideration of arguments and, possibly, an internal acceptance of their position (Nemeth, 1986). Majorities tend to have a greater impact on public conformity, whereas minorities tend to have more effect on private conformity (Chaiken & Stangor, 1987).

Research has found that the most persuasive individuals and minorities tend to be those who hold to their dissenting position in an unwavering, self-assured manner (Nemeth & Wachtler, 1974). It also helps if they are not perceived to be arguing in their own interests, dogmatic and inflexible, or psychologically disturbed. In addition, one has a better chance of influencing a group if one first conforms to it. Deviance is better received if it comes on the foundation of having built up ample *interpersonal credits* among those with whom one disagrees (Hollander, 1958).

Historically, minority perspectives and deviant behaviors generally have not been readily tolerated. People tend to have little patience or kindness for anyone trying to upset the applecart. Greedy corporations have been known to fire employees who dare to protest their inhumane working conditions. By the same token, striking labor groups have been known to crack the skulls of fellow workers who refuse to take part in a work action. More than a few deviants have felt the noose tighten around their necks or have otherwise gone the way of public execution. Though people who hold dissenting opinions are often seen as competent and honest, they are usually not liked (Bassili & Provencal, 1988). Deviance is most accepted from high-status persons, most expected from low-status persons, but is rarely tolerated from intermediate-status persons. The latter have neither the credit of the highs, nor do they not have anything to lose like the lows.

Not only does violation of a norm invite public opprobrium, it also can result in self-punishment. Breaching a social norm is psychologically painful. In a study by Milgram and Sabini (1978), research assistants asked subway riders to give up their seats for them. Making such a request was reported to be extremely unnerving, even though the worst response one typically got was a simple "no." We fear punishment, or reproach ourselves, for breaking social norms. Unless one has a combative nature and thick skin, it is no fun jeopardizing the acceptance of valued others, no fun being socially ostracized (see Williams, 1997; Williams, Forgas, & Hippel, 2015).

Yet, in every realm of life there are people who accept being outsiders, often to society's benefit. John Lennon, of Beatle fame, put his nonconformity this way (his words laden with a heavy Liverpuddlian accent):

> I'm not gonna change the way I look or the way I feel to conform to anything. I've always been a freak. So I've been a freak all my life and I have to live like that, you know. I'm one of those people.

But if defiance is painful, conformity is too. One sulks over having to go along with some ridiculous or repugnant norm, and if conformity doesn't cause actual pain, it can produce a harmful numbness. It can destroy one's soul, according to British novelist Virginia Woolf: "Once conform, once do what other people do because they do it, and a lethargy steals over the finer nerves and faculties of the soul. She becomes an outer show and inward emptiness; dull, callous, and indifferent."

Clearly, healthy social life requires a deft balance between conformity and autonomy, between compliance and defiance. Chief among the things one must learn in life is when to go along and conform and when to stop in one's tracks and resist the trends and influence of social groups. Solomon Asch (1955) worried about the degree of conformity he found in his research:

> Life in society requires consensus as an indispensable condition. But consensus, to be productive, requires that each individual contribute independently out of his experience and insight. When consensus comes under the dominance of conformity, the social process is polluted and the individual at the same time surrenders the powers on which his functioning as a feeling and thinking being depends. That we have found the tendency to conform in our society so strong that reasonably intelligent and well-meaning young people are willing to call white black is a matter of concern. It raises questions about our ways of education and about the values that guide our conduct.

(p. 34)

Perhaps we, like Asch, should worry too.

Revelation

Ubiquitous and irresistible norms govern social life. Groups exert tremendous normative influence over their members that only a few brave souls can defy.

What Do You Think?

It is often said that one should always be one's own person—saying what one truly thinks, and doing what one really wants. If so, then why does the pressure to conform feel so strong? Is there an advantage to being one of the crowd—one of the "sheeple"? Is there safety in numbers?

Chapter Reference

Asch, S. E. (1955, November). Opinions and social pressure. *Scientific American, 19*, 31–35.

Other References

Bassili, J. N., & Provencal, A. (1988). Perceiving minorities: A factor-analytic approach. *Personality and Social Psychology Bulletin, 14*, 5–15.

Bond, R. (2005). Group size and conformity. *Group Processes and Intergroup Relations, 8*, 331–354.

Chaiken, S., & Stangor, C. (1987). Attitudes and attitude change. *Annual Review of Psychology, 38*, 575–630.

Crutchfield, R. A. (1955). Conformity and character. *American Psychologist, 10*, 191–198.

Deutsch, M., & Gerard, H. B. (1955). A study of normative and informational social influences upon individual judgment. *Journal of Abnormal and Social Psychology, 51*, 629–636.

Gerard, H. B., Wilhelmy, R. A., & Conolley, E. S. (1968). Conformity and group size. *Journal of Personality and Social Psychology, 8*, 79–82.

Goodall, J. (1971). *Tiwi wives*. Seattle, WA: University of Washington Press.

Granberg, D., & Bartels, B. (2005). On being a lone dissenter. *Journal of Applied Social Psychology, 35*, 1849–1858.

Gregor, T. (1985). *Anxious pleasures: The sexual lives of the Amazonian people*. Chicago, IL: University of Chicago Press.

Herdt, G. H. (1981). *Guardians of the flutes: Idioms of masculinity*. New York: McGraw-Hill.

Hollander, E. P. (1958). Conformity, status, and idiosyncratic credits. *Psychological Review, 65*, 117–127.

Insko, C. A., Smith, R. H., Alicke, M. D., Wade, J., & Taylor, S. (1985). Conformity and group size: The concern with being right and the concern with being liked. *Personality and Social Psychology Bulletin, 11*, 41–50.

Jacobs, R. C., & Campbell, D. T. (1961). The perpetuation of an arbitrary tradition through several generations of a laboratory microculture. *Journal of Abnormal and Social Psychology, 62*, 649–658.

Langer, E. J., Blank, A., & Chanowitz, B. (1978). The mindlessness of ostensibly thoughtful action: The role of "placebic" information in interpersonal interaction. *Journal of Personality and Social Psychology, 36*, 635–642.

Leary, M., Tambor, E., Terdel, S., & Downs, D. (1995). Self-esteem as an interpersonal monitor: The sociometer hypothesis. *Journal of Personality and Social Psychology, 68*, 518–530.

Maass, A., & Clark, R. D., III. (1984). Hidden impact of minorities: Fifteen years of minority influence research. *Psychological Bulletin, 95*, 428–450.

Milgram, S., Bickman, L., & Berkowitz, L. (1969). Note on the drawing power of crowds of different size. *Journal of Personality and Social Psychology, 13*, 79–82.

Milgram, S., & Sabini, J. (1978). On maintaining urban norms: A field experiment in the subway. In A. Baum, J. E. Singer, & S. Valins (Eds.), *Advances in environmental psychology* (Vol. 1, pp. 9–14). Hillsdale, NJ: Lawrence Erlbaum.

Nemeth, C. J. (1986). Differential contributions of majority and minority influence. *Psychological Review, 93*, 23–32.

Nemeth, C., & Chiles, C. (1988). Modelling courage: The role of dissent in fostering independence. *European Journal of Social Psychology, 18*, 275–280.

Nemeth, C. J., & Wachtler, J. (1974). Creating the perceptions of consistency and confidence: A necessary condition for minority influence. *Sociometry, 37*, 529–540.

Robertson, I. (1987). *Sociology* (3rd ed.). New York: Worth Publishers.

Schachter, S. (1951). Deviation, rejection and communication. *Journal of Abnormal and Social Psychology, 46*, 190–207.

Sherif, M. (1936). *The psychology of social norms*. New York: Harper.

Williams, K. D. (1997). Social ostracism. In R. M. Kowalski (Ed.), *Aversive interpersonal behaviors* (pp. 133–170). New York: Plenum.

Williams, K. D., Forgas, J. P., & Hippel, W. V. (2015). *The social outcast: Ostracism, social exclusion, rejection, and bullying*. New York: Psychology Press.

More to Explore

Grant, A., & Sandberg, S. (2016). *Originals: How non-conformists move the world*. New York: Viking.

2 Clashing Cognitions

When Actions Prompt Attitudes

"The most merciful thing in the world . . . is the inability of the human mind to correlate all its contents."

—H. P. Lovecraft (1890–1937), American cult fiction writer

Background

The expression "sour grapes" is commonly used to describe the ungracious attitude of a sore loser toward a worthy winner. However, the dictionary definition is a little different. It can be traced all the way back to a classic fable entitled "The Fox and the Grapes," by the Greek story-teller Aesop. The fable tells of a hungry fox rummaging about for scraps of food. Glancing up, the fox catches sight of a mouth-watering bunch of grapes growing from a vine coiled around a tree. He valiantly tries to climb the tall tree to get to them. Alas, his limbs are poorly suited to scaling tree trunks, and he keeps sliding back to the ground. In the end, exhausted by his fruitless endeavors, the fox grumpily gives up. As he scampers away he consoles himself with the follow-ing thought: "I bet those grapes weren't ripe anyhow!" Thus, we are dealing here, not so much with grapes of wrath, as with grapes of *rationalization*. That is, Aesop's fable suggests that, when matters turn out badly because of something we have done, we tend to minimize how bad they actually were to make ourselves feel better.

A vivid real-life example of this tendency comes from a field study of a doomsday cult (Festinger, Riecken, & Schachter, 1956). Led by Mrs. Marian Keech—a charismatic housewife from Minnesota—members of this cult came to the conclusion that the world as we know it would end on December 21, 1954. At God's behest, all dry land would be deluged, and all earthly creatures drowned. On the eve of the apocalypse, however, the faithful few would be transported by flying saucer to another planet, where they would take up residence until the terrestrial flood-waters had subsided.

The cult's dire predictions were, thankfully, disconfirmed. The question that intrigued the researchers (who had infiltrated the group in search of the answer) was how cult members would react to the disconfirmation. Would they begin to doubt the doctrines of the cult? Many did. They walked away disillusioned, forever skeptical of suburban saviors. However, many others stubbornly maintained their faith. Having committed themselves to the cause for many months, and having renounced all worldly possessions, they preferred to explain away this happy ending. They concluded that God had spared the wayward world, thanks to the piety and fidelity shown by the cult members. Cheered by this ingenious (not to mention flattering) rationalization, cult members set about proselytizing unbelievers harder than ever. Their renewed zeal seems to have been motivated by a need for social validation. If only they could get other people to agree with them, then they would be reassured that their beliefs had been right all along.

People engage in rationalization, not only when farfetched prophecies fail, but also in more everyday situations. For example, after choosing one option over another, they increase their preference for the chosen option over the unchosen option (Brehm, 1956). They regard tasks on which they have performed poorly as less important than those on which they have performed well (Crocker & Major, 1989). And they even justify a lack of charity toward victims by blaming them for their plight (Lerner, 1980).

Now suppose that you were a social psychologist seeking to develop a general theory of rationalization—one capable of making sense of all the findings previously listed. How would you proceed? You might choose to focus on the fact that rationalization is always, at some level, the making of later thoughts and deeds consistent with earlier ones. For example, while it makes little *logical* sense to proselytize on behalf of a doomsday cult whose prophecies have been disconfirmed, it makes plenty of *psychological* sense if people have already spent several months proselytizing on the cult's behalf. Persevering allows them to avoid the embarrassment of admitting how wrong they were in the first place. Hence, understanding rationalization in terms of consistency gives social psychologists a way of analyzing its many manifestations.

Several theories of psychological consistency have been proposed over the years. However, the theory of *cognitive dissonance*, set forth by Festinger (1957), remains unrivaled in scope and influence. Festinger proposed that pairs of *cognitions* (an inclusive term for thoughts and feelings) can be consonant, dissonant, or irrelevant with respect to one another. Consonant cognitions are those that psychologically imply one another. For example, "I helped the old lady across the street" and "I am a helpful person" are consonant beliefs. Dissonant cognitions are those that psychologically imply the reverse of one another, as do the beliefs "I refrained from helping the old lady across the street" and "I am a helpful person." Finally, irrelevant cognitions are those that carry no psychological implications for one another, as with "I helped the old lady across the street" and "I am good at math."

According to Festinger, the presence of dissonant cognitions gives rise to a state of unpleasant psychological tension. Moreover, the greater the number of dissonant cognitions, and the greater their importance to the individual, the more intense the resulting tension will be. Once the tension has been aroused, the individual is motivated to alleviate it. In particular, he or she tries to find ways to resolve the cognitive dissonance responsible for the tension. Several tactics are available, all of which involve rationalization in one form or another (Abelson, 1963).

Festinger never went so far as to stipulate how dissonance reduction was to be achieved in different settings. He merely asserted that it would be achieved—one way or another. Nonetheless, he did make one very specific prediction concerning the preconditions for arousing cognitive dissonance. This prediction applies in settings where people are induced to behave in a manner that contradicts one of their important attitudes, that is, when they are induced to perform a *counter-attitudinal* act. For example, suppose that Miguel liked a movie, but then told Maria, who was considering going to see it, that the movie was rubbish. The act of lying would be counter to Miguel's true attitude. The thought associated with this act, "I told Maria that the movie was rubbish," would then clash with Miguel's preexisting thought, "I liked the movie."

Festinger's (1957) prediction was that performing a counter-attitudinal act would arouse cognitive dissonance only if the incentive for performing it was just sufficient to get the job done. For example, Miguel might well experience cognitive dissonance if, in a moment of selfishness, he voluntarily told Maria that the movie was rubbish so that she would attend a different movie with him, one he hadn't seen already. However, if some Mafia don had bundled Miguel into the back of a car and had threatened to rub him out unless he told Maria that the movie was rubbish (beginning to sound like a Woody Allen movie?), then no cognitive dissonance would result.

Now, one way people can reduce cognitive dissonance is to shift their attitudes so that they better accord with their behavior. For example, Miguel might conclude, after lying to Maria about not liking the movie, that he had not really liked the movie after all. This revision of opinion would serve to clear his conscience. Festinger predicted that, whenever people strive to reduce cognitive dissonance by shifting their attitudes, their attitudes will shift more when they are given a smaller incentive to behave counter-attitudinally than when they are given a larger one.

Note that this flies in the face of what one might intuitively expect. Indeed, the received wisdom in Festinger's time was that the principles of reward and punishment that govern animal behavior should also govern human behavior. On this view, a larger incentive, known to produce more behavior change in animals, ought also to induce more attitude change in humans. The theory of cognitive dissonance suggests, however, that the human mind does not operate like this. On the contrary, a smaller incentive should produce more attitude change, as it implies that a person is freely undertaking a counter-attitudinal act.

Putting matters to the empirical test, Festinger joined forces with an undergraduate student of his, Carlsmith, to conduct an ingenious experiment in which participants were persuaded to do something inconsistent with their attitudes after being given either a large or small incentive to do so.

What They Did

Festinger and Carlsmith (1959) began by having their participants—71 male psychology undergraduates at Stanford University—perform a pair of mind-numbing tasks. After being told they were taking part in a study involving "measures of performance," participants spent the first half hour diligently filling a tray with spools, then emptying it, over and over again, using only one hand. The next half hour brought no relief. They spent it repeatedly rotating 48 square pegs on a board a quarter turn clockwise, one peg after the other. To compound their tedium, participants were not given any specific performance goals, but simply told to work at their own pace. As they yawned their way through both tasks, an experimenter with a stopwatch sat in the background, busying himself taking notes.

Once they had turned their last peg, participants no doubt breathed a sigh of relief. In actuality, however, the study was only just beginning. The researchers had no interest in participants' ability to manipulate spools or pegs. They simply wanted to make participants regard the study— that is, the initial stage of the real study—in a negative light. What they were really interested in was how participants' attitudes toward this study would change in response to experimental manipulations.

To reinforce the impression that the study had indeed concluded, the experimenter reset his stopwatch, and began debriefing participants about its purpose. As part of an elaborate cover story, the experimenter claimed that the study was about how the presence or absence of positive expectations affected fine motor coordination. He went on to say that participants, like him, had been assigned to the no-expectation condition, in which they had received no information about the study before taking part. He alleged that an additional positive-expectation condition also existed, in which participants, prior to taking part, were informed (falsely) that the study was interesting and fun. The experimenter further claimed that this information was normally imparted by an experimental confederate pretending to be a student who had just completed the study himself. The pretense was necessary, argued the experimenter, because participants would be more likely to accept the testimony of a fellow student than the assurances of a professor. (Keep in mind that the entire debriefing was fake. The real study had nothing to do with expectations, and there was no such confederate. The elaborate deception merely served to make subsequent experimental manipulations seem sensible.)

At this point, the experimenter, who had up until now come across as confident and fluent, affected an air of hesitancy and worry. He explained, with evident embarrassment, that his confederate had failed to turn up. The confederate's absence had left him in the lurch because the next participant, who was assigned to the positive expectation condition, was now waiting to begin. He now humbly asked participants for a favor: Would they mind filling in for the absent confederate? And would they be available on future occasions to do the same?

If participants showed any signs of reluctance the experimenter reassured them that the favor would not take very long, and that they would need to be available in the future only rarely. With these reassurances, all participants volunteered their services. The experimenter then explained that their role would involve striking up a casual conversation with the other participant, and conveying the impression that the study was interesting and fun. A sheet of paper detailing what to say in this regard was provided. The experimenter then escorted participants to the office where the other participant, a female undergraduate, was waiting.

This presumed other participant was actually a confederate of the experimenter. In the conversation that ensued, she responded in a preplanned way. She began by letting participants do most of the talking. When the subject of the study came up, and participants began singing its praises, she indignantly expressed surprise. A friend of hers, she claimed, had already taken part in the study, and had found it exceedingly dull, and had advised her to get out of it if at all possible. In response to this challenge, participants had been instructed to reaffirm their conviction that the study was engaging and fun, and that the confederate would certainly enjoy it. To verify that these conversations proceeded as planned, the researchers secretly recorded them on tape for later inspection.

Given that this study had more twists and turns than a boardwalk roller coaster, let's take stock for a moment. Participants had taken part in a very boring study. They had come away with a very negative impression of it. Yet they now found themselves voluntarily misleading a participant of the opposite sex into believing that the study had been interesting and fun. Clearly, what participants privately believed ("I disliked the study") and what they publicly did ("I claimed the study was enjoyable") were at odds with one another. In short, cognitive dissonance had been created, and as a consequence participants would have experienced an unpleasant inner tension. Festinger and Carlsmith predicted that participants would attempt to relieve this tension by bringing the clashing cognitions that were causing it back into harmony. One way to do this was to adopt a more favorable attitude toward the study.

Inducing cognitive dissonance in an experimental setting would have been no small achievement in itself. However, Festinger and Carlsmith also wished to test whether they could also prevent cognitive dissonance from occurring by manipulating the magnitude of the incentive offered to participants for behaving contrary to their attitudes. They predicted that a large incentive would reduce or eliminate cognitive dissonance because it would provide participants with an additional cognition consonant with their deceptive behavior, namely, "I am doing this because of the large incentive I will receive." The large incentive would give them a justification for having misled the confederate.

Thus, the experimenter offered one group of participants a generous $20, and another group a paltry $1, for trying to convince the female confederate that the study would be interesting and fun. (One should bear in mind that this was back in the 1950s, when $20 was a considerable sum of money, even for well-to-do Stanford undergraduates!) A third group of participants—the *control* group, who also endured the tedium of the earlier task—were spared having to deceive a female confederate afterward. This group's results provided a baseline against which results from the other two groups could be compared.

The experimental manipulations over, the researchers needed to measure participants' final attitudes toward the study. However, there was a difficulty. How could they be sure that what participants reported reflected their true feelings and not simply what they felt they should report? Suppose you participated in a boring experiment and then had to tell the next participant that it was interesting. You might then report to an experimenter that you too had found it interesting simply to avoid an embarrassing scene, or out of gratitude for the money he had given you for helping him out. To safeguard against such possibilities, the experimenter did not attempt to measure participants' attitudes himself. Instead, he delegated this responsibility to a second confederate, seemingly unassociated with the prior proceedings. The experimenter mentioned in passing that some psychology students down the hall were conducting surveys. The supposed purpose of these surveys was to assess how the quality of studies conducted in the department of psychology could be improved. Hence, if participants had any comments or complaints, here was their opportunity.

The experimenter escorted participants down to the interviewer's office, commenting along the way that the study had, in general, been well received. This comment was to help participants persuade themselves that the study was indeed enjoyable, if cognitive dissonance was already pushing them in that direction. After the experimenter bade them farewell, the second confederate, posing as a student interviewer, proceeded to ask participants how interesting they had found the study, how much they had learned from it, how scientifically important they had thought it was, and how eager they would be to take part in a similar study. Participants expressed their attitudes, in both cases, using rating scales that ranged from –5 (*not at all*) to +5 (*extremely*).

Here the study truly ended. Participants were questioned afterward about whether they had suspected its true purpose. On these grounds, five participants were eliminated. Six more suffered the same fate for failing to comply with instructions. This left 60 participants, with 20 in each experimental group.

What They Found

As predicted, the participants who were paid $1 to misrepresent the study ended up with significantly more positive attitudes toward the study than baseline participants did. These $1 participants changed their attitudes to be more consistent with what they had openly declared to be true, presumably to reduce cognitive dissonance. However, the attitudes of the participants paid $20 to do the same did not show a similar shift. The provision of a larger incentive evidently forestalled cognitive dissonance. In sum, both of the researchers' main predictions were clearly confirmed (Figure 2).

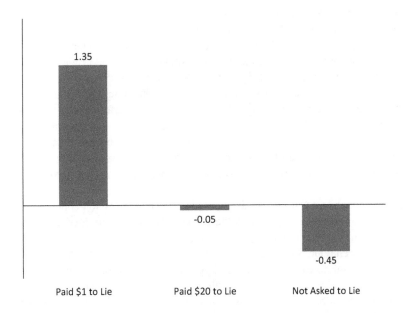

Figure 2 Participants' ratings of how much they liked a boring "study," when paid $1 or $20 to lie that the study had been interesting, or when not asked to lie

The same pattern of results emerged for participants' ratings of their willingness to participate in a similar experiment, although here the pattern was less pronounced. This is to be expected, given that the manipulation of cognitive dissonance was principally designed to influence attitudes, not behavior. The remaining two measures, which assessed the perceived educational value and scientific importance of the study, differed little across the study's three conditions. This is also to be expected given that these measures tapped attitudes that were at best peripherally related to how participants behaved. Changing these attitudes would not, in consequence, have allowed participants to reduce the cognitive dissonance induced by their behavior.

So What?

First of all, the study shows how rationalization can be profitably understood in terms of cognitive consistency. Festinger and Carlsmith (1959) engineered a situation in which uncomfortably dissonant cognitions were created and then showed that participants responded by taking advantage of an available means of harmonizing them, namely by changing their attitudes. This finding supports the hypothesis that keeping cognitions consonant is a primary human motivation and one that can have a powerful impact on our beliefs and feelings (Gawronski, 2012). Indeed, keeping cognitions consonant may be more important than fulfilling other desires. The French wartime leader Charles de Gaulle once publicly declared that he would give up smoking for good, and duly did so. When asked how he had managed to resist his subsequent nicotine cravings, he replied, "De Gaulle cannot go back on his word!" Public commitments of this sort keep people honest because if they renege on them the dissonance they experience will be especially acute.

The study also demonstrated that it is not only attitudes that give rise to actions, but also actions that give rise to attitudes (see the "What Do You Think?" question). In many cases, it may even be easier to change people's minds by inducing them to perform a counter-attitudinal act than by having them carefully consider persuasive arguments. Do you think the participants in the present study could have been talked into regarding the boring tasks that they had performed as interesting? It seems unlikely. Demonstrations of cognitive dissonance also highlight the potential irrationality of the persuasion process. Our attitudes are changed not only by objective facts but also by subjective motivations.

Indeed, cognitive dissonance has been used as a deliberate instrument of indoctrination. For example, during the Korean War, Chinese communists took charge of many prison camps. There, they set about inducing captive American soldiers to engage in what might be called trivial acts of defection. For example, they had them publicly endorse mildly pro-communist statements such as "America is not perfect." As you might expect, such tactics did not initially create much cognitive dissonance or attitude change. However, their Chinese captors were only just getting started. They proceeded to increase by barely noticeable degrees the magnitude of the pro-communist gestures that the American soldiers performed. Bit by bit, these prisoners of war found themselves doing more and more pro-communist things, like drafting Maoist tracts, with only minimal inducement. The eventual result was a substantial pro-communist shift in ideology (Schein, 1956).

Finally, Festinger and Carlsmith's study showed that, when trying to get people to change their minds, the subtle approach is superior to the blatant. The larger the incentive, the smaller the dissonance. This finding has practical implications for, among other things, how to effectively manage children's behavior. Suppose, for example, that little Amélie dislikes the taste of spinach and refuses point blank to eat it. What should you do? Your best move may be to induce her to eat just a little (that is, engage in some mildly counter-attitudinal behavior), thereby allowing cognitive dissonance to bring about a more pro-spinach attitude. But how should you motivate Amélie to take that very first bite? Promising her chocolate cake might seem like a good tactic. However, the present study suggests that such an in-your-face bribe would only short-circuit any useful cognitive dissonance that might be created. Amélie would instead learn that spinach is a yucky food, only worth consuming to get a yummy dessert. (The motivation-sapping properties of overt reward are pursued in Chapter 9.)

A superior tactic would be to give Amélie an inducement that was just enough to get her to taste her spinach—a little gentle encouragement perhaps. She would then be more likely to conclude that she is eating the spinach because she likes it. The same lesson applies to the stick as to the carrot: The milder the punishment, the greater its persuasiveness. If children are severely warned, as opposed to softly told, not to play with a forbidden toy, they later come to like that toy more, and are more likely to play with it when adults are not around (Aronson & Carlsmith, 1963; Freedman, 1965). This effect may be due either to their inclination to express their autonomy in defiance of restrictive authority (Brehm & Brehm, 1981) or to their understanding that what is forbidden is usually attractive (Bushman, 1996). At any rate, such inverse correlations between persuasion and consequence size highlight the pitfalls of trying to explain human behavior and attitudes too simplistically.

Afterthoughts

The theory of cognitive dissonance gives us a way of making sense of many aspects of human thinking and behavior that might otherwise remain perplexing. Nevertheless, the theory has been criticized and revised over the years (Harmon-Jones & Mills, 1999). We now briefly touch on some of these developments in order to give the reader a sense of how social psychological theories evolve over time as research progresses.

Soon after the present study appeared in the literature, a few researchers questioned whether its findings were genuine. They either pointed out various confounds that might have compromised the study's validity (Chapanis & Chapanis, 1964) or else conducted other studies whose findings seemed at odds with dissonance theory (Rosenberg, 1965). However, more than 50 years later, countless studies have soundly confirmed that dissonance effects are real and can be reliably replicated (Cooper, 2007).

Convinced that they were dealing with real phenomena, social psychologists then began debating how best to interpret it. Festinger (1957) proposed, as we have seen, that counter-attitudinal acts give rise to unpleasant arousal, and that attitude change is one way to eliminate that arousal. Bem (1967) disagreed with this account, proposing that the underlying dynamics were far simpler. He contended that we come to know our own attitudes in the same way that we come to know the attitudes of other people, namely, by observing behavior. He argued that we do not so much peer inside our own souls to discover how we feel, as watch what we do and then make an informed guess. On this view, the knowledge that I dislike spinach would come from the innumerable times I have complained about it, refused to eat it, and so on, rather than from any perception of my own feelings. Counter-attitudinal behavior causes attitude change by leading people to calmly infer that they hold attitudes that match their counter-attitudinal behavior. Participants in the Festinger and Carlsmith study were well aware of their telling the female confederate that the study was interesting. This, according to Bem, led them to conclude that they too also found the initial tasks interesting (or at least more interesting than they otherwise would have). In other words, attitudes change through simple self-perception, without arousing any unpleasant inner tension.

Both Festinger and Bem's theories make intuitive sense. Which then is correct? The contemporary consensus is that both are correct, but under different circumstances. Cognitive dissonance is believed to occur when people perform extremely counter-attitudinal acts, whereas self-perception is believed to occur when people perform mildly counter-attitudinal acts (Fazio, Zanna, & Cooper, 1977). So if I hate pizza, and you subtly induce me to eat some, then I will come to like pizza more as a way of resolving the dissonance created internally. However, if

I only slightly dislike pizza, and you subtly induce me to eat some, then I will come to like pizza more by noting my pizza-eating behavior and inferring a pizza-loving disposition. But how can we be sure that unpleasant arousal *ever* plays a role in dissonance? The definitive proof comes from studies in which attitude change is eliminated after participants have been given another way to explain where their unpleasant arousal has come from (Losch & Cacioppo, 1990; Zanna & Cooper, 1974). For example, if participants are told that a pill they have just ingested is enough to explain their unpleasant inner tension, then their attitudes no longer shift.

Researchers have also tried to clarify the conditions necessary for cognitive dissonance to occur. Festinger (1957) had already established that people respond better to nudges than shoves, but later research established that they must also (a) *freely* perform the counter-attitudinal act; (b) *foresee* that the act will have *negative consequences*; and (c) *attribute* unpleasant arousal to the *act itself* (Goethals, Cooper, & Naficy, 1979; Linder, Cooper, & Jones, 1967; Zanna, Higgins, & Taves, 1978). All these conditions were met in the original Festinger and Carlsmith study. Such findings also inspired Cooper and Fazio (1984) to reformulate Festinger's theory. They argued that cognitive inconsistency per se was irrelevant to the production of dissonance effects. The phenomena attributed to cognitive inconsistency only occurred, they claimed, when people believed that they had freely chosen to bring about unwanted consequences that they had foreseen.

By way of illustration, imagine a mirror-image version of the Festinger and Carlsmith study. Here participants begin by performing two enjoyable tasks. They then voluntarily tell a female confederate that these tasks were boring. Will these participants now go on to develop less positive attitudes toward the tasks? We suspect not, or at least not to the same degree. The fact that the anticipated consequences of telling the lie are not negative (a nice, as opposed to nasty, surprise now awaits the confederate) removes the need for rationalization. Nonetheless, the level of cognitive inconsistency is no less than it was in the original study; its polarity has merely been reversed. The results of such thought experiments are backed up by actual research showing that if an act, freely undertaken, has foreseeable unwanted consequences, attitude change occurs, even if that act is consistent with one's original attitudes (Scher & Cooper, 1989).

However, Festinger may have the last laugh. More recent research implicates cognitive consistency after all. For one thing, cognitive dissonance effects appear to be confined to people who value consistency as a personality trait (Cialdini, Trost, & Newsom, 1995). In addition, shifts in attitude occur even when people perform acts that do not have any immediate negative consequences. For example, persuading participants to freely write down, on a later discarded piece of paper, that they like an unpleasant tasting beverage, leads them to rate that beverage more favorably later (Harmon-Jones, Brehm, Greenberg, Simon, & Nelson, 1996). Moreover, if participants are induced to make a private speech in favor of condom use, and are then reminded about their past failures to use condoms, they later purchase more condoms by way of atonement (Stone, Aronson, Crain, Winslow, & Fried, 1994). Festinger's (1957) original theory can accommodate such findings; Cooper and Fazio's (1984) reformulation cannot. Ironically, studies of cognitive consistency have themselves yielded inconsistent findings!

However, if we assume that some valued aspect of the self is threatened by all manipulations of cognitive dissonance, and that people then take steps to restore their damaged self-image, then a degree of theoretical integration may be possible. The desire to maintain a positive self-image is a primary human motivation (Sedikides & Gregg, 2008). Evidence that it lies behind cognitive dissonance comes from studies in which participants are given the opportunity to affirm their self-image. Suppose for the sake of argument that participants in the Festinger and Carlsmith study had been allowed to contribute to their favorite charity immediately after lying to the female confederate. It is likely that this act would have sufficed to make them feel better about themselves, thereby removing any motivation to affirm their self-image by revising their opinion of the boring study (proving that they are not just shameless liars). In actual studies run along similar lines, the shifts of attitude that usually follow manipulations of cognitive dissonance are eliminated by an opportunity to perform a good deed or affirm an important value (Steele, 1988). Hence, the underlying motivation seems not so much about resolving inconsistency as about maintaining a positive self-image.

A neat compromise viewpoint is also available. Cognitions are not so much mutually consonant or dissonant with one another (as Festinger originally claimed) as they are consonant or dissonant with some *valued aspect of the self*—such as honesty, competence, personal consistency, or whatever (Aronson, 1969). On this view, the dissonant cognitions in the Festinger and Carlsmith study were not so much "I disliked the study" and "I claimed the study was enjoyable," but rather "I am a truthful person" and "I lied by claiming the study was enjoyable." The advantage of this formulation is that it retains the idea of cognitive inconsistency in Festinger's original theory while specifying what makes cognitions important in the first place, namely, relevance to self-image.

Yet even the role of self-image in cognitive dissonance remains unclear. There is no direct evidence, for example, that performing counter-attitudinal acts makes people temporarily think poorly of themselves. Instead, they merely seem to experience a generalized sense of uneasiness or discomfort (Elliot & Devine, 1994; Harmon-Jones, 2000). Furthermore, one curious extension of the Festinger and Carlsmith study found that if participants attempted to convince a confederate, truthfully, that the original task had been boring, they later rated the task as having been more enjoyable too (Girandola, 1997). If compromised moral principles are the ultimate source of cognitive dissonance, then why should truthfulness lead to greater attitude change than deceit?

So there we have it. Oscar Wilde's remark that truth is rarely pure and never simple certainly applies to cognitive dissonance theory. However, there is no denying that successive incarnations of the theory have thrown progressively more light on our understanding of human motivation, and that social psychologists will continue to unravel the mysteries that remain for many years to come.

Revelation

If you wish to change somebody's opinion, subtly induce him or her to act at odds with it. This tactic works because people readily rationalize objectionable actions for which they feel responsible by adjusting their attitudes to match them.

What Do You Think?

In *A Song to Myself*, the American poet Walt Whitman wrote the following lines: "Do I contradict myself? Very well then I contradict myself. (I am large, I contain multitudes.)" Do you feel the same way? Should one make peace with one's inconsistencies, or try to resolve them?

Chapter Reference

Festinger, L., & Carlsmith, J. (1959). Cognitive consequences of forced compliance. *Journal of Abnormal and Social Psychology, 58*, 203–10.

Other References

Abelson, R. P. (1963). Computer simulation of "Hot Cognition." In S. Tomkins & S. Messick (Eds.), *Computer simulation of personality* (pp. 277–298). New York: Wiley-Blackwell.

Aronson, E. (1969). The theory of cognitive dissonance: A current perspective. In L. Berkowitz (Ed.), *Advances in experimental social psychology* (Vol. 4, pp. 1–34). New York: Academic Press.

Aronson, E., & Carlsmith, J. M. (1963). Effects of the severity of threat on the devaluation of forbidden behavior. *Journal of Abnormal and Social Psychology, 12*, 16–27.

Bem, D. J. (1967). Self-perception: An alternative interpretation of cognitive dissonance phenomena. *Psychological Review, 74*, 183–200.

Brehm, J. W. (1956). Post-decision changes in desirability of alternatives. *Journal of Abnormal and Social Psychology, 52*, 384–389.

Brehm, S. S., & Brehm, J. W. (1981). *Psychological reactance*. New York: Academic Press.

Bushman, B. J. (1996). Forbidden fruit versus tainted fruit: Effect of warning labels on attraction to television violence. *Journal of Experimental Psychology: Applied, 2*, 207–226.

Chapanis, N., & Chapanis, A. (1964). Cognitive dissonance: Five years later. *Psychological Bulletin, 61*, 1–22.

Cialdini, R. B., Trost, M. R., & Newsom, J. T. (1995). Preference of consistency: The development of a valid measure and the discovery of surprising behavioral implications. *Journal of Personality and Social Psychology, 69*, 318–328.

Cooper, J. (2007). *Cognitive dissonance: 50 years of a classic theory*. Thousand Oaks, CA: SAGE Publishing.

Cooper, J., & Fazio, R. (1984). A new look at dissonance theory. In L. Berkowitz (Ed.), *Advances in experimental social psychology* (Vol. 17, pp. 229–267). New York: Academic Press.

Crocker, J., & Major, B. (1989). Social stigma and self-esteem: The self-protective properties of stigma. *Psychological Review, 96*, 608–630.

Elliot, A. J., & Devine, P. G. (1994). On the motivational nature of cognitive dissonance: Dissonance as psychological discomfort. *Journal of Personality and Social Psychology, 67*, 382–394.

Fazio, R. H., Zanna, M. P., & Cooper, J. (1977). Dissonance and self-perception: An integrative view of each theory's proper domain of application. *Journal of Experimental Social Psychology, 13*, 464–479.

Festinger, L. (1957). *A theory of cognitive dissonance*. Stanford, CA: Stanford University Press.

Festinger, L., Riecken, H. W., & Schachter, S. (1956). *When prophecy fails: A social and psychological study of a modern group that predicted the destruction of the world*. New York: Harper Torchbooks.

Freedman, J. L. (1965). Long-term behavioral effects of cognitive dissonance. *Journal of Experimental Social Psychology, 1*, 145–155.

Gawronski, B. (2012). Back to the future of dissonance theory: Cognitive dissonance as a core motive. *Social Cognition, 30*, 652–668.

Girandola, F. (1997). Double forced compliance and cognitive dissonance theory. *Journal of Social Psychology, 137*, 594–605.

Goethals, G., Cooper, J., & Naficy, A. (1979). Role of foreseen, foreseeable, and unforeseeable behavioral consequences in the arousal of cognitive dissonance. *Journal of Personality and Social Psychology, 37*, 1179–1185.

Harmon-Jones, E. (2000). Cognitive dissonance and experienced negative affect: Evidence that dissonance increases negative affect even in the absence of aversive consequences. *Personality and Social Psychology Bulletin, 26*, 1490–1501.

Harmon-Jones, E., Brehm, J. W., Greenberg, J., Simon, L., & Nelson, D. E. (1996). Evidence that the production of aversive consequences is not necessary to create cognitive dissonance. *Journal of Personality and Social Psychology, 70*, 5–16.

Harmon-Jones, E., & Mills, J. (1999). *Cognitive dissonance: Progress on a pivotal theory in social psychology*. Washington, DC: American Psychological Association.

Lerner, M. J. (1980). *The belief in a just world: A fundamental delusion*. New York: Plenum.

Linder, D., Cooper, J., & Jones, E. (1967). Decision freedom as a determinant of the role of incentive magnitude in attitude change. *Journal of Personality and Social Psychology, 6*, 245–254.

Losch, M. E., & Cacioppo, J. T. (1990). Cognitive dissonance may enhance sympathetic tonus, but attitudes are changed to reduce negative affect rather than arousal. *Journal of Experimental Social Psychology, 26*, 289–304.

Rosenberg, M. (1965). When dissonance fails: On eliminating evaluation apprehension from attitude measurement. *Journal of Personality and Social Psychology, 1*, 28–42.

Schein, E. (1956). The Chinese indoctrination program for prisoners of war: A study of attempted "brainwashing". *Psychiatry, 19*, 149–172.

Scher, S. J., & Cooper, J. (1989). Motivation basis of dissonance: The singular role of behavioral consequences. *Journal of Personality and Social Psychology, 56*, 899–906.

Sedikides, C., & Gregg, A. P. (2008). Self-enhancement: Food for thought. *Perspectives on Psychological Science, 3*, 102–116.

Steele, C. M. (1988). The psychology of self-affirmation: Sustaining the integrity of the self. In L. Berkowitz (Ed.), *Advances in experimental social psychology* (Vol. 21, pp. 261–302). New York: Academic Press.

Stone, J., Aronson, E., Crain, A. L., Winslow, M. P., & Fried, C. B. (1994). Inducing hypocrisy as a means for encouraging young adults to use condoms. *Personality and Social Psychology Bulletin, 20*, 116–128.

Zanna, M. P., & Cooper, J. (1974). Dissonance and the pill: An attribution approach to studying the arousal properties of dissonance. *Journal of Personality and Social Psychology, 29*, 703–709.

Zanna, M. P., Higgins, E., & Taves, P. (1978). Is dissonance phenomenologically aversive? *Journal of Experimental Social Psychology, 12*, 530–538.

More to Explore

Gawronski, B. (2012). Back to the future of dissonance theory: Cognitive dissonance as a core motive. *Social Cognition, 30*, 652–668.

3 Baptism of Fire

When Suffering Leads to Liking

"Fanaticism consists in redoubling your effort when you have forgotten your aim."
—George Santayana (1863–1952), Spanish-American philosopher

Background

Chapter 2 showed that, when we are led, with minimal inducement, to behave in a manner inconsistent with our attitudes, our attitudes often shift to become more consistent with our behavior (Festinger & Carlsmith, 1959). This is one way of reducing the unpleasant cognitive dissonance that comes from knowing we have willingly done something embarrassing or immoral. Because the deed cannot be denied, nor responsibility for it evaded, we preserve our dignity or integrity by adopting an attitude that justifies the deed, and by believing that we held that attitude all along.

However, cognitive dissonance can also arise, and be resolved, by other means. Consider the identical twins, Jess and Tess. Normally inseparable, the pair happened to attend different showings of the same movie. Whereas Jess paid an extravagant $20 for an advance screening, Tess paid a paltry $5 for a bargain matinee. Unfortunately the movie they watched turned out to be rather disappointing—at least, that was the subsequent consensus of moviegoers and critics alike. Some days later Jess and Tess got around to discussing their respective cinematic experiences. Although they usually agreed about everything, they found that they disagreed about the merits of the movie. Whereas Tess echoed the misgivings of the majority, Jess was enthusiastic in her praise.

The twins' difference of opinion can be explained by the difference in how much each spent. Jess prided herself on being a sensible spender. Hence, admitting that she had willingly wasted a sizeable sum on a lousy movie would have been too much for her to bear. The most convenient way to avoid making this admission was to regard the movie in retrospect as better than it had been. Tess, too, prided herself on being a sensible spender. However, having spent a smaller sum to see the movie, she did not feel any great need to revise her opinion of it upward.

Cognitive dissonance theory can explain why Jess came to like the movie more than Tess did. However, note that the counter-attitudinal behavior creating the dissonance (forking out $20) took place *prior* to the formation of the attitude (the impression of the movie), not after it, as happened in the study reported in Chapter 2. This inverted sequence of events points to the operation of a different class of dissonance effect. It boils down to this: If we first attain something at considerable cost, we later become biased toward evaluating it favorably. For Jess and Tess, the cost was monetary. But other costs can also arouse dissonance—effort exerted, trouble taken, pain suffered. In all cases, the greater the hardship endured, the greater the subsequent change in attitude.

This conclusion may strike you as plausible enough. Perhaps you have already observed a correlation between the amount of work people put into something and how much they value the result. For instance, someone who has worked diligently to get a degree is liable to prize it more than someone who has worked only half-heartedly to get it. However, such correlations on their own are not enough to prove an *effort-justification effect*—namely, that the harder you work for something, the more you like it. This is so for two reasons. First, the amount of work people put in often determines the quality of the result. For example, if a student works hard on a term paper, his or her favorable opinion of the finished product may reflect its consequent quality, rather than any attempt on his or her part to justify the effort exerted. Second, people who strive harder to attain a result are likely to have initially placed greater value on attaining that result. So suppose that Chun-Ju does her level best to make the school volleyball team whereas Yi-Ying barely tries at all. Both nonetheless make the volleyball team. It turns out that Chun-Ju later appreciates being on the team more than Yi-Ying does. Was this due to the greater effort Chun-Ju put in? Not necessarily. Chun-Ju might have originally liked the idea of being a team member more, and then tried harder to make the team as a consequence. Hence, observation alone can provide only circumstantial evidence for an effort-justification effect.

What is a social psychologist to do? He or she needs to conduct an experiment in which the cost of attaining an outcome is varied while everything else—including the quality of the outcome attained, and the intensity of the original desire to attain it—is held constant. Under such circumstances, differences in outcome evaluation can be confidently attributed to differences in initial cost, and to nothing else.

Aronson and Mills (1959) set about obtaining the relevant data. They concentrated on a common but often significant social event: joining the ranks of an established group. Realizing that becoming a new group member can sometimes be a challenging experience, the researchers predicted that the more severe a person's initiation into a group, the more they would come to like that group and value being a member.

What They Did

To test their hypotheses cleanly, Aronson and Mills had to artificially create a social group that satisfied two conditions. First, it had to afford a suitable pretext for an initiation procedure whose severity could be varied. Second, it had to be interesting enough for participants to want to join even after they learned about the initiation procedure. To meet these challenges, the researchers created a group whose alleged purpose was to discuss on a weekly basis a most intriguing topic: sex. Sixty-three female college students volunteered to become members.

The initiation procedure consisted of an *embarrassment test* that was supposed to determine whether participants felt comfortable talking openly about sex. Across the study's three conditions, the magnitude of the embarrassment that participants experienced during the initiation was systematically manipulated. In the severe-initiation condition, participants had to say aloud 12 highly obscene words (including some four-letter ones) and then read aloud two passages of prose depicting lurid sexual activity. To make matters worse, they had to do this in front of the male experimenter, who was closely monitoring them for any signs of hesitation or blushing. In the mild-initiation condition, participants were given the far less daunting task of reading aloud five mildly sex-related words (e.g., virgin, petting). In a final control condition, the initiation procedure was omitted completely. In both mild-initiation and severe-initiation conditions, the experimenter explained that the embarrassment test was necessary in order to ensure that all participants would contribute in equal measure to the group discussion. The reason, he claimed, was that the dynamics of the discussion process were under scrutiny, and that reluctance to speak would distort these dynamics. Importantly, the experimenter emphasized that participants were under no obligation to take the test, although they could not become group members without doing so. This ensured that participants only took the test voluntarily (a known necessary condition for cognitive dissonance to occur; Linder, Cooper, & Jones, 1967). The fact that there was no pressure placed on participants to undergo the initiation may ease some of the reader's ethical concerns about the study. One participant did indeed exercise her prerogative not to take the embarrassment test.

The experimenter also explained to participants that, in an effort to reduce the embarrassment caused by discussing sex face to face, he had opted to put all participants in separate rooms and have them communicate over an intercom system via microphone and headphones. However, this was merely an elaborate deception aimed at keeping an important fact under wraps, namely, that the discussion group did not actually exist! In reality, all participants listened through their headphones to the same recorded discussion taking place between supposed group members.

Why the elaborate deception? Why not just use a real group? The answer is that the researchers were trying to cut down on irrelevant variation in their experiment. Such variation makes the effects of the manipulation harder to detect—much as the background hiss on a radio makes a channel harder to hear. If participants had interacted in person, then the ensuing discussion would have been difficult to regulate, and would have introduced much irrelevant variation into the experiment. However, with all participants listening to the same discussion, it was all removed in a single stroke.

Of course, to maintain this clever deception, the researchers had to keep participants from joining in the discussion. To achieve this, they first asked participants whether or not they had ever read a book called *Sexual Behavior in Animals*. All replied in the negative. The experimenter then explained to participants that they could not join in the current discussion because the other group members had already read the book, and introducing someone who hadn't could distort the dynamics of the discussion. (Participants had earlier been told that the discussion group had been meeting for several weeks, so this revelation did not strike them as odd.) Nevertheless, participants were informed that they could still listen in on the group discussion to get a feel for what the group was like.

Participants were led to believe that a group meeting was already in progress. The experimenter interrupted the group over the microphone, and explained to them that a new member (whose name he gave) would be listening. At the precise moment when participants donned their headphones, three prerecorded voices introduced themselves, and then settled back into their discussion.

So what juicy topics did these fictitious group members address? Participants hoping to deepen their understanding of sexuality were in for a monumental disappointment. The researchers' own description of the recording illustrates why:

> The recording . . . was deliberately designed to be as dull and as banal as possible . . . participants spoke dryly and haltingly on secondary sex behavior in lower animals, inadvertently contradicted themselves and one another, mumbled several non sequiturs, started sentences that they never finished, hemmed, hawed, and in general conducted one of the most worthless and uninteresting discussions imaginable.
>
> (Aronson & Mills, 1959, p. 179)

Once the discussion had finished, participants were asked to fill out a questionnaire about what they thought of both the discussion and of the other group members. They were told that everybody in the group had done the same. The main prediction was that participants in the severe-initiation condition, because they had experienced more cognitive dissonance, would come to think more highly of the group discussion, and of the group members themselves.

The cover story and carefully choreographed procedures proved remarkably successful. Only one participant, when questioned afterward, expressed any definite suspicions about the nonexistence of the discussion group (her data were discarded). It is also noteworthy that, when the real purpose of the study was at last revealed to participants, none were dismayed either at having been deceived or at having been put through the initiation procedure. In fact, the researchers reported that most participants were intrigued by the study, even returning at the end of the term to learn about the results.

What They Found

The results were clear-cut. Compared to participants in the mild-initiation and no-initiation conditions, participants in the severe-initiation condition rated both the discussion and the discussants more favorably, providing powerful evidence for the effort justification effect (Figure 3). As predicted, the more severe participants' initiation into a group, the more they said they liked that group. Why? Most likely because of the cognitive dissonance they experienced. Specifically, participants' knew that (a) they had freely submitted to an unpleasant initiation procedure; and (b) that group membership was a disappointment. Unable to deny the freedom of their actions or the unpleasantness of the initiation, they instead looked back on group membership through rose-tinted glasses, and concluded that being part of the group was a worthwhile experience. (See Chapter 17, for more on perceptual bias, and Chapter 21, for more on retrospective bias.)

Two other experimental findings deserve comment. First, there were no differences between the mild-initiation and no-initiation conditions with regard to how participants rated the discussion and the discussants. It seems that the mild-initiation condition caused participants hardly any embarrassment, with the result that little cognitive dissonance was created. The researchers might have preferred liking for the group to rise in step with severity of initiation, but it was difficult for them to predict in advance what increment in severity would correspond to what increment in liking. Second, initiation severity had a greater influence on participants' opinions about the quality of the discussion than on their opinions about the likability of the group members. This may have been because derogating the quality of the discussion was more crucial to reducing dissonance. Alternatively, participants may simply have been reluctant to directly criticize fellow students.

It has been pointed out that other psychological mechanisms could perhaps have accounted for the findings obtained in the present study. For example, participants in the severe-initiation

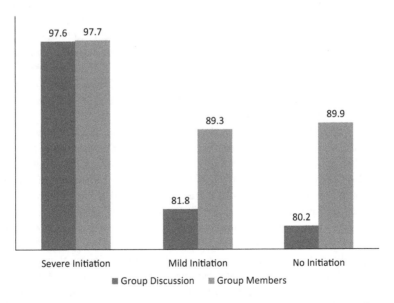

Figure 3 Participants' ratings of the group discussion, and of other group members, after undergoing a severe initiation or mild initiation into the group, or no initiation

condition might have formed a more positive impression of the group discussion because it seemed decidedly pleasant in comparison to the mortifying test they had just been put through. Or again, these participants, despite experiencing embarrassment, might still have had their interest in sexual topics piqued, and thus looked upon the tedious discussion of animal courtship more favorably. Happily, subsequent research has ruled out even these alternative explanations. In a rigorous replication study (Gerard & Mathewson, 1966), initiation severity was manipulated by administering to participants different levels of safe but unpleasant electric shock (unlike in the famous Milgram studies of obedience, where *no* electric shocks were actually administered; see Chapter 4). The merit of this new manipulation, from a scientific perspective, was that the content of the initiation procedure was no longer related to the content of the discussion group. This permitted several possible confounds to be simultaneously eliminated. In addition, the researchers manipulated whether participants did or did not believe that they were part of the group whose members and discussion they later evaluated. This permitted the researchers to tease apart the effects of otherwise identical negative experiences—one linked to group initiation, the other not—on later attitudes toward the group. Several other precautions were also taken. Despite this extra degree of rigor, the results obtained were strongly consistent with an effort-justification effect.

So What?

The study demonstrated that the overcoming of painful obstacles en route to becoming a group member makes people value group membership more, not less. This helps us to understand why, in everyday life, loyalty to a group can increase over time even in the face of seemingly substantial and repeated incentives to leave.

Common sense holds that the way to make people join a group, and ensure that they remain members, is to remove all possible obstacles to joining, and to generously reward long-term fidelity. In one sense, this is obviously true. If I do not have to do anything special to join a group, and am paid handsomely for being a member, why should I not join it? Yet, although such powerful incentives are effective in shaping our behavior, they do not necessarily lead us to *internalize* feelings of loyalty to a group. That is, you can bribe people into belonging to a group but you cannot bribe them into feeling committed to it. If you want to transform how people truly feel, you would be wise to adopt a more indirect approach. The present study documents one tactic that someone in a position of power can employ: induce people to willingly undergo some hardship as a precondition for joining a group. Cognitive dissonance will then ensure that people's private attitudes toward the group shift in a positive direction. Hence, group membership need not be maintained through the provision of incentives; the process of self-justification ensures that people come to value group membership for its own sake.

The problem, of course, is how to motivate people to take the first big step toward membership. Sometimes the allure of the group is sufficient on its own. The promise of a pay raise, status boost, or unique opportunity can inspire would-be members to endure any preliminary hardships they encounter. Ironically, it is precisely those who are originally more motivated to join a group who will be prepared to endure initiations of greater severity, thereby reinforcing their already positive attitude toward group membership. This is an example of how social conditions can conspire to make preexisting attitudes more extreme, creating a self-reinforcing loop (Abelson, 1995). Consider also, in this connection, the case of a prospective group member called upon at first to make a small sacrifice for the privilege of group membership, but then gradually seduced into making much larger sacrifices. Each increment along the way is so small that it is never possible, having made the previous sacrifice, not to justify making the next one also. Such a slippery slope can snare even people who were not initially so keen to become model group members. (See Chapter 4 for how a slippery slope has also been used to explain obedience to authority.)

There is evidence to suggest that the slope need not even be so slippery for commitment to take root. Making a token concession at first can lead a person to a more consequential concession later. In one study, for example, undergraduate participants were asked whether they would show up at seven in the morning to take part in research on thinking processes. Half the participants were immediately informed of the early starting time, whereas the other half were informed of it only after first agreeing to take part in the research itself. This trivial difference in the wording of the request made a substantial difference to the number of participants who complied with it. Whereas less than a quarter of those immediately informed of the early starting time showed up, more than half of those who first verbally committed to the research did (Cialdini, Cacioppo, Bassett, & Miller, 1978).

Salespeople often use similar techniques to get customers to part with their hard-earned cash. One of the authors (APG) learned from an investigative journalist about how a dodgy car finance company used compliance techniques to sweeten deals for themselves at the expense of their customers. For example, as a matter of sales policy, they had customers unnecessarily wait for hours while their finance deal was supposedly being negotiated upstairs. Can you see how this might elicit their acceptance of the dealership's final offer?

Given the various subtle means by which commitment can be strengthened, can you now begin to appreciate how people can get sucked into unsavory organizations whose practices and beliefs strike outsiders as absurd and extremist? Nonetheless, we must not lose sight of the fact that effort-justification phenomena are not limited to fringe organizations; they abound in mainstream society too. Think of all the social institutions that require sacrifices as a precondition for joining their ranks. College fraternities haze new members in fiendish ways; the military puts new recruits through purgatorial boot camps; and bleary-eyed interns slave night and day before becoming medical doctors. The rationale for such harsh preconditions on group membership is unclear until one realizes their potential for arousing cognitive dissonance. That dissonance can be resolved by members adopting a more positive attitude toward the group, which in turn facilitates greater loyalty, obedience, and esprit de corps, all of which promote group cohesion.

An analysis of 19th-century utopian cults by Kanter (1972) underscored the central roles of effort-justification and commitment in keeping groups together. She found that cults requiring their members to make significant sacrifices were more successful. For example, cults that had their members surrender all their personal belongings lasted much longer than those that did not. Hence, the experimental findings of Aronson and Mills are nicely borne out by historical data.

Afterthoughts

In concluding our discussion of the effort justification effect, let us once more consider the plight of Jess, who spent all that money to see such a disappointing movie. Suppose that Jess had sufficient acquaintance with dissonance theory not to let the $20 she paid influence her judgment. Halfway through the movie, she bravely admitted to herself that she had made a mistake. What, rationally, should she do now? Stay or leave? You might suspect that, having paid so much, she would be better off staying. However, a little thought makes it clear that Jess should leave as soon as she can. After all, she cannot get a refund no matter what she does. However, if she leaves, she will at least no longer have to sit through a boring movie. With the money already spent, the only thing that matters is the quality of Jess's life from now on. Hence, she should walk out of the movie posthaste. She would thereby avoid a common behavioral trap called the *sunk cost error*—the irrational tendency to honor an irrevocable loss to the detriment of one's present and future welfare (see Arkes & Blumer, 1985). In experimental tests, for example, people tend to keep investing well past the break-even point, even when the investment climate has obviously become unfavorable (Rubin & Brockner, 1975).

Irrationally sitting through a boring movie because you paid for the privilege of doing so is a relatively minor instance of the sunk cost error. Matters start to get more serious when high-ranking officials persist in squandering public funds on pointless projects to justify all the public funds they have already squandered. One famous example is the Tennessee-Tombigee Waterway. Costing $2 billion to build, and requiring more earth to be displaced than the Panama Canal, it today stretches 234 miles from Alabama to Mississippi. Midway through construction, however, it was concluded that the estimated economic value of the waterway would be far less than the amount required to complete it. Nonetheless, Alabama Senator Jeremiah Denton had these words to say in defense of forging ahead anyhow: "To terminate a project in which $1.1 billion has been invested represents an unconscionable mishandling of taxpayers' dollars" (cited in Dawes, 1988, p. 23). The good Senator appears to have overlooked the fact that the original $1.1 billion was gone forever, and that spending another $0.9 billion would only mishandle taxpayers' dollars further. Today, the so-called Tenn-Tom is used mainly as a shipping route for coal and timber products, and has failed to live up to its predicted usefulness.

Another potential boondoggle is the United States' F-35 stealth fighter jet, the most expensive (and possibly most error ridden) military weapons system in history. The project has been criticized at every turn, and yet it is now out of research and development and into production, and is estimated to ultimately cost as much as $1.5 *trillion*. Could it be that the sunk cost error—throwing good money after bad money—is again being committed? Time will tell. At any rate, we should never—whether as individuals or collectives—unwisely maintain our commitments to profligate endeavors. Rather, we should deliberately cut our losses and move on. This can be difficult, given our relative aversion to incurring sure losses (Tversky & Shafir, 1992). Indeed, because the sunk cost error tends to be a self-justifying process, it helps to have a more objective second party oversee ongoing investment decisions (Gunia, Sivanathan, & Galinsky, 2009).

Revelation

When people voluntarily undergo an unpleasant experience to achieve something, they come to value that something more, not less. This helps explain why people become committed members of groups even when membership entails considerable initial sacrifice and offers scant subsequent reward.

What Do You Think?

It is often said that "winners never quit, and quitters never win." But isn't failing to quit, when progress is impossible or unlikely, a recipe for losing? To succeed in life, isn't it more a matter of "knowing when to hold 'em, and knowing when to fold 'em"—just as in a game of poker?

Chapter Reference

Aronson, E., & Mills, J. (1959). The effect of severity of initiation on liking for a group. *Journal of Abnormal and Social Psychology, 59*, 177–181.

Other References

Abelson, R. P. (1995). Attitude extremity. In R. E. Petty & J. A. Krosnick (Eds.), *Attitude strength: Antecedents and consequences* (pp. 25–41). Hillsdale, NJ: Lawrence Erlbaum Associates.

Arkes, H., & Blumer, C. (1985). The psychology of sunk cost. *Organization Behavior and Human Decision Processes, 35*, 124–140.

Cialdini, R., Cacioppo, J., Bassett, R., & Miller, J. (1978). Low-ball procedure for producing compliance: Commitment then cost. *Journal of Personality and Social Psychology*, *36*, 463–476.

Dawes, R. M. (1988). *Rational choice in an uncertain world*. San Diego, CA: Harcourt Brace.

Festinger, L., & Carlsmith, J. (1959). Cognitive consequences of forced compliance. *Journal of Abnormal and Social Psychology*, *58*, 203–210.

Gerard, H. B., & Mathewson, G. C. (1966). The effects of severity of initiation on liking for a group: A replication. *Journal of Experimental Social Psychology*, *2*, 278–287.

Gunia, B. C., Sivanathan, N., & Galinsky, A. D. (2009). Vicarious entrapment: Your sunk costs, my escalation of commitment. *Journal of Experimental Social Psychology*, *45*, 1238–1244.

Kanter, R. M. (1972). *Commitment and community: Communes and utopias in sociological perspective*. Cambridge, MA: Harvard University Press.

Linder, D., Cooper, J., & Jones, E. (1967). Decision freedom as a determinant of the role of incentive magnitude in attitude change. *Journal of Personality and Social Psychology*, *6*, 245–254.

Rubin, J. Z., & Brockner, J. (1975). Factors affecting entrapment in waiting situations: The Rosenkrantz and Guildenstern effect. *Journal of Personality and Social Psychology*, *31*, 1054–1063.

Tversky, A., & Shafir, E. (1992). The disjunction effect in choice under uncertainty. *Psychological Science*, *3*, 305–309.

More to Explore

Tavris, C., & Aronson, E. (2008). *Mistakes were made (but not by me): Why we justify foolish beliefs, bad decisions, and hurtful acts*. Boston, MA: Mariner Books.

4 Just Following Orders

A Shocking Demonstration of Obedience to Authority

"Obedience, bane of all genius, virtue, freedom, truth, makes slaves of men, and, of the human frame, a mechanized automaton."

—Percy Bysshe Shelley (1792–1822), English poet

Background

Whenever you do something because someone tells you to do it—whether or not you want to do it—that is *obedience*. Obedience is often a good thing. It permits society to function smoothly and to accomplish large-scale goals that require hierarchical coordination. Leaders tell followers what to do, the followers do it, and things get done. The ancient Greek philosopher, Socrates, extolled the importance of obedience to the state, and stoically accepted an Athenian jury's order to drink poisonous hemlock (for the sin of corrupting the minds of young people). Yet obedience is not always a good thing. Indeed, Plato, mindful of his mentor's fate, questioned the wisdom of obeying unjust laws. History has been replete with poignant examples of obedience-turned-tragedy, thereby instilling the spirit of rebellion in the enlightenati of later generations.

During the height of the Vietnam War, an American Bravo company swept through a defenseless hamlet, My Lai, slaughtering all the natives in sight because they were suspected of siding with the enemy. One of the invading soldiers admitted in a sobering testimony to pushing men, women, and children into a ravine and shooting them, because he was ordered to do so by the officer in charge (Milgram, 1974). That officer, Lieutenant Benjamin Calley, defended his own actions—he, too, was just following orders. In 1978, more than 900 People's Temple devotees of the Reverend Jim Jones obeyed his command to commit mass suicide by drinking cyanide-laced Kool-Aid (although it appeared afterward that some had done so at gunpoint, most had submitted willingly). In 1993, impassioned disciples of David Koresh followed his charge to fire on approaching law enforcement officers and remained barricaded in their Waco, Texas compound for weeks. (Of course, the raiding government troops were likewise being obedient to their superiors.) The standoff ended when the compound was burned to the ground, leaving about 80 Branch Davidian cultists dead, among them 20 children. This is but a fraction of the deplorable historical episodes that have inspired the following kind of quote: "When you think of the long and gloomy history of man, you will find that far more, and far more hideous, crimes have been committed in the name of obedience than have ever been committed in the name of rebellion" (Snow, 1961, p. 24).

Social psychologists are well aware of the horrors of history and the world around them. The *zeitgeist* (spirit of the times) and the *ortgeist* (spirit of a place) greatly influence what social psychologists choose to study. When the U.S. government makes some calamitous decision, as it did during the 1961 Bay of Pigs fiasco, social psychologists feel compelled to study the pitfalls of group decision making. When a woman is raped on a barroom pool table in full view of unresponsive barflies, social psychologists are driven to study bystander intervention (or lack thereof—see Chapter 5). When it transpires that women on the whole earn less than their male peers do, social psychologists commit to research on gender stereotypes. Social psychology is perhaps more influenced by ongoing social events than any other field of scientific inquiry.

Social psychologist Stanley Milgram (1963) sought to explain one of the most shameful episodes of human history. As a young assistant professor at Yale University, Milgram had been captivated by the Nuremberg war trials, especially by the trial of Adolf Eichmann, an alleged architect of the Final Solution—the Nazi's abhorrent attempt to exterminate the Jews of Europe. Eichmann, by all appearances a normal man, repeatedly testified to the Jerusalem court that he had simply been obeying orders, and it was the ordinary demeanor of men like Eichmann that led the social commentator Hannah Arendt to write, in 1965, about the *banality of evil* (the fact that it can be committed by everyday people—like you and me). Eichmann's plea fascinated Milgram. Had this been an incomprehensively evil man or simply someone who was just following orders? Was Eichmann driven by unspeakably perverse passions, a deranged ideologue known to fulminate against Jews, or was he an ordinary person who just happened to get caught up in a vortex of hatred and vengeance? Just how banal is evil?

The starting point of what is arguably the most famous (or infamous) of all social psychological experiments was a simple observation by its designer:

> It has been reliably established that from 1933–1945 millions of innocent persons were systematically slaughtered on command. Gas chambers were built, death camps were guarded, and daily quotas of corpses were produced with the same efficiency as the manufacture of appliances. These inhumane policies may have originated in the mind of a single person, but they could only be carried out on a massive scale if a very large number of people obeyed orders.
>
> (Milgram, 1974, p. 467)

This observation provoked obvious questions. What caused those who perpetrated the Final Solution to obey the heinous orders they received? More generally, how inclined are people to obey authority figures, and what factors mitigate or exacerbate such an inclination?

Milgram began as a firm believer in cultural differences. He suspected that the apparent blind obedience on the part of the Nazis during World War II reflected a distinct, and probably rare, German character. In an effort to demonstrate this point, he devised a unique measure of obedience. Specifically, he *operationalized* obedience (that is, he defined it in terms of how he would measure it) as the intensity of shock one person, a presumed teacher, would willingly give another person, a presumed learner, at the behest of an authority figure, during what was claimed to be an experiment on the effects of punishment on learning. Crucially, the required level of shock increased as the experiment continued—up to a lethal maximum. Having developed this measure of obedience, Milgram speculated that very few of his participants would administer even moderate shocks, let alone intense shocks: "You would get only a very, very small portion of people going out to the end of the shock generator, and they would constitute a pathological fringe" (Meyer, 1970, pp. 3–4).

Milgram started out studying adults from the community surrounding Yale University, a reasonably representative sample of the population at large. These participants—the rank and file of ordinary Americans—were to serve as a baseline against which he would later compare German participants expected to possess more Nazi-like characteristics. However, as it turned out, Milgram never got around to studying Germans per se. The results he obtained from the people next door were too startling.

What He Did

Milgram (1963) conducted scores of obedience experiments, altogether involving more than 1,000 participants. Many of these studies replicated his fundamental findings, and many served to identify important *moderators* (influences on) and *boundary conditions* (limits) of those findings. We begin by describing Milgram's basic paradigm and the exact procedure of his first published study on this front.

Advertising in local newspapers, Milgram paid $4.50 (significant money in the early 1960s—the equivalent of $35 in 2016!) to each of 40 men—who ranged from 20 to 50 years old and were from all walks of life—to participate in a study on memory in an elegant laboratory at Yale University. Each participant arrived at the lab at about the same time as did a mild-mannered and amiable 47-year-old accountant, a research *confederate* who posed as a second participant. The experimenter—a stern-looking 31-year-old male high school biology teacher, wearing a gray technician's coat (not Milgram himself)—began by presenting both men with a *cover story* (stated rationale for the study) concerning the presumed relation between punishment and learning:

> We know very little about the effect of punishment on learning, because almost no truly scientific studies have been made of it on human beings. For instance, we don't know how much punishment is best for learning—and we don't know how much difference it makes as to who is giving the punishment, whether an adult learns best from a younger or older person than himself—or many things of the sort. So in this study we are bringing together a number of adults of different occupations and ages. And we're asking some of them to be teachers and some to be learners. We want to find out just what effect different people have on each other as teachers and learners, and also what effect punishment will have on learning in this situation. Therefore, I'm going to ask one of you to be the teacher here tonight and the other to be the learner.
>
> (Milgram, 1974, p. 468)

At this point the two participants (the real one and the confederate posing as a participant) drew slips of paper from a hat to determine their respective roles. However, the drawing was rigged so that the real participant was always assigned the teacher role. Then the two participants followed the experimenter to an adjoining room where the learner sat down and had his arm strapped into place.

The experimenter explained that the straps were designed to prevent any undue movement, or any attempt at escape. An electrode, allegedly connected to a shock generator in the adjacent room, was attached to the learner's wrist, and buffered by electrode paste "to avoid blisters and burns." As part of the elaborate subterfuge, the learner asked, with apparent nervousness, if the shocks would be painful, to which the experimenter coolly replied that the shocks, though quite painful, would cause no lasting damage. (In subsequent studies, the learner also mentioned that he had a "heart condition.") Thus, the participant was made fully aware of the learner's unenviable predicament.

The experimenter then apprised the participant of his task. He was to read a list of paired words (*blue–sky*, *nice–day*, *wild–duck*, etc.) over a microphone to the learner in the next room. The learner's task was allegedly to memorize the word pairs. The participant would then read the first word of each pair along with four words (e.g., "blue" . . . "ink," "sky," "box," "lamp") and the learner would indicate which of the four words he believed was originally paired with the first word by pressing one of four switches in front of him. One of four numbers would then light up on an answer box in the next room where the participant sat, indicating the learner's response. The answer box was located conveniently above a very authentic-looking shock generator.

The instrument panel of the shock generator included 30 identical lever switches, each with its own industrially engraved voltage designation. The first switch (on the far left) indicated 15 volts, the second 30 volts, the third 45 volts, and so on all the way up to 450 volts. The first three switches carried the label *Slight Shock*. Moving to the right, subsequent triplets of switches carried the labels *Moderate Shock, Strong Shock, Very Strong Shock, Intense Shock, Extremely Intense Shock*, and *Danger: Severe Shock*. The final two switches were ominously marked *XXX*. (The original title for this chapter was simply "XXX," but it's not that sort of chapter!) Whenever a switch was pressed, a pilot light went on, an electric buzz was heard, a blue light (labeled *voltage energizer*) flashed, and a dial on a voltage meter swung rightward.

To make matters even more convincing, all participants were given a sample shock. An electrode was applied to their wrists, the third switch was pressed, and a real 45-volt shock was delivered. Their reactions proved to them that the shock was intense. In fact, they often estimated that they had received a higher level of shock. The participant was told that whenever the learner gave an incorrect answer, the participant was to deliver a shock to him, by throwing one of the switches, and was to "start from 15 volts and increase the shock level one step each time the learner gives a wrong answer" (Milgram, 1974, p. 469).

The participant was instructed to administer shocks in this way until the learner got all of the word pairs correct, even if this required going through the list several times. Unknown to the participant, however, the learner followed a predetermined schedule of responses, answering correctly on only about a quarter of the trials. In this particular study, the learner was heard to pound on the wall after seemingly receiving a 300-volt shock, but gave no further answers thereafter. The experimenter coolly instructed the typically puzzled and alarmed participant to treat this absence of a response as a wrong answer and to advance to the next level of shock, 315 volts. The learner pounded on the wall again after seemingly receiving this level of shock, but after that, nothing more was heard from him. Deathly silence reigned.

Participants instinctively turned to the experimenter for advice on whether they should proceed. They often objected to continuing to shock the unresponsive learner. The experimenter responded with a preordained sequence of five statements, made in a polite but firm tone of voice: "Please continue," "Please go on," "The experiment requires that you continue," "It is absolutely essential that you continue," and "You have no other choice, you must go on." To any participant expressing concern about the learner's physical condition, the experimenter would matter-of-factly reply: "Although the shocks may be painful, there is no physical damage, so please go on." If the participant said he wanted to quit the procedure, the experimenter retorted: "Whether the learner likes it or not, you must go on until he has learned all the word pairs correctly. So please go on."

Milgram collected various types of data in this study. Photographs of the participant were taken through one-way mirrors; notes were kept by the experimenter, and sometimes by additional observers, on any of the participant's eccentric behaviors; and recordings were made of the time that elapsed between when the learner responded and when the participant pressed a shock lever, and of the duration of each lever press. However, the main dependent variable was the maximum shock a participant would administer before refusing to go on. Milgram's primary objective was to see how far participants would go in their obedience to the experimenter, the authority figure in the situation.

When the experiment was over, the participant was presented with open-ended questions, projective measures (inkblots), and attitude scales about his experience as a teacher. The participant was then *debriefed* (the true purpose of the study was explained), after which the learner reintroduced himself and revealed that he was, in fact, a research accomplice, who had not received any shocks or suffered any harm during the ordeal. The filmed expressions of the unsuspecting teachers when they received this revelation shows *them* being shocked.

What He Found

Imagine 100 people that you know with diverse backgrounds and assorted personality traits going through Milgram's procedure. What percentage of the 100 would likely obey the experimenter and deliver a 15-volt shock to a fellow participant? How many would proceed to 30 volts, 45 volts, 60 volts, and so on? What percentage do you imagine would deliver intense or extremely intense shocks to a fellow human being, even after he demanded to be let out, pounded on the wall, and then fell silent? What percentage would go all the way to deliver 450-volt "XXX" shocks? When Milgram posed such questions to his colleagues and Yale University psychology majors, he found that the vast majority predicted that few people would go beyond "Very Strong Shock" levels and that only an insignificant few (0 to 3%) would continue obediently to the maximum level of shock. Also, 40 psychiatrists at a nearby medical school, contemplating a similar follow-up study, predicted that less than 1%—only the most twisted and sadistic—would deliver the highest possible shock. Naturally, when people were asked to predict how *they* would act in such a situation, none imagined themselves delivering any more than the most minimal shocks.

In light of these predictions, Milgram's (1963) actual results were astounding. *Not one* of the 40 participants stopped prior to delivering the 300-volt shock, the point at which the learner audibly pounded on the wall. Five of the 40 participants refused to go on at that point. Four more participants refused to go on after delivering 315 volts of shock and hearing the learner once again pound on the wall. Two participants then quit delivering shocks at 330 volts, and one more at each of the next three shock levels (345, 360, and 375 volts) when the learner was no longer pounding on the wall or saying anything. But that was it. The remaining 26 participants proceeded to 390, 405, 420, 435, and 450 volts of shock. In other words, 65% of "ordinary" people punished the learner (for failing to correctly remember word pairs) with the most extreme and potentially deadly levels of shock (*Danger: Severe Shock* and *XXX*; Figure 4). These participants often expressed discomfort, fear, reluctance, and indignation, although some remained oddly serene. Milgram (1974) commented on their demeanor during the ordeal:

> [When] the experimenter called a halt to the proceedings, many obedient [participants] heaved sighs of relief, mopped their brows, rubbed their fingers over their eyes, or nervously fumbled cigarettes. Some shook their heads, apparently in regret. Some remained calm throughout the experiment, and displayed only minimal signs of tension from beginning to end.
>
> (p. 470)

A few further results from Milgram's subsequent studies (1965) are noteworthy. As mentioned, once Milgram stumbled upon his unanticipated results, he attempted to identify factors responsible for greater or lesser obedience within his general paradigm. For example, he surmised that the *prestige* of the sponsoring institution (namely, Yale University) may have contributed to his dramatic results; so he moved his study to a shabby commercial building in downtown Bridgeport, Connecticut, and found that more than half the participants there also obeyed to the bitter end, only a minor reduction. Milgram also wondered about the effect that the physical or psychological distance between the participant and either the experimenter or the learner might have on his results. Thus, in one study, instead of having the experimenter physically present to give instructions, Milgram had him give instructions either by telephone or tape recorder. Here, only 16% of the participants went all the way (and some participants cheated by giving reduced shocks). In another study, the learner was placed one and a half feet away from the participant in the same room—adding visual cues of pain to the audible cues that were present in the initial study. In that situation, about 40%, rather than 65%, gave extreme shocks—again a reduction, but still less than you might expect. In perhaps the most startling condition, where the experimenter ordered the teacher to manually force the reluctant learner's hand onto a shock plate (a plastic shield prevented the teacher himself from receiving the presumed shock), obedience still reached 30%!

With indefatigable curiosity, Milgram also tested the effects of group pressure on obedience by having *three* teachers (two of them were research confederates) deliver shocks together (the real participant was by *chance* the one to actually press the shock levers). When the other two teachers

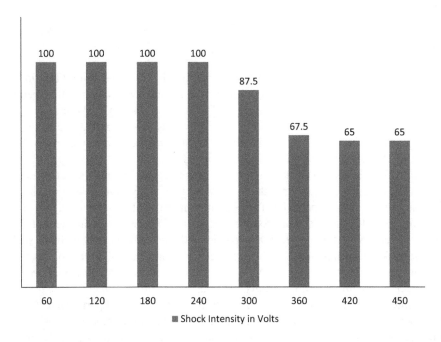

Figure 4 Percentage of participants who kept on obeying the experimenter's instruction to shock a learner, as the level of shock intensity increased

submissively obeyed the experimenter and showed no sympathy for the distressed learner, the true participant tended to do the same (72% delivered extreme shocks). However, when the other two teachers defied the experimenter (quitting at 150 and 210 volts, respectively), the true participants showed considerably more backbone (only 10% delivered extreme shocks). (See Chapter 1 for more on the effects of having a defiant ally.) Interestingly, when participants put through the procedure of the original study were allowed to choose the shock level they would give for each wrong answer, only 1 in 40 ever resorted to 450 volts. Yet when a participant was put in a subsidiary role where he stood by while another participant (actually a confederate) pressed the shock lever, the sobering 65% mentioned earlier jumped to an alarming 93%. Participants in passive roles seldom did anything substantial to stop the shocks. Might this explain why, during World War II, ordinary Germans stood by while the Nazis carried out systematic slaughter? On the other hand, there was one condition (also conducted in Bridgeport) where obedience did decline: If the participant was a friend or relative of the learner, only 15% went to 450 volts. This makes sense, and on the surface, looks like good news. But perhaps it only means that Nazis would have been less likely to obey instructions to harm other Nazis.

Finally, to the chagrin of anyone wanting to extol the importance of a person's moral mettle in such a situation, Milgram found that personality traits and demographic variables had little effect on his general results. Participants high on the trait of *authoritarianism* (rigid deference to authority and lack of sympathy for the weak and oppressed) did obey slightly more than those low on the same trait. Roman Catholics obeyed slightly more than Protestants or Jews. And those with less education and income obeyed slightly more than those with more education and income. Even so, most of what the person brought into Milgram's laboratory (including whether they were male or female) had little to do with what they did in his laboratory, with that very authentic-looking voltage generator sitting in front of them and the imperious experimenter nearby.

So What?

Milgram's (1963) findings sent shockwaves through academia and the world beyond. They led many to conclude that the average person—you and me—can be easily prodded into committing brutal and inhumane acts given the presence of an impassive and unyielding authority figure. In Milgram's words: "A substantial proportion of people do what they are told to do, irrespective of the content of the act and without limitations of conscience, so long as they perceive that the command comes from a legitimate authority" (1965, pp. 74–75). Milgram's results are an antidote to moral self-complacency, making it harder for us to assume that we could never act like Adolf Eichmann in Nazi Germany, Lt. Calley in My Lai, the suicide victims in Jonestown, Guyana, or the Branch Dividian cultists in Waco, Texas.

Although we would like to think of ourselves as free agents, relatively impervious to situational pressures, this is evidently not the case. Milgram's study reveals how much power the situation can exert over one's behavior. This is a bitter pill to swallow, and it is a rare person who would admit, as did the novelist Kurt Vonnegut Jr., that "If I'd been born in Germany I suppose I would have been a Nazi, bopping Jews and gypsies and Poles around, leaving boots sticking out of the snow-banks, warming myself with my sweetly virtuous insides" (1966, p. 69).

It is important to note that, although Milgram identified various situational *moderators* (factors that affect the magnitude) of his results, his research did little to elucidate the psychological *mediators* (intervening causes) of those results. Why, specifically, did participants feel so compelled to obey the experimenter even though, in many cases, they were so obviously distressed? Milgram's research did not provide many insights at the conceptual or theoretical level. Nonetheless, there has been no shortage of post hoc explanations.

One is that Milgram's participants were, in fact, depraved and gleefully merciless, or at least casually indifferent. Yet consider how much strain and distress they evidently suffered during the ordeal. Milgram noted how many of them succumbed to fits of nervous laughter, sweated profusely, and begged the experimenter to stop. Clearly, his participants *did* feel concern for the victim, even if that concern was, in truth, more selfish than unselfish (but see Chapter 18). To claim that they were merciless or indifferent is to commit the *fundamental attribution error*— exaggerating the dispositional determinants of behavior while downplaying the situational determinants of behavior (Ross & Nisbett, 2011; see Chapter 10).

Another explanation points to the role of *norms*—societal expectations concerning how one should and should not behave (see Chapter 1). The *norm of obedience*, for example, dictates that people should obey those who have legitimate authority. The *norm of social responsibility*, in contrast, demands that people help others in distress. Each of these norms tends to arise or be salient in different situations, as when a police officer orders one to use a crosswalk (obedience) or when one encounters a lost child (social responsibility). In the situation Milgram created, these two norms were pitted against each other. Opposing psychological forces collided: Participants did not want to suffer any disapproval or scorn for refusing to obey, nor did they want to suffer distress over knowingly hurting another person. The institutional setting and the experimenter's forceful words ("You must continue. . . . It is absolutely essential that you continue") emphasized the norm of obedience. Less austere surroundings and different words ("Be careful not to hurt the learner. . . . Be sensitive to his feelings and welfare") would have underscored the expectation to be compassionate and might have produced different behaviors (although, see Haslam, Loughnan, & Perry, 2014). Unfortunately, the norm of obedience often overshadows the norm of social responsibility in everyday circumstances, with regrettable outcomes.

The concepts of *low-balling* and *foot-in-the-door* have also been offered to explain Milgram's results. One gets low-balled when one commits to a particular course of action (such as agreeing to buy a cherry-red "classic" from a used car salesman) that proves to be more costly or less attractive than one originally expected (the fail-safe warranty turns out not to be part of the deal; see Cialdini, 2000). The savvy influence peddler gets his foot in the door when he convinces his patsy to make a small commitment that later makes it psychologically difficult to forego a larger commitment (Cialdini, Cacioppo, Bassett, & Miller, 1978; see Chapters 2 and 3). In Milgram's scenario, participants unknowingly committed themselves to a course of action that initially seemed quite benign (the shocks were weak and were intended to improve learning) and meritorious (from a scientific standpoint). How could the participants have known that the learner was going to make so many mistakes and that the shocks would quickly become so intense? Furthermore, if the teacher obeyed the experimenter at 45 volts, what reason could he give himself for disobeying at 60 volts, and if he obeyed at 390 volts, why disobey at 405 volts? If participants had to increase the shocks in 100-volt (instead of 15-volt) increments, would they still have been so obedient? Apparently, the gradual step-by-step nature of their obedience to the experimenter's escalating requests kept participants from disobeying. They were on a slippery slope, with no time to think (Gilbert, 1981). Their innocuous acts quickly mutated into unconscionable ones. As sometimes happens in life outside the lab, innocence devolved into evil.

Finally, perhaps Milgram's participants went to such shocking extremes (sorry, we just couldn't resist) because they were *authorized* to do so. In fact, Milgram (1974) described participants as entering into an *agentic state*—seeing themselves as mere instruments or agents of the experimenter, helpless cogs in the machinery of the situation. Participants were led to focus on details of the task and not on its higher-level implications (Vallacher & Wegner, 1987). When they asked, "Who's responsible?," the experimenter stated clearly "I'm responsible," thus absolving them of at least some of the responsibility for their actions.

Perhaps none of these explanations is completely satisfying. However, the blunt truth remains: It was the situation (the experimenter's words, the nature of the task, and the trappings of the lab) that in large part made participants do what they did. Sobering is the fact that the critical features of Milgram's procedures often have analogies in everyday life.

Afterthoughts

Were Milgram's (1963) methods excessive? Did he overstep critical ethical boundaries by putting his participants through unnecessary psychological torture? Well, he could have done worse. By way of comparison, about 40 years earlier a researcher by the name of Carney Landis (1924) studied the facial expressions of strong emotions and was quite cavalier in how he went about producing them. For example, to arouse fear, Landis put a participant's hand (sight unseen) into a bucket of water containing three frogs (imagine it is *your* hand and you have no idea what those slimy, warty, leggy things in the water are). To produce pain, he sent a strong current of electricity through the water (ouch!). To startle his charges, he set off firecrackers under their chairs. He also exposed his ill-fated participants to pornographic pictures in order to create yet other emotions: shock, arousal, or possibly disgust. As a finale, Landis commanded each of his participants to use a dull butter knife to decapitate a live rat (perhaps saying "the experiment requires it . . . you have no choice . . . please go on"). A participant who refused was still required to watch as Landis did the beheading himself. The point of this detailed description is to point out that today such research would be unequivocally considered unethical and prohibited by ethics committees everywhere.

Milgram's research is less blatantly unscrupulous, but not beyond reproof. In fact, his research has become almost synonymous with issues regarding the fair treatment of human participants, and he probably spent more time and energy than any other social psychologist responding to criticisms regarding ethics (Baumrind, 1964, 1985, and Milgram, 1964, 1977). The primary question is whether Milgram's results, as compelling as they were, justified the psychological cost to participants. Undoubtedly, Milgram put at least some of his participants through extreme duress, which even he admitted:

> I observed a mature and initially poised businessman enter the laboratory smiling and confident. Within 20 minutes he was reduced to a twitching, stuttering wreck, rapidly approaching a point of nervous collapse. He constantly pulled on his earlobe, and twisted his hands. At one point he pushed his fist into his forehead and muttered: "Oh God, let's stop it." And yet he continued to respond to every word of the experimenter, and obeyed to the end.
>
> (Milgram, 1963, p. 376)

Milgram's participants were not warned about upcoming procedures, something that would have compromised the purpose of the study. Furthermore, he deceived his participants in many ways. Most seriously, he led them to believe that they were perilously harming another human being. Even after a friendly reconciliation with the supposed victim and a thorough debriefing, participants were left forever knowing that they were *capable* of such perniciousness. Clearly, they had not asked for such disconcerting insights into their own psyches. Even granting the wisdom of the age-old mandate to "know thyself," most people would rather do so without being deceived.

Milgram countered the profusion of objections with the fact that a follow-up mail survey revealed that defiant and obedient participants alike said that they were glad they had taken part in the study (but note the connection between this finding and the results of the study described in Chapter 3). Nearly 85% indicated that they would be willing to participate in further similar experiments. Milgram also managed to find psychiatrists who would attest to the lack of any harmful long-term effects on his participants. On the other hand, some more recent historical investigations suggest that Milgram may not have properly debriefed all participants (Perry, 2013). But regardless, the ethical furor has resulted in permanent changes in how research participants should be treated. It became the majority opinion that strict ethical guidelines should thereafter protect human participants from the wiles of overzealous researchers. Such guidelines have become plenteous: a judicious cost-benefit analysis, use of deception only when justified, avoidance of unnecessary harm, informed consent, and a thorough debriefing. Few today would contend the merits of these guidelines. However, more than a few miss the opportunity Milgram had, and took, to put human participants to such a dramatic test, and with such sensational results.

Given the ethical concerns that Milgram's study raises, special obstacles arise when testing its replicability. Burger (2009), however, had an idea. He noted that, in the original Milgram studies, participants who got as far as administering the 150-volt shock went on to administer the highest level of shock four-fifths of the time. Hence, the original study could be replicated up to the 150-volt level, still quite meaningfully, but also more ethically, given that participants would not be under nearly so much stress. And indeed, Burger's reasonable compromise secured approval from his ethics committee. The result: Whereas 82% of Milgram's participants obeyed up to 150-volt level, 70% of Burger's participants did—nearly comparable results. In addition, some evidence also emerged that personality mattered: Participants who scored higher in *empathic concern* obeyed somewhat less.

Burger's (2009) research builds on previous studies that also employed alterative paradigms in which orders to harm were given, and which were also less stressful to participants. These also revealed surprisingly high levels of obedience. In one study, an unknown doctor telephoned 22 nurses and ordered them to give double the safe dosage of an uncommon drug to patients. All but one complied—before an alert research assistant intervened to stop them (Hofling, Brotzman, Dalrymple, Graves, & Pierce, 1966). In another series of studies, Dutch students were instructed to place job applicants under stress so they would fail a test, and remain unemployed (Meeus & Raaijmakers, 1995). Again, the vast majority complied. Such converging findings strengthen the conclusion that obedience to authority is not limited to New Haven, Connecticut, in the 1960s.

One final observation is worth making. Milgram did not systematically vary who the *learner* was—he always had the same middle-aged guy play the role. This leaves some interesting questions unanswered. For example, although male and female teachers obeyed the experimenter's instructions to shock the learner to about the same degree, what if Milgram had enlisted a *female* learner? Would both males and females have punished *her* with the same level of shocks? Would damsels in distress have inspired male teachers in particular to defy their orders? Or would members of both genders have discriminated in their own favor (with males shocking males less than females and vice versa)? Recent research (Reicher, Haslam, & Smith, 2012) suggests that the degree to which participants identify with the learner (as a member of the community) as opposed to the experimenter (as a representative of science) plays a role in their willingness to obey. If so, then obedience may be strongly influenced by group dynamics. It may only be strangers, or members of outgroups, whom we consent to harm. Those we know or identify with may stimulate our rebellious instincts.

Revelation

The power of the situation can incline people to willingly obey authority figures, with the result that they sometimes commit the most heinous of acts.

What Do You Think?

Just following orders has led many people to commit evil. So just when are we obliged to follow orders? If people never followed orders—say they gave up completely believing in the authority of government—would the world be a better or worse place? Also, how does Arendt's (1965) concept of the banality of evil manifest in today's world? Does evil tend to be more banal or dramatic?

Chapter Reference

Milgram, S. (1963). The behavioral study of obedience. *Journal of Abnormal and Social Psychology, 67,* 371–378.

Other References

Arendt, H. (1965). *Eichmann in Jerusalem: A report on the banality of evil* (rev ed.). New York: Viking Press.

Baumrind, D. (1964). Some thoughts on the ethics of research: After reading Milgram's "Behavioral Study of Obedience." *American Psychologist, 19,* 421–423.

Baumrind, D. (1985). Research using intentional deception: Ethical issues revisited. *American Psychologist, 40,* 165–174.

Burger, J. M. (2009). Replicating Milgram: Would people still obey today? *American Psychologist, 64,* 1–11.

Cialdini, R. B. (2000). *Influence: Science and practice* (4th ed.). New York: Allyn & Bacon.

Cialdini, R., Cacioppo, J., Bassett, R., & Miller, J. (1978). Low-ball procedure for producing compliance: Commitment then cost. *Journal of Personality and Social Psychology, 36,* 463–476.

Gilbert, S. J. (1981). Another look at the Milgram obedience studies: The role of a graduated series of shocks. *Personality and Social Psychology Bulletin, 7,* 690–695.

Haslam, N., Loughnan, S., & Perry, G. (2014). Meta-Milgram: An empirical synthesis of the obedience experiments. *PLoS One, 9*(4), 93927.

Hofling, C. K., Brotzman, E., Dalrymple, S., Graves, N., & Pierce, C. M. (1966). An experimental study in nurse-physician relationships. *The Journal of Nervous and Mental Disease, 143,* 171–180.

Landis, C. (1924). Studies of emotional reactions: General behavior and facial expressions. *Comparative Psychology, 4*, 447–509.

Meeus, W. H. J., & Raaijmakers, Q. A. W. (1995). Obedience in modern society: The Utrecht Studies. *Journal of Social Issues, 51*, 155–175.

Meyer, P. (1970, February). If Hitler asked you to electrocute a stranger would you? . . . What if Mr. Milgram asked you? *Esquire*, 72–73.

Milgram, S. (1964). Issues in the study of obedience: A reply to Baumrind. *American Psychologist, 19*, 848–852.

Milgram, S. (1965). Some conditions of obedience and disobedience to authority. *Human Relations, 18*, 57–76.

Milgram, S. (1974). *Obedience to authority: An experimental review*. New York: Harper & Row.

Milgram, S. (1977, October). Subjects' experiences: The neglected factor in the ethics of experimentation. *Hastings Center Report*, 19–23.

Perry, G. (2013). *Behind the shock machine: The untold story of the notorious Milgram psychology experiments*. New York: The New Press.

Reicher, S. D., Haslam, S. A., & Smith, J. R. (2012). Working toward the experimenter: Reconceptualizing obedience within the Milgram paradigm as identification-based followership. *Perspectives on Psychological Science, 7*, 315–324.

Ross, L., & Nisbett, R. E. (2011). *The person and the situation: Perspectives of social psychology*. London: Pinter & Martin.

Snow, C. P. (1961). Either-or. *Progressive*, 24.

Vallacher, R. R., & Wegner, D. M. (1987). What do people think they're doing? Action identification and human behavior. *Psychological Review, 94*, 3–15.

Vonnegut, K., Jr. (1966). *Mother night*. New York: Dell.

More to Explore

Perry, G. (2013). *Behind the shock machine: The untold story of the notorious Milgram psychology experiments*. New York: The New Press.

5 "Who, Me?"

The Failure of Bystanders to Intervene in Emergencies

"I have always depended on the kindness of strangers."
—Blanche Dubois in *A Streetcar Named Desire* by American playwright Tennessee Williams
(1911–1982)

Background

This chapter's study is grounded in the tragic story of Kitty Genovese. The *New York Times* (March 27, 1964) reported it this way:

> For more than half an hour thirty-eight respectable, law-abiding citizens in Queens watched a killer stalk and stab a woman in three separate attacks in Kew Gardens. Twice the sound of their voices and the sudden glow of their bedroom lights interrupted him and frightened him off. Each time he returned, sought her out and stabbed her again. Not one person telephoned the police during the assault; one witness called after the woman was dead.

During this fatal ordeal, Kitty Genovese screamed numerous pleas, including "Oh, my God! He stabbed me! Please help me!" One onlooker started to call the police, but his wife stopped him: "Don't, thirty people have probably called by now." Another neighbor, after calling a friend in another county for advice, went to the top of his building, across several rooftops, and down into another building, where he asked an elderly woman to call the police. The police later found him in his apartment, guilt-ridden and drunk (Rosenthal, 1964).

Although the Kitty Genovese incident is legendary, it does not stand alone in the annals of hero-less situations. Similar occurrences, equally shocking, surface in the news from time to time. Latané and Darley (1970) described how a teenage boy was gutted with a knife as he rode home on the subway. Eleven other riders watched as he bled to death. None of them came to his aid, even after his attackers had fled the subway car. In another example, a young switchboard operator was beaten and raped while alone in her office. Breaking free, she ran naked and bleeding to the street, screaming for help. Forty onlookers watched—but did not intervene—as, in broad daylight, the rapist tried to drag the woman back upstairs. Fortunately, in this case, two policemen happened by, did not turn the same blind eye, and dutifully arrested the assailant.

Social commentators—journalists, professors, ministers—have a field day probing for the causes of such seemingly callous indifference to the plight of others. Why don't people help in these situations? With so many witnesses, you'd think that at least one would get involved, even if just to pick up the phone and dial 911. Does big-city life turn decent folk into zombie-like bystanders, too jaded to concern themselves with fellow human beings? Do such tragedies reflect an insidious moral decay in our culture?

John Darley and Bibb Latané (1968) put their money on a social psychological explanation. They argued that people witnessing an emergency, especially something as petrifying as a stabbing, are in a state of conflict. Humanitarian norms and the whisperings of their conscience prompt them to intervene; at the same time, a host of fears, both rational and irrational, hold them back. After all, one could get hurt while helping, experience public embarrassment, or get tangled in police procedures. How might features of the *situation* dictate the way such a conflict is resolved?

Darley and Latané surmised that the presence of other people witnessing the same emergency, rather than spurring one to action, might actually discourage one from helping, and for several reasons. First, seeing that others are not helping may lead one to define the situation as a non-emergency, and so feel no obligation to help. "It's probably just a lover's spat." Collective inaction begets further collective inaction. Second, one may not know how others are responding. This may lead one to infer that others are in fact helping, making one's own involvement unnecessary. Darley and Latané referred to this phenomenon as *pluralistic ignorance* (see also Prentice & Miller, 1999). In fact, many of those who observed the assault on Kitty Genovese, upon seeing lights and silhouettes in nearby apartment windows, knew that others were also watching, but had no way of knowing how they were reacting. Pluralistic ignorance prevailed. Finally, nonintervention may occur due to what Darley and Latané termed a *diffusion of responsibility*. Failure to help occurs because the responsibility for helping is spread among a number of observers, as is any blame for not taking action. An ironic implication is that, had the brutal attack and Kitty Genovese's pleas for help been observed by a single night owl, who believed that he or she alone was witnessing this vicious assault, it might have been prevented from ending so tragically. The pressure to intervene would have focused uniquely on that one witness.

A quote from Evans (1980) described a discussion between Darley and Latané (recalled years later by Darley) when the Genovese murder was still a hot news item:

> Latané and I, shocked as anybody else, met over dinner a few days after this terrible incident had occurred and began to analyze this process in social psychological terms. . . . First, social psychologists ask not how are people different or why are the people who failed to respond monsters, but how all people are the same and how might anybody in that situation be influenced to not respond. Second, we asked: What influences reach the person from the group? We argued for a several-step model in which a person first had to define the situation. Emergencies don't come wearing signs saying "I am an emergency." In defining an event as an emergency, one looks at other people to see their reactions to the situation and interpret the meaning that lies behind their actions. Third, when multiple people are present, the responsibility to intervene does not focus clearly on any one person . . . You feel a diffusion of responsibility in that situation and you're less likely to take responsibility. We argued that these two processes, definition and diffusion, working together, might well account for a good deal of what happened.
>
> (pp. 216–217)

This discussion led Darley and Latané to hypothesize that the more bystanders there are to an emergency, the less likely, or the more slowly, any one bystander will intervene. They then put this hypothesis to an empirical test.

What They Did

Darley and Latane's (1968) experiment required a bit of staging and theatrics. Just how does one conduct an experiment in which (a) an emergency occurs, (b) participants are blocked from communicating with others and knowing about their behavior, and (c) it is possible for the experimenter to assess the frequency and speed of participants' reactions to the emergency?

Seventy-two New York University students (males and females) participated in Darley and Latané's study. Upon arriving for the experiment, a participant found himself or herself in a long corridor with doors opening to a series of small rooms (a significant detail). An experimenter took the participant to one of the rooms (leaving the contents of the other rooms to the imagination) and seated her at a table on which a microphone and pair of headphones lay. The participant filled out an information form and then listened to instructions presented by the experimenter over an intercom.

Participants were told that the study was concerned with the kinds of personal problems that normal college students face in a high-pressure urban environment (remember, these were NYU students). They were also told that the study was designed to avoid any embarrassments that arise from discussing personal problems with strangers. They would each remain anonymous, seated in separate rooms rather than face-to-face. They were further told that, because an outside listener might inhibit the discussion, the experimenter would not be eavesdropping. He would get their reactions afterward, by questionnaire. It was explained that each person would talk in turn, disclosing personal problems, via microphone, to those seated in the other rooms down the hall. Next, each person would, in turn, comment on what the others had said, and finally there would be an open discussion. Importantly, the flow of the conversation would be regulated. That is, each participant's microphone would be on for only two minutes, during his or her turn, while the other microphones would be off, so that only one participant would be heard over the network at a time.

Unknown to participants, however, the two-minute inputs of others were tape recordings. In other words, participants thought they were listening to the live verbal disclosures of other participants when in fact these others were merely recorded scripts. One of these alleged others—we will call him the *victim*, for reasons that will make sense in a moment—spoke first. He began by describing a few commonplace problems, like having a hard time getting adjusted to New York City and his studies. He also mentioned, hesitantly and with apparent embarrassment, that he sometimes experienced seizures, especially when studying hard or taking an exam. One by one, the other "participants" also divulged some of their own problems, but with no mention of proneness to epileptic fits. Finally, the real participant, playing his or her own unwitting part in the elaborate charade, divulged some personal trials and tribulations. When it was again the victim's turn to talk, he made a few relatively calm comments, and then, becoming noticeably louder and more incoherent, continued:

> I-er-urn-think I-I need-er-if-if could-er-er-somebody er-er-er-er-er-er-er give me a little help here because-er-I-er-I-er-er-h-h-having a-a-a real problemer-right now and I-er-if somebody could help me out it would-it-would-er-er s-s-sure be-sure good . . . because-er-there-er-er-a cause I-er-l-uh-I've got a-a one of the-er-sei-er-er-things coming on and-and-and I could reallyer-use some help if somebody would-er-give me a little h-help-uh-er-erer-er-er c-could somebody-er-er-help-er-uh-uh-uh (choking sounds) . . . I'm gonna die-er-er-I'm . . . gonna die-er-help-er-er-seizure-er-[chokes, then quiet].
>
> (Darley & Latané, 1968, p. 379)

You've got to admit, social psychology has its inspired moments!

Despite all this elaborate theater, the main dependent variables were simple. First, did participants notify the experimenter at the end of the hall that an emergency was taking place? And second, if they did, how long did it take them to do so? As soon as a participant reported the presumed fit, or if he or she failed to do so in six minutes, the experiment was stopped and he or she was *debriefed* (the true nature of the study was revealed and any ill feelings were sympathetically addressed).

Participants then completed a battery of questionnaires, which measured *Machiavellianism* (cold-hearted ruthlessness), *anomie* (lack of personal values), *authoritarianism* (deference to authority and disdain for the downtrodden), *social desirability* (the tendency to seek approval), and *social responsibility* (social compassion and helpfulness). These additional assessments allowed a comparison between the influences of personality and situational factors on helping behavior. We should point out, however, that these personality variables might have been better measured in a separate context, perhaps prior to the experiment, in an apparently unrelated session. Non-helpers especially may have exaggerated their standing on some of these personality dimensions in order to compensate for their embarrassing inaction earlier. This could have obscured any real differences in personality capable of accounting for differences in helping.

Knowing that experiments involve the deliberate manipulation of one or more independent variables, you might be wondering what exactly was manipulated in this study. Well, think back to Darley and Latané's (1968) diffusion-of-responsibility hypothesis: The more bystanders to an emergency, the less likely or more slowly any one bystander will help. This hypothesis led Darley and Latané to manipulate *perceived group size*. To this end, they varied both the assistant's comments before the experiment and the number of voices heard speaking in the first round of the group discussion. Participants were led to believe that the group consisted of two people (just them and the victim), three people (them, the victim, and one other participant), or six people (them, the victim, and four other participants). Keep in mind that the only real people were the participants themselves; the others were merely tape recordings.

The composition of the three-person groups was also manipulated. In one variation, the taped bystander's voice was that of a female, in another that of a male, and in another that of a male who just happened (wink!) to mention that he was a premedical student who occasionally worked in the emergency ward (just the kind of person trained to deal with unexpected seizures). Thus, the major independent variables were group size and group composition, while the major dependent variables were whether and how fast a participant came to the victim's aid by reporting the seizure to the experimenter.

What They Found

Participants reported being genuinely convinced of, and affected by, the victim's seizure—a matter of *experimental realism* (the participants felt psychologically drawn into the experiment). Whether or not participants intervened, they clearly believed the sudden epileptic fit to be real and serious, saying things like: "My God, he's having a fit!" "It's just my kind of luck, something has to happen to me!" or "Oh God, what should I do?" Unbeknownst to participants, the experimenter could hear these various comments over the intercom. Also, to the experimenter down the hall, participants said things like: "Hey, I think Number 1 is very sick. He's having a fit or something." And when the experimenter checked the situation and reported that "Everything is under control," they were apparently relieved, although they would still ask "Is he being taken care of?" or "He's all right, isn't he?" Like the participants in Milgram's (1963) obedience study (see Chapter 4), they seemed genuinely upset and concerned.

The number of others that participants believed were present had a profound effect on whether and how promptly they helped. Specifically, 85% of participants who believed they were alone reported the emergency before the victim was cut off (that is, within 2 minutes), whereas only 31% of those who believed that four others were present did so. Moreover, 100% of the participants in the two-person groups, but only 62% of those in the six-person groups, ever reported the emergency (Figure 5). In fact, at any point in time, more participants in two-person than three-person groups, and more participants in three-person than six-person groups, reported the incident. Also, the fewer individuals that participants thought were present, the faster they responded.

Interestingly, participants in the three-person groups were equally likely to respond, and responded equally quickly, regardless of whether they believed the other participant (besides the victim) to be male, female, or medically competent. Also, even though males are often given the duty of responding to emergencies, or are regarded as more inclined to assume the role of rescuer in dire situations, male participants in this study were no more likely than females to help, nor did they help more quickly. This may have been because helping in this study involved merely reporting a crisis.

Did some additional factor in this experiment account for helping? It seems not. Participants indicated which thoughts—from a list presented to them—they had had during the emergency (e.g., "I didn't know exactly what was happening" or "I didn't know what to do"). There were no significant differences in their reported thoughts across the three conditions. Although participants in the three-person and six-person groups reported that they were fully aware that others were present to hear the fit, they claimed that this had no effect on their behavior. Research has found, however, that we often do not know the true causes of our behavior (Nisbett & Bellows, 1977; see Chapter 14). The nice thing about an experiment is that it allows one to isolate exactly what does cause something. In this case, because participants had been randomly assigned to different conditions, nothing other than the participants' awareness of the number of others present could explain the group differences in helping, despite their apparent lack of insight regarding its influence.

Finally, just as was the case in a number of other classic studies documenting the power of the situation (see Chapters 4 and 8), none of the personality measures was significantly related to the likelihood or speed of participants' responses. In fact, only one variable besides group size correlated with speed of helping: The larger the community a participant grew up in, the less likely

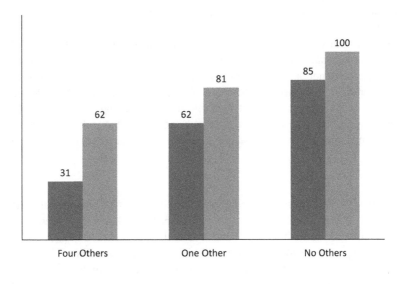

Figure 5 Percentage of participants who went to help a bogus victim, during his apparent epileptic fit or ever, when they believed that four others, one other, or no others also heard him

he or she was to help. Make of this finding what you will, but the more important result is that it was something *outside* of the person—namely, the number of others present—and not simply something *inside* the person—like a disposition to be compassionate and responsible—that determined how a person behaved in response to the desperate heaving of a fellow student who, by his own account, was "gonna die."

So What?

According to Darley and Latané (1968), participants in this study experienced an *avoidance–avoidance conflict* (a type of conflict you want to avoid!). They were obviously concerned about the stammering victim, and would likely have been ashamed of themselves had they not taken action, but they also did not want to make fools of themselves by jumping to conclusions. For those in the two-person groups ("It's just me and this guy croaking in another room") the conflict was easily resolved: "My help in this situation is crucial." But for those who believed that others were present ("There are four or five of us listening to this guy unfold") the anticipated embarrassment of helping, should no help in fact be needed, increased, thereby leading them to restrain their humanitarian instincts, and heightening their internal conflict. "Should I let the guy continue to suffer, even die, or should I alarm the experimenter and risk embarrassing myself?" It was not that the participants consciously decided not to intervene. Rather, they mentally vacillated between two negative alternatives and never actually did anything. Then, after several minutes had passed, it was illogical or simply too late to help.

Darley and Latané's results cast doubt on explanations for bystander unresponsiveness that refer to apathy or indifference. Such reasoning asserts that crowds of people who stand by and do nothing when others are suffering before their very eyes are somehow different from the rest of us: desensitized by modern culture or just naturally uncaring. Why else would someone watch passively as someone else gets hacked to death? However, dispositional explanations of this sort may be too convenient, allowing us to deny that we, as persons of unimpeachable character or infinite benevolence, would ever fail to help in a similar situation. Indeed, none of the personality variables implicated in such pat, self-protective accounts were found in the present study to have anything to do with whether or how quickly participants helped.

The significance of this study is quite apparent if you reconsider the grievous case of Kitty Genovese, or the equally lamentable cases of the subway rider or switchboard operator described earlier. These unfortunates were not only victims of their heartless assailants; they were also victims of the influence that pluralistic ignorance or a diffusion of responsibility can have on helping in an emergency. This dynamic is not uncommon and deserves our understanding. Just as we are encouraged to learn CPR and to recycle plastic, should we not also be encouraged to understand and resist the situational pressures that inhibit helping? Bystanders need not be so unresponsive, crowds so unhelpful.

Afterthoughts

Darley and Latané's (1968) study ingeniously captured the critical features of certain types of emergencies, such as the Genovese murder, in which spectators knew that others were watching, could neither communicate with them nor know how they were reacting, and were uncertain as to whether it was up to them to help. Further studies along the same lines followed. In one by Latané and Rodin (1969), participants were busy filling out questionnaires when a young female experimenter left to get more materials from an adjacent room. The unsuspecting participants heard her drag a chair across the floor of the other room, climb onto it, and then emit a piercing scream, after which there was a loud crash that sounded like a bookcase overturning, followed by the ominous thud of a body hitting the floor. Next they heard the woman moaning in pain and crying out, "Oh my God! My ankle! I can't move it! I think it's broken!" (All of these sound effects were carefully tape-recorded beforehand and played back from the other room once the woman arrived there.) Think about it: How would you have responded as a participant in this study? Would you have rushed to the woman's aid, regardless of the number of observers present? Well, predictably, the woman received help 70% of the time from solitary participants, 40% of the time from either member of two-person groups, and a mere 7% of the time when the other member of the pair was a deliberately unresponsive experimental confederate.

More than 50 follow-up studies, conducted either in the laboratory or in field settings, have confirmed the inverse relationship between group size and helping (see Latané & Nida, 1981). A more recent meta-analysis—which involved statistically summarizing the results of many individual studies—concurred (Fischer et al., 2011). The meta-analysis also found, perhaps reassuringly, that more *serious* emergencies (those in which the dangers were physical and the perpetrators were present) resulted in *less* bystander apathy, probably because such situations were less ambiguous.

Yet, to be sure, Darley and Latané's study, and numerous replications, do not shed light on all aspects of helping or failing to help. New questions on this topic crop up as quickly as old ones are answered. (That a sense of enlightenment begets a sense of ignorance is not uncommon in science.) One question: How are people socialized to be helpful? Coates, Pusser, and Goodman (1976) found that certain TV shows, like *Sesame Street*, promote helpful behavior in preschoolers by providing likable models that they can imitate. In contrast, ostentatiously rewarding children for helping is a counterproductive strategy (Fabes, Fultz, Eisenberg, May-Plumlee, & Christopher, 1989; see Chapter 9).

Another question: Does one's mood influence one's tendency to help? Levin and Isen (1975) demonstrated that adults whose spirits were lifted upon finding a dime planted in the coin return of a public telephone (remember those days?) were subsequently more inclined to help a passerby who *accidentally* dropped a folder of papers. Also, Cunningham (1979) found that people leave larger tips on sunny days than on cloudy or rainy days (the *sunny Samaritan effect*). Furthermore, Harris, Benson, and Hall (1975) found that Catholics on the way into confession (presumably burdened by guilt) donated more money to the March of Dimes than did those coming out of confession (their guilt resolved).

A final question: Does gender or race affect helping? Eagly and Crowley (1986) found that men generally help more than women, and are more likely to assist strangers. This is especially true when there are onlookers, when there is potential danger involved in helping, and when the person in need is female. On this latter point, West, Whitney, and Schnedler (1975) found that when a motorist was seen to be changing a flat tire along a highway, 25% of cars stopped when the motorist was female, but only 2% stopped when the motorist was male. (Would the same be found today?) In addition, Brigham and Richardson (1979) found that White convenience store clerks allowed a customer, who discovered that he or she did not have enough money to purchase a product, to do so anyway two-thirds of the time if the customer was a White man or woman, or a Black woman, but only one-third of the time if the customer was a Black man. Indeed, one's similarity to a victim is a good predictor of whether one will intervene (Levine, Evans, Prosser, & Reicher, 2005). In fact, here, the key finding *reverses*: The more bystanders there are, the *more* one is inclined to assist a friend or fellow group member (Levine & Crowther, 2008; see also Chapter 7). This is perhaps because one knows that one is *supposed* to help them, and fears looking like a coward when others are onlooking. Hence, bystander apathy in crowds—as in the Kitty Genovese case—may be a phenomenon confined to strangers.

These and other questions and findings suggest that helping in an emergency and helping more generally is a multifaceted phenomenon, a complex function of many variables. Also, identifying the social conditions that facilitate helping does not establish why people want to help in the first place. Chapter 18 addresses the deeper motivational question of whether helping is ever done for purely unselfish reasons.

Revelation

The more witnesses there are to an emergency, the less likely it is that any one of them will help. This is because individuals are often not privy to others' reactions, or because they do not feel uniquely responsible for preventing tragic outcomes.

What Do You Think?

Have you ever needed to help or rescue someone in dire need? Describe factors that would prompt you to help, and factors that would prevent you from helping, in an emergency? Suppose that, after reading this chapter, you encounter an emergency situation where lots of other bystanders are present. Knowing what you know now, would you feel you were more inclined to intervene, or more obliged to do so?

Chapter Reference

Darley, J. M., & Latané, B. (1968). Bystander intervention in emergencies: Diffusion of responsibility. *Journal of Personality and Social Psychology*, 8, 377–383.

Other References

Brigham, J. C., & Richardson, C. B. (1979). Race, sex, and helping in the market place. *Journal of Applied Social Psychology*, 9, 314–322.

Coates, B., Pusser, H. E., & Goodman, I. (1976). The influence of "Sesame Street" and "Mister Rogers' Neighborhood" on children's social behavior in the preschool. *Child Development*, 47, 138–144.

Cunningham, M. R. (1979). Weather, mood, and helping behavior: Quasi-experiments with the sunshine Samaritan. *Journal of Personality and Social Psychology*, 37, 1947–1956.

Eagly, A. H., & Crowley, M. (1986). Gender and helping behavior: A meta-analytic review of the social psychological literature. *Psychological Bulletin*, 100, 283–308.

Evans, R. I. (1980). *The making of social psychology: Discussions with creative contributors*. New York: Gardner Press.

Fabes, R. A., Fultz, J., Eisenberg, N., May-Plumlee, T., & Christopher, F. C. (1989). Effects of rewards on children's prosocial motivation: A socialization study. *Developmental Psychology*, 25, 509–515.

Fischer, P., Krueger, J., Greitemeyer, T., Kastenmüller, A., Vogrincic, C., Frey, D., Heene, M., Wicher, M., & Kainbacher, M. (2011). The bystander-effect: A meta-analytic review on bystander intervention in dangerous and non-dangerous emergencies. *Psychological Bulletin*, 137, 517–537.

Harris, M. B., Benson, J. M., & Hall, C. L. (1975). The effects of confession on altruism. *Journal of Social Psychology*, 96, 187–192.

Latané, B., & Darley, J. M. (1970). *The unresponsive bystander: Why doesn't he help?* New York: Appleton-Century-Crofts.

Latané, B., & Nida, S. (1981). Ten years of research on group size and helping. *Psychological Bulletin*, 89, 308–324.

Latané, B., & Rodin, J. (1969). A lady in distress: Inhibiting effects of friends and strangers on bystander intervention. *Journal of Experimental Social Psychology*, 5, 189–202.

Levin, P. F., & Isen, A. M. (1975). Further studies on the effect of feeling good on helping. *Sociometry*, 38, 141–147.

Levine, M., & Crowther, S. (2008). The responsive bystander: How social group membership and group size can encourage as well as inhibit bystander intervention. *Journal of Personality and Social Psychology*, 96, 1429–1439.

Levine, R. M., Evans, D., Prosser, A., & Reicher, S. (2005). Identity and emergency intervention: How social group membership and inclusiveness of group boundaries shape helping behavior. *Personality and Social Psychology Bulletin*, 31, 443–453.

Milgram, S. (1963). Behavioral study of obedience. *Journal of Abnormal and Social Psychology, 67,* 371–378.

Nisbett, R. E., & Bellows, N. (1977). Verbal reports about causal influences on social judgments: Private access versus public theories. *Journal of Personality and Social Psychology, 35,* 613–624.

Prentice, D. A., & Miller, D. T. (Eds.). (1999). *Cultural divides: Understanding and overcoming group conflict.* New York: Russell Sage Foundation.

Rosenthal, A. M. (1964). *Thirty-eight witnesses.* New York: McGraw-Hill.

West, S. G., Whitney, G., & Schnedler, R. (1975). Helping a motorist in distress: The effects of sex, race, and neighborhood. *Journal of Personality and Social Psychology, 31,* 691–698.

More to Explore

Cook, K. (2014). *Kitty Genovese: The murder, the bystanders, and the crime that changed* America. New York: W. W. Norton.

6 Of Roaches and Men
Social Enhancement and Inhibition of Performance

"The chief difference between mankind and the cockroach is that the one continually bitches over his fate while the other stoically plods on, uncomplaining, with never a glance backward nor a sigh for what might have been."

—Jean Shepherd (1921–1999), American storyteller and actor

Background

The following *creepy* study is part of a research tradition that began over a century ago, when in 1898 Norman Triplett published "The Dynamogenic Factors in Pacemaking and Competition" in the nascent *American Journal of Psychology*. There are two things worth mentioning about Triplett. First, he loved bicycle racing. He frequently took part in competitions, savored his role as a spectator, and was a noted authority on the sport. In fact, it was his rapt inspection of the 1897 records book of the League of American Wheelmen that led him to notice an apparent pattern: Cyclists who competed against or were paced by others seemed to perform better than those who raced against the clock alone. This, Triplett (1898) concluded, was because the "presence of another rider is a stimulus to the racer in arousing the competitive instinct . . . the means of releasing or freeing nervous energy for him that he cannot of himself release" (p. 516).

The second thing to mention about Triplett is that he was, evidently, a natural-born experimentalist. Venturing beyond casual observation and speculation, he cajoled 40 local children into winding up fishing reels, each affixed to a Y-shaped frame, as fast as they could. Sometimes he had them do this alone, sometimes in pairs. (Imagine what the neighbors thought: Something *reely fishy* is going on!) Just as he predicted, winding times were generally faster when the children wound together. The data suggested that the mere presence of other children resulted in enhanced performance. Triplett's interest in social influences on performance, and his attempt to investigate such influences experimentally, distinguished him as an important forebear of social psychology (see Stroebe, 2012, for an historical critique).

Following Triplett's inspiration, hundreds of studies have looked at the relationship between the presence of others and an individual's performance on a task. Bond and Titus (1983) conducted a *meta-analysis* (quantitative summary) of some 241 of these studies. Various types of performance had been investigated: doing simple arithmetic, making complex calculations, putting on clothes, memorizing nonsense syllables, learning a finger maze, crossing out vowels, shooting pool, and eating. Studies have focused on the influence of coactors (others working simultaneously on the same or even a different task) and on the effects of performing in front of an audience. Interestingly, results show that the presence of other people only sometimes enhances performance (referred to as *social facilitation*); at other times it impairs performance (*social inhibition*). For example, whereas participants cross out the vowels in a newspaper column faster in the presence of others, they memorize nonsense syllables (like "bir" or "koh") slower in the presence of others. For a long time, investigators were perplexed by such inconsistent findings.

Then, in 1965, Robert Zajonc (whose Polish name rhymes with "science") offered an elegant solution to the puzzle. He proposed that the presence of other people serves to heighten *arousal* (of the physiological, not sexual, sort—unless the other people happen to be naked!). Reviving an old behaviorist principle of learning, he also suggested that heightened arousal facilitates *dominant* (simple, well-learned) responses, but inhibits *nondominant* (complex, novel) responses. For example, if you are a fast and proficient typist, others watching you will spur you to an even nimbler performance, but if you are a slow and clumsy typist, others hanging over your shoulders will turn your fingers into soggy French fries!

Numerous studies have now demonstrated this particular interaction (the social facilitation of dominant responses and social inhibition of nondominant responses), but one of the classics is Zajonc and Sales (1966). Male students practiced pronouncing 10 different Turkish words (actually seven-letter nonsense words). Two of these words were presented once, two twice, two four times, two eight times, and two sixteen times, all in a random order. Participants then began the subliminal (unconscious) perception phase of the study. A tachistoscope was used to present the words again, this time very briefly, and the participant's task on each trial was to guess which word was presented. Each was flashed for only one-tenth of a second. Nonetheless, participants correctly guessed the words about 90% of the time. Non-words—31 different configurations of irregular black lines—were also presented on other trials, but only for 1/100th of a second in each case. At this even shorter exposure, however, participants could not tell the difference between words and non-words. These extra trials allowed the researchers to estimate participants' tendency to guess. Altogether the participants saw four blocks of 41 stimuli: 10 pseudo-Turkish words and 31 pseudo-pseudo-Turkish words.

Some participants went through this guessing procedure alone (the use of an automated slide projector and a tape recorder made the presence of the experimenter unnecessary), whereas others went through the procedure in the presence of other (unknown) students, passively seated a few feet away. These students, actually confederates in the study, had casually mentioned to participants that they were observing the study with the permission of the experimenter. Zajonc and Sales predicted that the presence of an audience would facilitate dominant responses, namely, guessing Turkish words that had been more frequently practiced (8 or 16 times), and inhibit nondominant responses, namely, guessing Turkish words that had been practiced less frequently (once or twice). This is exactly what they found.

This and other rigorous studies lent credibility to Zajonc's parsimonious explanation for so-called mere presence effects. Yet these results still left room for plausible alternative explanations. For example, perhaps the presence of others creates apprehension in participants, spurring them to try harder at a task, but impairing their performance if the task is relatively challenging. Or, perhaps participants are more motivated by the need for approval and spend more time self-monitoring in the presence of others, thereby distracting them and yielding the same pattern of results. Such explanations raise questions about the cause and generalizability of mere presence effects. To what extent are more complex cognitive processes (such as apprehension or self-awareness) responsible for them? Would it be possible to demonstrate such effects with members of another species, including ones that have less going on upstairs? Would Zajonc's theory accurately predict mere presence effects in, say, apes, monkeys, dogs, or mice? Or even in one of the least brainy creatures ever to scurry across the face of the Earth: *cockroaches*? Why not round up a few and find out?

What They Did

Zajonc, Heingartner, and Herman (1969) predicted that, even among roaches, simply being in the presence of other roaches would facilitate performance on a simple task and inhibit performance on a complex task. The researchers initially envisioned an uncomplicated experimental design, in which roaches would run down a straight runway (a relatively easy task) or through a slightly more complex maze (a relatively difficult task), either alone or in tandem (with one other roach). (This is referred to as a *2 × 2* design, with two levels of each of two independent variables.) However, they realized that the tandem condition contained a potential confound: If the roaches ran faster with a partner, it might be because the two had *aroused* each other (as suggested by Zajonc) or because they had *directed* each other using mysterious roach body language, perhaps with a subtle shake of the legs or a timely touch of the feelers. Foreseeing this possibility, Zajonc and his colleagues engineered an additional condition in which roaches performed in front of an audience of spectator roaches. (Little known fact: A group of roaches is technically called an *intrusion*.) Though spectator roaches might influence the performing roaches by their mere presence, it is unlikely that they would provide any task-relevant behavioral cues.

The participants in this study were 72 adult female cockroaches (*Blatta orientalis*, to be entomologically correct). Although they signed no consent forms, the participants were nonetheless treated ethically. The experimenter thoughtfully maintained them in agreeably dark quarters on a delicious diet of sliced apples. From which university dormitory they were obtained, alas, the scientific paper is silent.

The basic apparatus was a clear plexiglass cube, about 20 inches along each edge, outfitted to house either a winding maze or a straight runway. The former, of course, would be a more challenging route for a running roach. A 150-watt floodlight, shone into a start box, served as a noxious stimulus (roaches, unlike moths, hate bright lights). A darkened goal box at the other end of the runway or maze beckoned to them. The route featured guillotine gates and clear runway tubes. See-through audience boxes, positioned along most of the walls of the runway or maze were added in some conditions. These contained small apertures that allowed the transmission of olfactory (smell-related) cues: One whiff would signal any fellow roaches nearby, in case the lights dazzled them.

Turning on the floodlight and opening a guillotine door spurred the roaches to motion. The crucial variable was the time it took the roaches to get through the runway or maze and enter the goal box (a final guillotine door snapped shut just after the roach's last leg crossed the threshold of the goal box).

What They Found

Zajonc and his colleagues, retiring back to their roach-free offices to analyze their data, found strong support for their hypotheses. Roaches that negotiated the more complex maze in tandem took more time than roaches that negotiated it alone, whereas roaches that traversed the simpler runway in tandem took less time than roaches that traversed it alone. The same pattern of results emerged when comparing the audience condition to the solitary condition: The presence of a roach audience inhibited maze performance but facilitated runway performance (Figure 6). Thus, the coactive and audience roaches had similar effects on performance. This finding (the lack of a significant three-way interaction) was critical, for it eliminated the possibility that the observed effects were due to specific behavioral cues. It is highly unlikely that the audience roaches were communicating—through sound or gesture—hints to the performing roaches on the runway but not in the maze. This strongly suggests that it was the mere presence of other roaches that mattered, nothing else.

Worth mentioning is another of Zajonc and his colleagues' (1969) experiments, in which roaches traveled through either a runway or a maze, in both cases flanked by mirrors, while being exposed either to a fragrant egg carton left for a few days in the roach colony or to a fresh egg carton bearing not a trace of *eau de roach*. Again, the runway versus maze manipulation provided a simple versus complex task. The mirrors conveyed the false impression that fellow roaches were present (the roaches were hardly so smart as to recognize themselves). The egg carton—fragrant or fresh—was a manipulation of olfactory cues, again suggesting, in a different

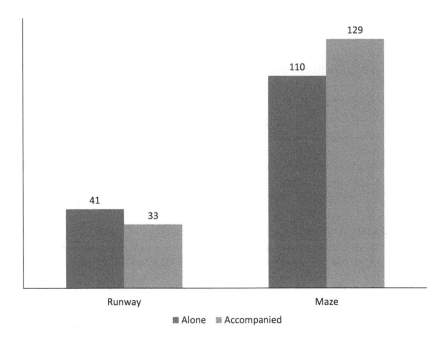

Figure 6 Number of seconds that it took roaches to travel down a runway or to negotiate a maze, when alone or accompanied by other roaches

way, that other roaches were present or absent. The results of this experiment were not so conclusive, but the inclusion of mirrors and the manipulation of odor did highlight an interesting question: What minimal features are sufficient to produce mere presence effects? For example, would roaches perform differently (faster in the runway, but slower in the maze) in the presence of dead or anaesthetized roaches (assuming that these immobile companions would not unduly alarm them)?

So What?

"So what?" is an easy question to ask in response to research involving roaches. However, bear in mind that this research is backed up by dozens of other studies on mere presence effects (e.g., Michaels, Blommel, Brocato, Linkous, & Rowe, 1982). Most of these have involved human participants, but comparable effects have been documented in dogs, birds, fish, rats, armadillos, fruit flies, centipedes, and ants (e.g., Chen, 1937, found that ants dig twice as much dirt in the presence of other ants than when alone). Also bear in mind that Zajonc and his colleagues (1969) were not attempting to understand the richness of human social behavior based upon observations of *Blatta orientalis* alone. That is, they were not interested in generalizing directly from roaches to human beings. Rather, they sought to show that it is *possible* for mere presence effects to occur in the absence of elaborate cognitive mediation. Hence, they conducted an experiment that allowed them to rule out such variables as evaluation-apprehension, self-monitoring, or some sort of approval-seeking as necessary causes of mere presence effects. Unless one is willing to argue that the lowly roach is swayed by many of the same passions and vulnerabilities that beset college sophomores, they succeeded in doing just that. All that is needed to explain why the mere presence of others can help or hinder performance is *physiological arousal*—which is known to improve performance on easy tasks and hamper performance on hard tasks. And although humans and roaches undoubtedly differ in many ways—the latter being more likely to survive a nuclear holocaust, for example—both still find other members of their species arousing.

Relevant here is an article by Mook (1980), provocatively titled "In Defense of External Invalidity." Mook astutely pointed out that experimental research serves a variety of objectives, only one of which is to generalize from one population or setting to another. Instead, one often wants to demonstrate that an effect is simply *possible*—that it can be obtained even in the somewhat contrived conditions of the laboratory. Also, one often wants only to *test a hypothesis* generated by a particular theory, without initially caring about generalizability. In our roach study, for example, Zajonc and colleagues showed it was possible that performance can be enhanced or impeded by the mere presence of others without much cognition being involved. They also implicitly tested every theory claiming that something other than arousal was necessary, and showed them all to be false. In other words, the artificiality of the laboratory, or the peculiar characteristics of, say, college sophomores, is often not a problem. In fact, laboratory experiments have the advantage of permitting particular variables to be isolated by paring down the complexity of the situation (see our Introduction). In everyday life there is often simply too much going on to figure out exactly what causes what. The laboratory, therefore, provides a means of discovering rare social psychological truths, as the many experimental studies in this book illustrate.

Afterthoughts

Science unfolds in a *dialectical* manner. A theory is asserted, then found wanting in some respect, then modified or replaced (see Cialdini, 1995). Sometimes support is discovered for competing explanations, in which case it is often concluded that an effect can occur for more than one reason. For example, is it indeed the mere presence of others (sans cognitive mediation) that produces social facilitation and inhibition? Or is some kind of cognitive mediation, such as concern over being judged by others, also responsible for such effects? A study by Cottrell, Wack, Sekevak, and Rittle (1968) found that participants performing a task in front of an audience showed the typical interaction pattern (social facilitation of dominant responses, and inhibition of nondominant responses), but not if the others were blindfolded, supporting the claim that mere presence effects in humans are mediated by evaluation apprehension (see also Aiello & Svec, 1993). However, Markus (1978) also found that evaluation apprehension was not always necessary for mere presence effects in humans.

Nonetheless, the findings of the roach study cast doubt on the necessity of explaining mere presence effects in terms of something so human as evaluation apprehension (though, to our knowledge, nobody has tried the blindfold trick with roaches!). But what then, if not performance anxiety, might cause roaches to change their pace (sometimes going faster, sometimes slower) in the presence of other roaches? Sanders and Baron (1975) suggested that they get distracted. The distraction caused by coactors or an audience creates a conflict between focusing on the task and focusing on the others present. This conflict then raises arousal, thereby facilitating dominant and inhibiting nondominant responses. Indeed, sudden noises or flashes of light have been found to produce the same pattern of enhancement or impairment. Thus, we might conclude that a small mix of variables mediates social facilitation and inhibition: the mere presence of others, distraction, and at least with humans, concerns about being evaluated (Geen, 1991; Guerin, 1993; Kent, 1996).

One thing to keep in mind about mere presence effects is that the complexity of a given task falls along a continuum. Arousal, too, falls on a continuum, from very low to very high. The implication is that the higher the arousal, the more dominant the response must be for performance to be facilitated. However, it is possible that arousal can be too high, disturbing performance on even relatively simple or well-practiced tasks. Consider, for example, competitive sporting events. It is well documented that sports teams tend to play better at *home* where, presumably, they feel more encouraged and possibly aroused than do their beleaguered opponents. Even so, Baumeister and Showers (1986) have empirically determined that when a given contest is particularly crucial and challenging—the final game of a major league baseball playoff, for example—playing at home is statistically a *disadvantage*. Indeed, one can think of examples of a person's feeling so aroused that even the simplest of tasks is all but impossible to accomplish. On the other hand, some people relish the big occasion. Narcissists (those who regard themselves as superior to others) perform better when opportunities for glory present themselves, whereas non-narcissists tend to choke more under the pressure (Wallace & Baumeister, 2002).

Findings of social facilitation and inhibition fit with a more general insight: People greatly affect the person. All sorts of interesting things happen when we fall in among other *homo sapiens*. Their norms dictate our perceptions and behaviors (see Chapter 1); we feel less personally responsible and culpable in their company (see Chapter 5); we look among them for self-flattering connections (see Chapter 11); we lose our sense of self among them (see Chapter 12); we tend to like them more the more we encounter them (see Chapter 13); and they assuage our fear of death (see Chapter 27). This theme—that people affect the person—is fascinating because of the subtle and manifold ways in which it plays itself out.

Revelation

The mere presence of others enhances performance on simple tasks but impairs performance on complex tasks. This can occur even in the absence of complex mediating cognitions.

What Do You Think?

How has the mere presence of other people sometimes inhibited and sometimes enhanced your performance on particular tasks? Have you ever choked under pressure or even had a panic attack when others were around? Also, how do you feel about the fact that you share psychological dynamics in common with the humble cockroach? Moreover, do cockroaches run faster in the presence of humans, or humans in the presence of cockroaches? Devise an experimental design to test this.

Chapter Reference

Zajonc, R. B., Heingartner, A., & Herman, E. M. (1969). Social enhancement and impairment of performance in the cockroach. *Journal of Personality and Social Psychology, 13*, 83–92.

Other References

Aiello, J. R., & Svec, C. M. (1993). Computer monitoring of work performance: Extending the social facilitation framework to electronic presence. *Journal of Applied Social Psychology, 23*, 537–548.

Baumeister, R. F., & Showers, C. J. (1986). A review of paradoxical performance effects: Choking under pressure in sports and mental tests. *European Journal of Social Psychology, 16*, 361–383.

Bond, C. F., Jr., & Titus, L. T. (1983). Social facilitation: A meta-analysis of 241 studies. *Psychological Bulletin, 94*, 265–292.

Chen, S. C. (1937). Social modification of the activity of ants in nest-building. *Physiological Zoology, 10*, 420–436.

Cialdini, R. B. (1995). A full-cycle approach to social psychology. In G. C. Bronnigan & M. R. Merrens (Eds.), *The social psychologist: Research adventures* (pp. 52–73). New York: McGraw-Hill.

Cottrell, N. B., Wack, D. L., Sekevak, G. J., & Rittle, R. H. (1968). Social facilitation of dominant responses by the presence of an audience and the mere presence of others. *Journal of Personality and Social Psychology, 9*, 245–250.

Geen, R. G. (1991). Social motivation. *Annual Review of Psychology, 42,* 377–399.

Guerin, B. (1993). *Social facilitation.* Cambridge: Cambridge University Press.

Kent, M. V. (1996). Presence of others. In A. P. Hare, H. H. Blumberg, M. F. Davies, & M. V. Kent (Eds.), *Small groups: An introduction* (pp. 41–57). Westport, CT: Praeger.

Markus, H. (1978). The effect of mere presence on social facilitation: An unobtrusive test. *Journal of Experimental Social Psychology, 14,* 389–397.

Michaels, J. W., Blommel, J. M., Brocato, R. M., Linkous, R. A., & Rowe, J. S. (1982). Social facilitation and inhibition in a natural setting. *Replications in Social Psychology, 12,* 21–24.

Mook, D. G. (1980). In defense of external invalidity. *American Psychologist, 38,* 379–388.

Sanders, G. S., & Baron, R. S. (1975). The motivating effects of distraction on task performance. *Journal of Personality and Social Psychology, 32,* 956–963.

Stroebe, W. (2012). The truth about Triplett (1898), but nobody seems to care. *Perspectives on Psychological Science, 7,* 54–57.

Triplett, N. (1898). The dynamogenic factors in pacemaking and competition. *American Journal of Psychology, 9,* 507–533.

Wallace, H. M., & Baumeister, R. F. (2002). The performance of narcissists rises and falls with perceived opportunity for glory. *Journal of Personality and Social Psychology, 82,* 819–834.

Zajonc, R. B. (1965). Social facilitation. *Science, 149,* 269–274.

Zajonc, R. B., & Sales, S. M. (1966). Social facilitation of dominant and subordinate responses. *Journal of Experimental Social Psychology, 2,* 160–168.

More to Explore

Weisinger, H., & Pawlin-Fry, J. P. (2015). *Performing under pressure: The science of doing your best when it matters most.* New York: Crown Business.

7 Us and Them

Discrimination on the Basis of Trivial Social Categorization

"Now, the Star-Belly Sneetches had bellies with stars. The Plain-Belly Sneetches had none upon thars . . . You might think such a thing wouldn't matter at all. But, because they had stars, all the Star-Belly Sneetches would brag, 'We're the best kind of Sneetch on the beaches.'"
—*The Sneetches*, Dr. Seuss (1904–1991), American writer and cartoonist

Background

In the summer of 1954, Sherif, Harvey, White, Hood, and Sherif (1961) set out to test Sherif's newly proposed *realistic conflict theory*, which states that prejudice and discrimination arise between groups whenever those groups compete for scarce valuable resources. Sherif arranged to have 11 boys (all White, middle class, and Protestant) bused from Oklahoma City to a Boy Scout camp in Oklahoma's Robbers Cave State Park, about 100 miles away. The next day, 11 more boys (with similar backgrounds) made the same trip. At the spacious 200-acre park, the two groups of boys were initially kept apart. Neither group knew of the other's existence. During the first week, activities such as hiking, swimming, cooking, and bunking together served to establish group identities and loyalties. The boys chose names for their respective groups—the *Eagles* and the *Rattlers*—and made group-identifying shirts and flags for themselves. They spontaneously established distinct group *norms* (common expectations and behaviors; see Chapter 1).

During the second week, the two groups were brought into contact in a park pavilion. Group members were told that they would be competing in baseball and tug-of-war, vying for individual prizes and a handsome team trophy. The ensuing contests quickly led to animosity and hostility. The groups staked out separate territories and began taunting each other. The Eagles made the first move by burning the Rattlers' flag. The Rattlers retaliated by ransacking the Eagles' cabin, flipping beds and stealing personal property. The groups had to be physically separated to prevent the hostilities from escalating. During a cooling off period, the boys listed traits of each group. They tended to characterize their own group favorably and the other group unfavorably. It was clear that the Eagles didn't like the Rattlers, and vice versa.

A final phase of the study brought the Eagles and Rattlers together to work on common goals. They worked shoulder-to-shoulder to dislodge a school bus that was stuck in the mud and combined their wits to solve a water supply problem. This cooperation served to reduce the conflict that had arisen during the previous competition. *Social categorization* (dividing into *us* and *them*), competition (in the form of sporting events and prizes for winners), and cooperation (working together on common problems) all had their expected effects. Sherif and his colleagues thus demonstrated that it is possible to produce prejudice and discrimination by putting groups of research participants into competitive situations, and also possible to resolve conflict by having the groups work together toward shared goals.

An important feature of this study is that the two groups were deliberately thrust into competition. But what would have happened if the two groups had not been made to compete? What if they had been aware of each other, but nothing more? Would prejudice and discrimination still have occurred?

Fourteen years later, on April 4, 1968, civil rights leader Dr. Martin Luther King, Jr., was assassinated. That evening, Jane Elliott, a third-grade teacher in Riceville, Iowa, was watching the news on TV as she ironed material for a teepee that she planned to use the next day in a lesson on Native Americans. An interview with a Black leader caught her attention. A White reporter, microphone thrust forward, was demanding, "When our leader [meaning President John F. Kennedy] was killed several years ago, his widow held us together. Who's going to control your people?" Notice how the reporter used the words "our" versus "your" and "held" versus "control."

The next day Elliott decided that she would combine her lesson on Native Americans with a lesson about Dr. King. As she attempted to discuss racism with her class of all-White small-town 8-year-olds, she realized that they were not grasping the significance of the issues at hand. So she asked the children whether they would like to participate in an exercise that would enable them to actually feel what it would be like to be treated differently. Anticipating a break from their regular lessons, the children were game.

Elliott began by matter-of-factly stating that blue-eyed children are superior to brown-eyed children. Melatonin makes children's eyes blue and also makes them smarter and better learners, she explained. She then had the blue-eyed children wrap a brown collar around the brown-eyed children's necks, rendering them more identifiable. She announced that blue-eyed children would be given special privileges, commensurate with their superiority. They would sit in the front of the classroom, get second helpings at lunch, enjoy extra time at recess, have access to a new jungle gym on the playground, and be allowed to drink from the classroom water fountain. Brown-eyed children were denied these privileges. Furthermore, Elliott purposefully singled out brown-eyed children for their faults and mistakes, while making reference to their inferior eye color.

The children's behavior quickly changed. The blue-eyed children became more cheerful and animated. They also became arrogant and bossy toward the brown-eyed children. The brown-eyed children became withdrawn, timid, and subservient. They huddled together on the edges of the playground, feeling ashamed and angry, and they suddenly performed worse on academic tasks in the classroom. It was a long day for the brown-eyed children. The next morning, Elliott changed her tune. She claimed that she (being blue-eyed herself) had lied: Brown-eyed children were, in fact, superior to blue-eyed children. The intergroup dynamics of the previous day were reversed. However, they were not as dramatic, given that the brown-eyed children had just personally experienced the pain of prejudice and discrimination.

Jane Elliott's classroom exercise received a mix of reactions from her colleagues and the surrounding community. Some thought she was ingenious and courageous to do what she did, whereas others wondered what gave her the right to put innocent children through such an anguishing procedure. Although Negroes (a common term at the time) were perhaps familiar with such treatment, the White children of Riceville were not. Controversy aside, Elliott soon appeared on the Johnny Carson Show and, 15 years later, on Oprah. Elliott is also credited with being the founder of modern-day diversity training (Peters, 1987).

Worth noting is that Elliott's classroom exercise did not feature the sort of provoked competition that the Robbers Cave study did. Instead, Elliott simply ascribed different traits and privileges to the blue-eyed and brown-eyed children. But were even these manipulations necessary to produce prejudice and discrimination? If the children had been explicitly recognized for having either blue eyes or brown eyes, and nothing more, would that have been enough to produce ill will between the two subgroups?

It is possible to imagine other ways to experimentally manipulate intergroup dynamics in order to demonstrate discrimination. Moreover, in the social world, there are countless examples of discrimination, based on differences in nationality, politics, religion, culture, race, ethnicity, gender, social class, occupation, sexual orientation, age, and so forth. But although the world is divided into myriad social groups, some group divisions produce more conflict than others. For example, whereas the racial divide between Whites and Blacks sometimes degenerates into violence, the sports divide between Lakers and Celtics hardly ever does. Still less do lovers of, for example, different types of art come to blows. Or do they? In this regard, Tajfel and his colleagues (1970, 1971) raised a fundamental question: What are the *minimal* intergroup differences required to produce discrimination? The prevailing assumption had been that either personality differences or social tensions were necessary. Self-interest and competition for limited resources were also presumed to be necessary. But were these assumptions correct? Surely, in mature adults with no prior grievances against one another, mere *social categorization* ("I belong to this group; you belong to that group") would not be enough to produce discrimination. Or would it?

To investigate these questions, Tajfel, Billig, Bundy, and Flament (1971) set out to create what would come to be known as the *minimal group paradigm* (MGP): a situation where one would not intuitively expect discrimination to occur. To this end, they sought to create groups based on arbitrary and seemingly trivial distinctions. There would be no history (e.g., preexisting hostility) between the groups. Also, group members would have no direct contact with members of their own group (their *ingroup*) or members of the other group (their *outgroup*). They wouldn't even know who was in either group, only what group they themselves were in. Moreover, group members' behaviors would in no way be able to benefit themselves, whether directly or through interpersonal reciprocity. Furthermore, there would be no anticipation of future interactions within or between the groups. Why would members of such groups ever discriminate against one another?

What They Did

Tajfel and his colleagues (1970, 1971) conducted two experiments. In Experiment 1, the participants were 64 boys, 14–15 years old, from a suburb outside of Bristol in the United Kingdom. All the boys were from the same school and knew each other well. The boys were told that the experiment was concerned with visual judgments. Accordingly, 40 clusters of varying numbers of dots were flashed onto a large projection screen, one cluster at a time, for a split second (too quickly for the boys to accurately count the dots). Each boy estimated the number of dots in each cluster, writing his estimates on an answer sheet.

One of the experimenters then pretended to score the boys' judgments, after which each of the boys was randomly assigned to one of two groups. Half the boys were told that they had tended to overestimate the number of dots in the clusters; the other half of the boys were told that they tended to underestimate the number of dots. Importantly, what the boys were told had nothing to do with the actual accuracy of their estimates. However, because the boys could not accurately count the dots, they could be effectively led to believe that they were either "underestimators" or "overestimators"—in the grand scheme of things, a fairly trivial designation.

After being told what group he was in, each boy was asked to allocate points to other boys in the group. An answer booklet contained several matrices organized into a top row and a bottom row, with different pairs of numbers all along. One number of the pair was the amount of reward or penalty that would be allotted to one other individual; the other number was the amount of reward or penalty to be allotted to a second individual. Negative numbers, such as *-14*, indicated a penalty; positive numbers, such as *23*, indicated a reward. Each point that participants allotted was worth one-tenth of a penny (this was back in the days when a penny still meant something). In each matrix, the top and bottom rows stood respectively for rewards and penalties to be awarded to either (a) two ingroup members, (b) two outgroup members, or (c) an ingroup member and an outgroup member. Thus, the boys had to choose a pair of numbers from each matrix, indicating how much they wanted to allocate to each of two boys. They didn't know the identity of each boy to whom they were giving money, but they did know each boy's group membership.

It was stressed to the boys that they would not be rewarding or penalizing themselves. However, they were informed that, at the end of the task, they would receive the amount of money that others had awarded them.

In Experiment 2, Tajfel and his colleagues divided 48 of the aforementioned boys on the basis of their alleged artistic preferences. The boys were shown 12 color slides, six of paintings by Paul Klee (a Swiss painter who died in 1940) and six of paintings by Wassily Kandinsky (a Russian painter who died in 1944). The names "Klee" and "Kandinsky" were written on the blackboard, but the painters' signatures did not appear on the paintings. For each pair of paintings, the boys were asked which one they preferred. They were then given bogus feedback, as in Experiment 1, and randomly assigned to either the "group preferring Klee" or the "group preferring Kandinsky."

Each boy was then asked to make reward allocations, just as they did in Experiment 1. However, this time Tajfel and his colleagues were interested in which of three allocation strategies was most preferred: (a) the largest reward for members of both groups ("maximum joint profit"), (b) the largest reward for an ingroup member regardless of the reward for the outgroup member ("largest possible reward to ingroup"), or (c) the largest possible difference in reward between the two groups, favoring the ingroup ("maximum difference").

What They Found

In Experiment 1 (involving dot estimation), Tajfel and his colleagues were primarily interested in what the boys would do when they were allocating one amount to a member of their own group and another amount to a member of the other group. They found that a large majority of the boys gave more money to ingroup members than to outgroup members.

In Experiment 2 (involving artistic preferences), they found that 34 of the boys (72.3%) allocated points in favor of their own group, four of the boys (8.5%) allotted points equally to the two groups, and nine of the boys (19.2%) allocated points in favor of the other group (Figure 7). This replicated the results of Experiment 1. But a subtler finding also emerged. Surprisingly, maximizing the difference in profits between the two groups was the most favored allocation strategy, while maximizing joint profits was the least favored strategy (with the strategy of favoring the ingroup falling in between). In other words, the boys chose a suboptimal strategy from a strictly selfish point of view. Evidently, most important to most boys was the absolute difference between what their group members would receive and what the other group members would receive. Otherwise put, they sacrificed *absolute* rewards for ingroup members just so members of the outgroup got *relatively* less. How mean!

Thus, Tajfel and his colleagues found, in both experiments, that classifying individuals into trivial social categories was enough to produce *ingroup favoritism*. They also found, in their second experiment, that participants chose the allocation strategy of maximizing the difference in outcomes of ingroup and outgroup members over that of maximizing overall rewards to the two groups. These results occurred despite the fact that the two groups were based on completely arbitrary distinctions, there was no history between the groups, and there was no room for self-interest in the allocation of points. Trivial social categorization led to ingroup favoritism and maximum group distinctiveness.

So What?

Evidently, it doesn't take much—the most trivial social distinction—to produce intergroup discrimination. This is alarming given that malevolent discrimination has, historically, been among the worst problems facing humanity. It is a ubiquitous and seemingly interminable social plague. If the MGP can produce discrimination, then the more profound distinctions involving race,

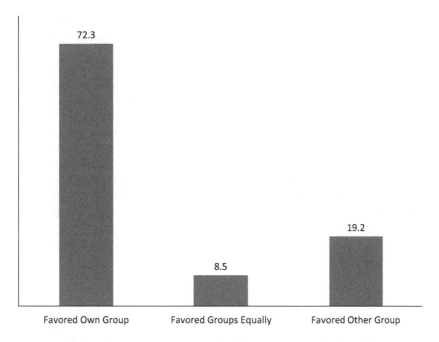

Figure 7 Percentage of participants whose point allocations favored their own group, their own and the other group equally, or the other group

nationality, religion, and so forth are likely to produce even more discrimination (see Mook, 1983). The fact that discrimination is so spontaneous and inevitable is a sobering revelation.

Since Tajfel and his colleagues (1970, 1971) introduced the MGP, a standard version has evolved. Typically, participants engage in a computer-based dot-estimation task. For example, a participant might estimate the number of dots in 10 rapidly presented dot patterns. This is referred to as the Numerical Style Estimation Test (NEST). Participants are led to believe that people's estimation styles vary, with about half of people overestimating and about half of people underestimating the number of dots in a cluster. Importantly, participants are told that one's estimation style is not related to any other cognitive tendency or personality trait. The computer then provides random feedback, indicating that the participant is either an overestimator or an underestimator. The feedback, of course, is bogus. NEST does not actually assess any perceptual tendency; it merely provides a means of establishing two distinct groups. The resulting groups have no history. Also, no one knows who in particular is in one's ingroup or who is in one's outgroup. Allocations are based on code numbers, not names. The participant is reminded of his own group membership as the experiment continues, so that he knows whether he is dealing with an ingroup or outgroup member while engaged in the task that follows. This task involves distributing some valuable resource (such as points that can be converted to money) among ingroup and outgroup members. Participants are led to believe that they will receive any resources group members allocate to them. All group members remain anonymous so that allocations will not be influenced by favoritism toward specific individuals or by reciprocity (in which allocations made are based on allocations received).

The MGP has been found to produce numerous other effects besides ingroup favoritism. One such effect has to do with perceptions of variability among ingroup and outgroup members. People tend to perceive more homogeneity among outgroup members ("They're all the same") and more heterogeneity among ingroup members ("We are richly diverse"; see Ostrom & Sedikedes, 1992). This *outgroup homogeneity effect* is qualified by the relative positivity or negativity of given traits. That is, *we* are all the same more when it comes to positive traits, while *they* are all the same more when it comes to negative traits.

To be sure, the results of Tajfel's research are not beyond dispute. Indeed, one should always be thinking critically about the findings of science, including the findings of social psychology. For example, what role might *demand characteristics* (guesses about what the experimenters are up to; see Chapter 13) have played in this study? Perhaps the boys were simply living up to what they thought the experimenters expected of them—that they would favor their ingroup. Also, while we have not yet mentioned it, the ingroup favoritism found in this study was moderated by what appeared to be a sense of fairness. The boys did not show ingroup favoritism at every turn; they departed from this trend in ways that showed that they were also interested in "being fair." Is this *positive* finding regarding fairness not as important as the *negative* finding regarding discrimination? Furthermore, what else might have moderated this finding of ingroup favoritism? For example, what role might age or culture have played? Quite possibly, the participants— adolescent boys from the United Kingdom—were influenced by their youthful selfishness or by their competitive Western culture (see Brown, 2001).

Afterthoughts

Where is the theory in all of this? Keep in mind, scientific theories play an integral role in empirical research. Theories serve to summarize large bodies of research findings. They define the relationships among particular variables. They suggest hypotheses for future research. Research then either supports or fails to support the theory. Theories are rarely immediately discarded when they are not supported; they tend to have a *protective belt*, which gives them the "benefit of the doubt" (a point emphasized by famed philosopher of science, Imre Lakatos; see Larvor, 1998). However, theories can fall out of favor or be discarded altogether if enough disconfirming evidence emerges (Popper, 2002). At any rate, theories are important. As Kurt Lewin, the father of social psychology, once quipped: "There is nothing so practical as a good theory" (1952, p. 169).

The MGP represents a research technique for creating relatively trivial group distinctions and allowing one to test the ramifications of those distinctions. However, it is not a theory. Indeed, Tajfel and his colleagues were surprised by their own results. They had presumed that, like the rest of us, they would have to make groups more meaningful, with a history of interaction, and some competition, before any consequential discrimination emerged. But as it turned out, this was not the case. But given that discrimination does reliably occur under such minimal conditions, a theory is now required. Nearly a decade after Tajfel and his colleagues (1970, 1971) introduced the MGP, Tajfel and Turner (1979) proposed *social identity theory* (SIT), which claims that there are three cognitive processes relevant to one's being a member of a group: *social categorization*, *social identification*, and *social comparison*. Social categorization involves recognizing which group one (or someone else) does or does not belong to. As demonstrated by Tajfel and his colleagues, the most minimal distinctions can lead to social categorization, without any preexisting intergroup history. Social identification occurs when group members agree with ingroup attitudes, conform to ingroup norms, share ingroup goals, and participate in ingroup activities. Finally, social comparison leads to contrasting perceptions of ingroup and outgroup members. As research on the MGP demonstrates, such perceptions tend to be biased in favor of ingroups.

But why, exactly, does ingroup favoritism occur? SIT claims that we favor ingroups and derogate outgroups because we seek *positive distinctiveness*. That is, as individuals we want our groups to be better than other groups because we want to have relatively positive social identities. Importantly, a person's identity is claimed to have two aspects, one personal and one social. One's *personal identity* has to do with self-perceived traits and individual outcomes, unrelated to group memberships. One's *social identity*, in contrast, derives from social categorization along with social comparison. When we belong to successful and well-regarded social groups, we acquire a positive social identity. When we belong to unsuccessful and maligned groups, our social identity suffers. The combination of our personal and social identities results in our overall identity. Our overall identity in turn impacts our self-esteem. That is, the way we *think* about ourselves has consequences for how we *feel* about ourselves. We are motivated to possess positive social identities because we want to feel good about ourselves (Abrams & Hogg, 2006; Rubin & Hewstone, 1998). It works the other way around too. If one manipulates a person's self-esteem (making them feel relatively good or bad about themselves), they will then be less or more inclined to derogate and discriminate against outgroup members (e.g., Crocker, Thompson, McGraw, & Ingerman, 1987; see Chapter 11 for more on group identity and self-esteem).

Given our fundamental desire to feel good about ourselves, how can we ever hope to significantly reduce—let alone eliminate—prejudice and discrimination? What chance do we have of ever living in a harmonious utopian world? One solution would be for everyone to recognize that they belong to one all-inclusive ingroup, namely, humanity. This worldwide ingroup would need to be more salient and important than any lesser ingroup-outgroup distinctions. It may be far-fetched, but consider what would happen if the Earth was attacked by extraterrestrials. Earthlings would then represent one big ingroup, and the aliens would represent one big outgroup. We would suddenly identify with all fellow Earthlings. We would desperately cooperate to defend our race, brushing aside mundane (down-to-Earth) differences. The Earth's problems regarding intergroup conflicts would be solved (or at least ignored). Of course, we would still have a serious intergroup conflict problem on our hands: We would now be engaged in interplanetary warfare! (For more about identifying with all of humanity, see McFarland, Webb, & Brown, 2012.)

Finally, it is worth noting that Tajfel's classic study was no "one-hit wonder." Scores of MGP studies followed and continue to appear. Tajfel's study has inspired 45 years of research that has reliably shown that people favor members of their ingroup in their perceptions, attitudes, and behaviors. In just the past five years there have been a variety of studies that demonstrate MGP-produced biases. For example, Ratner, Dotsch, Wigboldus, van Knippenberg, and Amodio (2014) demonstrated that we form different mental images of MGP-produced ingroup and outgroup members. Specifically, visualizations of ingroup members are found to elicit more favorable impressions (e.g., ingroup faces are trusted more than outgroup faces). Moreover, Young and Hugenberg (2010) found that we are more motivated to accurately process the facial expressions of ingroups members than outgroups members. Think how this might influence a perceiver's degree of empathy. Finally, Abrams, Randsley de Moura, and Travaglino (2013) found that people forgive serious transgressions by ingroup leaders more than outgroup leaders. Think how this might bias members of different political parties. These are but a few recent MGP findings. Tajfel's experiments involving the MGP will no doubt have an ongoing legacy.

Revelation

People readily categorize themselves into ingroups and outgroups. To bolster their self-esteem, they favor their ingroup, even when categorizations are based on contrived and trivial experimental manipulations.

What Do You Think?

Is every negative generalization necessarily a prejudicial stereotype? Can one ever legitimately say that some group is generally bad in some respect? Is it a prejudice stereotype to say that Blacks are bad at math? That Asians are bad at basketball? Both? Neither? Also, will the world ever be free of prejudice and discrimination—why or why not?

Chapter Reference

Tajfel, H., Billig, M. G., Bundy, R. P., & Flament, C. (1971). Social categorization and intergroup behavior. *European Journal of Social Psychology*, *1*, 149–178.

Other References

Abrams, D., & Hogg, M. A. (2006). Comments on the motivational status of self-esteem in social identity and intergroup discrimination. *European Journal of Social Psychology*, *18*, 317–334.

Abrams, D., Randsley de Moura, G., & Travaglino, G. A. (2013). A double standard when group members behave badly: Transgression credit to ingroup leaders. *Journal of Personality and Social Psychology*, *105*, 799–815.

Brown, R. (2001). *Group processes: Dynamics within and between groups* (2nd ed.). Cambridge, MA: Wiley-Blackwell.

Crocker, J., Thompson, L. L., McGraw, K. M., & Ingerman, C. (1987). Downward social comparison, prejudice, and evaluations of others: Effects of self-esteem and threat. *Journal of Personality and Social Psychology*, *52*, 907–916.

Larvor, B. (1998). *Lakatos: An introduction*. London: Routledge.

Lewin, K. (1952). *Field theory in social science: Selected theoretical papers*. New York: Harper & Row.

McFarland, S., Webb, M., & Brown, D. (2012). All humanity is my ingroup: A measure and studies of identification with all humanity. *Journal of Personality and Social Psychology*, *103*, 830–853.

Mook, D. G. (1983). In defense of external invalidity. *American Psychologist*, *38*, 379–381.

Ostrom, T. M., & Sedikedes, C. (1992). Outgroup homogeneity effects in natural and minimal groups. *Psychological Bulletin*, *112*, 536–552.

Peters, W. (1987). *A class divided*. New Haven, CT: Yale University Press.

Popper, K. (2002). *The logic of scientific discoveries* (2nd ed.). New York: Routledge.

Ratner, K. G., Dotsch, R., Wigboldus, D. H., van Knippenberg, A. D., & Amodio, D. M. (2014). Visualizing minimal ingroup and outgroup faces: Implications for impressions, attitudes, and behaviors. *Journal of Personality and Social Psychology*, *106*, 897–911.

Rubin, M., & Hewstone, M. (1998). Social identity theory's self-esteem hypothesis: A review and some suggestions for clarification. *Personality and Social Psychology Review*, *2*, 40–62.

Sherif, M., Harvey, O. J., White, B. J., Hood, W., & Sherif, C. W. (1961). *Intergroup conflict and cooperation: The Robbers Cave experiment* (pp. 155–184). Norman, OK: The University Book Exchange.

Tajfel, H. (1970). Experiments in intergroup discrimination. *Scientific American*, *223*, 96–102.

Tajfel, H., & Turner, J. C. (1979). An integrative theory of intergroup conflict. In W. G. Austin & S. Worchel (Eds.), *The social psychology of intergroup relations* (pp. 33–47). Monterey, CA: Brooks/Cole.

Young, S. G., & Hugenberg, K. (2010). Mere social categorization modulates identification of facial expressions of emotion. *Journal of Personality and Social Psychology*, *99*, 964–977.

More to Explore

Greenwald, A. G., & Pettigrew, T. F. (2014). With malice toward none and charity toward some: Ingroup favoritism enables discrimination. *American Psychologist*, *69*, 645–655.

8　The Sauntering Samaritan

When Context Conquers Character

"If we see someone who needs help, do we stop? There is so much suffering and poverty, and a great need for good Samaritans."

—Pope Francis (1936–), current Pope of the Roman Catholic Church

Background

The experiments in this book might be dubbed *empirical parables* (Ross & Nisbett, 2011). They are empirical in the sense that their findings derive from careful data collection; parables because they offer a profound, sometimes even moral, punch line. We now describe an experiment that is based on an actual parable, one that has no doubt inspired many a Sunday sermon:

"And who is my neighbor?" Jesus replied, "A man was going down from Jericho, and he fell among robbers, who stripped him and beat him, and departed, leaving him half dead. Now by chance a priest was going down the road; and when he saw him he passed by on the other side. So likewise a Levite, when he came to the place and saw him, passed by on the other side. But a Samaritan, as he journeyed, came to where he was; and when he saw him, he had compassion, and went to him and bound his wounds, pouring on oil and wine; then he set him on his own beast and brought him to an inn, and took care of him. And the next day he took out two denarii and gave them to the innkeeper, saying, "Take care of him; and whatever more you spend, I will repay you when I come back." Which of these three, do you think, proved neighbor to him who fell among the robbers? He said, "The one who showed mercy on him." And Jesus said to him, "Go and do likewise."

(Luke 10: 29–37 RSV, as cited in Darley & Batson, 1973, pp. 100–101)

What comes to mind when you contemplate this parable? Convictions about the importance of helping people in distress? Differences among people in their penchant for doing good deeds? Suspicions that we are attempting to convert you?

To the minds of two prominent social psychologists, John Darley and Daniel Batson (1973), there came the realization that this short biblical narrative features two types of variables known to influence people's behavior: *dispositional variables* (stable, enduring characteristics of a person) and *situational variables* (aspects of the physical or social environment). Although Jesus seems to have been emphasizing differences in the dispositions of the unhelpful Levite and priest and the more compassionate Samaritan, features of the situation itself, which might have influenced decisions to help, can also be read into this iconic scenario. For example, the priest and Levite, religious functionaries preoccupied with temple ceremonies and other liturgical matters, were perhaps more burdened with social obligations and a demanding schedule than was the Samaritan. In the words of Darley and Batson:

> One can imagine the priest and Levite, prominent public figures, hurrying along with little black books full of meetings and appointments, glancing furtively at their sundials. In contrast, the Samaritan would likely have far fewer and less important people counting on him to be at a particular place at a particular time, and therefore might be expected to be in less of a hurry than the prominent priest or Levite.
>
> (p. 101)

So, mindful of the Good Samaritan parable, Darley and Batson sought to examine the relative effects of dispositional and situational variables on helping behavior. Darley and Latané (1968) had already conducted acclaimed experiments on bystander intervention in emergency situations (see Chapter 5). These experiments suggested that at least one feature of the situation, namely the number of people present, greatly influences whether or not one will help someone in trouble. Their concept of *diffusion of responsibility* served as a possible explanation for why it is that the more people there are to witness an emergency the less likely it is that any one of them will intervene. At the same time, researchers in general were having bad luck finding personality characteristics associated with helping behavior. Such variables as *social desirability* (trying to please others and behave in a socially acceptable manner) and *social responsibility* (feeling an obligation to help others in need), which were expected to strongly predict helping, in fact hardly predicted it at all. Furthermore, Mischel (1968) had just vigorously challenged the overused *trait* concept and entrenched notions of cross-situational consistency in behavior, citing, for example, Hartshorne and May's (1928) discovery that moral behavior is not a solid fixture of personality: A child's honesty in one situation was found to be virtually unrelated to his or her honesty in another situation.

Such findings and prevailing themes were brought together in a profound way in Darley and Batson's (1973) *Jerusalem to Jericho* study, in which variables that might affect helping behavior were theoretically identified (drawing hints from careful biblical exegesis!) and then ingeniously *operationalized* (defined in terms of how one would experimentally manipulate or measure them). Darley and Batson examined two situational variables: whether or not the *norm of social responsibility* was made salient to participants, and *how much of a hurry* those participants were in. They also examined the dispositional variable of *religiosity* (how religious a person is). Darley and Batson wondered: What are the relative influences of these variables on helping? Was the Samaritan a better "neighbor to him who fell among the robbers" because he was more benevolently motivated? Or were the priest and Levite simply worse neighbors to the pitiable traveler to Jericho because they had greater social responsibilities and a busier agenda?

What They Did

The participants were 67 students at Princeton Theological Seminary (where Batson, himself an ordained minister, had received his doctoral training). The study, said to be concerned with religious education and vocations, had two parts. In the first part, participants completed several questionnaires concerning religious issues and their motives for being religious. Statistical analysis of their responses revealed that the questions measured three somewhat distinct *factors* (underlying dimensions). The first two factors were *religion as a means* and *religion as an end*. These reflect a distinction made by the eminent personality psychologist, Gordon Allport (1961), between *extrinsic religion* (which is primarily conventional and pragmatic) and *intrinsic religion* (which centers on faith and religious values). The third religiosity factor, promoted by Batson as an addition to Allport's two-factor model, was *religion as a quest* (which involves one's search for meaning in life). Darley and Batson hypothesized that people who are religious for intrinsic reasons or as part of a quest for meaning would be more inclined to help someone in distress, whereas people who are religious in order to gain extrinsic rewards would be less inclined to do so.

The second part of the study contained the experimental manipulations. Participants were asked to give a brief talk on the jobs they thought seminary graduates would excel at or on the parable of the Good Samaritan (a printed copy of the parable was provided in case they were unfamiliar with it). A research assistant then casually explained:

> Since they're rather tight on space in this building, we're using a free office in the building next door for recording the talks. Let me show you how to get there [draws and explains map on 3 × 5 card]. This is where Professor Steiner's office is. If you go in this door [points at map] . . . another of Professor Steiner's assistants will get you set up for recording your talk.
>
> (Darley & Batson, 1973, p. 103)

This miniature drama ended with the assistant saying one of three things: "Oh, you're late. They were expecting you a few minutes ago. We'd better get moving. The assistant should be waiting for you so you'd better hurry. It shouldn't take but just a minute" (the *high-hurry* condition) or "The assistant is ready for you, so please go right over" (the *intermediate-hurry* condition) or "It'll be a few minutes before they're ready for you, but you might as well head on over. If you have to wait over there it shouldn't be long" (the *low-hurry* condition; Darley & Batson, 1973, p. 104).

Thus, the study featured a *2x3* design: There were two levels of one independent variable (the topic of the talk they were asked to give) and three levels of another independent variable (how hurried they were made to feel). Each participant was randomly assigned to one of the six resulting conditions.

On the way through the alley that separated the two buildings, each participant encountered a person (a second research confederate) who was sitting slumped over in a doorway, head down, eyes closed, not moving, and coughing and groaning. If the participant asked what was wrong or offered any help, the seemingly groggy confederate responded:

> Oh, thank you [cough]. . . . No, it's all right. [Pause] I've got this respiratory condition [cough]. . . . The doctor's given me these pills to take, and I just took one. . . . If I just sit here and rest for a few minutes I'll be O.K. . . . Thanks very much for stopping though [smiles weekly].
>
> (Darley & Batson, 1973, p. 104) (Imagine being the thespian confederate in this experiment!)

The confederate was *blind* to (not told about) the participant's religiosity score, how hurried he was, or what talk he was assigned to give. This prevented him from having a biasing influence on the participant's behavior. Incidentally, this part of the study took place over the course of a very chilly December in New Jersey, making the confederate's apparent plight all the more miserable.

The dependent variable was whether, and how much, a participant would offer assistance. To this end, the confederate in the alley rated the participant's behavior, according to the following scale: *0* if he apparently did not notice the victim; *1* if he noticed but did not offer help; *2* if he did not stop, but indirectly sought help (e.g., told someone else that the person needed help); *3* if he stopped and asked if the victim needed help; *4* if he stopped, took the victim inside, and left; and *5* if he took the victim inside and stayed with him.

The participant then met an assistant in the second building and was given time to prepare and privately record his brief speech. Afterward, he completed a questionnaire on personal and social ethics, which contained such questions as "When was the last time you saw a person who seemed to be in need of help?" and "When was the last time you stopped to help someone in need?" These questions served to verify participants' perceptions of the situation in the alley (referred to as a *manipulation check*).

Participants were then thoroughly debriefed. Darley and Batson claimed that: "All [participants] seemed readily to understand the necessity for the deception, and none indicated any resentment to it" (p. 104). One wonders, however, if a disproportionate number of the participants who failed to help—especially those who unhurriedly went to preach about the Good Samaritan—subsequently felt ill-suited for the ministry, and opted instead for a less pastoral career, perhaps one on Wall Street. . . .

What They Found

Darley and Batson (1973) predicted that the topic of the talk participants readied themselves to give (Good Samaritan vs. vocational opportunities) would not affect their behavior, even though this prediction flies in the face of theories that emphasize the importance of normative influences. In other words, Darley and Batson hypothesized that, regardless of whether or not the norm of social responsibility was emphasized, participants would help equally. They did predict, however, that how *rushed* participants were would markedly sway their behavior. In particular, participants in more of a hurry would offer less help. Finally, they predicted that participants who were intrinsically religiously motivated or whose faith took the form of an existential quest would demonstrate more good will than would those who were extrinsically religiously motivated.

As it turned out, 40% of the participants offered some help. Importantly, the hurry manipulation profoundly affected participants' responses. Averaging across both talk topics, help was offered by 63% of those in the low-hurry condition, 45% of those in the intermediate-hurry condition, but only 10% of those in the high-hurry condition (Figure 8). At the same time, 53% of

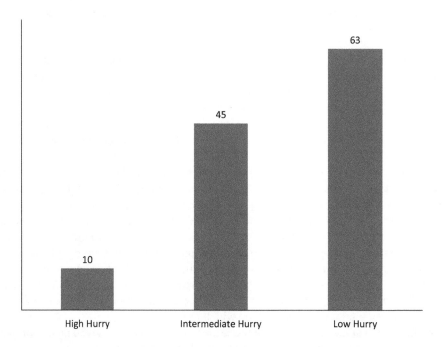

Figure 8 Percentage of participants who, on the way to give a sermon, offered help to a man slumped in an alley, depending on how much of a hurry they were in

those asked to talk about the Good Samaritan parable offered help, while 29% of those asked to speak on the vocational strengths of seminarians offered help, a difference that Darley and Batson concluded did not meet their criteria of statistical significance. However, percentage-wise, it looks non-trivial. Indeed, a re-analysis by Greenwald (1975), using more focused tests, did find it to be statistically significant. Thus, both of the situational manipulations—the hurry manipulation and the talk manipulation—influenced helping behavior.

In contrast, religiosity (the dispositional variable) was generally unrelated to whether participants offered to help. The only exception was religion as quest, which did predict the kind of help that was offered. However, it did so in a manner *opposite* to what Darley and Batson had predicted, luring them into a labyrinth of *post hoc* logic in their discussion.

At any rate, Darley and Batson's results led them to a provocative conclusion:

> A person not in a hurry may stop and offer help to a person in distress. A person in a hurry is likely to keep going. Ironically, he is likely to keep going even if he is hurrying to speak on the parable of the Good Samaritan, thus inadvertently confirming the point of the parable. (Indeed, on several occasions, a seminary student going to give his talk on the parable of the Good Samaritan literally stepped over the victim as he hurried on his way!)
>
> (p. 107)

So What?

Some of the most remarkable social psychological experiments have been those that have attempted to examine and challenge oft-repeated adages or deeply entrenched assumptions. Darley and Batson's (1973) experiment was a perfect example. It demonstrated how subtle aspects of a situation can at times influence consequential behaviors in a way that relevant personality variables do not. Thus, the study contradicted our general proclivity to make dispositional attributions for others' behaviors (Ross, 1977; see Chapter 10). Although we might assume that someone who is subdued at a party is typically bashful or that someone who drops a few quarters into a beggar's cap is characteristically magnanimous (dispositional attributions), situational factors may in fact be responsible for such behaviors (perhaps the party music was depressing or a friend did not show up, and maybe the person ringing the charity bell was charmingly good-humored or irresistibly attractive). The causes of behavior are often to be found in the *situation* rather than the *person*, and the only way to know is to do the relevant experiment (sometimes with some wholesome Biblical inspiration!).

Were you surprised (even disturbed) that 60% of the seminarians (who, remember, were training to do God's work) failed to offer any help at all? Given that all of the participants noticed the victim in the alleyway (as revealed by their answers to the questions at the end of the study), should we say that those who did not help were undeniably coldhearted? A follow-up study by Batson and his colleagues (1978) may help to answer this question. Their study followed procedures that were similar to those in the Darley and Batson (1973) study and likewise found that participants in a hurry were less likely to help (40%) than were those who were not (65%). However, this study further determined that the difference occurred primarily for participants who thought their research participation was essential to the experimenter. When participants were led to believe that the researcher was not counting on their participation, those in a hurry were just about as likely to help (70%) as those not in a hurry (80%). In other words, the hurry and participation variables combined to predict helping. When participation seemed essential, there was a difference of 25% (65% minus 40%) between the high-hurry and low-hurry conditions. However, when participation seemed optional, the difference was only 10% (80% minus 70%)—a difference between differences (technically known as an *interaction*).

This latter finding suggested that the participants in these studies may have wanted to help both the experimenter and the victim and decided upon a course of action only after a cost–benefit analysis. The non-helpers in Darley and Batson's study were perhaps, indeed, still being Good Samaritans, but toward the *experimenter*, whom they had committed to help, rather than toward the victim, who was more incidental to their goals. Being in a hurry may have prevented them from acknowledging the needs of the victim, or even if they had enough time to acknowledge them, they may have concluded that their ethical obligation to the experimenter was paramount.

Perhaps the priest and the Levite in Jesus's parable can be similarly pardoned. It is conceivable that they may have made the decision to bypass the man who had fallen among robbers because their business in Jericho imposed an even greater obligation on them. Perhaps Jesus would have made a stronger case (especially to any social psychologists in his audience!) if he had mentioned in his parable that neither the priest nor the Levite (nor the Samaritan) were *not* attending to more pressing business.

Afterthoughts

In their book, *The Person and the Situation*, Ross and Nisbett (2011) described the many successful attempts of social psychology to show the power of situations to influence behavior, and the general failure of personality variables to do the same. Researchers are often able to demonstrate that a particular contextual variable (that laypeople may fail to appreciate) has a substantial impact on behavior, whereas traits or personality differences (that people may believe are decisive) prove to have trivial effects.

Ross and Nisbett also reminded us of the attention that Kurt Lewin—one of the early giants in the field—brought to apparently minor, though materially important, details of a social situation. These *channel factors*, as he called them, are any critical facilitators of, or barriers to, behavior. In Darley and Batson's (1973) study, time pressure was a channel factor. It was a subtly manipulated, but quite powerful, determinant of compassionate behavior. There may be other channel factors affecting Good Samaritan behavior. For example, Huston, Ruggiero, Conner, and Geis (1981) conducted in-depth interviews with people who had intervened in dangerous crime episodes (bank holdups, armed robberies, and street muggings) or who had passively stood by. Their investigation revealed that those who threw caution to the wind were relatively taller and heavier, had more life-saving, medical, or police training, or were more apt to describe themselves as strong and aggressive. In other words, these Good Samaritans were not necessarily more motivated by humanitarian concerns, just physically stronger and better trained.

A final point to make is that the *social* psychologist (who focuses more on external determinants of behavior) and the *personality* psychologist (who focuses more on internal determinants of behavior) are typically one and the same person. Many psychologists feel comfortable donning both hats. In fact, one often finds these two disciplines wedded together within psychology departments at universities. (Indeed, the flagship journal of the field is named the *Journal of Personality and Social Psychology*.) Yet if one considers the pure form of each approach, one begins to see what strange bedfellows they are. To the social psychologist, differences among people represent *noise*. Personality differences mask the *signal* (produced by the experimental manipulation) that the social psychologist is hunting for. Randomly assigning research participants to the different conditions in an experiment (so that, in all likelihood, the participants in one condition are no different from the participants in another condition on any given dimension) is the primary way of nullifying such noise. In contrast, it is precisely these noisy but often persistent differences among people that are of interest to the personality psychologist. Alert to people's unique traits, they instead view situational differences as the source of unwanted noise. Fortunately, many psychologists are able to adroitly pursue both approaches simultaneously. Instead of pitting situational and dispositional variables against each other, to see which better explains behavior, they attempt to see how the two add to or, better yet, *interact* with each other, mindful of the famous Lewinian formula, $B = f(P, E)$. Behavior is a function of both the person *and* his or her environment. They are interested, for example, in how a change in the situation will affect behavior, but only for *some* people, or, conversely, how certain types of people behave in certain ways, but only in *some* situations. They are also interested in how people tend to seek out or create different situations that in turn affect them (referred to as *niche-building*). Darley and Batson's study is a precious examination of the impact of both the person and the person's situation on a critical human behavior: helping someone who is apparently in great distress.

Revelation

Small, subtle, seemingly trivial situational variables often have a greater impact on behavior than do the personality variables that we more readily, but often mistakenly, regard as influential. Something as simple as time pressure can impact something as vital as compassionate behavior.

What Do You Think?

In the Biblical parable, the Samaritan was praised for assisting a Judean—a foreigner. Should we help strangers as much as we do friends, and immigrants as much as natives? Should one give half one's income away to help the neediest? Where do our obligations begin and end? Also, describe how a particular channel factor determined a significant behavior in your own or another person's life.

Chapter Reference

Darley, J. M., & Batson, C. D. (1973). "From Jerusalem to Jericho": A study of situational and dispositional variables in helping behavior. *Journal of Personality and Social Psychology, 27*, 100–108.

Other References

Allport, G. W. (1961). *Pattern and growth in personality*. New York: Holt, Rinehart & Winston.

Batson, C. D., Cochran, P. J., Biederman, M. F., Blosser, J. L., Ryan, M. J., & Vogt, B. (1978). Failure to help when in a hurry: Callousness or conflict? *Personality and Social Psychology Bulletin, 4*, 97–101.

Darley, J. M., & Latané, B. (1968). Bystander intervention in emergencies: Diffusion of responsibility. *Journal of Personality and Social Psychology, 8*, 377–383.

Greenwald, A. G. (1975). Does the Good Samaritan parable increase helping? A comment on Darley and Batson's no-effect conclusion. *Journal of Personality and Social Psychology, 32*, 578–583.

Hartshorne, H., & May, M. A. (1928). *Studies in the nature of character*. Vol. 1. New York: Palgrave Macmillan.

Huston, T. L., Ruggiero, M., Conner, R., & Geis, G. (1981). Bystander intervention into crime: A study based on naturally-occurring episodes. *Social Psychology Quarterly, 44*, 14–23.

Mischel, W. (1968). *Personality and assessment*. New York: Wiley-Blackwell.

Ross, L. (1977). The intuitive psychologist and his shortcomings: Distortions in the attributional process. In L. Berkowitz (Ed.), *Advances in experimental social psychology* (Vol. 10, pp. 174–221). New York: Academic Press.

Ross, L., & Nisbett, R. E. (2011). *The person and the situation: Perspectives of social* psychology. London: Pinter & Martin.

More to Explore

Gladwell, M. (2002). *The tipping point: How little things can make a big difference*. Boston, MA: Back Bay Books.

9 Taking the Magic Out of the Markers
The Hidden Cost of Rewards

"Work is more fun than fun."

—Noel Coward (1899–1973), English lyricist and playwright

Background

There is a heartwarming tale about an elderly gentleman who, while feeding pigeons from his favorite park bench, is one day confronted by a mob of nasty teenagers. For several minutes, they cruelly make fun of him. He endures the episode stoically, hoping that it will soon be over and never repeated. Alas, when he returns to his bench the following day, the teenagers are there again. Indeed, their taunts start to become a regular feature of his visits to the park. The gentleman eventually decides that enough is enough, and hatches a clever plan to put an end to their mischief. The next time they make fun of him, he does something wholly unexpected. He pays each of them a dollar for their trouble. The astonished teenagers conclude that the old guy must be going senile. He continues to show the same unaccountable generosity day after day, and no matter how badly the teenagers treat him, they still get paid. Then one day, without a word of explanation, he abruptly stops distributing cash. His tormenters are outraged. Why should they bother to taunt somebody who pays them nothing for the privilege? With a disdainful air, they part company with him forever. Smiling, the gentleman returns to feeding his pigeons.

Readers may recognize in this anecdote some familiar themes. Remember how smaller incentives can cause larger shifts in opinion (see Chapter 2), and how obstacles to group membership make people value membership more (Chapter 3)? Such quirky findings contradict our everyday expectations about how rewards and punishments work. In the anecdote, further quirkiness emerges. A temporary reward (money) undermines interest in an activity (taunting) instead of strengthening it. This chapter unpacks this paradoxical point and describes an experiment that tests its validity in an important applied setting.

According to pop psychology gurus, the main problem with human motivation is that it is in such short supply (e.g., Durand, 2000). If only people could get sufficiently motivated, the argument runs, all manner of social and personal ills would soon be overcome. Bulging waistlines would recede, flagging test scores would soar, and the poor and underprivileged would start living the American Dream. Finding effective ways to cultivate motivation is, therefore, a top priority. How should this be accomplished?

Motivations can be divided into two basic types. On the one hand, we can wish to do something for its own sake, for the joy and satisfaction that the activity itself affords. On the other hand, we can wish to do something as a means to an end, for the desirable consequences it promises. In the former case, we are said to be *intrinsically* motivated, in the latter, *extrinsically* motivated. For example, if the authors of the present volume wrote out of sheer intellectual and literary enthusiasm, their motivation would be intrinsic. However, if they wrote with a view to lining their pockets with royalties, their motivation would be extrinsic. (Of course, it's not always one or the other! But the point is that there are two possible types.) Now, if you wished to encourage someone to do something, you could focus on increasing either their intrinsic or extrinsic motivation. Which strategy would serve you best?

Consider the issue in practical terms. Imagine you are a piano teacher whose task it is to turn giddy youngsters into accomplished musicians. If you chose to motivate your pupils intrinsically, you would try to make your lessons as engaging as possible. You might, for example, teach them a series of popular tunes, or use musical games to educational effect. Your goal would be to stimulate pupils' enthusiasm, capitalizing upon their natural desire to make music.

If, however, you chose to extrinsically motivate your pupils, you would adopt an altogether different approach. Your first step would be to perform a behavioral analysis of piano instruction, that is, to find out what rewards promote, or what punishments impede, behaviors associated with making musical progress (e.g., practicing regularly, showing up on time, hitting the right notes). Your guiding assumption would be that the motivation to perform any behavior depends on external contingencies, that is, on the objective consequences of performing it. If doing something has pleasant consequences, people will tend to do it more often, whereas if doing something has unpleasant consequences, people will tend to do it less often (Skinner, 1953). So, in terms of our piano-playing example, if Ashok gets candy every time he practices, he will likely practice more diligently; or, if Madhumita gets scolded every time she arrives late, her punctuality will likely improve. By implementing and adjusting contingencies with sufficient rigor, Ashok and Madhumita can be made to do, and made to want to do, most of what is required of them as novice musicians. Their motivation can be maintained by the deft use of carrots and sticks.

Some *behaviorists* (as those who advocate this carrot-and-stick approach are called) contend that only reward should be used as a motivator because punishment has several drawbacks. First, punishment is ineffective. The pain and anxiety that it creates disrupt the overall learning process. Second, punishment is inefficient. It gets rid of unwanted behaviors but does not establish specific new ones. Third, punishment is unethical. It hurts, and therefore should only be used as a last resort. Thus, rapping Ashok or Madhumita on the knuckles for playing the wrong notes does not help them to concentrate, nor does it teach them how to play the right notes, nor does it respect their rights as individuals.

By comparison, rewarding people for doing the right thing seems to be a far more enlightened and constructive approach. Rewards motivate effectively; they are nice to receive; they are a fitting recompense for hard work. Indeed, the received wisdom in Western culture is that rewards are marvelous inventions. Look around and you will see incentive systems everywhere—gold stars for perfect scores, bonuses for working overtime, Nobel prizes for inspired research.

However, are rewards as beneficial as they are made out to be? Indisputably, they work. When contingencies that deliver rewards are implemented, people want to get the job done and they work toward doing so. So where is the problem? Consider again our pair of fledgling pianists, Ashok and Madhumita. The purpose of teaching them is not only to get them to follow instructions while they are being taught, but also to instill in them a love for the instrument—producing a life-long desire to keep playing piano after instruction has ceased. Which motivational approach, intrinsic or extrinsic, is best suited to achieving this long-term goal? The intrinsic approach, trying to get pupils to play piano for its own sake, seems to be a promising one, given that its intent is to sow seeds of interest that will later bear fruit. But what about the extrinsic approach? If pupils are initially given rewards for, say, playing "Boogie-Woogie," and those rewards are then withdrawn, will pupils thereafter be more likely to play Boogie-Woogie than if they had never been rewarded for doing so? It seems possible. The rewards might get pupils into the swing of things, to provide them with the motivational momentum they need to get started and to keep going. Alas, exactly the opposite seems to be true.

What They Did

Lepper, Greene, and Nisbett (1973) suspected that conditionally rewarding people for engaging in an activity would not only fail to promote their interest in it, but would actually *undermine* their interest in it. To test this hypothesis experimentally, the researchers adopted the following strategy. First, they identified an activity, X, that people engaged in spontaneously. Second, they measured how often people engaged in X when the opportunity arose (an indirect measure of interest). Third, they provided some people, but not others, with a reward for engaging in X. Half the time, this reward was expected (they were told they would receive it), whereas half the time, it was unexpected (its receipt came as a surprise). The impact of these manipulations on how often people subsequently engaged in X was then assessed.

Lepper and his colleagues predicted that people in the expected-reward condition would engage in X *less often* than they had originally. They reasoned that such people would attribute engaging in X to the forthcoming reward rather than to any personal inclination. This self-perception would then undermine their motivation for engaging in X. In contrast, Lepper and his colleagues predicted that people in both the no-reward condition and the unexpected-reward condition would engage in X *just as often* as they had before. Interest would not be lost because participants would believe they had engaged in X because they wanted to, rather than because of the reward. The inclusion of the unexpected-reward condition was important because it allowed the researchers to test whether it was the *expectation* of a reward, and not just the receipt of a reward, that undermined motivation.

The study was conducted in a nursery school, a practical setting appropriate for testing the effects of conditional rewards. The 51 participants were children from middle-income families between the ages of 3 and 5. Two-thirds were girls. The classroom format was such that the children were free throughout the day to engage in any of a number of recreational activities. One of these was the target activity: playing with magic markers. (These are known outside the United States as "felt-tip pens.") It was chosen because (a) children found it interesting, (b) their level of interest could be easily measured (in terms of time spent playing with the markers), and (c) the activity did not look out of place alongside other classroom activities.

The experimental setup was as follows. Several magic markers, together with a sheaf of drawing paper, were placed on a table to the side of the classroom. Two observers, neatly hidden behind a one-way mirror, recorded the length of time that children spent at the table playing with the markers. If these grown-up observers had been visible, the children's behavior might have been inadvertently influenced, and the results of the study compromised. Both observers were kept unaware of the experimental condition to which the children had been assigned, to guard against possible recording bias.

The children's initial interest in magic markers was assessed by how often they played with them for the first hour of class on three consecutive days. This provided a *baseline* to which subsequent levels of interest could be compared. This was followed by an interval of three to four weeks, during which the experimental manipulations were administered. Children's eventual interest in playing with magic markers was then assessed on three further consecutive days. Their eventual interest thus reflected the impact of the experimental manipulations.

These manipulations ran as follows. In the expected-reward condition, children received an award for the quality of their drawings, having been told in advance that they would. In the unexpected-reward condition, children received the same award, but without being told beforehand that they would. In the no-reward condition, children did not receive any reward, nor were they told that they would. Note that the actual quality of their drawings was not taken into account. Children were assigned to one of the three conditions at random.

Implementing the manipulations involved a little theater. One by one, the children were approached by a friendly experimenter who chatted and played with them for a while. This experimenter then invited each child to come to a surprise room with him. Although several children refused his invitation (perhaps justifiably—he was, after all, a stranger), the majority accepted. On arriving at this surprise room, each child was told to sit down at a small table on which magic markers and drawing paper had been placed. The experimenter then told children that another "grown-up" would shortly be coming by to see what kinds of pictures young children liked to draw.

It was here that the differences between the conditions were introduced. Children in the expected-reward condition were told that the grown-up would be giving out "Good Player Awards" for good quality drawings. The awards were designed to look highly appealing to youngsters. They took the form of colorful 3×5-inch cards, decorated with a flashy gold star and red ribbon, with a space for the child's name and that of the school. The experimenter showed children a sample award, and asked whether they would like to win it. Children in the unexpected-reward and no-reward conditions were not shown this award; they were merely asked whether they would like to draw a picture for the grown-up who would shortly be arriving.

The "grown-up" (also unaware of the experimental conditions) then arrived to play his part. Dismissing the first experimenter, he sat down across the table from the children, and invited them to start drawing. Throughout the 6 minutes of allotted drawing time the grown-up attempted to show interest in, though not necessarily approval of, the children's performance.

Once they had finished drawing, children in the no-reward condition were immediately sent back to class, reassured they had done a good job. However, children in both the expected and unexpected reward conditions stayed on to receive their Good Player Award to much fanfare and applause. The second experimenter proudly inscribed their names and the name of their school on each award. The children were then invited to pin their coveted awards on an Honor Roll board (which featured a display of similar awards) so that everyone would know what good players they were.

What They Found

What effect did these manipulations have on the children's behavior a few days later? As predicted, children who drew with the magic markers hoping to earn a Good Player Award were subsequently less interested in those markers than children who were either given the award unexpectedly, or given no award at all. The effect was quite pronounced. Children in the expected-reward condition ended up playing with the markers only about half as often as children in the other two conditions (Figure 9).

Given that children's baseline interest in playing with magic markers had also been assessed, it was possible to analyze whether, within each of the three conditions, their interest rose or fell as a consequence of the manipulation. Again in line with predictions, children in the expected-reward condition showed a significant decrease in interest, whereas children in the other conditions showed no real change.

Some interesting secondary findings also emerged. First, when children in the unexpected-reward condition were split into those who had, and had not, originally been interested in playing with magic markers, those who had not been became more interested in playing with them. Perhaps receiving the Good Player Award out of the blue had left them with a favorable impression of the activity. In contrast, when children in the expected-reward condition were split in the same way, those who had originally been particularly interested in playing with magic markers became less interested in playing with them (though the interest of both declined). This result suggests that the more interesting the activity, the more extrinsic rewards undermine intrinsic interest in it.

One final striking finding emerged. The manipulation also affected the quality of the pictures that the children drew (as judged by three raters unaware of the condition to which they had been assigned). In the expected-reward condition, children drew poorer quality pictures than in both

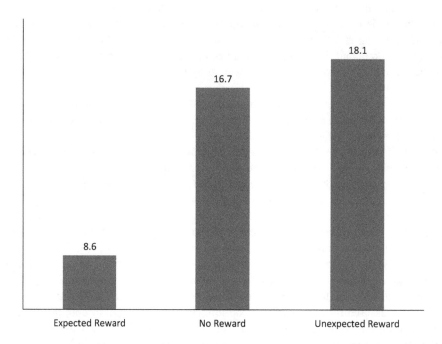

Figure 9 Percentage of time that child participants played with magic markers after being given an expected reward, no reward, or an unexpected reward

other conditions. Apparently, the ill effects of extrinsic reward were not limited to undermining interest, but also extended to compromising performance.

So What?

This study shows that making the receipt of a reward conditional on the performance of an activity ultimately reduces people's interest in performing that activity. Rewards do alter behavior effectively in the short-term. In the long-term, however, they have the side effect of making people grow weary of activities that they would otherwise continue to enjoy.

The researchers determined that extrinsic rewards could undermine preschoolers' motivation to engage in a fun activity. Does this effect generalize? Indeed it does. Literature reviews confirm that many kinds of incentives reduce enthusiasm for many kinds of tasks (Deci, Koestner, & Ryan, 1999). Moreover, the young and the old alike are susceptible (although tangible incentives affect the young to a greater degree). Next we describe two concrete examples of how extrinsic rewards can sap one's interest in an activity.

The first concerns smoking. One large study tested the effectiveness of different self-help methods for kicking the habit (Curry, Wagner, & Grothaus, 1991). Some participants received a prize for turning in weekly progress reports on how much they had been smoking; some received personalized feedback to help them abstain; some received both; and some received neither. A week later, it was the participants in the prize alone (reward) condition who were doing best. However, three months later the picture had radically changed. Now, participants in the prize alone condition were doing the worst, puffing away even more often than those who had received neither prize nor feedback. Moreover, saliva tests revealed that these extrinsically rewarded participants lied twice as often as everyone else about how much they were smoking.

The second example concerns good behavior in children. Conscientious parents strive to raise their sons and daughters to be cooperative and caring. However, if extrinsic rewards undermine intrinsic motivation, then the use of bribery and flattery for this purpose may ultimately backfire, spawning little devils instead of darling angels. Indeed, the empirical evidence bears out this suspicion. For example, children who receive tangible rewards from their mothers are less likely to help both at home and in the lab, and children frequently praised for doing the right thing become less likely to do it as time passes (Fabes, Fultz, Eisenberg, May-Plumlee, & Christopher, 1989; Grusec, 1991). Although interpretation of these studies is complicated (maybe troublesome kids require more bribery), other research does indicate that rewarding people for doing good deeds makes them less likely to see themselves as likely to perform them spontaneously (Kunda & Schwartz, 1983).

Why do extrinsic rewards undermine intrinsic motivation? Three different answers, not mutually exclusive, have been proposed. The first, sketched out earlier, and supported by the Kunda and Schwartz (1983) study, has to do with self-perception. When we receive a reward for doing *X*, we infer that we are doing *X* for that reward and not for its own sake. In the absence of the reward, we see less of a reason to do *X*. Once the reward is taken away, therefore, we act in accord with our self-perception, and stop doing *X*. Lepper and his colleagues (1973) dubbed this process *overjustification*, because the extrinsic reward provides, as it were, *too much reason* for doing *X*.

A second possibility is that whenever some *X* is portrayed as a means to an end, it comes to be regarded as undesirable, because means to an end often are undesirable. We know this from everyday life. We brush and floss to avoid tooth decay, we dust and vacuum to keep our house clean, and we grunt and sweat to stay fit. Consequently, whenever we do *X* to get a reward, we are implicitly reminded of all the other times we did something undesirable to get a reward, and *X* automatically conjures up negative connotations. Lepper, Sagotsky, Dafoe, and Greene (1982) conducted a clever experiment to test this possibility. They noted first that preschool children loved to play, not only with magic markers, but also with pastel crayons. They then set up two reward contingencies. Half the children were told that, in order to play with the markers, they would first have to play with the crayons; the other half were told the opposite. The result? Two weeks later, children spent less time playing with the drawing utensil that was a means to an end (a precondition) for playing with the other.

A third possibility is that extrinsic rewards are perceived as unpleasantly controlling. Unlike lower animals, we do not just blindly respond to carrots and sticks. We also understand and respond to the contingencies that govern their delivery. Suppose, for example, that Jack kisses his dog, Duchess, only when she fetches a stick for him. This is liable to train Duchess to fetch the stick, in accordance with well-established principles of instrumental conditioning. Duchess—an obedient pooch—will raise no objection. However, suppose that Jack now kisses his girlfriend Jill only when she fetches him a beer from the fridge. It is unlikely that Jill will be as compliant as a canine. She will almost certainly resent Jack being so transparently manipulative. Hence, Jill's intrinsic motivation for beer-fetching, and her frequency of doing so, is likely to decrease, not increase.

The example above is facetious, but the principle is not. To the extent that a situation is perceived as undermining our free will, we will tend to withdraw from it or rebel against it (Brehm & Brehm, 1981). Whenever we work in order to obtain rewards, it feels like something outside of ourselves is determining what we do, not our inner being. We feel like pawns rather than persons. According to self-determination theory (Ryan & Deci, 2000), this leaves our fundamental need for *autonomy* unsatisfied. (The theory also postulated two other fundamental needs: for *relatedness* and *efficacy*). Extrinsic rewards therefore fall into the same category as threats, deadlines, inspections, and evaluations. All have a corrosive impact on intrinsic motivation (Kohn, 1999).

In fairness to extrinsic rewards, it should be pointed out that they are not only controlling. They also provide valuable feedback about people's level of performance. This could conceivably promote intrinsic motivation, assuming that people are keen on developing their skills. However, given that such feedback could also be given in the absence of extrinsic rewards, it is hardly a compelling defense of their use.

Afterthoughts

The harmful consequences of extrinsic rewards are not, unfortunately, limited to undermining intrinsic motivation. Recall that, in the present study, children hoping to receive a Good Player Award also drew poorer quality pictures. The effect is no fluke. For example, in another study, the ability of student journalists to think up catchy headlines was monitored over time. Some were paid for each headline they produced, others not. It transpired that paid students quickly reached a point at which they stopped improving, whereas unpaid students continued to improve (Deci, 1971). Indeed, whenever people perform a variety of tasks that require creative input, the result is less original and inspired when rewards have been promised in return (Amabile, Hennessey, & Grossman, 1986).

Extrinsic rewards also impair one's ability to solve problems. In one classic study, participants were presented with matches, a box of thumbtacks, and a candle, and asked to mount the candle on a wall (so that when the candle is lit the melted wax does not drip on the floor) using only these materials. (Can you do it? Hint: Use *all* the materials!) Participants offered incentives of varying magnitudes to solve this problem took nearly one-and-a-half times as long as participants offered nothing (Glucksberg, 1962). Another study found that the offer of incentives interfered with participants' ability to discover a nonobvious rule (a particular sequence of key presses), and that participants were reluctant to abandon incorrect rules that had secured them rewards earlier (Schwartz, 1982).

This undermining of creativity and problem solving presumably occurs because people are preoccupied with the prospect of receiving the reward. Tunnel vision makes people think and act greedily and inflexibly, thereby impairing their performance in settings that call for the cool-headed consideration of complex possibilities. Indeed, when rewards are at stake, people generally choose the task that will secure those rewards most easily (Pittman, Emery, & Boggiano, 1982).

We could keep telling cautionary tales about the ill effects of incentives. For example, even toddlers become less caring if rewarded with a toy cube for doing so (Warneken & Tomasello, 2008). However, it is better to light a candle than to curse the darkness. The pragmatic question is: How can intrinsic motivation be enhanced? In particular, what would make students approach their studies with a curious and enthusiastic mindset? This is an especially crucial question given that good grades are probably one of the most demotivating of incentives. (Just ask any college student how interested they are in learning something that will not appear on an exam!)

One promising approach is to add features to a prescribed learning activity in order to satisfy a student's underlying needs for stimulation, mastery, and autonomy. For example, take an activity as potentially uninviting as learning how to use arithmetical operators (e.g., $+$, $-$, $\times$, $\div$) in their correct hierarchical order, and how to add parentheses that override the hierarchy if necessary. (It's the sort of task that leaves many students non-plussed!) Cordova and Lepper (1996) had grade school children play a computer game in which success depended on correct use of numbers and operators made available to them. In brief, the children had to generate the biggest number they could on each turn so that they would advance as quickly as possible toward a target number. The game as it stands is already potentially appealing (and likely an improvement over teaching arithmetic conventions verbally). However, the researchers added three features to the task in an attempt to make it more appealing still. First, they personalized the game. Rather than make general announcements, the computer addressed children by name at various key junctures (e.g., "May the force be with you, Commander Constantine!"). Second, the game was contextualized by embedding it in a fantasy scenario called *Space Quest*. Now the goal was not only to attain an arbitrary numerical target, but rather also to reach the planet Ektar and pick up precious titanium deposits before the aliens did, thereby saving the Earth from a global energy crisis. Third, incidental aspects of the game were made more controllable. For example, the children could choose the type of spacecraft they would travel in (e.g., Starship) and what its name would be (e.g., Enterprise NCC 1701). Results showed that each of these enhancements increased children's intrinsic motivation. Thanks to their greater involvement with the task, children generated more complex arithmetic formulas, which in turn increased their rate of learning. Furthermore, children who played the enhanced games showed higher levels of aspiration, and greater feelings of competence, than children who played the unenhanced equivalents. If comparable adaptations could be made to educational curricula across the board, taking into account what students at each stage are interested in, formal tuition might become less of a chore and strict discipline less of a necessity.

We have so far spent this chapter being critical of extrinsic motivation. However, before closing, we should mention two arguments that might be made in its favor. First, it provides an economical way of making people behave in desirable ways. A well-meaning person in a position of power may use carrots (or sticks) to pursue laudable goals when those under him or her have a preference for pursuing questionable ones. For example, a novice teacher faced with a class of pupils who enjoys misbehaving may need to establish order by dishing out rewards and punishments in a systematic fashion. Once that basic goal has been achieved, he or she can move on to nurturing his or her academic interests. Second, and implied by the previous point, not all intrinsic aspirations are worthy of being nurtured. For example, some people may get a kick out of badmouthing others behind their back, committing criminal offences, or cheating on their partner. Such activities are unlikely to afford either them or others lasting happiness. It seems right, therefore, that extrinsic controls on such behavior should be applied, either formally or informally.

Revelation

Receiving a reward for doing something makes people want to do it more. However, when the reward is withdrawn, people want to do it even less than they did before receiving the reward.

What Do You Think?

As a student, what was your most enjoyable and/or successful learning experience? Were you motivated by extrinsic rewards or intrinsic rewards, and in either case, of what type? What lessons would you apply from this experience, if you had to teach students today?

Chapter Reference

Lepper, M., Greene, D., & Nisbett, R. E. (1973). Undermining children's intrinsic interest with extrinsic reward: A test of the "overjustification" hypothesis. *Journal of Personality and Social Psychology, 28,* 129–137.

Other References

Amabile, T. M., Hennessey, B. A., & Grossman, B. S. (1986). Influences on creativity: The effects of contracted-for reward. *Journal of Personality and Social Psychology, 50,* 14–23.

Brehm, S. S., & Brehm, J. W. (1981). *Psychological reactance: A theory of freedom and control.* New York: Academic Press.

Cordova, D. I., & Lepper, M. R. (1996). Intrinsic motivation and the process of learning: Beneficial effects of contextualization, personalization, and choice. *Journal of Educational Psychology, 88,* 715–730.

Curry, S. J., Wagner, E. H., & Grothaus, L. C. (1991). Intrinsic and extrinsic motivation for smoking cessation. *Journal of Consulting and Clinical Psychology, 58*, 310–316.

Deci, E. L. (1971). Effects of externally mediated rewards on intrinsic motivation. *Journal of Personality and Social Psychology, 18*, 105–115.

Deci, E. L., Koestner, R., & Ryan, R. M. (1999). A meta-analytic review of experiments examining the effects of extrinsic rewards on intrinsic motivation. *Psychological Bulletin, 125*, 627–668.

Durand, D. (2000). *Perpetual motivation.* New York: ProBalance Inc.

Fabes, R. A., Fultz, J., Eisenberg, N., May-Plumlee, T., & Christopher, F. C. (1989). Effects of rewards on children's prosocial motivation: A socialization study. *Developmental Psychology, 25*, 509–515.

Glucksberg, S. (1962). The influence of strength of drive on functional fixedness and perceptual recognition. *Journal of Experimental Psychology, 63*, 34–41.

Grusec, J. E. (1991). Socializing concern for others in the home. *Developmental Psychology, 27*, 338–342.

Kohn, A. (1999). *Punished by rewards.* Boston: Houghton Mifflin.

Kunda, Z., & Schwartz, S. H. (1983). Undermining intrinsic moral motivation: External reward and self-presentation. *Journal of Personality and Social Psychology, 45*, 763–771.

Lepper, M. R., Sagotsky, G., Dafoe, J. L., & Greene, D. (1982). Consequences of superfluous social constraints: Effects on young children of social inferences and subsequent intrinsic interest. *Journal of Personality and Social Psychology, 42*, 51–65.

Pittman, T. S., Emery, J., & Boggiano, A. K. (1982). Intrinsic and extrinsic motivational orientations: Reward-induced changes in preference for complexity. *Journal of Personality and Social Psychology, 42*, 789–797.

Ryan, R. M., & Deci, E. L. (2000). Self-determination theory and the facilitation of intrinsic motivation, social development, and well-being. *American Psychologist, 55*, 68–78.

Schwartz, B. (1982). Reinforcement-induced behavioral stereotype: How not to teach people to discover rules. *Journal of Experimental Psychology: General, 111*, 23–59.

Skinner, B. F. (1953). *Science and human behavior.* New York: Macmillan.

Warneken, F., & Tomasello, M. (2008). Extrinsic rewards undermine altruistic tendencies in 20-month-olds. *Developmental Psychology, 44*, 1785–1788.

More to Explore

Pink, D. H. (2011). *Drive: The surprising truth about what motivates us.* New York: Riverhead Books.

10 The Burglar's Situation

Actor-Observer Differences in Explaining Behavior

"People have got to know whether or not their president is a crook. Well, I'm not a crook."
—Richard Nixon (1913–1994), former (crooked) U.S. President

Background

You are in line at a supermarket, resisting rows of candy bars. Your eyes scan a tabloid headline (*Pet Pig Devours Wedding Cake*) when the woman in front of you suddenly becomes irate. She is trying to get a double-coupon discount on an already discounted item (or something like that) and the cashier is explaining that it does not work that way. The woman refuses to budge (as the line behind her grows) and insists on talking to the manager. She starts to ramble incoherently about customer service and the policies of other supermarkets. You step back a foot or two as her voice falters and then becomes loud again. Will she do something dramatic? Is she mentally ill, or did she simply wake up on the wrong side of bed? What is it about this woman that is causing her to act this way?

Later the same day you find yourself in what others might view as a similar situation (although you don't see the parallel). You are a student returning a textbook that you discovered you do not need. The book is still in the bag—your hectic schedule has kept you from returning it sooner. A cashier explains that you have missed the 30-day return deadline: "I'll say it one more time: you're too late for a refund. I'm sorry!" But late by only a week, you reason, less if you count Sunday and a holiday on Monday when the bookstore was closed. Rigid, maybe even illegal, policies have you steaming. "Sorry is not enough," you assert, "I want to talk to a manager and I'm not moving until I do!" Those behind you retreat as your anger swells and finds its targets: "Snobby cashier, over-priced textbooks, capitalism!" The other customers have little sympathy for you, however. They believe that you have been irresponsible, you are being unreasonable, and you are becoming belligerent. Just as your focus was on the woman in front of you, their focus is on you.

The preceding vignettes highlight what has been referred to as the *actor-observer bias*. Jones and Nisbett (1971, 1972) were among the first to argue that *actors* (those performing certain behaviors) and *observers* (those witnessing others performing certain behaviors) often offer different *causal attributions* (explanations). The idea is that actors tend to attribute the cause of their behavior to precipitating events and external stimuli, whereas observers tend to attribute an actor's behavior to his or her personality. As a result, we are said to recognize the pressures we ourselves are under, but not the similar pressures felt by others. The one side of this bias has been dubbed the *fundamental attribution error*—as social perceivers, we tend to explain others' actions in terms of personality traits rather than situational factors (Ross, 1977). One of the virtues of social psychology is that it calls attention to this potential error by revealing the ubiquitous and often powerful external influences on human behavior.

A study by West and his colleagues (1975) was perhaps the most dramatic demonstration of the actor-observer bias. West and his colleagues were enthralled by the Watergate scandal, which dominated the news and rocked the nation a few years earlier. In June of 1972, five men were arrested for burgling the Democratic National Committee headquarters at the Watergate apartments in Washington, DC. The bungled break-in and attempted cover-up came to light during that year's presidential campaign. Congressional impeachment hearings followed, culminating in the resignation of President Nixon in 1974. It was a scandal of grand proportions that begged for explanation. The press attributed the crimes to the paranoid and amoral qualities of the Nixon administration, whereas Nixonites defended the actions by claiming that they were a natural reaction to the nefarious objectives of the radical left. A single event occurred but different outsider and insider explanations followed. Some saw the devil in the perpetrators, some in the situation. (See Chapter 17 for more on how identical events can produce quite different perceptions.)

These disparate accounts of the Watergate imbroglio seemed again to be a case of the actor-observer bias. Intrigued by this, West and his colleagues (1975) sought to elicit Watergate-like behavior from research participants, and then examine their explanations, as well as the explanations of others, for such behaviors. Would the actors tend more toward *situationalism* (claiming that outside forces are at work) and the perceivers more toward *dispositionalism* (believing the cause lies within the person)?

What They Did

West and his colleagues (1975) conducted two studies. In the first, an experimenter (known by many to be a local private investigator) invited each of 80 criminology students, a mix of males and females, to either his home or a local restaurant to discuss a project he was working on. Every participant accepted this mysterious invitation.

A *confederate* (research accomplice) accompanied the experimenter to the clandestine meeting. In B-movie fashion, the private eye carried a briefcase (handcuffed to his wrist?) containing detailed plans for the burglary of a local advertising agency (a *job* was going *down!*). The unsuspecting participants were randomly assigned to one of four experimental conditions. In one condition, the Internal Revenue Service (IRS) was said to be sponsoring the burglary. The reputed ad agency was allegedly harboring a set of bogus accounting records, used to defraud the U.S. government out of millions of tax dollars a year. The agency was allegedly a front for a Miami investment firm. The records were copies of coveted originals; they needed to be microfilmed so that the IRS could obtain a search warrant and subpoena to seize the originals. (Note: this was in the days before everyone had a smartphone. Instead, spies used a special-issue Minox camera with 11 × 8-mm film.) The participants were told that the IRS would guarantee them immunity from prosecution if they got caught. (If all this sounds farfetched now, it didn't to the aspiring criminologist being briefed by the businesslike private eye in a dimly lit corner of a smoky local restaurant!)

A second experimental condition was identical, except that participants were warned that there would be no immunity from prosecution if they were apprehended. In a third experimental condition, the cover story described how a second ad agency was secretly offering $8,000 for a copy of a set of designs developed by the first agency. If the burglary succeeded, the participant's under-the-table cut would be $2,000 (a small fortune for a financially strapped college student in the mid-1970s). In a final experimental condition, participants were told that they would break and enter but not actually steal anything, simply to see if the burglary plans of the private eye were feasible. None of the participants protested discussing the proposed crime.

In all of these conditions, the research accomplice was introduced as a member of the burglary team. He would serve as an outside lookout. The private eye (the experimenter) would monitor police calls from an office inside the building. A third member of the team (not present), said to be a lock-and-safe expert with extensive military intelligence training, would also abet the crime. The participant would serve as an inside lookout and do the actual microfilming.

The experimenter and confederate presented the participant with aerial photographs of the building and local area, lists of routes and times of city and state police patrols, and blueprints of the building. All this gave the appearance of a well-planned, professional job. Participants were given a chance to ask questions, most of which were about technical details of the plan. Then a second meeting was arranged. The participant was given time to think things over before committing to the crime or not. The confederate, unaware of the researchers' hypotheses, was on hand to record the participant's decision to join the team or not, and his or her rationale either way.

Anyone with ethical scruples will be glad to know that a break-in never took place. Whether participants agreed or refused to perform the burglary, and what reasons they gave for their decision, were the main dependent variables. Once this information was obtained, they were carefully debriefed and the deception was explained.

What an elaborate ruse! We wish there was hidden-camera footage. Indeed, this first study alone would have been a vivid enough demonstration of compliance. However, a second study was necessary to more fully examine the actor-observer bias. The behaviors and explanations of actors had been recorded. It was now necessary to obtain data on the perceptions of observers.

The 238 participants in the second study (all students in introductory psychology classes) were each given a detailed description of one of the four conditions of the first study. Each was asked: "If 100 students were presented with the proposal, how many would you guess would agree to participate?" In response to a second question, "Would you do it?," each was asked to respond *yes, maybe,* or *no,* and to write comments. Finally, half of the participants were presented with the following scenario: "Suppose John, an undergraduate at FSU [the study was conducted at Florida State University], after listening to the proposal previously described, agreed to participate. In two or three sentences, briefly describe why John made this decision." The other half of the participants responded to the same scenario, except that John refused instead of agreed. The purpose of this second study was to examine observers' explanations of a person's agreeing or refusing to illegally break into a presumed local company and steal information. Comparing these explanations to those given by the participants in the first study represented a direct investigation of the actor-observer bias.

What They Found

The results of the first study are perhaps reassuring to anyone concerned about the ethical standards of college students in the mid-1970s: The majority of those solicited were unwilling to participate in the burglary. However, agreement rates varied from condition to condition. Four participants in the $2,000-reward condition (20%), two in the let's-just-see-if-it-will-work condition (10%), and only one in the government-sponsorship-but-no-immunity condition (5%) agreed to assist in the break-in and copy the desired documents. The differences among these conditions are not statistically significant (the power of the study to detect significant differences is low given the relatively small number of participants). However, 9 of the 20 participants (45%) in the government-sponsorship-with-immunity-if-caught condition agreed to participate. Because participants were randomly assigned to the four conditions, and because all extraneous variables were carefully controlled, it can be assumed that the greater compliance in the last condition was due to the features of the condition itself. Evidently, the prospect of immunity, or its interaction with government sponsorship, represented a powerful situation that produced alarming rates of compliance.

Did observers in the second study believe that they, if put in the same situation, would have joined the crime team? As it turned out, so few thought they would that West and his colleagues (1975) decided to combine *yes* with *maybe* answers to allow for a more meaningful analysis.

(That participants generally believed that they would not have taken part in the burglary is reminiscent of what people imagine they would or would not do in situations that call upon good character; see Chapter 4.) Observers also were more inclined to think that they would have helped pull off the burglary if there was government sponsorship and immunity than in the other conditions. Interestingly, there were no overall differences between males and females in rates of agreement to participate in the break-in (which is inconsistent with the fact that males are several times more criminally inclined than females in every society ever studied; Wilson & Herrnstein, 1998). Yet males, merely reading about the situation, were almost twice as likely as females to report that they would have gone along with the caper (consistent with men's greater criminality).

However, compliance is not the main story of this chapter; attributions are. Actors' and observers' attributions for why the actor in the situation or John (the hypothetical FSU student) agreed or refused to take part in the burglary were *coded* (put into one or more categories, allowing statistical comparisons). A *1* indicated a dispositional attribution, *3* a situational attribution, and *2* a combination of both. Which type of attribution was more common among actors? What about among observers? Was there an actor-observer bias?

There was. Actors made relatively more situational attributions, whereas observers made relatively more distributional attributions. This effect varied a bit depending upon the condition—government sponsorship with or without immunity, reward, or control—but this did not take away from the striking overall actor-observer difference, which, by the way, occurred for attributions for both agreeing and for refusing to engage in the crime (Figure 10). Thus, West and his colleagues were able to ingeniously demonstrate an actor-observer bias.

So What?

Under certain circumstances (e.g., with government backing and immunity from prosecution) nearly half the participants—who, remember, were students seeking a career in criminology, not

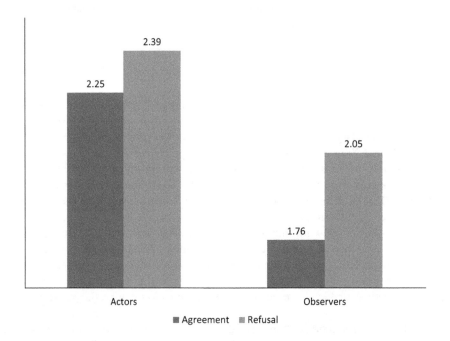

Figure 10 The degree to which actors and observers attributed actors' agreement or refusal to take part in a burglary to situational rather than dispositional factors

delinquents destined for a career in crime—said they would be willing to help pull off a plainly illegal act: breaking into a company's private headquarters to steal confidential documents. Why? Perhaps this was a case of the *foot-in-the-door phenomenon* (getting a person to agree to a large request by first having him or her agree to a small request), illustrated in a study by Freedman and Fraser (1966). In that study, a member of an alleged "Committee for Safe Driving" approached women in their homes and asked them if they would allow a large, unsightly "Drive Carefully" sign to be staked into their front lawn. Not surprisingly, only 17% agreed to the request. However, that was not the only condition. Women who had agreed two weeks earlier to display a 3 × 3-inch sticker in a car or house window complied 76% of the time with the request to erect the larger sign. So also did nearly half of participants who had earlier agreed to sign a petition either related or unrelated to safe driving. Evidently, getting a foot in the door is an effective technique for inducing compliance. It is possible that, in West and colleagues' (1975) first study, agreeing to attend a meeting, in the private eye's home or the shadowy backroom of a nearby restaurant, was tantamount to acquiescing to doing something shady. However, the foot-in-the-door concept does not explain the *pattern* of compliance across the experimental conditions. Compliance was exceptionally high in only one of the conditions, that which featured the imprimatur of the IRS and the promise of immunity. Evidently, these features, perhaps along with a foot in the door, set the stage for Watergate-like behavior.

Compliance aside, what explains the actor-observer bias found by West and his colleagues (1975)? Jones and Davis' (1965) *theory of correspondent inference* holds that we are inclined to believe that a person's behavior stems from, or corresponds to, his or her dispositional characteristics if the behavior is *unflattering* (indulgence in criminal escapades tends to be so), *out of role* (burglary and theft are not formal college requirements), and *freely chosen* (which was the case in West and others' study). However, the theory does not state that we should make more correspondent inferences in our judgments of others than of ourselves. Yet a number of studies have found that we do.

In a study by Ross, Amabile, and Steinmetz (1977), featuring a simulated TV quiz game, participants were randomly assigned to be either questioners or contestants. Questioners each created 10 challenging but fair questions. Contestants answered as many as possible (usually getting about 4 out of 10 correct). Interestingly, contestants subsequently judged the questioners to be significantly more knowledgeable than they were, and audience members shared this impression. Again, this makes no sense. The participants were randomly assigned to the two roles—based on the laws of probability neither the questioners nor the contestants would have been any more or less erudite.

In another study, by Saulnier and Perlman (1981), when prisoners were asked why they committed their crimes, they emphasized situational factors ("I was out of work, so I robbed the bank" or "the Devil made me do it"). However, their counselors cited characteristics of the inmates' personalities ("he's antisocial" or "she's impulsive"). Furthermore, Nisbett, Caputo, Legant, and Maracek (1973) had male college students explain why they liked their current girlfriends and why their best friends liked their girlfriends. They tended to explain their own choice in terms of qualities of the girlfriend (part of the situation) but their friend's choice in terms of his personality. Thus, a number of studies have found evidence for an actor-observer bias.

Again, what accounts for this bias? Perhaps it seems depends on what is salient, on what captures one's attention. Going back to Ross and colleagues' (1977) study, the contestants and outside observers alike saw that the questioners knew all the answers to rather tough questions (they seemed to forget that the questioners were drawing on areas of personal expertise). The contestants saw themselves, and observers saw contestants, struggling for answers, and 6 out of 10 times giving the wrong one. Prior random assignment to the two roles—questioner or contestant—was ignored. Even the contestant, who as an actor would normally be more focused on external factors, was apparently aware of only selective aspects of the situation (the difficulty of the esoteric questions or maybe the condescending smile of the questioner).

The same holds true in any example of the actor-observer bias. When we consider our own behaviors the focus of our attention is more on its context. What events preceded our actions? What are we responding to right now? How is the situation responding back? The effect of the external world on us is subjectively obvious. This is one reason why we generally do not believe that trait labels apply to us (Nisbett and others, 1973). Other people have traits, we have situations, or so we believe. When we view others' behaviors, we see them lifted out of context. Lacking information about their life history or current circumstances, we reflexively assume that what they do reflects who they are.

But, still, so what? (This is always a legitimate question when reviewing social psychological research.) So we sometimes explain our own and others' behaviors differently, chalking the former up to external influences and the latter to internal impulses. So we commit the fundamental attribution error even when we are given contextual information about a person's behavior? Well, consider a maxim of social psychology: People do not interact with reality; they interact with their *perception* of reality (see Chapters 14, 15, 17, and 21 for examples of how people mentally construct their own social reality). Assuming this maxim to be valid, what happens if we, as individuals or a society, readily view others as the principal cause of, and therefore hold them responsible for, their behavior (even when they have been swamped by external influences)? What happens when we excuse our own behavior as being the product of the situation (even when we are, in fact, the primary cause of it)? Might we tend to unfairly explain the plight of rape victims, homeless people, disadvantaged minorities, and other unfortunates in predominantly dispositional terms? Does an actor-observer bias leave us less sympathetic and charitable, more fixated on trying to change individuals instead of the social order? Might the actor-observer bias perpetuate self-righteousness and social coldness? And yet, the opposite bias might be just as foolhardy: failing to hold people responsible when doing so is justified. Is it true that the observer is always wrong and the actor always right? Might the socially disadvantaged, for example, be partly responsible for their plight? The problem in all of this is that the truth about causality and responsibility is difficult to establish. Nonetheless, if understanding ourselves and others, and rewarding and punishing our own and others' actions, are in any way central to the lives we lead, then comprehending and counteracting attributional biases, of any sort, are vital.

Afterthoughts

West and his colleagues' (1975) research (much like Milgram's, 1963, *obedience to authority* research—see Chapter 4) is ethically suspect. Recall the results of their first study. A significant number of criminology students indicated their willingness to engage in criminal activity. Afterward, they were told that the experiment was a setup to see how much they would comply. Think about it: Would not this invitation, however delicately made, be potentially very upsetting, especially to those who had agreed to participate in the break-in? Would not the knowledge of what one was poised to do threaten to create embarrassment or guilt? Watergate had been repeatedly condemned in the press, and here one was, preparing to act much as a disgraced Watergate convict (Cook, 1975). Furthermore, was not this a case of entrapment? Were the participants in this study looking to enter a life of crime, or did individuals they respected and trusted thrust the opportunity upon them?

To be sure, West and his colleagues (1975) went to great lengths to allay ethical concerns. They had a lawyer-psychologist help plan and implement the study. They did not force anyone into anything or have them actually act illegally. They provided a careful debriefing. They noted that participants seemed not to suffer any psychological trauma. Finally, they had the State Attorney's Office review the experiment and declare that its procedures were legally acceptable. Still, concerns remained.

A longer discussion of ethical issues could be offered, but the simple (though difficult) balance is always this: the value of the information gained from the research against concerns for the rights and dignity of the participants. West and his colleagues (1975) believed that their research addressed important questions. What situational factors might induce normally law-abiding citizens to engage in illegal activities that violate the civil rights of others? How can we trust the press, those working in the legal system, or even ourselves to supply valid explanations for given behaviors? You be the judge: Does a contribution to scientific knowledge ever warrant deception and inducement to engage in bad actions?

Ethical considerations aside, it is important to note that experimental social psychology is an ongoing and collective enterprise. Particular theories are at times validated and at other times invalidated by independent researchers. A theory that receives consistent empirical support is seen as valid, whereas one that receives scant or sporadic support falls by the wayside. No single study, without adequate replication, is enough to establish the validity of a particular theory or effect. Even "classic" studies must be complemented by a host of other—though perhaps less rigorous, dramatic, or famous—similar studies. In this regard, a valuable tool in the social psychologist's methodological arsenal is *meta-analysis*, a quantitative summary of the results of numerous studies that test a particular hypothesis. (Single empirical studies are sometimes referred to as *primary research*; quantitative reviews of numerous studies having a common focus are sometimes referred to as *secondary research*.) A meta-analysis reveals the range and average of the *effect sizes* (significant differences produced by experimental manipulations) found in such studies. It is also useful in identifying variables that *moderate* (increase or decrease) an effect of interest, thereby resolving inconsistencies in research results (see the Introduction to this book).

Indeed, Malle (2006) conducted a meta-analytic review of some 173 studies on the actor-observer bias published between 1971 and 2004. The results of his analysis produced a significant twist in the story of the actor-observer bias (which he refers to as an *asymmetry*). His findings are at odds with the contention that "evidence for the actor-observer effect is plentiful" (Fiske & Taylor, 1991, p. 73) and that "the actor-observer bias is pervasive" (Aronson, 2002, p. 168). In particular, Malle found that some studies (like the one conducted by West and his colleagues, 1975) provide support for the actor-observer bias, some provide no support at all, and some provide support for an opposite bias (in which actors are more inclined to explain behaviors in dispositional terms and observers are more inclined to explain behaviors in situational terms). However, according to Malle's (2006) meta-analysis, overall there is *no* actor-observer bias!

Disappointed? Well, consider this important question: What produced the *variance* in the results of all those 173 studies of the actor-observer bias? Fortunately, Malle (2006) was able to conduct a *moderator analysis* and identify a number of significant variables, perhaps the most important of which is the *valence* of the behavior being explained. To the point: "The asymmetry held for negative events, but a reverse asymmetry held for positive events" (Malle, 2006, p. 895). When actors were considering their *negative* behaviors, they tended to give situational explanations, whereas when they were considering others' *negative* behaviors, they tended to give dispositional explanations. Oppositely, when explaining their own *positive* behaviors, they tended to give dispositional explanations, whereas when they were considering others' *positive* behaviors they tended to give situational explanations. Thus, Malle found that there is no simple actor-observer bias; rather, there are two separate biases. There is an actor-observer difference for positive events and an opposite actor-observer difference for negative events. Furthermore, this *interaction* (difference of differences) is apparently self-serving: As social perceivers we tend to take personal credit for our positive but not our negative behaviors, whereas we tend to hold others responsible for their negative behaviors but not their positive behaviors.

Self-serving attributions are not uncommon, although we tend to be biased in recognizing them! That is, we tend to think that others are more prone to attributional biases than we ourselves are (Pronin, Lin, & Ross, 2002). Such self-serving biases are common in the educational realm, as when teachers take personal credit for a student's progress, but blame the student for a lack of progress (Beckman, 1970). They are also common in the business world, as when CEOs claim credit for 83% of positive company outcomes and accept blame for only 19% of negative company outcomes (Salancik & Meindl, 1984). Furthermore, they are common in sports, as when athletes and coaches attribute their victories to skill and hard work and their defeats to bad calls and bad luck (Lau & Russell, 1980; see also Chapter 17). And whether self-serving or not, it's interesting how athletes often publically thank the Lord for a personal victory, but do not publically blame the Lord for a defeat!

Revelation

Our explanations of behaviors are often biased. We tend to attribute our positive behaviors to dispositional causes and our negative behaviors to situational causes, whereas we tend to make the opposite attributions when observing others' behaviors.

What Do You Think?

When you think of other people—especially when you attempt to explain their behaviors—do you tend to do so in dispositional or situational terms? For example, who makes more dispositional attributions (and fewer situational attributions): Democrats or Republicans? Why?

Chapter Reference

West, S. G., Gunn, S. P., & Chernicky, P. (1975). Ubiquitous Watergate: An attributional analysis. *Journal of Personality and Social Psychology, 32*, 55–65.

Other References

Aronson, E. (2002). *The social animal* (8th ed.). New York: Worth Publishers.

Beckman, L. (1970). Effects of students' performance on teachers' and observers' attributions of causality. *Journal of Educational Psychology, 61*, 76–82.

Cook, S. W. (1975). A comment on the ethical issues involved in West, Gunn, and Chernicky's "Ubiquitous Watergate: An attributional analysis." *Journal of Personality and Social Psychology, 32*, 66–68.

Fiske, S. T., & Taylor, S. E. (1991). *Social cognition* (2nd ed.). New York: McGraw-Hill.

Freedman, J. L., & Fraser, S. C. (1966). Compliance without pressure: The foot-in-the-door technique. *Journal of Personality and Social Psychology, 4*, 195–202.

Jones, E. E., & Davis, K. E. (1965). A theory of correspondent inferences: From acts to dispositions. In L. Berkowitz (Ed.), *Advances in experimental social psychology* (Vol. 2, pp. 219–266). New York: Academic press.

Jones, E. E., & Nisbett, R. E. (1971). *The actor and the observer: Divergent perspectives on the causes of behavior*. Moristown, NJ: General Learning Press.

Jones, E. E., & Nisbett, R. E. (1972). The actor and the observer: Divergent perspectives of the causes of behavior. In E. E. Jones, D. E. Kanouse, H. H. Kelley, R. E. Nisbett, S. Valins, & B. Weiner (Eds.), *Attribution: Perceiving the causes of behavior* (pp. 79–94). Morristown, NJ: General Learning Press.

Lau, R. R., & Russell, D. (1980). Attribution in the sports pages: A field test of some current hypotheses about attributional research. *Journal of Personality and Social Psychology, 39*, 29–38.

Malle, B. F. (2006). The actor-observer asymmetry in attribution: A (surprising) meta-analysis. *Psychological Bulletin, 132*, 895–919.

Milgram, S. (1963). Behavioral study of obedience. *Journal of Abnormal and Social Psychology, 67*, 371–378.

Nisbett, R. E., Caputo, C., Legant, P., & Marecek, J. (1973). Behavior as seen by the actor and as seen by the observer. *Journal of Personality and Social Psychology, 27*, 154–164.

Pronin, E., Lin, D. Y., & Ross, L. (2002). The bias blind spot: Perceptions of bias in self versus others. *Personality and Social Psychology Bulletin, 28*, 369–381.

Ross, L. (1977). The intuitive psychologist and his shortcomings: Distortions in the attributional process. In L. Berkowitz (Ed.), *Advances in experimental social psychology* (Vol. 10, pp. 174–221). New York: Academic Press.

Ross, L., Amabile, T. M., & Steinmetz, J. L. (1977). Social roles, social control, and biases in social perception processes. *Journal of Personality and Social Psychology, 35*, 485–494.

Salancik, G., & Meindl, J. R. (1984). Corporate attributions as strategic illusions of management control. *Administrative Science Quarterly, 29*, 238–254.

Saulnier, K., & Perlman, D. (1981). The actor-observer bias is alive and well in prison. *Personality and Social Psychology Bulletin, 7*, 559–564.

Wilson, J. Q., & Herrnstein, R. J. (1998). *Crime and human nature: The definitive study of the causes of crime*. New York: Free Press.

More to Explore

Ross, L., & Nisbett, R. E. (2011). *The person and the situation: Perspectives of social psychology*. London: Pinter & Martin.

11 We're Number One!

Basking in Others' Glory

"Showing off is the fool's idea of glory."
　　　　　　　　　　　　　—Bruce Lee (1940–1973), American martial artist and actor

Background

It is not uncommon for us to highlight our virtues and accomplishments, hoping that others will like and respect us more. True, we may on occasion admit to a few personal foibles or failures, particularly among those who know us well (Tice, Butler, Muraven, & Stillwell, 1995). However, some form of self-enhancement, direct or indirect, is more typical. We seek to persuade ourselves, and those who might listen, that we are uniquely talented, irresistibly charming, and perfectly lovable (Sedikides & Gregg, 2008). It is a rare person, perhaps only one suffering from severe depression or bereft of self-esteem, who is not his or her own best public relations agent. Think about it: Do you honestly report your modest IQ at job interviews, or reveal your embarrassing birthmark on a first date? Even members of *collectivistic* societies, where public self-promotion is frowned upon, show the same fondness for the letters and characters in their own name that *individualistic* Westerners do (Kitayama & Karasawa, 1997), and have an inclination to regard themselves as above-average on traits valued by collectivistic cultures (Sedikides, Gaertner, & Toguchi, 2003).

A subtler example of our tendency to self-enhance is our attempt to capitalize on another person's victory or fame, even when we have little if anything to do with it ourselves. Think of how we may use tangential associations to our advantage. We inject into a conversation the fact that we share the same birthday as a movie celebrity. Or mention with unabashed pride that we hail from the state that has produced the most vice presidents. (I once heard someone brag that the oldest inland open-air market in the U.S. continues to operate in none other than his own hometown—wow, fascinating!) In such cases, we publicize the positive links—however tenuous they might be—emanating from our being. Studies show that feeling respected and admired (even independently of being liked and appreciated) is associated with higher self-esteem (Mahadevan, Gregg, Sedikides, & De Waal-Andrews, 2016). But why earn respect and admiration yourself when you can piggyback conveniently on that of others?

Another example of self-enhancement by association is when we lay claim to the glory of a sports team's victory. The following scene recently caught my eye: A camera pans through an intoxicated L.A. crowd and zeroes in on a spectator whose bald head is a painted mosaic of blue and yellow. He's emphatically holding up his index finger and chanting "We're number one! We're number one!" As Cialdini et al. (1976) pointed out, the chant is always: "'*We're* number one,' never '*They're* number one.'"

Cialdini and his colleagues (1976) referred to the previous phenomenon as *Basking in Reflected Glory* (or *BIRGing* for short). To investigate BIRGing (in the first of several studies), they went to seven different universities (Arizona State, Louisiana State, Notre Dame, Michigan, Pittsburgh, Ohio State, and Southern California) and secretly noted the clothing of introductory psychology students each Monday during football season. Taking note of whether a particular university won or lost their previous Saturday game, they recorded how many students wore jackets, sweatshirts, T-shirts, or buttons that displayed either the university's name or insignia, or the football team's nickname or mascot (wearing school colors did not count, nor did university notebooks and book covers). Their findings were clear-cut: Students showed off their scholastic affiliation more after their school's football team had won than after it had lost. Moreover, the correlation between the number of students displaying their school and the margin of victory was a noteworthy $r = .43$ (where 0 denotes no correlation, and 1 a perfect correlation; Robert Cialdini, personal communication). In other words, the more lopsided the score, the more students on the victorious side displayed their school affiliation (and the less those on the losing side displayed theirs). This was just as true for home games (for which it might be argued that cheers from the stands helped to bring about the victory) as it was for away games (which fewer students would have attended).

What explains such findings? Perhaps students believed, consciously or not, that others would regard them more favorably if they flaunted their scholastic affiliation when their team won. The public flattery would boost their self-esteem. We seem to have an intuitive sense, accurate or not, that we are evaluated based not just on who we are as individuals, but also on who or what we are associated with. We imagine that being seen with VIPs will add an inch or two to our own social stature. We also sense that others will like us more when we communicate good news than when we bear bad news, even when we have obviously played no role in matters. We are reluctant to deliver a gloomy message, not because we feel guilty or sorrowful, but because we fear that we, though blameless, will be negatively evaluated as a result. (Mae, Carlston, and Skowronski, 1999, found something similar. When a communicator badmouths or praises someone, the described traits get automatically transferred onto the communicator as time passes. The target of the comments is forgotten, and a simple associative link persists.)

Cialdini and his colleagues (1976) pointed out, however, that the tendency to wear university-related clothing following football team wins might have nothing to do with efforts to exploit an incidental affiliation for egotistical ends. Perhaps doing so simply expresses one's school pride, or is an uncomplicated means of feeling good. In other words, people may BIRG for purely *intrapersonal* reasons (for private rather than public rewards). It is easy to imagine Notre Dame students wearing their *Fightin' Irish* sweatshirts in the privacy of their own dorm rooms, without necessarily wanting others to notice them doing so. However, Cialdini and his colleagues (1976) sought to demonstrate that BIRGing occurs, at least in part, for *interpersonal* reasons as well. It is a means of boosting one's self-esteem by winning others' respect and admiration or garnering other social benefits.

What They Did

Cialdini and his colleagues (1976, Study 2) examined students' use of *pronouns* in their descriptions of the outcomes of football games with rival universities. They predicted that students would tend to use "we" more in references to school victories ("we won") and "they" more in references to defeats ("they lost"). They further predicted that this pattern of results would be exaggerated for participants whose self-esteem had recently been attacked.

One hundred seventy-three undergraduates at a large university (boasting a nationally ranked football team) were randomly selected from the university's telephone directory. During a three-day period midway through the 1974 football season, they were contacted by phone by research assistants who identified themselves as employees of a regional survey center with headquarters in an out-of-state city. Ninety-three percent of those called agreed to participate in the survey. The caller said he was conducting a survey of college students' knowledge of campus issues and proceeded to ask six questions about campus life. A typical question: "What percentage of students at your school are married—would you say it's closer to 20% or 35%?" ("I haven't the foggiest idea" was not an option). After participants answered the six questions, the caller told them either that they had done very well compared to other students (getting five out of six questions correct) or that they had done relatively poorly (getting only one out of six correct). These randomized remarks served to experimentally manipulate participants' *state* self-esteem (how they felt about themselves in the moment rather than over time). Presumably, the participants in the first condition experienced a slight boost in how they felt about themselves, whereas participants in the second condition experienced a slight deflation in how they felt about themselves. (Including a *manipulation check* demonstrating that the experimental manipulation did, indeed, have an effect would have enhanced this study.)

The caller then mentioned that there would be a few more questions, the first of which had to do with campus athletics. Half the participants were asked about a football victory: "In the first game of the season, your school's football team played the University of Houston. Can you tell me the outcome of that game?" The other half were asked about a defeat: "In the first game of the season, your school's football team played the University of Missouri. Can you tell me the outcome of that game?" If a participant did not know the results of the game, a new participant was called. Otherwise his or her verbatim account of the outcome was recorded.

The dependent variable was whether participants gave "we" responses (e.g., "We won" or "We got beat") or non-"we" responses (e.g., "The score was 14–6, Missouri" or "They lost"). Again, Cialdini and his colleagues (1976) predicted that participants would give more "we" responses when describing a victory than when describing a defeat, and that this effect would be greater for participants who had failed the campus issues survey. Those participants, in particular, were expected to emphasize their affiliation with a winning team ("we") and distance themselves from a losing team ("they"), in order to prop up their flagging self-esteem.

What They Found

Cialdini and his colleagues (1976) found precisely what they had predicted. Usage of "we" was more common in descriptions of team victories than in descriptions of team defeats. Importantly, however, this occurred *only* among those whose egos had been bruised. For those who presumably experienced a blow to their self-esteem, "we" was used 40% of the time for victories and only 14% of the time for defeats. For those whose egos had presumably been bolstered, "we" usage was almost identical for victories and defeats (Figure 11). This pattern of results supports the contention that, when feasible, people highlight, though perhaps not intentionally, trivial links between themselves and successful others in order to impress others and feel better about themselves.

Notice the difference between Study 1 and Study 2. Study 1 demonstrated a correlation between football team victories and the wearing of the team or sponsoring school's clothing. Study 2 built on Study 1 by experimentally manipulating whether a research participant was contemplating a team win or loss and by testing a theoretical claim about the mediating role of self-esteem in the tendency to BIRG. Ideally, science works precisely in this manner. It starts with careful observation of correlated variables, and then moves on to experimental research that allows for sound causal inferences. It also moves back and forth between the so-called real world and the laboratory (see Cialdini, 1995).

A final study served to document a further nuance of BIRGing. Benefits should accrue to the BIRGer only if he or she can boast of an association that is *not* shared by the observer. As an example of this, Cialdini and his colleagues (1976) pointed out that when Californians brag about their state's idyllic climate, they are more likely to do so to people from other states (North Dakota, say) than to fellow Californians. In other words, BIRGing should occur more readily

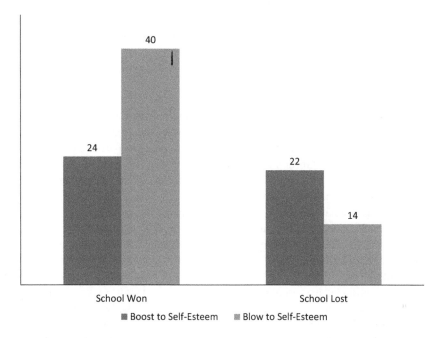

Figure 11 Percentage of participants who used "we" to describe the outcome of their school's football game after they had received a boost or blow to their self-esteem

when one's connection with a celebrated entity is stronger than the observer's connection. In order to test this assertion, an experimenter called participants, inquiring, as in the second study, about campus issues, including the outcome of a recent school football game. He identified himself as an employee of either the university survey center located on campus, or the regional survey center located in an out-of-state city. Although the results of this study did not quite reach conventional levels of statistical significance, the trend was clear. Participants were more likely to use "we" to describe school victories and other language (such as "they") to describe school defeats when they were talking to a presumed out-of-state caller versus a campus caller. This marginal result reinforces the claim that BIRGing is not only about wanting to feel good—it is also about wanting to feel good by impressing others (especially those who do not share the same source of pride).

Thus, in the last study, the origin of the caller (on campus or out-of-state) was a notable *moderator* of the BIRGing effect. Variable *C* moderates the link between *A* and *B* if the strength or direction of that link changes when *C* changes. Note how moderation is different from *mediation*. In both, a link between *A* and *B* depends on some third factor. However, with mediation, the *A*–*B* link cannot occur unless that third factor is present. With moderation it can, though when the factor is present, the *A*–*B* link gets stronger or weaker. Think of the relationship between your dentist and the pain he or she causes. Whereas the dental drill mediates the link between your dentist and your pain (no drill, no pain), a local anesthetic moderates the link between the two (it reduces the intensity of the pain, hopefully).

These more technical details aside, all three studies by Cialdini and his colleagues (1976) showed that participants were more likely to publicly identify themselves with their university's football team after it had recently been victorious. In addition, this identification appeared to hinge on how positively or negatively participants evaluated themselves in the moment. Finally, there are some signs that people make known their links to successful groups at least in part because they believe that observers recognize such links and will evaluate them positively as a result. This belief and the desire to enjoy a favorable social image (especially after that image has been tarnished) appear to foster the BIRGing tendency.

So What?

The research of Cialdini and his colleagues illustrates an important truth: One's identity includes both "I" and "we"—personal attributes as well as social connections and group memberships. One's family, friends, ethnic group, religious affiliations, political party, and professional peers are all part of who one is. As Gordon Allport (1954), one of social psychology's prime movers, put it: "Attachment to one's own being is basic to human life . . . and along with this beloved self go all of the person's basic memberships" (p. 30).

This theme is captured in Tajfel (1979) and Turner's (1985) *social identity theory*, which highlights the role that group identification plays in achieving positive self-esteem (see Chapters 7 and 26). We feel better about ourselves when our group (which social psychologists call the *ingroup*) has positive distinctiveness, that is, when it appears superior to other groups to which we do not belong or identify with (*outgroups*). Thus, self-esteem is more than just one's personal self-evaluation. It has a collective aspect (Turner, Hogg, Oakes, Reicher, & Wetherell, 1987). Moreover, how one categorizes oneself can be flexibly rooted in the immediate context—an idea emphasized by *self-categorization theory*. For example, if you are one of only a few males in a class of psychology students, or one of only a few females in a class of physics students, you will be more likely to think of yourself in terms of your gender while in that class. That is, for purely perceptual reasons, gender will stand out, quite apart from whether gender politics is or is not a feature of your long-term identity. Self-categorization theory also stipulates that there is a trade-off in how you see yourself and others—either as stand-alone individuals *or* as a representative of a group. Consider, for example, the divisive 2016 presidential election. Avid supporters of Donald Trump or Hillary Clinton—especially when airing their differences in public crowds—hardly seemed to be thinking of themselves or of rival supporters as individuals. Rather, they seemed to be thinking of everyone involved as interchangeable members of the pro-Trump or pro-Clinton factions, and to collectively coordinate their partisan activities on that basis.

But getting back to BIRGing, how did Trump or Clinton supporters (and maybe you were one of them) feel after their preferred candidate was or was not elected? Probably either exuberant or deflated. And yet, their *personal* role in the candidates' success or failure was minimal. Merely being associated with someone else's success or failure can have a dramatic effect on self-esteem. Whomever you root for represents you. If you are an American, and Michael Phelps wins more Olympic gold medals than anyone in history, you are a winner too (as if you yourself have logged thousands of laps in the swimming pool). And if you are Brazilian, you are certainly not disappointed if Brazil has just won the World Cup in soccer (even if you don't own a soccer ball). We psychologically internalize our team's outcomes. In fact, believe it or not, a sports fan watching a live basketball game in which his team wins is subsequently more likely to predict that he will do well on a task (any task) than if his team loses. In other words, his team's winning boosts his self-confidence (Hirt, Zillman, Erickson, & Kennedy, 1992).

But keep this in mind: Although we try to associate with winners (and those who are otherwise successful), we sometimes find ourselves inadvertently and unwillingly affiliated with losers (as did Brazilian soccer fans when Germany trounced Brazil 7–1 in 2014). When this happens, we have a couple of options. One is to make excuses. For example, we can explain a sports loss on poor officiating (see Chapter 17). If excuses do not work, we can distance ourselves from defeated or unpopular individuals or ingroups. That is, we can *Cut Off Reflected Failure* (CORF).

In an investigation of CORFing, Snyder, Lassergard, and Ford (1986) had participants work on intellectual problems together in a small group, the "Blue Team." Afterward they were given bogus feedback: Some were told that they had essentially failed (scoring below 70% of people in their age group), others that they had succeeded magnificently (scoring above 90% of others in their age group). A control group of participants was not given any feedback. On their way out, participants were told that there was a box of team badges by the door, and that they could take and wear one of the badges if they wished. About 50% of the participants given no feedback took a badge. But get this: Whereas a mere 10% of the participants in the low-scoring group took a badge (the few that did not CORF), a full 70% of the participants in the high-scoring group took a badge (the many who BIRGed). The upshot of research on CORFing is that we tend to distance ourselves from losers (or a losing ingroup). We do not want to suffer unfavorable associations or, worse, harmful consequences. Logically, CORFing is the opposite of BIRGing. But you will notice that, in the above study, the CORFing effect (−40%) was even stronger than the BIRGing effect (+20%). This suggests that deflecting negative affiliations, to protect self-esteem, is more important than reflecting positive affiliations, to promote self-esteem. And indeed, in many domains, it is more imperative to counteract what is bad than to cultivate what is good (Baumeister, Bratslavsky, Finkenauer, & Vohs, 2001).

Afterthoughts

Cialdini and his colleagues (1976) explored how we compare the performance of ingroups to that of outgroups, and how our self-esteem and social awareness factor into the comparison. That is precisely what is happening when, for example, we anxiously watch the score in a playoff game involving our favorite team volley back and forth. Who is going to win? If we win: pride and joy. If we lose: heartache and humiliation. Again, "we" is a prominent part of "I."

However, we also engage in direct *social comparison*: We compare ourselves, as individuals, to other individuals (Tesser, 1988). Recall how in elementary school you were curious about how well (or poorly) your friend did on a spelling test compared to you, and how as an adult the mere sight of someone else's dazzling new Lexus (or dilapidated Taurus) causes you to reflect on the relative quality of your own car. An important question: How does social comparison affect how we feel about ourselves? After all, although we might delight in someone else's glory, we might also suffer jealousy over it (Salovey & Rodin, 1984).

William James (1907), one of psychology's trailblazers, noted that some social comparisons are more relevant than others. It depends on what matters to your identity:

> I, who for the time have staked my all on being a psychologist, am mortified if others know much more psychology than I. But I am content to wallow in the grossest ignorance of Greek. My deficiencies there give me no sense of personal humiliation at all. Had I "pretensions" to be a linguist, it would have been just the reverse.
>
> (p. 310)

Thus, we tend to like someone who performs better than us on something of little personal relevance. In more personally significant arenas, however, we prefer others to be slightly inferior to us (if they are too inferior then the comparison is not seen as legitimate).

However, matters may be subtler. Tesser's (1988) *self-evaluation maintenance model* notes that how one feels depends, not only on whether the dimension of evaluation does or does not pertain to one's personal identity, but also on whether the comparison person is close (a friend or relative) or distant (a stranger or foe). For example, an aspiring comedian may feel more psychological threatened by a friend's hilarious jokes than by a stranger's. By the same token, however, he may feel more psychologically uplifted by a friend's (comedy-unrelated) job promotion than by a stranger's.

At any rate, we all want to be admired and appreciated, and to avoid headaches and heartaches in our social encounters (Leary, Tambor, Terdel, & Downs, 1995; Mahadevan and others, 2016). To this end, we try to present ourselves in the best possible light, a process referred to as *impression management* (Schlenker, 1980). We attempt to influence others' impressions of us by selectively displaying certain behaviors. According to renowned sociologist Irving Goffman (1959), social interactions represent a kind of theatrical performance in which one presents a *line*: carefully chosen words and deeds meant to express a certain self. We each seek to minimize our social blunders and agonizing embarrassments—Goffman refers to this as *face work*—and we have a repertoire of face-saving devices when these occur.

In fact, BIRGing is only one of several impression management techniques (although one of the least obvious and intentional ones). Jones and Pittman (1982) have identified a grab bag of other ploys. One is *ingratiation*: We give others our attention, conform to their opinions, shower them with flattery, give them favors, and pretend to overlook their flaws, all in order to be liked. We too know "how to win friends and influence people" (Dale Carnegie, 1994). Another ploy is *self-handicapping*: We do or say things that will enable us to either excuse a subsequent failure or take credit for an unlikely success. For example, we get intoxicated the night before a big exam or mention before a musical audition that we have a sore throat and possibly a fever. (As a long distance runner, I am always amazed at how many of us toeing the start line of a race are not expecting—or so we tell others—to run our best, given the taxing workout we ran the day before.) Yet another strategy is *exemplification*. Although we risk appearing sanctimonious, we nevertheless let it be known, through melodramatic self-denial and suffering, how morally exemplary we are ("You go on, I'll finish up here. I'll just quickly clear off the table, wash and dry all the dishes, sweep the floor, make us some coffee, bring out desserts . . . "). These are but a few of our schemes to manage others' impressions of us.

Interestingly, face-saving devices and impression management techniques can also occur in collusion. When we notice someone picking their nose, we tactfully ask them if they need a tissue. When we trip over our own two feet, a friend continues talking as if nothing embarrassing has happened. We help one another—especially in close relationships—maintain a favorable impression and positive self-esteem.

People differ in their inclinations to monitor their behaviors and employ such strategies; some people are high, and some people are low, in *self-monitoring* (Snyder, 1987). Such strategies require energy and skill, however. Maintaining one's mask is no easy task. Perhaps this is why we often fall back on the more effortless maneuver of basking in someone else's exultation.

Revelation

Groups and institutions we are socially connected to are part of our identity and impact our self-esteem. We personalize their successes and failures, trumpeting the former and dissociating ourselves from the latter.

What Do You Think?

Today, you likely belong to many different social groups. Over time, you have joined some, and left others. To what extent do you think you join or leave groups based on your social reputation? For example, would you support some teams no matter how badly they performed? Also, describe various impression management techniques that you and your family members and friends have used. Would you describe yourself as high or low in self-monitoring?

Chapter Reference

Cialdini, R. B., Borden, R. J., Thorne, A., Walker, M. R., Freeman, S., & Sloan, L. R. (1976). Basking in reflected glory: Three (football) field studies. *Journal of Personality and Social Psychology, 34*, 366–375.

Other References

Allport, G. W. (1954). *The nature of prejudice*. Reading, MA: Addison-Wesley.

Baumeister, R. F., Bratslavsky, E., Finkenauer, C., & Vohs, K. D. (2001). Bad is stronger than good. *Review of General Psychology*, *5*, 323–370.

Carnegie, D. (1994). *How to win friends and influence people*. New York: Pocket Books.

Cialdini, R. B. (1995). A full-cycle approach to social psychology. In G. C. Brannigan & M. R. Merrens (Eds.), *The social psychologists: Research adventures* (pp. 52–73). New York: McGraw-Hill.

Goffman, E. (1959). *The presentation of self in everyday life*. Garden City, NY: Doubleday.

Hirt, E. R., Zillman, D., Erickson, G. A., & Kennedy, C. (1992). Costs and benefits of allegiance: Changes in fans' self-ascribed competencies after team victory versus defeat. *Journal of Personality and Social Psychology*, *63*, 724–738.

James, W. (1907). *Pragmatism*. New York: Longmans, Green.

Jones, E. E., & Pittman, T. (1982). Toward a general theory of strategic self-presentation. In J. Suls (Ed.), *Psychological perspectives on the self* (Vol. 1, pp. 231–262). Hillsdale, NJ: Lawrence Erlbaum Associates.

Kitayama, S., & Karasawa, M. (1997). Implicit self-esteem in Japan: Name letters and birthday numbers. *Personality and Social Psychology Bulletin*, *23*, 736–742.

Leary, M., Tambor, E., Terdel, S., & Downs, D. (1995). Self-esteem as an interpersonal monitor: The sociometer hypothesis. *Journal of Personality and Social Psychology*, *68*, 518–530.

Mae, L., Carlston, D. E., & Skowronski, J. J. (1999). Spontaneous trait transfer to familiar communications: Is a little knowledge a dangerous thing? *Journal of Personality and Social Psychology*, *77*, 233–246.

Mahadevan, N., Gregg, A. P., Sedikides, C., & De Waal-Andrews, W. (2016). Winner, losers, insiders, and outsiders: Comparing hierometer and sociometer theories of self-regard. *Frontiers in Psychology*, *7*, 1–19.

Salovey, P., & Rodin, J. (1984). Some antecedents and consequences of social-comparison jealousy. *Journal of Personality and Social Psychology*, *47*, 780–792.

Schlenker, B. R. (1980). *Impression management: The self-concept, social identity, and interpersonal relations*. Monterey, CA: Brooks/Cole.

Sedikides, C., Gaertner, L., & Toguchi, Y. (2003). Pancultural self-enhancement. *Journal of Personality and Social Psychology*, *84*, 60–79.

Sedikides, C., & Gregg, A. P. (2008). Self-enhancement: Food for thought. *Perspectives on Psychological Science*, *3*, 102–116.

Snyder, C. R., Lassergard, M., & Ford, C. E. (1986). Distancing after group success and failure: Basking in reflected glory and cutting off reflected failure. *Journal of Personality and Social Psychology*, *51*, 382–388.

Snyder, M. (1987). *Public appearances/private realities: The psychology of self-monitoring*. New York: W. H. Freeman.

Tajfel, H. (1979). Individuals and groups in social psychology. *British Journal of Social and Clinical Psychology*, *18*, 183–190.

Tesser, A. (1988). Toward a self-evaluation maintenance model of social behavior. In L. Berkowitz (Ed.), *Advances in experimental social psychology* (Vol. 21, pp. 181–227). New York: Academic Press.

Tice, D. M., Butler, J. L., Muraven, M. B., & Stillwell, A. M. (1995). When modesty prevails: Differential favorability of self-presentation to friends and strangers. *Journal of Personality and Social Psychology*, *69*, 1120–1138.

Turner, J. C. (1985). Social categorization and the self-concept: A social-cognitive theory of group behavior. In E. J. Lawler (Ed.), *Advances in group processes* (Vol. 2, pp. 77–122). Greenwich, CT: JAI Press.

Turner, J. C., Hogg, M., Oakes, P., Reicher, S., & Wetherell, M. (1987). *Rediscovering the social group: A self-categorization theory*. Oxford, England: Basil Blackwell.

More to Explore

Gilovich, T., & Ross, L. (2016). *The wisest one in the room: How you can benefit from social psychology's most powerful insights*. New York: Free Press.

12 Hooded Hoodlums

The Role of Deindividuation in Antisocial Behavior

"To be a member of a crowd is closely akin to alcohol intoxication."
—Aldous Huxley (1894–1963), English novelist

Background

Consider the phenomenon of *suicide baiting*. A despondent soul is perched upon a window ledge, eight floors up. A passerby happens to look up and notice him, and instinctively stops, which provokes others to do the same. A growing number of curious individuals stare upward as the desperate person inches forward, resolved to jump. The burgeoning rush-hour crowd quickly transforms into an unruly mob of several hundred people. Police arrive on the scene, hoping to diffuse the situation and rescue the victim above. However, a sudden shout—"Let the fool jump!"—emanates from the horde and hangs in the growing darkness. Someone shouts a more imperative "Jump!" from another indistinct niche in the mass. Debris is thrown at an arriving ambulance. Jeers and other malicious exhortations follow, and before long a taunting chorus bellows: "Jump! Jump! Jump!"

You might wonder: Why do otherwise conscientious people sometimes behave in such a callous manner? Why do they sometimes violate their own ethical standards and social norms to engage in cruel behaviors? Answers to such pressing questions have implicated an array of possible causes: genetic defects, arrested moral development, pent up rage, media influences, a bleak economy, social disintegration, and so on. A number of social psychologists have suggested that simply being immersed in a large group is enough to induce impetuous, wanton behavior. Indeed, Le Bon (1896) described how an individual immersed in a crowd "descends several rungs in the ladder of civilization" (p. 36). Festinger, Pepitone, and Newcomb (1952) picked up on this theme and proposed the idea that uninhibited, antisocial behavior is performed by group members who are temporarily not seen, either by themselves or others, as individuals. Such a state of *deindividuation* involves a mix of possible features: increased physiological arousal, reduced self-awareness, a sense of anonymity, a collapse of self-control, and greater sensitivity to social cues.

Zimbardo (1969) sought to demonstrate deindividuation empirically. He led female participants to believe that they were giving electric shocks to another woman (in reality, a research confederate, who was never actually shocked; see Chapter 4). They did so either alone or in groups. When in groups, they were informed that the experimenter could not tell who was giving the shocks or how hefty the shocks were. Furthermore, participants wore either oversized lab coats that resembled hooded Ku Klux Klan outfits (rendering them anonymous) or normal clothes and an ID badge (making them readily identifiable). Finally, some participants interacted with an affable confederate, others with an obnoxious one.

Zimbardo found that being in a group and being anonymous increased the duration of the shocks participants gave, consistent with the concept of deindividuation. Also significant: The identifiable participants shocked the unlikable woman more than they did the likable woman, whereas the anonymous participants gave the same levels of shock to both women. Apparently, being anonymous resulted in greater, as well as more indiscriminate, hostility.

However, not all researchers would agree that Zimbardo's participants experienced deindividuation. Alternative explanations for group-based antisocial behavior suggest themselves. Perhaps *modeling* is a crucial mechanism. Does a sinister type of contagion occur in a group, with one member's impulsive behavior triggering the same in other members? When electric power is lost at a shopping mall, does one start plundering costly merchandise simply because others are doing the same? Researchers have also wondered about the role of *responsibility*. Would intentionally altering a group member's responsibility (by explicitly assigning responsibility to someone else in the group) spur that person to greater extremes of unrestrained behavior? A creative study by Diener, Fraser, Beaman, and Kelem (1976) addressed such questions. And they did so on the spookiest night of the year: Halloween.

What They Did

The study was ambitious in scope and setting. It involved a grand total of 1,352 children, visiting 27 different homes across Seattle, Washington, on Halloween night. This study was an example of a *quasi*-experiment. It featured some of the critical features of a true experiment (such as deliberate manipulation of independent variables) but not others (such as perfect random assignment of participants to conditions or absolute control over nuisance variables). The study thus traded some *internal validity* (the ability to draw confident causal inferences) for *ecological validity* (the ability to claim that the results were obtained in a realistic everyday setting, rather than in an artificial laboratory setting). That said, contrary to commonplace assumptions, experiments do not *need* to generalize (see the Introduction, and Chapter 6, for more on this).

All 27 homes were set up similarly: On one end of a low table inside the front door was a large bowl of bite-sized candy bars; at the other end was a bowl of pennies and nickels. Children randomly arrived on trick-or-treat night either alone or in groups. In each home, a different woman (actually a research accomplice) greeted the children, complimented them on their costumes, and otherwise acted in a friendly manner. On some occasions, the children (both those who came alone and those who came in groups) were deliberately identified. The woman asked each child what his or her name was and where he or she lived, and then repeated the information back to the child. On other occasions, children (alone or in groups) were not asked to identify themselves or say where they lived. They remained anonymous. The woman then told the children that they should take just *one* candy. If a child asked about the bowl filled with coins, she simply repeated her instruction to take only one candy.

In a number of homes, the woman also declared that the smallest child (if the children had arrived in a group) would be responsible for any extra candy or money that was taken. There were three variations of this *shifted responsibility* condition: Sometimes all the children, including the one made responsible, remained anonymous; sometimes the responsible child was identified while the other children in the group remained anonymous; and sometimes all the children, including the responsible child, were identified. It was suspected that shifting responsibility to the smallest child would make transgressions more likely, because the bigger children could blame him or her if they were found out, and the smallest child was unlikely to contest the issue.

After these various manipulations were in place, the woman casually mentioned that she needed to return to her work in another room. What the children did not know was that a research assistant was observing them through a peephole in a decorative backdrop, recording how much candy and money they took.

What They Found

For the sake of simplicity, each child was scored as having *transgressed* (taken more than they should have) or not. About a third of the children took money, extra candy, or both. More importantly, and as predicted, anonymity and group presence each exerted a significant *main effect* (each alone affected the number of transgressions, in both cases increasing them). Most notably, however, these two factors significantly *interacted* (the effect of one factor depended on the effect of the other). Specifically, 8% of the children stole either money or extra candy when they were alone; 21% stole something when they were anonymous *or* part of a group; and 57% stole something when they were anonymous *and* part of a group. Thus, children stole the most when they were members of anonymous groups (Figure 12). Another striking finding was that a full 80% of the children swiped extra candy or money when they were in a group, anonymous, *and* relieved of responsibility.

Diener and his colleagues (1976) also wanted to determine whether the effect of being in a group was attributable to modeling. Does being in a group in and of itself cause one to transgress more freely, or is the effect of the group on an individual's behavior mediated by his or her observing other group members transgress? Diener and his colleagues found clear evidence of the latter. Transgression rates were notably higher in groups in which the *first* child—or *initiator*—stole money or extra candy compared to groups in which the initiator took only a single piece of candy. However, on average, initiators in groups of children also swiped more candy or money than children who were alone, suggesting that modeling was not solely responsible for the group transgression rate. Something occurred in the anonymous groups besides modeling—presumably deindividuation—to coax kids into antisocial behavior. Apparently, being anonymous and being in a group influenced the initiator's behavior, and then his or her actions created a behavioral *norm* that was followed by the other children in the group (see Chapter 1).

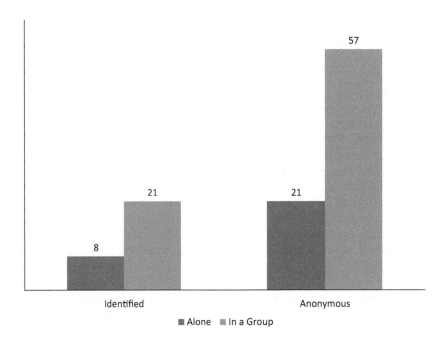

Figure 12 Percentage of trick-or-treaters who stole, when alone or in a group, and when identified or anonymous

So What?

Diener and his colleagues (1976) were able to show that an interaction of group membership, anonymity, and altered responsibility can lead to a sharp escalation of forbidden behaviors. Roving in a small pack of other children, and keeping their real identity secret by dressing up as a witch, mummy, or pirate costume (keep in mind, this was the 1970s, long before *Harry Potter* or *Frozen* costumes), led individual children to make a grab for extra candy bars and dig freely into a nearby bowl of coins. Those children were further emboldened if another child was held responsible for their malfeasance.

Such minor transgressions provide a model for more serious crime. Indeed, deindividuation can pose very real problems. Historical examples of mob behavior abound. These range from the vigilante lynchings and other acts of violence against Blacks in the United States in the early 1900s; to *Kristallnacht*, a 1938 uprising in which Nazi hoodlums attacked Jews, looted their property, and burned their synagogues; to the riots in Watts, Harlem, and Newark in reaction to White racism in the 1960s. Sports fans—especially hockey, soccer, and American football enthusiasts—are also notorious for their uproarious and sometimes tragic mob behavior. Even joyous victory celebrations have been known to turn calamitous, as when an NBA team clinches the championship and its home city erupts into a bacchanal of vandalism, arson, looting, and assault. In a similar manner, an outrageous injustice can trigger bedlam. Recall the 2014 riots following the police shooting of Michael Brown in Ferguson, Missouri. Furthermore, wearing a disguise seems to precipitate violence. Silke (2003) found that, in over 40% of some 500 cases of violent interpersonal attacks in Northern Ireland, the perpetrator of the attack wore a mask to disguise his identity. Wearing a disguise was found to be related to inflicting more serious injuries, attacks on a greater number of people, a greater number of threats toward victims afterward, and more vandalism. To the extent that antisocial events are predictable, preventive measures can be taken, such as beefing up the show of police force (although the tactics involved in police militarization are controversial). Yet often the sparks that ignite unruly crowd behavior occur unpredictably. It is always easier to postdict than predict such social upheavals.

An intriguing archival study by Mann (1981) attempted such backward predicting of factors associated with suicide baiting (portrayed at the beginning of this chapter). Mann scoured 15 years of the *New York Times* and *Chicago Tribune* for reports of cases in which crowds were present when an individual publicly threatened and in some cases committed suicide by leaping from a high place. Mann coded the content of these reports for such variables as location of the incident, position of the victim, date and time of day, duration of the episode, and crowd size, and then compared the baiting episodes to the non-baiting episodes. He found that a number of factors correlated with baiting. Specifically, baiting occurred more often in large crowds (over 300 people), in which individual baiters were relatively anonymous and likely to experience increased arousal and diminished self-awareness. Baiting was also more common under the cover of darkness (a majority of the incidents occurred at night), which would, again, make baiters feel more anonymous. The distance between the victim and the crowd also predicted baiting. The mockery and dares that typify baiting tended not to occur when the victim was too close to the crowd (just a few floors above the street) or when the victim was too far away (many floors above street level or on a bridge). Apparently, baiting requires that the victim be at some optimal distance (though hardly optimal from the victim's point of view!). Finally, baiting was more prevalent in longer episodes (those that lasted more than 2 hours), which perhaps allowed time for deindividuation to set in and deviant behavior to escalate. It is also plausible that longer episodes fostered a sense of frustration and irritation, even a need for closure ("Come on, jump, I've gotta get home to dinner!"). Evidently, a host of external factors combine to cause individuals to join in a baiting chorus. Although it is easy to characterize those involved as cold-hearted and sadistic, and to imagine that "I would never do such a thing," one should not discount the power of the prevailing social situation.

Afterthoughts

The research literature on deindividuation is not self-contained or well defined. The causes, manifestations, and consequences of deindividuation need more rigorous study. Researchers have been quick to assert that just about any instance of uninhibited behavior reflects deindividuation. For example, stimulus-rich environments (a glitzy casino or Bourbon Street during the Mardi Gras) or even drug-induced alterations in consciousness have been claimed to produce deindividuation. It has also been suggested that *total institutions* (those that control many aspects of one's behavior), such as hospitals, prisons, and military boot camps, alienate people from their personal identities. Such institutions, with their standard uniforms, identification bracelets, codes of conduct, routine schedules, and general lack of freedom, strip people of their individuality.

The deindividuation concept has also been applied to victims as well as aggressors. In Chapter 4 we described how Milgram (1963) found that a teacher was more willing to shock a learner when the two could not see each other. Note how hoods were often placed over criminals when they were publicly hanged in the United States. What purpose did this serve? On a lighter note, Turner, Layton, and Simons (1975) found that drivers were more likely to honk at a stalled motorist when a curtain was drawn across the back window compared to when there was no such curtain.

Some researchers have even portrayed deindividuation as a potentially good thing, emphasizing that being absorbed in a group can liberate one from self-strangulating shyness. *Encounter groups*, with their intense interpersonal dynamics, have been extolled for having the same type of liberating effect. Even being part of the jubilant anarchy of, say, Times Square goers on New Year's Eve can give rise to a euphoric sense of freedom or unaccountability. Researchers have also found that when environmental cues make social responsibility salient, deindividuation can lead to more altruistic behavior (Johnson & Downing, 1979; Spivey & Prentice-Dunn, 1990). For the most part, however, researchers have warned of the dark side of deindividuation, claiming that it leads to unprincipled and harmful behaviors.

But let's back up. Uninhibited behavior in groups occurs for at least two general reasons. An anonymous group member might feel that he or she can get away with certain behaviors (by going undetected), or that he or she will not be held personally responsible for collective behaviors (*diffusion of responsibility*; see Chapter 5). Either way, public self-awareness is reduced. The individual feels less conspicuous. He or she is less likely to be singled out, evaluated, criticized, or punished, and so is less concerned about approval, embarrassment, or retaliation by others. As in the fantasy of being invisible, behavior may be dramatically altered. Technically, however, getting away with bad behavior is not, in and of itself, deindividuation.

By definition, deindividuation occurs when *private self-awareness* is reduced. The truly deindividuated person is alleged to pay scant attention to personal values and moral codes. He or she is claimed to be inordinately sensitive to cues in the immediate environment. Seeing others smash through storefront windows and escape with stereos and TVs during a looting spree, the deindividuated person is held to automatically join in, heedless of personal ethical qualms. The perpetrator is temporarily unaware of being an individual. Behavior is released from cognitive control as one becomes immersed in the pulsating crowd.

In favor of this point of view is research that investigates what happens under opposite conditions—where people are made to focus on themselves, thereby increasing private self-awareness (Silvia & Duval, 2001). Here, people become aware of their personal standards, and are less likely to act in a way that violates them.

However, there is another interpretation of deindividuation phenomena (Reicher, Spears, & Postmes, 1995). It is not so much that a person loses all contact with their sane self, and turns into a berserk automaton. Rather, the way in which they *categorize* themselves changes, such that their *social identity* comes to overshadow their *personal identity*. As a result, their construal of a situation, and what it is moral to do in that situation, reflects group standards rather than private standards. But that is very different from claiming that their moral compass altogether disappears.

Indeed, a *meta-analysis* (quantitative summary) of 60 deindividuation studies suggests that factors such as anonymity and group size alone have only a modest effect overall on antisocial behavior (Postmes & Spears, 1998). This leaves open the possibility that group norms play a crucial role too (see Chapter 1). For example, the trick-or-treaters studied by Diener and colleagues (1976) may have felt they were *entitled* to more than just a single candy each (which does sounds a bit stingy). In an anonymous group, with costumes reinforcing their collective identity, a take-just-a-little-bit-more norm could well have come to the fore.

Besides, what's the point of dressing up for Halloween in a pirate outfit if you can't bring home some booty?

Revelation

Being immersed in a group can lead to heightened arousal, a sense of anonymity, reduced self-awareness, and the automatic modeling of others' behaviors. Such a state of deindividuation can result in unrestrained—often aggressive and destructive—behavior.

What Do You Think?

Recount a personal experience of deindividuation—describe the situation and how you (and others) were affected by that situation. Also, under the cover of darkness, people sometimes turn antisocial. That said, doesn't nighttime still have its own special allure? Creatures of the night can be creepy, true; but they can also be mysterious, enchanting, and romantic. Can the cover of dark help us escape the glare of our everyday identities?

Chapter Reference

Diener, E., Fraser, S. C., Beaman, A. L., & Kelem, R. T. (1976). Effects of deindividuation variables on stealing among Halloween trick-or-treaters. *Journal of Personality and Social Psychology, 33*, 178–183.

Other References

Festinger, L., Pepitone, A., & Newcomb, T. (1952). Some consequences of deindividuation in a group. *Journal of Abnormal and Social Psychology, 47*, 382–389.

Johnson, R. D., & Downing, L. L. (1979). Deindividuation and valence of cues: Effects on prosocial and antisocial behavior. *Journal of Personality and Social Psychology, 37*, 1532–1538.

Le Bon, G. (1896). *The crowd: A study of the popular mind.* London: Ernest Benn.

Mann, L. (1981). The baiting crowd in episodes of threatened suicide. *Journal of Personality and Social Psychology, 41*, 703–709.

Milgram, S. (1963). Behavioral study of obedience. *Journal of Abnormal and Social Psychology, 67*, 371–378.

Postmes, T., & Spears, R. (1998). Deinidividuation and antinormative behavior: A meta-analysis. *Psychological Bulletin, 123*, 238–259.

Reicher, S., Spears, R., & Postmes, T. (1995). A social identity model of deindividuation phenomena. *European Review of Social Psychology, 6*, 161–198.

Silke, A. (2003). Deindividuation, anonymity and violence: Findings from Northern Ireland. *Journal of Social Psychology, 143*, 493–499.

Silvia, P. J., & Duval, T. S. (2001). Objective self-awareness theory: Recent progress and enduring problems. *Personality and Social Psychology Review, 5*, 230–241.

Spivey, C. B., & Prentice-Dunn, S. (1990). Assessing the directionality of deindividuation behavior: Effects of deindividuation, modeling, and private self-consciousness on aggressive and prosocial responses. *Basic and Applied Social Psychology, 11*, 387–403.

Turner, C. W., Layton, J. F., & Simons, L. S. (1975). Naturalistic studies of aggressive behavior: Aggressive stimuli, victim visibility, and horn honking. *Journal of Personality and Social Psychology, 31*, 1098–1107.

Zimbardo, P. G. (1969). The human choice: Individuation, reason, and order versus deindividuation, impulse, and chaos. *Nebraska Symposium on Motivation, 17*, 237–307.

More to Explore

Zimbardo, P. (2008). *The Lucifer effect: Understanding how good people turn evil*. New York: Random House Trade Publications.

13 Familiarity Breeds Liking

The Endearing Effects of Mere Exposure

"The song is best esteemed with which our ears are most acquainted."
—William Byrd (1543–1623), English composer

Background

Consider the following Turkish words: *Iktitaf, Jandara, Afworbu, Biwojni, Civadra*. What do you imagine they mean? It's hard to say, right? Perhaps one seems a little more positive, another a little more negative. But right now they are basically "blank slates"—waiting to mean something in your mind.

Well, *doğrusu* (to be honest), they are not really Turkish words. They are made-up words used by Robert Zajonc (1968) in a classic demonstration of the *mere exposure effect*—the tendency to like neutral stimuli better the more often one encounters them. Zajonc flashed such pseudo-words to participants 1, 2, 5, 10, or 25 times, having them pronounce each one as they went along. Afterward, they rated how positive or negative they thought the meaning of each word was. He found that participants rated the more frequently presented words more positively. He also tested for the same effect using other novel stimuli, such as diagrams that look like Chinese calligraphy to the untrained eye. He again flashed each for a varying number of times, and again found that those presented more often were preferred. But was it only meaningless words or symbols that are liked more when repeated? Ever the enthusiastic experimentalist, Zajonc also helped to conduct a logistically more complicated study that involved flesh-and-blood people as stimuli (Saegart, Swap, & Zajonc, 1973). Here, participants were ushered from one room to the next, where they sampled a variety of pleasant and unpleasant drinks. In the process, each participant met each of the other participants more or less frequently (none had known each other previously). The interactions involved brief, face-to-face contact with no talking. Following these room-to-room migrations, the participants evaluated each other. Their evaluations were more favorable when they had met frequently, and less favorable when they had met infrequently. Incidentally, the taste of the liquids, pleasant or unpleasant, didn't matter: Sheer contact explained everything. This is another example of the mere exposure effect. Whether stimuli are nonsense words, ideographs, or people, the more they are encountered, the more they tend to be liked.

A shortcoming of these earlier studies, however, is that they each represented a *within-participants design*, in which each participant experiences more than one level of a particular variable. For example, a person might work on a frustratingly difficult crossword puzzle in an uncomfortably hot room and then later work on a different, yet equally challenging, crossword puzzle in a comfortable air-conditioned room (the dependent variable in each case might be how long he or she persists in working on each puzzle). Another example is the study described earlier, in which participants were exposed to different alleged Turkish words more or less frequently. One concern with either study (or any study involving a within-participants design) is that the results might have been due to participants' intuitions about its purpose. Participants' hunches may have led them to produce results they believed were expected by the experimenters. (Suspicions about a study's purpose can also cause participants to work against expected results, either deliberately or unwittingly.) Indeed, previous research had found that participants reported liking stimuli more even if they had simply *imagined* seeing them more frequently (Stang, 1974). This suggests that the mere exposure effect could have been an artifact of participants' suspicions about the purpose of the study and what it should reveal.

It is now well-recognized that certain cues in an experiment—referred to as *demand* characteristics—can prompt guesses and motives in participants that influence their behavior and bias research results (Orne, 1962). Demand characteristics are a vexing and ever-present problem in experiments involving people (as opposed to, say, fruit flies). Fortunately, there are several ways to guard against demand characteristics. A credible *cover story* (stated but misleading rationale for the study) helps. It prevents participants from feeling any need to figure out the real purpose of the experiment. Also, post-experimental inquiries serve to reveal demand characteristics, allowing researchers to eliminate them from future studies. Such inquiries often begin with broad, open-ended questions ("Do you have any thoughts or questions about this study?") and proceed to more pointed questions ("When indicating which of the Turkish words you liked best, were you aware that some had been presented to you more frequently than others? Did you believe that they were Turkish words?"). Yet another way to purge a study of demand characteristics is to change the design of the study altogether, from a within-participants design to a *between-participants* design, in which each group of participants is exposed to only one set of conditions. They are unaware of what participants in other conditions are exposed to (or even that there are other conditions), and are therefore less inclined to imagine that the experimenter is making comparisons across groups.

For example, in order to study the effects of light intensity on ping-pong performance, one might, in a within-participants design, have each participant play one game under full illumination and another under reduced illumination (randomly switching the order for different participants). Unfortunately, in this design, participants might well easily realize that illumination is the main focus of the study, and might alter their behaviors accordingly. In contrast, in a between-participants design, each group of participants would play a game under either high *or* low illumination (not both). This arrangement would prevent them from suspecting that light intensity is being manipulated. Again, a good cover story would also prevent suspicion: "This study is a product analysis of a newly designed ping-pong ball. Simply play the best you can while we videotape your performance." Only a telepathic participant would then surmise: "Hey, this study is really about the effect of light intensity on ping-pong performance" and therefore attempt to play better or worse.

The point is that there was a need in the 1970s for research that would render implausible any explanations for the mere exposure effect that implicated demand characteristics. Social psychologists interested in this issue wanted to be sure that it was the number of exposures, and not participants' suspicions, that were affecting liking for stimuli. Mita, Dermer, and Knight (1977) came up with a creative way of doing just that. They succinctly described the purpose of their study: "to test the mere-exposure hypothesis so that there was virtually no possibility of sensitizing participants to the frequency-effect hypothesis" (p. 597). They capitalized on two facts that many people considered trivial. First, when people view their own faces, they usually do so in a mirror, whereas others normally see their faces directly (this was before the current era of the smart phone *selfie*!). Second, people's faces are not completely symmetrical: One eyebrow is slightly bushier than the other eyebrow, or one side of the chin bears an unsightly pimple. As a result, the mirror image of a person's face is subtly different from the image that other people see. Mita and his colleagues (1977) incorporated these apparently trivial facts into their ingenious study.

What They Did

Even with the hints we have provided, it might be difficult to imagine a study that would dem-onstrate the mere exposure effect while eliminating demand characteristics. It often takes a good bit of experience and ingenuity to come up with the clever, if sometimes quirky, methodologies found in social psychology. Mita and his colleagues (1977) conducted two experiments. We will only describe the second, which was a more rigorous replication of the first. Replications are often necessary if one wants to publish one's research in a premier journal. They also help estab-lish the *reliability* (repeatability) and *boundary conditions* (limits) of a particular research finding (see the Introduction to the book).

At the University of Wisconsin, 38 women participated in a study on self-perception. Each was asked to bring along her boyfriend (each woman had indicated that she was dating or living with someone whom she believed was in love with her). As it happened, 10 of the women failed to bring a partner to the experiment, mostly because the partners were out of town, so they could provide only partial data (it's usually not easy to recruit couples into a study). In a preliminary session, a photo was taken of each woman. The film was then developed into two portrait-sized, black-and-white photographs that were the mirror images of one another. The two photos were subtly different, due to the fact that people's faces are not perfectly symmetrical, as mentioned previously. The *mirror* print was of how the woman appeared to herself in a mirror, whereas the *true* print was of how the woman appeared to others.

In the second session, each woman brought her boyfriend. He waited in another room while she was being tested, and was then tested himself while she waited (the two were not allowed to communicate while changing rooms). The woman sat at a table upon which the two photographs of her were displayed. She was shown the two photos five different times (she was asked to look away each time they were displayed, and nothing was said on each trial about whether a photo was the same as one previously shown). The left-right positioning of the mirror print and true print photos was randomized on each trial for each woman. The experimenter was not told which photos were mirror prints and which were true prints (a precaution that had not been taken in the first study). This was to ensure that he would not unduly influence her responses. On each trial, the woman's task was to simply indicate which of the photos she liked better, even if her deci-sion was based on trivial or ineffable differences. The women were not told the real purpose of the study or that the photographs were, in fact, mirror images of each other. After stating prefer-ences on five different trials, each woman was asked to provide reasons for her choices, in order to assess demand characteristics. She was also asked what she thought the purpose of the study was (these various responses were tape-recorded). She then changed rooms with her partner, who went through the same procedure of indicating photo preferences and being interviewed.

The design of the study was simple, as were its hypotheses. Mita and his fellow researchers predicted that the women would tend to prefer the mirror prints (which would present a likeness they would be most familiar with), whereas their partners would tend to prefer the true prints (which to them would be most familiar).

What They Found

On the first trial alone, 20 of the 28 women indicated that they preferred the mirror prints, whereas 17 of their 28 boyfriends indicated that they preferred the true prints. The first effect (women preferring the mirror print) was statistically significant, but the second effect (the majority of the boyfriends preferring the true print), although in the expected direction, was not. (This essentially replicated the results of the first study.) Moreover, the joint prediction—that the women would prefer the mirror prints *and* their boyfriends would prefer the true prints—was corroborated in 43% of the couples (significantly more than the 25% predicted by chance).

When Mita and his colleagues analyzed participants' responses across all five trials, they found even stronger confirmation of their hypotheses. In particular, 20 of the 28 women preferred the mirror prints, whereas 19 of their 28 boyfriends preferred the true prints. Both results are statistically significant (Figure 13). Thus, when aggregating across trials, a boyfriend-preference effect emerged. Furthermore, in 50% of the couples, both the woman-preference and the boyfriend-preference predictions were confirmed (double what chance would predict).

What reasons did participants give for their preferences? Did they come close to mentioning that they thought the two photos were mirror images of each other, that one of the photos was more familiar, and that it was for this reason that they preferred it? They did not. Instead, they seemed to invent reasons, mentioning that the photo they preferred was "more natural," had "better head tilt," "better eyes," a "straighter part," or looked "less mean." None of the participants mentioned anything about being exposed to either photograph more or less frequently. And only two participants reported noticing that the photos were mirror images of each other, and even then they indicated no knowledge of the study's hypotheses. In other words, Mita and his colleagues found no evidence of demand characteristics when probing for them.

So What?

Mita and his colleagues (1977) provided an elegantly simple test of the mere exposure hypothesis. The design of their study traded on a unique difference between conditions: The true and mirror images were almost indistinguishable, except that the two groups of participants (the women and their boyfriends) would have been exposed to each of them more or less frequently. Participants had no clue as to why they preferred certain photos or what the experiment was about. In fact, this experiment was so neatly done that even a trained social psychologist could probably have been a participant without figuring out its true purpose.

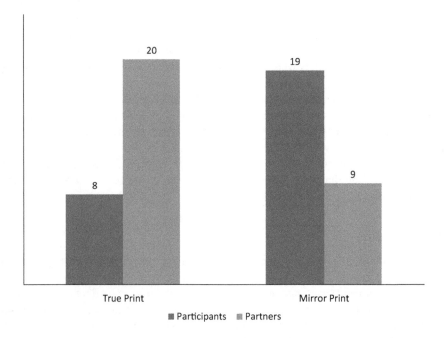

Figure 13 The number of participants, and the number of their partners, who most often preferred, over a series of trials, true or mirror prints of participants' faces

Several follow-up studies have illuminated conditions that *moderate* (affect the magnitude of) the mere exposure effect. For example, for at least some stimuli there seems to be an optimal range of exposure—often between a dozen to two dozen encounters (Bornstein, 1989). Greater exposure improves liking up to a point, but beyond that point, liking levels off. Indeed, if exposure continues, liking may actually transform into disliking. At first, one cannot get enough of *All About That Bass* by Megan Trainor, but after hearing it 73 times, one is liable to be somewhat less about that bass! Also, the nature of the stimulus has some bearing on whether and to what extent a mere exposure effect will emerge. For example, some studies find that repeated exposure to advertisements or product designs increases liking for them if they are complex, but not if they are simple (Cox & Cox, 1988, 2002). Little wonder then that one may never bore of Bach's labyrinthine organ works or Picasso's jigsaw-like paintings. In addition, mere exposure effects can be stronger for initially nice or neutral stimuli than for initially nasty stimuli. For example, people do not, despite repeated exposure, arrive at any greater appreciation for originally stinky odors, such as skunk poo or rancid cheese (Delplanque, Coppin, Bloesch, Cayeux, & Sander, 2015).

However, aside from these and a few other limiting conditions, the mere exposure effect is quite robust (Bornstein, 1989). That is, it is easy to replicate using a variety of stimuli and procedures. Also, the mere exposure effect readily occurs outside the laboratory. For example, it is partly due to the mere exposure effect that well-known, incumbent politicians (or politicians who are not well-known but spend oodles of money on media exposure) are preferred to unfamiliar ones. For example, Grush, McKeough, and Ahlering (1978) predicted 83% of the winners in a U.S. congressional election primary by calculating the amount of media coverage devoted to each candidate. Consider Donald Trump. He seemingly defied the odds in becoming the Republican candidate in the 2016 U.S. presidential election. But then again, he was *better recognized* in public than most of the other contenders, thanks to his starring on *The Apprentice*. Thereafter, he also dominated the news cycle (even if often unfavorably). Evidently, repeated names and sound bites win the political day (see Chapter 20). Consider also the Olympian efforts companies make to be the proud sponsors of the Olympic Games. Their goal, of course, is to present their product to millions of viewers ad infinitum. Thus, not only does the mere exposure effect occur naturally in our responses to songs on the radio and people we encounter in the elevator, it can also be wielded for political or financial gain.

Afterthoughts

Social psychology investigates how people perceive and influence one another. A common starting point is to examine some of the more elementary features of human interactions. This chapter demonstrates how being exposed to a loved one's face repeatedly affects liking for it. Chapter 6 explores what happens to one's performance on a task when others are present, and Chapter 12 investigates what happens to a person when he or she is immersed in a crowd. Such minimal situations—in which exposure but little if any interaction occurs—are important because they underlie and interact with more engaging and complex social psychological processes. They also reveal some of the automatic, nonconscious processes that govern human behavior.

About 25 years ago, following decades of waning respect for Sigmund Freud's theory of unconscious motivation, there was a resurrection in psychology of belief in nonconscious influences on human behavior. It was, once again, becoming clear that people often do not know what influences their thoughts, feelings, and behaviors. For example, they often cannot explain their choices (Nisbett & Wilson, 1977; see Chapter 14). Of course, many of our behaviors are quite deliberate and conscious, and we have a good understanding of what provokes them. A friend invites us to a fun party, so we go. Someone insults us, so we plot revenge. However, it is also the case that much of what we do is an automatic, unconscious response to prevailing stimuli. As such, we often do not understand our own responses or the very operation of our own minds.

Suppose, for example, you show people all the letters of the alphabet, and ask them to pick the five they most like the look of, and the five they least like the look of. The initial letters of their names are nearly always among their most preferred, and nearly never among their least preferred. And people will do this without realizing it (Hoorens, 2015). Similarly, although mere exposure effects occur relatively automatically and unconsciously, they nonetheless exert a powerful effect on human sentiments. In fact, such effects may even occur in animals. Research by Cross, Halcomb, and Matter (1967) found that rats who heard pieces by Mozart during infancy favored new pieces by Mozart over others by Schoenberg later on, whereas rats not exposed to Mozart did not show this preference! (See Chapter 23 for more about automatic social psychological processes.)

What explains such rudimentary influences upon our perceptions? Why does the mere exposure effect occur? Sociobiologists, who interpret social behavior in evolutionary terms, have suggested that there is a deep-rooted tendency in people to assume that what is familiar is safe, and that what is unfamiliar is dangerous. Liking familiar and seemingly safe stimuli, and avoiding unknown and unpredictable stimuli, is said to increase one's chances of survival and reproduction (thereby increasing the genes that underlie those preference in the gene pool). Bornstein (1989) asked this question:

> Who was likely to live longer, reproduce, and pass on genetic material (and inherited traits) to future generations, the cave dweller who had a healthy fear of the strange and unfamiliar beasts lurking outside, or the more risk-taking (albeit short-lived) fellow who, on spying an unfamiliar animal in the distance, decided that he wanted a closer look?
>
> (p. 282)

However, one might object to such an explanation by pointing out that curiosity about the unfamiliar and unknown, and the risk-taking that might follow, are likely to be adaptive traits as well. Nothing ventured, nothing gained. Would the human race have advanced or even survived without taking brave steps into the unknown? Furthermore, if everything familiar is liked, why does the word "new" generally have positive connotations, and "old" negative ones?

Social psychological explanations have suggested that frequent exposure leads to a sense of *familiarity*, which, in turn, might lead to an assumption of *similarity*. Plenty of research confirms that we like others who are similar to us (see Newcomb, 1961, for a classic demonstration of this). Cognitive explanations have pointed to the role of *recognition*. Frequent exposure makes objects more recognizable, which makes them more attractive. In other words, the conscious recognition of a stimulus *mediates* (is a necessary link in the causal chain) between exposure to a stimulus and one's emotional response to it. Studies have shown, however, that mere exposure can also occur subliminally—outside of conscious awareness—and still be efficacious (Bornstein & D'Agostino, 1992). Thus, conscious recognition seems not to be a necessary mediator of the mere exposure effect.

These competing explanations suggest that, with regard to the mere exposure effect, the *why* question has proven less tractable than the *when* question. This often happens. Determining when an effect occurs is part of describing it, whereas ascertaining why it occurs amounts to explaining it, a more difficult task. Psychology attempts to explain the causes of phenomena by conducting experiments. Mita and his collaborators did conduct an experiment (deliberately manipulating an independent variable and controlling extraneous variables), and so were in a position to infer causation. They could therefore say that more frequent exposure to a stimulus *causes* one to like it more. What they could not determine from their design, however, is what, if anything, mediates the causal link between exposure and liking.

A final afterthought: There is something reassuring about the mere exposure effect. Within limits, the more we are exposed to something that is initially novel, the more we come to like it.

In particular, the more often we encounter common decent folk, the more appealing they are to us. Repeated contact with someone is sufficient to increase our attraction to him or her. Contrary to what cynics would say, familiarity tends to breed liking, not contempt. Indeed, by and large, contact between different groups tends to reduce prejudice between them (although other preconditions need to be met; Pettigrew & Troop, 2006, 2008). This is quite a comforting thought, and all the more so the more one contemplates it!

Revelation

How we feel about a person (or any other stimulus) is influenced by a host of factors, but most basically, it is governed by mere exposure. We tend to like people more the more often we encounter them.

What Do You Think?

We like things that are familiar, and yet we crave novel experiences. Likewise, products can be advertised both on the basis of being around for ages or on the basis of being just released. What account for the seemingly contradictory appeal of both the old and the new?

Chapter Reference

Mita, T. H., Dermer, M., & Knight, J. (1977). Reversed facial images and the mere-exposure hypothesis. *Journal of Personality and Social Psychology, 35*, 597–601.

Other References

Bornstein, R. F. (1989). Exposure and affect: Overview and meta-analysis of research, 1968–1987. *Psychological Bulletin, 106*, 265–289.

Bornstein, R. F., & D'Agostino, P. R. (1992). Stimulus recognition and the mere exposure effect. *Journal of Personality and Social Psychology, 63*, 545–552.

Cox, D. S., & Cox, A. D. (1988). What does familiarity breed? Complexity as a moderator of repetition effects in advertisement evaluation. *Journal of Consumer Psychology, 15*, 111–116.

Cox, D., & Cox, A. D. (2002). Beyond first impressions: The effects of repeated exposure on consumer liking of visually complex and simple product designs. *Journal of the Academy of Marketing Science, 30*, 119–130.

Cross, H. A., Halcomb, C. G., & Matter, W. W. (1967). Imprinting or exposure learning in rats given early auditory stimulation. *Psychonomic Sciences, 7*, 233–234.

Delplanque, S., Coppin, G., Bloesch, L., Cayeux, I., & Sander, D. (2015). The mere exposure effect depends on an odor's initial pleasantness. *Frontiers in Psychology, 6*, 911.

Grush, J. E., McKeough, K. L., & Ahlering, R. F. (1978). Extrapolating laboratory exposure research to actual political elections. *Journal of Personality and Social Psychology, 36*, 257–270.

Hoorens, V. (2015). What's really in a name-letter effect? Name-letter preferences as indirect measures of self-esteem. *European Review of Social Psychology, 25*, 228–262.

Newcomb, T. M. (1961). *The acquaintance process*. New York: Holt.

Nisbett, R. E., & Wilson, T. D. (1977). Telling more than we can know: Verbal reports on mental processes. *Psychological Review, 84*, 231–259.

Orne, M. T. (1962). On the social psychology of the psychology experiment: With particular reference to demand characteristics and their implications. *American Psychologist, 17*, 776–783.

Pettigrew, T. F., & Tropp, L. R. (2006). A meta-analytic test of intergroup contact theory. *Journal of Personality and Social Psychology, 90*, 751–783.

Pettigrew, T. F., & Tropp, L. R. (2008). How does intergroup contact reduce prejudice? Meta-analytic tests of three mediators. *European Journal of Social Psychology, 38*, 922–934.

Saegart, S. C., Swap, W. C., & Zajonc, R. B. (1973). Exposure, context, and interpersonal attraction. *Journal of Personality and Social Psychology, 25*, 234–242.

Stang, D. J. (1974). Intuition as an artifact in mere exposure studies. *Journal of Personality and Social Psychology, 30*, 647–653.

Zajonc, R. B. (1968). Attitudinal effects of mere exposure. *Journal of Personality and Social Psychology Monographs, 9*, 1–27.

More to Explore

Schafer, J. (2015). *The like switch: An ex-FBI agent's guide to influencing, attracting, and winning people over*. New York: Touchstone.

14 Strangers to Ourselves

The Shortcomings of Introspection

"Consciousness is the mere surface of our mind, and of this, as of the globe, we do not know the interior, but only the crust."

—Arthur Schopenhauer (1788–1860), German philosopher

Background

Have you ever looked at a friend through a goldfish bowl? If not, try it—you will find that your friend appears upside down. In itself, this is not too surprising. What is surprising, however, is that your own eyes bend light rather like a goldfish bowl does. That is to say, although the image of an object lands upright on your cornea, it does a vertical flip within your eye, and reaches your retina upside down. Nonetheless, you do not normally perceive your friends to be hanging by their feet from the ground above. There is consequently a contradiction between how things are in the world and how they are presented to your visual system. This contradiction is brought out even more clearly by the following remarkable fact: If people wear special goggles that invert their field of vision, they start to see the world the right way up again after a few days (Stratton, 1897). Somehow, regardless of how the world actually is, the visual system is determined to make vertical sense of it.

Findings like these carry a profound implication: Our visual system does not simply reflect external reality but rather actively constructs it. Other neurological evidence supports this curious idea. Consider, for example, what happens when different parts of the occipital cortex (the outer layer of the brain toward the back of the head) are damaged. Several types of specific visual deficit then occur, many of an exceedingly odd character. Some brain-damaged patients cannot name objects that they can draw; others cannot draw objects that they can name; and still others cannot see the movement of objects that they can both name and draw (Blakemore, 1988). Normal perception, then, would appear to depend on distinct brain circuits making specialized interpretations of the world around us and weaving them together into a coherent fabric.

News of this constructive process comes as a surprise to anyone unacquainted with the science of vision. The reason is straightforward: We are not naturally aware of all the preparatory work that the brain does to produce a perception. We are only aware of the final result. The extent to which our unified experience is put together behind the scenes emerges solely under rare or artificial circumstances. Then, the limitations of our everyday intuitions are exposed, and we find ourselves grappling with the possibility that we see the world not as it is, but as we are.

The thesis of this chapter is that what is true of the visual system in particular is true of our mind in general. Our understanding of the outer world and everything in it—objects, people, groups—is a psychological construction. It is not a literal reflection of things as they are in themselves. Nevertheless, we mostly go about our lives assuming that it is, blithely endorsing what is called *naive realism*. As a result, we often fail to recognize that how we see things is often not how others do. For example, we generally tend to overestimate how likely others are to share our own beliefs, values, and habits—the so-called *false consensus effect* (Marks & Miller, 1987; Ross, Greene, & House, 1977).

The point is that, if conscious understanding is a psychological construction, we are not directly aware of the process itself. We can only infer that it is taking place by relying on indirect kinds of evidence, of the sort yielded by scientific investigation. A concise way of expressing the situation is that we are aware of the *products* of our mind (e.g., beliefs, feelings, desires, and judgments) but not of the *processes* that give rise to them. A major goal of social psychology is to characterize these processes by finding links between what goes on in the world and what goes on inside our heads.

Consider a commonplace activity that requires conscious understanding: the act of *explaining* your own thoughts and deeds. You might conclude, for example, that you nagged your boyfriend because you had a stressful day at work, or that a humorous movie put you in good mood, or that a childhood experience piqued your interest in psychology. Such explanations, as varied as they are, have one thing in common: They all refer to *causal factors* that you are aware of and can understand. This being so, a deep question arises: If much of mental life is invisibly constructed behind the scenes, how can we be sure that our everyday explanations are correct? Might not our limited awareness prevent us from grasping the real explanations?

Now suppose you wished to *test* whether our everyday explanations were correct or not. How would you proceed? Well, you would need to satisfy two criteria. First, you would need to show, beyond reasonable doubt, that some factor did (or did not) influence people's thoughts or actions. Second, you would need to show that, when explicitly questioned about this factor, people did not (or did) believe they had been influenced by it.

Imagine a simple psychology experiment in which participants are shown a photograph of a woman. Their task is to form an impression of her intelligence. There are two conditions. In one, the woman's hair is dyed black; in the other, it is dyed brown (everything else about the woman remains the same). Suppose it turns out that the woman with black hair is—for whatever reason— judged to be *dumber*. This would prove that hair color influenced participants' impressions. Suppose too that all participants, when later asked if hair color influenced their impressions, replied that it did *not*. This would prove that participants lacked conscious access to the mental processes underlying the formation of their impressions.

You would probably be surprised if black-haired women really were judged to be dumber than brunettes. However, if, in a variant of this experiment, blondes were judged to be dumber than brunettes, you would probably be less surprised. This is because, in Western society at least, everybody is familiar with the "dumb blonde" stereotype, and expects it to influence impressions. However, because there is no corresponding stereotype of dumb women with black hair, no one expects it to influence impressions. The point we wish to bring out here is that you may rely on commonplace stereotypes to predict the outcome of a hypothetical hair-color experiment. As a consequence, the accuracy of your predictions would depend on the accuracy of those stereotypes.

Indeed, the possibility arises that all people *ever* do when they explain their own thoughts and actions is to consult *intuitive theories* of what makes people tick—theories that are widely shared within a culture. (Stereotypes are one kind of intuitive theory.) It may seem as if we are *introspecting*—that is, reflectively looking "inwards"—to discover directly how our minds work; but we may actually just be drawing on those intuitive theories. It follows that the correctness of the explanations would depend solely on the correctness of those intuitive theories. Introspection itself would not *add* to self-knowledge.

Another interesting implication is this. Whether or not people had a thought or performed an action *themselves* would have little bearing on the correctness of their explanation for why they did so. *Observers*, to whom the provoking situation is merely described, would arrive at the same explanation as *subjects*, who experience the situation for themselves. This is because both observers and subjects would share the *same* intuitive theories, and it is these theories that would inform their explanations, not insights based on their own personal experience. For example, in the hair-color experiment mentioned previously, subjects who actually formed an impression of the woman, and observers to whom the experiment was merely described, would come to very similar conclusions about why the subjects had formed the impression that they did.

Social psychologists Nisbett and Bellows (1977) conducted a more complex experiment based upon the above logic. As you read the following details, keep in mind the researchers' two goals. The first was to show that people's verbal explanations for their mental processes are often mistaken. The second was to show that these mistaken verbal explanations are derived from widely shared intuitive theories.

What They Did

A total of 162 female university students participated. These were divided into two groups. First, 128 served as subjects. They were placed in a scenario where they received several items of information about a target person, and formed an impression of her. Second, 34 participants served as observers on the sidelines. These participants had the scenario described to them briefly. They were asked to guess what sorts of impressions they would have formed had they themselves been presented with the same items of information.

More specifically, the 128 subjects were asked to judge whether a young woman named Jill had the personality traits needed to become a staff member at a crisis center. (The scenario seemed real but was actually fictitious.) Each subject was handed an application folder containing three pages of information about Jill. The information was supposedly derived from three sources: an interview, a questionnaire, and a letter of recommendation. The portrait of Jill that emerged was of a well-adjusted and competent person, who could nonetheless be a little cool and aloof.

Against the background of all this personal data—which gave the study the appearance of realism—five of Jill's attributes were systematically varied. She was described as having, or as not having, each of the following: an attractive appearance; good academic credentials; a car accident some years earlier; the opportunity to meet participants in the near future; and the misfortune to accidentally spill coffee over an interviewer's desk. Each of these attributes was ascribed to Jill exactly half of the time, albeit in a rather complex way. In particular, the presence or absence of any one of Jill's five attributes was made independent of the presence or absence of any other. Why so? Because if the researchers had merely, say, led half the subjects to believe that Jill had all five attributes, and the other half to believe she had none, they would not have been able to rule out the possibility that any results obtained, for each of the five attributes, depended on the presence or absence of some combination of the remaining four. Hence, the researcher employed a *factorial* design, in which every possible combination of Jill possessing and not possessing each of the five attributes was featured (32 possible combinations!). Again, this prevented the effects of any attribute being *confounded* (mixed up with) the effects of any other. The upshot was that each participant received one of 32 descriptions of Jill.

Once subjects had finished reading the contents of the folder, they gave their opinions about how suitable a crisis center employee Jill would make. In particular, subjects rated how much Jill exhibited the following four traits: sympathy, flexibility, likability, and intelligence. Directly afterwards, subjects rated on 7-point scales how much they believed each of Jill's attributes had influenced their ratings of each of her traits. The researchers could now compare the actual impact of Jill's attributes on subjects' impressions to subjects' own judgments of their impact. *Actual impact* was indexed by subtracting subjects' average ratings of Jill when each attribute was present from their average ratings of her when that attribute was absent. *Judged impact* was indexed by taking subjects' average ratings of each attribute's impact when it was present.

The 34 observers, in contrast, only had the experimental scenario described to them (much as we have described it to you). They were asked to imagine having had access to information about a young female job candidate, and to estimate how their opinion of her *would* have shifted if she had possessed each of the five attributes systematically manipulated in the experiment. This was essentially a parallel index of judged impact. Observers responded using the same 7-point scales as subjects. This made the ratings given by the two groups—the subjects and the observers—directly comparable.

What They Found

As predicted, participants who served as subjects were largely mistaken about the impact that Jill's five attributes had on their impressions of her. For example, subjects who read that Jill had once been involved in a serious car accident claimed that the event had made them view her as a more sympathetic person. However, according to the ratings they later gave, this event had exerted no impact whatsoever. Conversely, subjects claimed that the prospect of meeting Jill had exerted little if any impact on their judgments of how sympathetic she was. However, subjects' later ratings revealed that the impact of this factor had been substantial. Much the same results were found for the ratings of Jill's flexibility and likability. Indeed, on 6 of 20 occasions, participants' ratings on average shifted in the *opposite* direction to that in which they on average believed they had. Thus, participants' perceptions of how their judgments of Jill had been swayed, and how their judgments of her actually had been swayed, bore little relation to one another.

The only exception pertained to ratings of Jill's intelligence. Here, an almost perfect correlation emerged between how subjects' judgments had actually shifted and how much they believed they had shifted. Why so? The researchers argued that there are explicit rules, widely known throughout a culture, for ascribing intelligence to people. Because subjects could readily recognize whether a given factor was relevant to intelligence, they could reliably guess whether they would have taken it into consideration, and therefore whether it would have had an impact on their judgments. In contrast, the rules for ascribing fuzzier traits like flexibility are ill-defined or absent. Hence, subjects had no sound basis for guessing whether a given factor had exerted an impact on their judgments in these cases. Introspection could not remedy the deficiency.

If subjects were generally unable to figure out how their judgments had been shaped, how did observers fare? As it turned out, they fared no better or worse than subjects themselves. The determinations of subjects and observers coincided almost exactly (Figure 14). This is quite remarkable given the obvious differences between the concrete judgmental task that subjects engaged in and the abstract scenario that observers read about. It provides powerful support for the hypothesis that people's ideas about how their minds work stem not from private insights but from public knowledge. Unfortunately, however, this public knowledge is often not accurate. It is based on intuitive theories, widely shared throughout society, that are often mistaken.

So What?

The significance of the present study can be brought out by drawing a distinction between two types of knowledge: *familiarity* and *expertise*. Consider a patient who suffers from a disease and the physician who treats him. The patient is familiar with the disease, being personally afflicted by it. In this sense, he might be said to "know" the disease better than the physician. Nonetheless, the patient's intimate acquaintance with the disease does not provide him with deep knowledge of how the disease developed, how it will progress, or how it should be treated. Yet the physician, who may never have suffered from that disease, is liable to be adept at understanding and treating it. In other words, when it comes to the body, familiarity does not guarantee expertise,

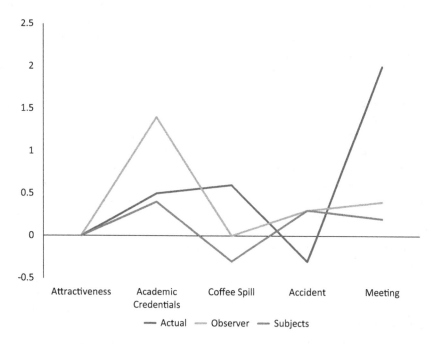

Figure 14 The actual effects of Jill's five attributes on subjects' judgments of her flexibility, and what subjects and observers judged those effects to be

nor is it even required for it. The same is true, we would argue, when it comes to the mind. The bare experience of, say, making a judgment, does not make someone an expert on the factors that shaped it. Moreover, someone who never made that judgment could nonetheless be such an expert. In the present study, for example, subjects were unable to determine how Jill's attributes had influenced their ratings, despite being familiar with what it was like to rate her suitability for a job. In contrast, the researchers, despite being unfamiliar with what it was like to rate her suitability for a job, were able to determine—by means of experimentation—how Jill's attributes had influenced subjects' ratings.

The upshot is that we are more of a mystery to ourselves than we realize. That is why social psychology exists as an objective science. It seeks to illuminate—by theorizing, measuring, and experimenting—how the human mind operates within the social world. Many of its most provocative discoveries would never have been unearthed by introspection alone. For example, have you ever suspected that engaging in an activity for a reward makes you enjoy it less? That you initially believe every statement that you comprehend? That changing your mind causes you to forget the opinions you held earlier? That common belief in free will is motivated by the desire to hold others morally responsible and to justify punishing criminals? Probably not, even though you are undoubtedly familiar with receiving rewards, comprehending statements, holding opinions, and the belief in free will. (See Chapters 9, 20, 21, and 29, respectively.)

The notion that real reasons for our thoughts and actions defy everyday understanding is, of course, hardly new. Psychoanalysts have long contended that much of what we think and do is *unconsciously* caused. Social psychologists agree that the real causes of behavior are often unconscious. However, they disagree about where they are to be located. Instead of locating them solely within the person, they also tend to locate them outside the person. So, whereas a psychoanalyst might explain war in terms of a largely unconscious death instinct, a social psychologist might do so in terms of social pressures to conform or obey (see Chapters 1 and 4), or people's penchant for identifying with their ingroup (see Chapter 7 and 11). Of course, social psychologists do not dismiss person-based explanations altogether; on the contrary, they recognize the continual interplay between an individual's personality and the social world. However, they are nonetheless apt to point out subtle aspects of situations that exert a surprisingly powerful impact (see, for example, Chapter 8).

The failure of introspection to detect social influence has been documented many times (Nisbett & Wilson, 1977a; Wilson & Stone, 1985). Consider the following study, which investigated people's awareness of the *halo effect*—the tendency for feelings about one thing to influence feelings about something else associated with it. Participants watched different videos of a college instructor who spoke with a pronounced Belgian accent. On one video, seen by half the participants, the instructor came across as warm, engaging, and likeable. On a second video, seen by the remaining half, he came across as cold, aloof, and unsympathetic. All participants then rated how appealing they found three specific features of the instructor, namely, his appearance, mannerisms, and accent. Note that these specific features remained the *same* regardless of his general demeanor (warm or cold). Nevertheless, participants regarded the instructor's appearance, mannerisms, and accent more favorably when his general demeanor was pleasant than when it was unpleasant. Moreover, participants were completely unaware that the instructor's general demeanor had shaped their opinion of his specific features. In fact, they reported exactly the opposite—that his specific features had shaped their opinion of his general demeanor (Nisbett & Wilson, 1977b).

The tendency to explain psychological states in terms of the wrong antecedent—*misattribution*—takes many forms. Some of these are as amusing are they are informative. In one study, male participants watched an erotic video (all for the sake of science, no doubt!). Before watching it, some did nothing, some exercised vigorously, and some exercised vigorously and then waited awhile. It turned out that participants in this last group later reported being most turned on by the video. The reason? Exercising had heightened participants' arousal, but because several minutes had passed, they no longer attributed that arousal to the exercise, but rather to the video, which happened to be the most noticeable stimulus in their environment (Cantor, Zillman, & Bryant, 1975). So, if you wish to use misattribution to your personal advantage, here is a suggestion: Bring your date to a scary movie, or on a rollercoaster ride. Then be sure to wait for a few minutes. Finally, make your move. With any luck, your unsuspecting date will misattribute his or her still-elevated arousal to you!

Our lack of introspective insight can also prevent us from recognizing how irrational our judgments can be. Consider, for example, the *above-average* bias. It is well established that most of us rate ourselves more favorably than is warranted on a variety of broadly desirable traits (Alicke & Govorun, 2005). Yet, most of us also consider ourselves better than our peers at avoiding this above-average bias, thereby ironically confirming its existence (Pronin, Lin, & Ross, 2002). Thus, we believe that our own perceptions of superiority are factually justified whereas those of our peers are the product of vanity.

In closing this section, we would like to briefly address two criticisms that have been leveled at the present study and others like it. The first begins by noting that there are always several valid explanations for what people think or do. As a result, when the explanations of researchers and participants conflict, it is not the participants who are mistaken, but the researchers, who have adopted too narrow a view of what constitutes a valid explanation. Admittedly, it is true that any thought or action can have multiple explanations and that these need not exclude one another. For example, my writing this chapter can be simultaneously explained in terms of personal motivation (sharing social psychology), economic reality (meeting market demand), or brain science (activated frontal cortex). However, what this criticism overlooks is that participants are not just theorizing at their leisure; they are asked specific questions about factors that have been experimentally proven to affect them. Whatever other valid explanations participants may privately entertain, they are still demonstrably mistaken about the impact of the factors they are questioned about.

The second criticism is that the accuracy of participants' verbal reports is misleadingly compromised by two cognitive defects: an inability to remember what factors affected them and an inability to articulate them. This criticism fails on two counts. First, it is not a sufficient explanation for the inaccuracy of verbal reports. The near-perfect match between the verbal reports of subjects and observers, for example, indicates people's overwhelming reliance on intuitive theories. Second, the criticism seems not so much to argue for the potential accuracy of verbal reports as to describe some additional reasons why they might be inaccurate. Poor memory and self-expression are further reasons to believe that people's verbal reports are likely to be wide of the mark.

Afterthoughts

Might our introspective insight into ourselves be more limited still? Could we be mistaken about what our true thoughts, feelings, and desires *are*, not merely what causes them? Freud certainly thought so. Unfortunately, his accounts of our hidden obsessions (e.g., lusting after our own mothers) were more brilliant than believable. Unawareness of our true selves may amount, more modestly, to something like the following. Although we may know for sure what thoughts, feelings, and desires we currently experience, we may still be mistaken about how long they will last or how typical they are of us (Gilbert, Pinel, Wilson, Blumberg, & Wheatley, 1998). That is, we may think that the contents of our consciousness reflect deep and abiding dispositions, but they turn out to be mere fleeting fancies, entertained one day, but forgotten the next.

Consider how we truly know that we love our romantic partner. Our immediate feelings may sometimes convince us that we do. But there are other occasions on which we recognize the need for a more objective appraisal (Bem, 1967). Have we behaved toward our partner like a lover is supposed to? Are we prepared to live with them for the rest of our lives? What is true love, anyhow? The answers to these questions are not subjectively obvious.

Now consider again what happens whenever we ask ourselves why we think and act the way we do. We come up with reasons that, as we have seen, are often erroneous. However, having come up with them, we may also use them as a source of information about our thoughts and actions. Unfortunately, the thoughts and actions implied by these reasons may not be the ones we have an underlying disposition to experience. Hence, the very act of explaining ourselves can put us out of touch with who we really are.

One indication that this is so is that the act of engaging in introspection undermines the link between what we say and what we do (Wilson, Dunn, Kraft, & Lisle, 1989). In one study, participants reported how they felt about their romantic partners. The correlation between the feelings they expressed and the ultimate fate of the relationship was then assessed. Normally, a reasonable correlation between the two was observed: Participants who liked their partner stayed with him or her, whereas those who did not, left. However, if participants had first asked themselves why they liked their romantic partners, then no correlation was observed. Introspection evidently disrupted participants' accurate perception of their underlying levels of love for their partner (Wilson & Kraft, 1993).

The pitfalls of introspection do not stop there. Based on the reasons we come up with, we may also make decisions. However, because these decisions fail to take account of our underlying dispositions, we may be setting ourselves up for disappointment. This possibility was nicely illustrated in another study (Wilson, Lisle, Schooler, Hodges, Klaaren, & LaFleur, 1993). Participants began by viewing posters depicting either fine art or pop art. Afterwards, some participants, but not others, wrote down reasons for why they liked or disliked each poster. All participants then rated how much they liked each poster. Next, participants were given the opportunity to privately choose one surplus poster to take home with them. Finally, 3 weeks later, the researchers telephoned participants to find out how satisfied they were with their chosen poster. Results showed that, normally, participants overwhelmingly preferred the fine art posters. However, if participants had first asked themselves why they liked the posters, they reported liking both types of posters about equally. In addition, those who had engaged in introspection reported being less satisfied with their poster at follow-up. Apparently, introspection had temporarily overridden participants' disposition to prefer fine art. However, this disposition had reasserted itself, leading them to ultimately regret their choice of a pop art poster. Note, however, that the disruptive effects of introspection are limited to circumstances where people are uncertain of their own attitudes: Strongly held attitudes are immune to self-reflective distortion (Wilson et al., 1989).

The general implication is that, given how poor we are at explaining our own behavior, introspection may hinder rather than help us acquire accurate self-knowledge. So, rather than get bogged down in unproductive navel-gazing, we might be better off exposing ourselves to a variety of circumstances and observing how we respond in each. This would enable us to compare our responses and thereby make informed guesses about what causes us to think and act in different ways. (Note that participants in the present study did not have this luxury; they had to determine how their attitudes toward Jill were determined by a unique set of circumstances and attributes.) Perhaps this is why travel broadens the mind: The environment is always changing, making it possible to observe a range of responses. This raises the intriguing possibility that backpacking across a distant continent may tell us more about ourselves than a year on a psychoanalyst's couch.

Revelation

The fact that we are aware of our own beliefs, feelings, and desires does not automatically make us experts on where they come from. Introspection is an unreliable guide to how the mind works, reflecting cultural truisms rather than providing infallible insights.

What Do You Think?

Here is a paradox. You have a set of beliefs about yourself. However, you also know that your self-knowledge is imperfect. Hence, you believe that some of your beliefs about yourself are false. But, by virtue of holding those beliefs about yourself, you must believe they are true. So you must regard some of your beliefs about yourself as both true and false. How is that possible? Also, how does one best gain insights into his or her innermost self, and how is such self-knowledge beneficial?

Chapter Reference

Nisbett, R. E., & Bellows, N. (1977). Verbal reports about causal influences on social judgments: Private access versus public theories. *Journal of Personality and Social Psychology, 35,* 613–624.

Other References

Alicke, M. D., & Govorun, O. (2005). The better-than-average effect. In M. D. Alicke, D. Dunning, & J. Krueger (Eds.), *The self in social judgment* (pp. 85–106). New York: Psychology Press.

Bem, D. J. (1967). Self-perception: An alternative interpretation of cognitive dissonance phenomena. *Psychological Review, 74,* 183–200.

Blakemore, C. (1988). *The mind machine.* London: BBC Books.

Cantor, J. R., Zillman, D., & Bryant, J. (1975). Enhancement of experienced sexual arousal in response to erotic stimuli through misattribution of unrelated residual excitation. *Journal of Personality and Social Psychology, 32*, 69–75.

Gilbert, D. T., Pinel, E. C., Wilson, T. D., Blumberg, S. J., & Wheatley, T. P. (1998). Immune neglect: A source of durability bias in affective forecasting. *Journal of Personality and Social Psychology, 75*, 617–638.

Marks, G., & Miller, N. (1987). Ten years of research on the false-consensus effect: An empirical and theoretical review. *Psychological Bulletin, 102*, 72–90. doi:10.1037/0033-2909.102.1.72

Nisbett, R. E., & Wilson, T. D. (1977a). Telling more than we can know: Verbal reports on mental processes. *Psychological Review, 84*, 231–259.

Nisbett, R. E., & Wilson, T. D. (1977b). The halo effect: Evidence for the unconscious alteration of judgments. *Journal of Personality and Social Psychology, 35*, 250–256.

Pronin, E., Lin, D. Y., & Ross, L. (2002). The bias blind spot: Perceptions of bias in self versus others. *Personality and Social Psychology Bulletin, 28*, 369–381.

Ross, L., Greene, D., & House, P. (1977). The false consensus phenomenon: An attributional bias in self-perception and social-perception processes. *Journal of Experimental Social Psychology, 13*, 279–301.

Stratton, G. M. (1897). Vision without inversion of the retinal image. *Psychological Review, 4*, 441–481.

Wilson, T. D., Dunn, D. S., Kraft, D., & Lisle, D. J. (1989). Introspection, attitude change, and attitude-behavior consistency: The disruptive effects of explaining why we feel the way we do. *Advances in Experimental Social Psychology, 22*, 287–343.

Wilson, T. D., & Kraft, D. (1993). Why do I love thee? Effects of repeated introspections about a dating relationship on attitudes toward the relationship. *Personality and Social Psychology Bulletin, 19*, 409–418.

Wilson, T. D., Lisle, D. J., Schooler, J. W., Hodges, S. D., Klaaren, K. J., & LaFleur, S. J. (1993). Introspecting about reasons can reduce post-choice satisfaction. *Personality and Social Psychology Bulletin, 19*, 409–418.

Wilson, T. D., & Stone, J. I. (1985). Limitations of self-knowledge: More on telling more than we can know. In P. Shaver (Ed.), *Review of personality and social psychology* (Vol. 6, pp. 167–183). Beverly Hills, CA: Sage.

More to Explore

Vazire, S., & Wilson, T. D. (Eds.). (2012). *Handbook of self knowledge*. New York: Guilford Press.

15 What Did You Expect?

The Behavioral Confirmation of the Physical Attractiveness Stereotype

> "Imaginations which people have of one another are the solid facts of society."
> —Charles Horton Cooley (1864–1929), American sociologist

Background

In George Bernard Shaw's celebrated play, *Pygmalion*, a raffish flower girl, Eliza Doolittle, is progressively transformed into a well-spoken lady, as she gradually meets the expectations of her snobby tutor, Professor Henry Higgins. In social psychology, this "Pygmalion effect" is more commonly called the *self-fulfilling prophecy*. According to Merton (1948):

> The self-fulfilling prophecy is, in the beginning, a false definition of the situation evoking a new behavior which makes the originally *false* conception come true. The specious validity of the self-fulfilling prophecy perpetuates a reign of error. For the prophet will cite the actual course of events as proof that he was right from the beginning.
>
> (p. 195)

The dynamics of the self-fulfilling prophecy typically involve *behavioral confirmation*, which Darley and Fazio (1980) described as a sequence that begins when a perceiver forms an expectation about a person, and then acts toward that person based on the expectation. The target person then interprets the perceiver's actions, and responds in a way that is consistent with the perceiver's expectation. Finally, the perceiver, based on the target's actions, continues to harbor the expectation, apparently confirmed. It is a chain reaction—one that occurs in a variety of social contexts.

For instance, introduce a guest speaker (without his knowledge) as "warm and friendly" and you will motivate the audience to express interest, which will then inspire the speaker to give a more animated, eloquent talk. But introduce him as a bit "cold and unfriendly" and you will produce an unsympathetic and reserved audience, which will, in turn, cause the speaker to give a cautious, lackluster talk. This is basically what Kelley (1950) found.

Or, randomly pull the names of some 1st and 2nd graders out of a hat and tell a teacher (who does not know the children) that, based on results from the "Harvard Test of Inflected Acquisition" (there really is no such test), those particular kids are on the verge of a substantial IQ spurt (even though the children are actually no different from other children). The teacher will then give them more attention in class, challenging work, detailed feedback, and emotional support. Eight months later, they will show greater progress than their peers, in terms of improved schoolwork (as appraised by the teachers) and higher IQ gains (on objective tests). This is basically what Rosenthal and Jacobson (1968) found. (However, see Jussim & Harber, 2005, for a more understated perspective on self-fulfilling prophecies in the classroom.)

Or, while interviewing a job applicant, whose ethnicity would "blend in nicely" with the rest of the company, sit close and make attentive eye contact with her, and ask questions that probe for positive information. She will then perform in a self-assured, bubbly manner, leading you to confidently announce that "She's just right for the position!" Alternatively, perhaps because the candidate's ethnicity would "stand out like a sore thumb," sit at a more professional distance, let her do the talking (after all, she's the one being interviewed), and ask questions that turn up uncomplimentary information. She will then perform in a more nervous, uninspired manner. This is similar to what Word, Zanna, and Cooper (1974) found.

Let us discuss this last study in more detail. Word and his colleagues had White participants interview White and Black job applicants. The applicants were actually trained *confederates* (individuals cooperating with the experimenter) who behaved according to a set script. Their verbal and nonverbal behaviors were practiced so as not to vary. The participants thought the researchers were studying the behaviors of the applicants, when in fact it was the interviewers (the participants themselves) who were being analyzed (a convincing *cover story* put participants of the scent). Interviewers were found to lean more toward, make more eye contact with, and say nicer things to the White applicants. They gave briefer interviews to, and sat further away from, the Black candidates. Having demonstrated this apparent racial discrimination, Word and his colleagues then trained interviewers to act accordingly—either warmly or coolly—toward White research participants playing the role of job applicants. Ratings by independent judges found that the White applicants performed more competently when they received the warm treatment, and less competently when they were treated as the Black applicants had previously been treated. (It is likewise significant that research confederates in Houston, Texas wearing "Gay and Proud" caps were treated more abruptly and negatively by job interviewers compared to confederates wearing "Texan and Proud" caps; Hebl, Foster, Mannix, and Dovidio, 2002. How might such treatment affect gay job applicants in real life situations?)

In all of these examples, behavior is reciprocated. Positive acts prompt positive responses and negative acts prompt negative ones. As a result, the perceiver retains his or her impression of the target person. Moreover, the target person may even come to internalize the perceiver's evaluation, especially if the perceiver is important to the target. "It's true what they think of me."

Snyder, Tanke, and Berscheid (1977) provided a classic experimental demonstration of behavioral confirmation. Surveying the field in the mid-1970s, they noted that social psychologists had been focusing too exclusively on cognition. A lot had been learned about the machinery of social cognition—for example, about how people explain their own or others' behaviors by attributing it to internal or external factors, and how people infer traits, from others' acts. Yet so far comparatively little was known about the *consequences* of attributions, impressions, expectations, and the like. Although research had documented how we cognitively bolster or protect the stereotypes we possess (overestimating the frequency of supportive examples, filling in informational gaps, interpreting ambiguous information as being consistent with our generalizations), not enough research had investigated how our perceptions shape our behaviors in actual encounters with others, and their behaviors in turn. Therefore, Snyder and his colleagues sought to remedy this defect.

In order to do this, they focused on the *physical attractiveness stereotype*: Beautiful people are supposedly good people (Dion, Berscheid, & Walster, 1972). If you show people three photos, one of a very attractive person, one of a so-so person, and one of an unattractive person, you will find that they tend to rate the persons quite differently. Physically attractive people are generally judged to possess more positive personality traits, hold more prestigious jobs, and be happier in their professional and social lives. (Okay, there is a slight downside too: They are also judged to be more vain, narcissistic, and unfaithful to their spouses.) Snyder and his colleagues chose the physical attractiveness stereotype because it is potent and because it is based—like gender, age, and race stereotypes—on superficial features that are easy to experimentally manipulate and present to others incidentally.

What They Did

Snyder and his colleagues (1977) sought to design a study that would mirror the way impressions are spontaneously formed and come to influence people's behaviors in everyday life. That is, they wanted their study to have *ecological validity*—to mimic the sorts of things people do and experience daily. (Although see Chapter 6, and the Introduction, for why ecological validity is not the be-all and end-all of experimental research.)

One hundred and two University of Minnesota students (an equal number of males and females) participated in the study. It was described as focusing on how people become acquainted through interactions that either do or do not involve nonverbal communication. This *cover story* provided a rationale for having unacquainted males and females arrive at separate rooms and have a telephone conversation that they agreed could be recorded. As part of this ruse, participants provided information about themselves, such as their academic major. They were each told that a folder of such information would be given to their partner to help jumpstart their conversation. Inserted unobtrusively into the folder given to each male was a photo allegedly of the female. In addition, a photo was taken of the male, consistent with the false claim that it would be given to his female partner. However, nothing about photos was ever mentioned and no photo was ever shown to the female participants.

The photo that each male participant received was drawn from a set provided by young women from nearby colleges who had posed to the tune of $5 (equivalent to $20 circa 2017). These photos had been rated by a separate group of college-age men as being very attractive (average rating of 8.1 on a 10-point scale: definite hottie territory) or very unattractive (average rating of 2.6: bad hair day, perhaps). (Ethics note: The women providing the photos all had consented in writing to the use of their pictures for research purposes. Moreover, none were informed of the attractiveness ratings they later received.) Thus, each male was tricked into believing that he would be conversing with either a near bombshell or a Plain Jane. In order to determine how much the photos shaped stereotypic impressions, Snyder and his colleagues had each male rate the particular female he was about to converse with on each of 27 personality traits (such as friendliness, enthusiasm, and trustworthiness). Keep in mind that their impressions would be based on the totality of information they had received in the folder, not just the experimentally manipulated photograph.

The male and female of each pair then engaged in a 10-minute, get-acquainted conversation, speaking though microphones and listening through headphones from separate rooms. (Three of the 51 conversations had to be interrupted and the participants immediately debriefed, because the males started commenting on the photos, perhaps saying "I'm noticing your big beautiful eyes and nice smile . . . like to go on a date?" This is technically known as participant attrition.) Afterward, the males again indicated their impressions of their partners on various trait dimensions, while the females rated themselves on the same dimensions and also indicated how comfortable they felt during their conversations, how physically attractive they believed their partners thought they were, and how much they thought their partners treated them the way males typically do. Finally, the male and female participants were carefully debriefed—an especially important step since the experimenter had deceived them.

Following this phase of the study, independent judges—who did not know the physical attractiveness of the males, the actual or perceived physical attractiveness of the females, or the hypotheses of the study—listened to the tracks of the tape-recorded conversations containing only the females' voices or only the males' voices. The judges rated how animated and enthusiastic the women and men each were, how intimate and personal their conversations were, and so on, allowing Snyder and his collaborators to examine in detail the process of behavioral confirmation.

What They Found

The males did indeed associate physical attractiveness with desirable personality characteristics (based on their ratings after being exposed to the photos, but before the actual conversations). The alleged attractive women were imagined to be relatively friendly, humorous, poised, and socially skilled. In contrast, the alleged unattractive women were imagined to be relatively unfriendly, serious, awkward, and socially inept. So far, so good: The experimental manipulation created the expected impressions (ones consistent with the physical attractiveness stereotype).

Furthermore, the men who talked with presumed attractive women were judged by those examining the tape-recorded conversations to be relatively bold, sociable, humorous, animated, confident, and sexually warm compared with their counterparts who chatted with the presumed unattractive women. Thus, the experiment not only changed the men's impressions of the women, it also changed their behavioral responses to the women, based on those impressions.

Finally, the most striking result: The judges rated the alleged attractive women as being more poised, animated, sociable, and sexually warm than they did the alleged unattractive women. (Remember, there is no reason to believe, given random assignment, that the two groups of women should have differed in actual attractiveness.) Importantly, on trait dimensions unrelated to the physical attractiveness stereotype, such as intelligence or sensitivity, no differences were found across the two conditions (Figure 15). Thus, all the elements of behavioral confirmation were found. Erroneous initial impressions and generalizations on the part of the males led to changes in their behaviors and to corresponding changes in the females' behaviors.

Snyder and his colleagues attempted to isolate *mediators* (more proximal causal factors) of the behavioral confirmation they found. They surmised that the degree of friendliness displayed

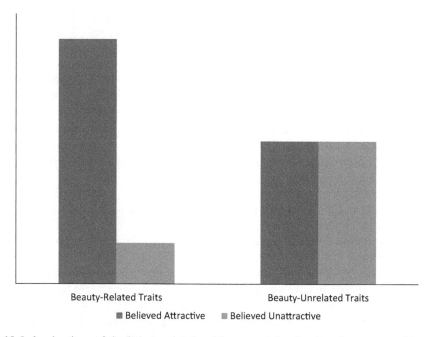

Figure 15 Judges' ratings of the beauty-related and beauty-unrelated traits of women speaking over an intercom to male participants who had been led to believe the women were attractive or unattractive. (*Note*: The figure is schematic because no means were provided in the orginal article.)

by the male perceivers was the key factor in evoking reciprocal friendliness in the target women (although friendliness per se was never actually measured). The ratings they obtained revealed that women thought to be attractive regarded their partners' images of them as being more accurate (even though they had no knowledge that those images were being influenced by photos of other women). Alleged attractive women also indicated that they regarded their partners' manner of interacting with them as being more typical of how men usually treated them. These perceptions perhaps help to explain why the women believed to be attractive responded so warmly to their male partners' friendly overtures. The presumed homely women had a cooler, more aloof reaction perhaps because it seemed to them that their partners had misperceived them and treated them in an unusually standoffish manner.

So What?

Snyder and his colleagues (1977) demonstrated important potential outcomes of stereotypic impressions. The young men's expectations governed their self-presentations, which induced female counterparts to behave accordingly. The men created the very behaviors they expected to encounter! The critical feature of the study was remarkably subtle: A photo was inconspicuously slipped into an information folder that males glanced through before striking up a phone conversation. Of course, the process would be more complicated in the "real world." There, expectations and behaviors would likely occur in both directions. The women would have expectations of their own, generating behaviors that would mold the behaviors of the men as well. Behavioral confirmation, where it occurred, would likely do so in a back-and-forth manner. The physical attractiveness stereotype would also normally overlap with other stereotypes, such as those pertaining to gender, age, social class, race, or ethnicity. In everyday life, it is often a confluence of impressions that evoke behaviors and responses to those behaviors.

Snyder and his colleagues (1977) demonstrated that initially mistaken expectations, based on commonplace stereotypes, can inadvertently turn those expectations into behavioral reality, in the context of an interpersonal interaction where those stereotypes apply. True, the researchers only demonstrated this under a restricted set of conditions. Hence, the results need not necessarily generalize to any given context. After all, there would be a lot more going on in the real world, and hence an abundance of additional factors could either facilitate or impede behavioral confirmation. But this is to miss the significance of the demonstration. Snyder et al. (1977) documented that behavioral confirmation *could* occur as a function of attractiveness stereotypes. Before their study, direct evidence of this was circumstantial.

Snyder and Swann (1978) demonstrated a similar dynamic in a study involving conversations between strangers. One member of each pair was led to believe that the other member was either hostile (likes contact sports; is insensitive and cruel) or non-hostile (likes poetry and sailing; is kind and cooperative). Judges evaluating the conversations found that partners randomly described as hostile ended up showing more hostility. Furthermore, when the presumed hostile and non-hostile persons conversed with new partners, who had no set expectations of them, the chain of events persisted—persons previously presumed to be either hostile or non-hostile maintained their demeanor.

Several other studies document behavioral confirmation. One by Curtis and Miller (1986) showed that if you merely believe that another person likes you, you might try to validate his or her reasons for liking you by behaving in a likable manner, which will cause him or her to, in reality, like you. But believing that someone dislikes you might lead to the opposite: giving him or her good reasons to actually dislike you. The process is circular.

Moreover, Miller, Brickman, and Bolen (1975), noticing what litter bugs children can be, told those in a particular class that they should be neat and clean. The admonition did increase how much litter the children put into wastebaskets, but only temporarily. However, when the researchers commended the children for *being* neat and tidy, on eight consecutive days, their environmental conscientiousness soared and persisted. "They think we're neat and clean—well, we'll show them that they're right!" Although we sometimes surrender, behaviorally, to negative labels, we also try to live up to positive ones.

Several of the foregoing studies provide good examples of what is referred to as schematic processing. A *schema* is an organized, structured set of cognitions that exerts influence over its possessor's perceptions and behaviors (it partly overlaps with the intuitive theories referred to in Chapters 14 and 21). Schemas influence how one responds to particular stimuli. One sees a pit bull, and all of his or her various thoughts about pit bulls spring to mind (including, hopefully, some that suggest caution). We have schemas related to the members of certain groups (stereotypes): Australians, TV evangelists, spelling bee champions, and so on. We also have schemas for individual people (like the schema you might have of a favorite aunt or uncle). We have schemas for particular occupations or social roles (prison guard or shaman). We even have schemas for social events (called *scripts*): weddings, restaurants, first dates, job interviews, and so forth. Scripts generally include information about what events occur, and in what sequence they occur, in given social situations. These manifold types of schemas influence inferences we draw, information we remember, and our expectations about the future. They also influence our behaviors. In the present study, the men's expectations regarding women's physical attractiveness served as schemas, influencing their behaviors, and the women's behaviors too.

When we encounter a person—a member of the Hell's Angels motorcycle club, say—our perceptions and behaviors are influenced both by our minds, filled as they are with myriad beliefs about Hell's Angels (perhaps thinking they are drug-dealing and violent), and by what we actually experience in our interaction with that person (who may unexpectedly appear law-abiding and friendly). In other words, what is outside in our environment interacts with what is inside our mind. Our preexisting thoughts do not completely determine our perceptions of reality (at least not normally), nor does reality typically influence us in a direct, unadulterated way. At times, one or the other is dominant, as when our preconceptions hold sway. This can be problematic. Though we cannot stop ourselves from believing things and thinking in generalities, we also cannot afford to harbor fallacious convictions that have no chance of being amended by incontrovertible experiences.

To be sure, schematic processing saves time and energy. You see someone that fits your homeless person, lumberjack, Muslim, or hippie-throwback schema, and that is pretty much all you may think you need to know. You are driving in a funeral procession, and that is pretty much all you may think you need to know. A script tells you what to do and how to be. You are on automatic pilot. No need to think a lot. Yet there are potential liabilities of schematic thinking, in the form of cognitive biases and errors, and inflexible modes of behavior. We may think that a person is lazy because, after all, he is "one of them" (even though he may be exceptionally hard working). We may think someone cannot handle a particular job because she is a woman (even though she may be eminently qualified for the position). We may refrain from mentioning to someone our love of the opera because that person is a supermarket butcher (even though that person is an avid patron of the fine arts). And so on: ignored information, wrong interpretations, and inaccurate predictions (see, for example, Cohen, 1981, for a good example of biased schematic processing).

The study by Snyder and his colleagues (1977) demonstrated how much one's thoughts can influence one's behaviors and how much one's behaviors can influence others' behaviors. Being told that someone is drop-dead gorgeous may turn our mental wheels in a way that affects our behavior (at least until we see the person for ourselves). Hearing that a particular person is secretive or delusional may channel our behavior so as to elicit sneaky or psychotic-like behavior from him or her. Of course, we are just as much the objects as we are the subjects of behavioral confirmation. How much of our own behavior is shaped by others' expectations?

Afterthoughts

It should be pointed out that in everyday life, unlike in the experimental laboratory, expectations are often rooted in reality (Jussim, 1991). Indeed, it has been argued that stereotype accuracy is one of the most robust and reliable effects in all of social psychology (see, for example, Jussim, Cain, Crawford, Harber, & Cohen, 2009). For example, if little Johnny has done poorly all semester, and his teacher develops warranted negative expectations about his academic capacity, it will hardly be surprising if her negative expectations end up coinciding with his future poor performance. That is, expectations can reflect reality as well as shape it. (Note that in several of the studies on behavioral confirmation mention in the "Background" section the researchers deliberately creating artificial expectations, which may be what led to such striking results in those studies.) That said, performance tends to improve, and motivation goes up, if students are encouraged to operate under the assumption that their abilities are malleable and capable of incremental improvement, rather than fixed and permanently tied to current levels of performance (Blackwell, Trzesniewski, & Dweck, 2007; Dweck, 1999).

It is also important to recognize that behavioral confirmation is far from assured in every context. If you discover that someone has cast you in a negative light, you may try to prove him or her wrong. You disagree with what you perceive is someone's impression of you, so you try to change it. For example, fervent Franklin expects tasty Tatyana to be "easy," and makes her an indecent proposal. Offended by his expectations, Tatyana kicks him in the groin, showing just how "difficult" she can be!

Nonetheless, genuine instances of behavioral confirmation remind us of two complementary themes running through social psychology. One theme is that people are quick (perhaps too quick) to attribute traits to others. Ample research has demonstrated people's fairly automatic tendency to assume that each person possesses stable, enduring traits that cause him or her to behave in a predictable manner, even across varied situations (Carlston & Skowronski, 1994; Gilbert, 1998). The other theme, iconoclastically articulated by personality psychologist Walter Mischel (1968), is that there is scant empirical evidence for pervasive cross-situational consistency in people's behavior, at least not as much as we intuitively think there is. People are not always the same in different situations; they are not as predictable as we imagine. Extroverts have their solitary days, and introverts occasionally come out of their shells.

The so-called *fundamental attribution error* involves unjustifiably attributing a person's behaviors to personality traits when situational constraints explain them better (Ross, 1977; although see Malle, 2006, and Chapter 10). However, what is interesting about the fundamental attribution error is that it is self-perpetuating. As Snyder and his colleagues (1977) explained, our believing that others possess certain traits may cause us to behave in certain consistent ways toward them. This may cause them, via behavioral confirmation, to behave in consistent ways in our presence. It is quite possibly our behaviors that are producing the consistencies in their behaviors. In others words, traits we believe exist in others may be largely due to the influence of our own consistent expectations and behaviors!

Finally, behavioral confirmation suggests a simple experiment you might try. Start by thinking the worst of the people you meet today. Believe that they are basically rotten, even when they are normally quite wholesome. See them as having malevolent ulterior motives. Give them the hard time they deserve. Let us know how they respond. Tomorrow, reverse your approach. Treat each person you meet as your best friend, someone that you have not seen for a long time and deeply miss. Lavish him or her with love and respect. Expect him or her to impress you with charm and goodness. Let us know what happens. Your findings should convince you—just as do the experimental demonstrations of social psychology—of the possibility and ready occurrence and significance of behavioral confirmation.

Revelation

Although our expectations of people are based on their behavior, it is likewise true that their behavior is the result of our expectations. Simply believing that someone is attractive may lead to their actually being attractive.

What Do You Think?

Give examples of how your expectations and resulting behaviors might have influenced others' behaviors, confirming your expectations, and of how others' expectations and resulting behaviors might have influenced your behaviors, confirming their expectations. Also, when people expect you to behave in particular way, do you feel inclined to live up to their expectations? In particular, if someone has a negative expectation of you, do you find yourselves inadvertently living up to it or rebelling against it?

Chapter Reference

Snyder, M., Tanke, E. D., & Berscheid, E. (1977). Social perception and interpersonal behavior: On the self-fulfilling nature of social stereotypes. *Journal of Personality and Social Psychology, 35*, 656–666.

Other References

Blackwell, L., Trzesniewski, K., & Dweck, C. S. (2007). Implicit theories of intelligence predict achievement across an adolescent transition: A longitudinal study and an intervention. *Child Development, 78*, 246–263.

Carlston, D. E., & Skowronski, J. J. (1994). Savings in the relearning of trait information as evidence for spontaneous inference generation. *Journal of Personality and Social Psychology, 66*, 840–856.

Cohen, C. E. (1981). Person categories and social perceptions: Testing some boundaries of the processing effects of prior knowledge. *Journal of Personality and Social Psychology, 40*, 441–452.

Curtis, R. C., & Miller, K. (1986). Believing another person likes or dislikes you: Behaviors making the beliefs come true. *Journal of Personality and Social Psychology, 51*, 284–290.

Darley, J. M., & Fazio, R. H. (1980). Expectancy confirmation processes arising in the social interaction sequence. *American Psychologist, 35*, 867–881.

Dion, K. K., Berscheid, E., & Walster, E. (1972). What is beautiful is good. *Journal of Personality and Social Psychology, 24*, 285–290.

Dweck, C. S. (1999). *Self-theories: The role in motivation, personality, and development*. Philadelphia, PA: Psychological Press.

Gilbert, D. T. (1998). Ordinary personology. In D. T. Gilbert, S. T. Fiske, & G. Lindzey (Eds.), *The handbook of social psychology* (4th ed., pp. 89–150). New York: McGraw-Hill.

Hebl, M. R., Foster, J. B., Mannix, L. M., & Dovidio, J. F. (2002). Formal and interpersonal discrimination: A field study of bias toward homosexual applicants. *Personality and Social Psychology Bulletin, 28*, 815–825.

Jussim, L. (1991). Social perception and social reality: A reflection-construction model. *Psychological Review, 98*, 54–73.

Jussim, L., Cain, T., Crawford, J., Harber, K., & Cohen, F. (2009). The unbearable accuracy of stereotypes. In T. Nelson (Ed.), *Handbook of prejudice, stereotyping, and discrimination* (pp. 199–227). Hillsdale, NJ: Erlbaum.

Jussim, L., & Harber, K. (2005). Teacher expectations and self-fulfilling prophecies: Knowns and unknowns, resolved and unresolved controversies. *Personality and Social Psychology Review, 9*, 131–155.

Kelley, H. H. (1950). The warm-cold variable in first impressions of persons. *Journal of Personality, 18*, 431–439.

Malle, B. F. (2006). The actor-observer asymmetry in attribution: A (surprising) meta-analysis. *Psychological Bulletin, 132*, 895–919.

Merton, R. (1948). The self-fulfilling prophecy. *Antioch Review, 8*, 193–210.

Miller, R. L., Brickman, P., & Bolen, D. (1975). Attribution versus persuasion as a means of modifying behavior. *Journal of Personality and Social Psychology, 31*, 430–441.

Mischel, W. (1968). *Personality and assessment*. New York: Wiley-Blackwell.

Rosenthal, R., & Jacobson, L. (1968). *Pygmalion in the classroom: Teacher expectation and pupils' intellectual development*. New York: Holt, Rinehart & Winston.

Ross, L. (1977). The intuitive psychologist and his shortcomings: Distortion in the attribution process. In L. Berkowitz (Ed.), *Advances in experimental social psychology* (Vol. 10, pp. 174–221). New York: Academic Press.

Snyder, M., & Swann, W. B., Jr. (1978). Behavioral confirmation in social interaction: From social perception to social reality. *Journal of Experimental Social Psychology, 14*, 148–162.

Word, C. O., Zanna, M. P., & Cooper, J. (1974). The nonverbal mediation of self-fulfilling prophecies in interracial interaction. *Journal of Experimental Social Psychology, 10*, 109–120.

More to Explore

Jussim, L. (2012). *Social perception and social reality: Why accuracy dominates bias and self-fulfilling prophecy*. New York: Oxford University Press.

16 The Calvinist's Conundrum

Unconsciously Engineering Good Omens

"[God] has mercy on whomever He chooses, and He hardens the heart of whomever He chooses."
—Romans 9:18, NRSV
—Saint Paul (5–67 C.E.), Apostle to the Gentiles

Background

In 16th-century France, a religious reformer named John Calvin broke away from the Catholic Church. He founded a Protestant faith whose roots lay in the teachings of Saint Paul and Saint Augustine. These saints had emphasized the absolute sovereignty of God (i.e., He was the ultimate boss) and the need for His grace (i.e., people could only be saved with His input). Calvin duly took on board these views and then pushed them as far as they would go. The result was an austere and uncompromising creed, capable of instilling much fear and trembling in its adherents.

Calvin preached that people were so inherently corrupt that nothing in their own nature could possibly make them love and worship God. He did accept, however, that some people were genuinely devout. How was this possible? The answer, according to Calvin, was that God had *predetermined* that this would be so. God had, before creating the world, decided to grant a lucky minority a special grace that would redeem them from their Original Sin (i.e., inherent wickedness), and so make it inevitable that they would worship God during their brief spell on Earth. So redeemed, these favored few—called God's Elect—would enjoy a wonderful future: an eternity in heaven with their beloved Creator. However, the vast majority of people, denied God's saving grace, would be consigned to a fearsome fate: everlasting agony in the fiery depths of hell.

What reasons did God have for deciding in advance who would be saved and who would be damned? Calvin was content to plead ignorance on this point. All that mattered, he claimed, was that God was God. Whatever He willed was good *by definition*. Still, Calvin did at least specify what God did *not* take into account: the efforts people made to live righteously. Whether or not they strove to live a life of virtue or vice had absolutely no bearing on their ultimate destiny. If people had not already been chosen by God their attempts to lead a virtuous life would come to nothing—they would roast regardless. According to Calvin, this was not unfair, because human beings were despicable to begin with, and therefore deserved to be damned. Only the receipt of God's grace could render them worthy of salvation.

Calvin's God—a master of suspense—had not seen fit to reveal to His earthly subjects whether heaven or hell awaited them. But he had not left them completely in the dark either. Certain *signs* were rumored to foretell their likely location beyond the grave. One indication of beckoning bliss was the tendency to lead an upright life. It was grounds for believing that they had *already* received the grace to be good, a privilege only God's Elect could receive. Calvin and his followers observed with satisfaction that they were the ones leading eminently upright lives: temperate, industrious, and frugal.

You may already sense the potential that Calvinism had to tie its adherents up in mental knots. Suppose that, as a devout Calvinist, you notice in yourself an urge to sin. Should you try to resist it? From one point of view, it should not matter whether you do or do not. Your fate has already been decided, so you might as well give in to your ungodliness. Yet what if you gallantly strive to overcome that sinful urge anyway? No good either. As mentioned earlier, Calvinism holds that willpower is irrelevant to salvation. Even worse, God's Elect should not even be tempted to sin, because God's grace should make righteousness in both thought and deed inescapable. Hence, the experience of temptation alone should bring beads of sweat to the brows of sincere Calvinists.

How did Calvinists cope with the temptations they surely felt? George Quattrone and Amos Tversky (1980) suggested that, although Calvinists did try to resist temptation, they *denied* that they were trying to do so. That is, they strove to be virtuous *unconsciously*. This psychological trick allowed them to interpret their virtue as a comforting sign of salvation rather than as a chilling sign of damnation.

The researchers saw this trick as one example of a general form of self-deception: the tendency to perform, without admitting it, actions *diagnostic* of (i.e., tending to indicate), but *causally unrelated* to (i.e., having no influence over), desired outcomes. In order to test whether this form of self-deception existed, the researchers reproduced a clever small-scale variant of the Calvinist's predicament in the laboratory.

What They Did

Participants in Quattrone and Tversky's study underwent a bogus medical exam, the results of which supposedly indicated their future medical status. The results of that exam could, of course, in no way influence their medical status. Participants' underlying condition would remain the same regardless of the exam's results. However, by making the results of the exam behavioral in nature, the researchers hoped to show that participants would alter its results so as to predict that their health prospects were promising. The researchers also hoped to show, by asking participants why they had behaved as they did, that they had no awareness of altering their exam results. This would be consistent with participants engaging in motivated self-deception—convincing themselves that the results of the exam were diagnostic of a favorable future medical status, even when they had fixed its results.

It happened like this. Thirty-eight undergraduate students signed up to take part in a study on the psychological and medical aspects of athletics. The female experimenter who greeted them explained that the purpose of the study was to investigate how, after a session of vigorous exercise, abrupt changes in body temperature would affect the cardiovascular system. Athletes sometimes take a cold shower immediately after working out. Could this refreshing activity nonetheless stress the heart, possibly damaging it in the long term? To add to the credibility of the cover story, the study was run in the physiology wing of the psychology department, where hi-tech equipment and bottled chemicals were much in evidence. The experimenter also wore the obligatory white lab coat.

Participants began with a *cold pressor test*: They placed both their forearms in a cooler full of ice water and kept them submerged for as long as they could. Though physically harmless, the cold pressor test proved challenging. The majority of participants felt compelled to withdraw their forearms in less than a minute. Nonetheless, for as long as they kept their forearms submerged, they rated their degree of discomfort every 5 seconds in response to prompts by the experimenter. These prompts took the form of letters, spoken aloud in alphabetical order. Participants replied to these prompts by saying aloud a number between 1 and 10, where 1 reflected no problem tolerating the cold, and 10 an inability to tolerate it further. The reason for prompting participants with ascending letters of the alphabet was to allow them to keep track of how long they had kept their hands submerged. This information would later enable them to make a crucial comparison.

So far as participants were concerned, the purpose of this phase of the study was to get a baseline measure of heart rate following an abrupt change in body temperature. The apparent purpose of the next phase was to determine whether a period of vigorous exercise would change these results. After finishing the cold pressor test, therefore, participants pedaled an exercise bicycle as hard as they could for 60 seconds. Then, after a short break, they completed a second cold pressor test. To ensure that participants remained convinced of the cover story, the experimenter went through the motions of measuring their pulse at appropriate intervals.

The true purpose of the study, of course, was not to measure the impact of temperature and exercise on heart rate, but rather to permit a test of the hypothesis that participants would alter their behavior unconsciously in order to make it diagnostic of some desired outcome. The behavior the researchers chose to focus on was participants' performance on the second cold pressor test. They made participants' performance on this task appear relevant to their future health prospects by persuading them during the break period that the ability to endure cold following a period of exercise had implications for cardiovascular fitness. The expectation was that participants would alter their performance on the second cold pressor test in the direction that implied greater coronary fitness.

How were participants led to believe that their performance on the second cold pressor test had a bearing on their future health prospects? During the break period, the experimenter gave participants a complimentary lecture. Participants assumed that this lecture was merely to occupy them usefully while they were waiting for the next phase of the study to begin. However, its real purpose was to convey bogus medical information that would motivate participants to engage in unconscious behavior that was diagnostic of preferred outcomes.

It was claimed in the lecture that the cold pressor test was used to study the psychophysics of pain. (Psychophysics is the branch of experimental psychology that investigates how the objective properties of stimuli relate to the subjective perceptions of them.) Participants were shown a graph illustrating the relation between forearm immersion time and levels of subjective discomfort. It was explained that this relation differed from person to person as a function of skin type and heart type. With respect to the heart type, participants were informed that everyone possessed one of two cardiovascular complexes, referred to, for the sake of brevity, as Type I or Type II hearts. A Type II heart was allegedly associated with a longer life span than a Type I heart, a fact vividly illustrated by another graph. The experimenter explained that, although people with Type I and Type II hearts did not normally differ in how much pain they could tolerate, a prior period of vigorous exercise could bring out the difference. The idea was to persuade participants that their performance on the second cold pressor test would have implications for how long they would live.

Then came the crucial point in the experiment. Half the participants were told that people with a Type II heart would be more tolerant of cold pressor pain after exercise, whereas the other half were told that such people would be less tolerant of it (in both cases, relative to people with a Type I heart). The prediction was this: Participants in the former condition would alter their behavior to show an increased tolerance for pain, whereas participants in the latter condition would alter their behavior to show a decreased tolerance for pain. Such shifts in tolerance would indicate that participants were motivated to manufacture evidence that a brighter future laid in store for them.

The seemingly odd way in which participants reported their levels of discomfort can now be seen to make sense. The alphabetized prompts, administered every 5 seconds, permitted them to compare how much time they spent tolerating pain during the first cold pressor test to how much time they spent tolerating it during the second. If they were motivated to unconsciously adjust their performance during the second test, they would now have guidelines for how to do it.

A different experimenter administered the second cold pressor test. This was done for two reasons. First, it was necessary to guard against the possibility that the experimenter, familiar with participants' earlier performance, might inadvertently influence their later performance, or record participants' responses with bias. Second, it was necessary to guard against the possibility that shifts in participants' performance would occur merely to please the experimenter, thereby complicating interpretation of the results. Participants were openly told that each experimenter would not know about the results collected by the other, so that neither would have the two pieces of information needed to infer their likely heart type. To reinforce this impression, the replacement experimenter dressed in casual clothing (instead of a white lab coat), suggesting that he was there solely for the purposes of administering the second test.

After the second cold pressor test had been completed, the experimenter gave participants a brief questionnaire to complete that contained two critical items. The first asked participants whether they believed they had a Type I or a Type II heart. The second asked them whether they had purposely tried to alter the amount of time they kept their forearms in the ice water during the second cold pressor test.

What They Found

Did participants shift their level of pain tolerance in the direction they believed was correlated with having a robust Type II heart? Yes. Participants told that people with a Type II heart were more tolerant of cold kept their forearms submerged for a longer time during the second cold pressor test. Conversely, participants told that people with a Type II heart were less tolerant of cold kept their forearms submerged for a shorter time during the second cold pressor test (Figure 16). Individual analyses revealed that roughly two-thirds of participants in both conditions showed the predicted shift, with the remaining third showing no shift at all (except for one who showed a shift in the opposite direction, enigmatically described by the researchers, without further elaboration, as a "suicidal" type!). Most participants were evidently altering their

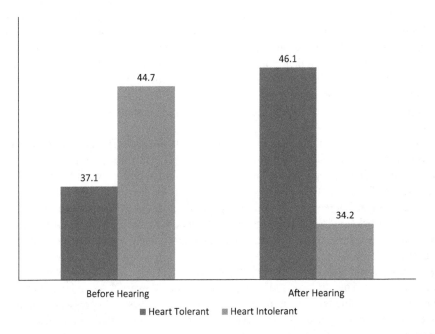

Figure 16 The number of seconds that participants kept their forearms in ice water, before and after hearing that a healthy heart is tolerant or intolerant of cold

behavior to make it diagnostic of favorable health prospects, even though this alteration obviously could not influence what sort of heart, Type I or Type II, they already had.

Were participants aware of changing the amount of time they kept their forearms submerged? By and large, no: 29 of the 38 participants denied attempting any change. (Interestingly, deniers and admitters did not differ in terms of their actual behavior. In both conditions, roughly the same proportion of participants altered their behavior, and to roughly the same extent.) The fact that most participants were not aware of altering their behavior on purpose, in conjunction with the fact that their behavior really did alter in the direction linked to better health prospects, suggests that they were engaging in self-deception. Such results are in line with the hypothesis that people will suppress awareness that they have deliberately performed a behavior whose results tend to be a sign of some desired outcome.

Participants who showed the predicted shift in pain tolerance were also asked *why* they had shifted. The typical response given was that the temperature of the water had changed. This is consistent with self-deception, attributing behavior to an external stimulus rather than to an internal motivation. However, it might be argued that participants were simply reluctant to publicly admit that they had deliberately modified their behavior. This contention, however, is less plausible in the light of a final set of findings. Of the 29 participants who denied intentionally altering how long they kept their hands immersed in the water, 20 of them (69%) also privately reported inferring that they had a Type II heart. In contrast, only two of the nine participants (22%) who admitted intentionally altering their responses also privately reported that inference. In other words, the majority of deniers privately inferred that their future health prospects were good, whereas the majority of admitters privately inferred that their future health prospects were poor. Thus, denial went hand in hand with comforting beliefs, and admission with disquieting ones. This suggests that participants' reports of their intentions were the result of genuine self-deception rather than superficial self-presentation.

So What?

It is often claimed in casual conversation that people deceive themselves with regard to their motives. Though this claim may be plausible in principle, the evidence for it is often weak. The great achievement of the present study was to demonstrate that self-deception exists in one particular form: not admitting to yourself that you have purposefully altered some sign to make it appear that some desired outcome is likely.

It is easy to think of real-world examples where this form of self-deception might operate. Suppose, for example, that you suspect you might be suffering from a serious disease one symptom of which is a loss of appetite. As matters stand either you have the disease or you do not—nothing you can do now is going change that. Nevertheless, do you not find yourself eating a little more than usual? Does not the knowledge that you are managing to eat a hearty dinner provide you with a measure of illusory reassurance?

Unfortunately, the unconscious steps that people take to reassure themselves can have grave repercussions. Suppose again that you suspect yourself of having a serious disease, but that the only way to know for sure is to undergo further medical testing. Unaccountably, you procrastinate, make excuses, and go about your daily business as usual. Why? Could it be because at some level you believe that not taking the tests is not only a sign of good health, but also a factor that can influence good health? In other words, do you feel that your likelihood of having the disease is increased by your taking the test or decreased by your not taking it? Rationally, this makes no sense at all, but the false logic can prove intuitively seductive. You kid yourself by refusing to admit that you are avoiding the medical tests out of concern for what they might reveal. To make such an admission, however, would prevent you from irrationally regarding not taking the tests as an indication of good health. The irony is that, although procrastination may provide some temporary psychological benefit, it may fatally delay the administration of critical medical treatment.

Our tendency to fabricate good omens expresses itself in other ways. Consider, for example, a second study conducted by Quattrone and Tversky (1980), published alongside the one reported here. In that study, the researchers attempted to provide an answer to a classic conundrum: Why do people bother to vote? Any individual vote has near zero chance of exerting a decisive impact in an election, so why turn out at all? Various explanations for this irrational behavior have been suggested. Typically, these appeal to a sense of civic duty or democratic idealism. However, Quattrone and Tversky (1980) put forward a different hypothesis. They argued that people vote because they believe that how they vote is a sign of how like-minded others will vote, and hence (by the twisted logic of self-deception) is an influence over how like-minded others will vote. Their results supported this curious hypothesis.

We conclude this section by describing another phenomenon that involves self-deception: *defensive self-handicapping* (Jones & Berglas, 1978). Oddly enough, people sometimes deliberately harm their chances of performing well on an important test. The reason? Fearing that failure is in the cards, but unwilling to conclude that they cannot succeed, people unconsciously prearrange circumstances so that they favor failure. This allows them to attribute failure, if it occurs, to those circumstances, and to deny responsibility for prearranging it. A prime example would be a student who lets his friends talk him into going drinking the night before a test, and who then blames his poor test performance on his hangover, which, of course, he never "meant" to cause. It seems that if people cannot change their performance to make it signify a desirable state of affairs (as participants in the present study did) they may try to change circumstances so that their performance at least does not signify an undesirable state of affairs. In the case of defensive self-handicapping, the undesirable state of affairs is the shame of admitting incompetence.

Afterthoughts

The present study documented one way that people deceive themselves with regard to their motives. Yet a puzzling question remains: How exactly does self-deception operate? In particular, how can people intend to do something yet be unaware that they are intending to do it?

Classic accounts of self-deception resolve the paradox by splitting the mind in two. An unconscious mind is postulated to possess an intelligence comparable to, or greater than, that of the conscious mind. This unconscious mind knows the true reasons for a person's behavior; indeed, it makes a person behave in those ways. Moreover, this unconscious mind keeps the conscious mind blissfully ignorant of all its activities. According to this view, the participants in the present study unconsciously knew that varying forearm immersion time would invalidate the cold pressor test. Nonetheless, their unconscious minds made the participants vary it anyhow, secure in the knowledge that their conscious minds would never find out.

This sort of account is highly problematic. It implies that there are two people inhabiting your head, one of whom is fooling the other. It boils down to invoking multiple personality disorder to explain self-deception, a rather drastic ploy. There is little evidence for such a sophisticated arrangement, but even if there were, it would in any case raise more questions than it answers. For example, if the unconscious mind deceives the conscious mind, why does it do so? Does it have a naturally deceitful character? And does the unconscious mind knowingly deceive the conscious mind? If so, would not that imply it was itself conscious? In addition, might there even be yet another unconscious mind deceiving it? The more one thinks about it, the more the split-mind account of self-deception seems to miss the essence of the phenomenon.

Greenwald (1988) provided a more plausible model of self-deception. The central contention of the model is that it is possible to avoid threatening information without exhaustively analyzing it first. An analogy to *junk mail*, of all things, makes this clear. When junk mail arrives, you do not need to open the envelope and read its contents in order to identify it. The telltale signs are already plain to see: bulk postage rates, low-quality paper, a flurry of exclamation marks. As a result, perfunctory inspection is enough to identify junk mail as such. The same is true of threatening information. It can be recognized as uncongenial on the basis of superficial cues. Moreover, once it has been so recognized, evasive mental maneuvers can be taken. If one has noticed the information, one can opt not to pay further attention to it; if one has paid attention to it, one can avoid trying to understand it; if one has understood it, one can refuse to draw logical inferences from it. In every case, one steers clear of realizations that create unpleasant feelings. Note how this solves the paradox of self-deception. If information perceived at a lower level of awareness has a negative ring to it then further processing at a higher level is avoided. The mechanism behind self-deception therefore involves not dwelling on information that shows signs of being uncongenial (Frey, 1986; Taylor, 1991).

Consider participants in the present study again. After the lecture, they presumably wanted to keep their forearms immersed in the ice water for a longer or shorter period of time (depending on which lecture they had heard). The likely result was a subtle strengthening or weakening of their resolve (see Chapter 24 for how goals can be unconsciously triggered). At some point thereafter, participants may have become dimly aware of a temptation to alter their results. However, they may have suppressed this awareness, let it pass out of their mind naturally, or chose not to elaborate upon its implications, because they realized that succumbing to this temptation would invalidate the test. Yet, the strength of their underlying resolve had perhaps already been influenced after hearing the lecture. Hence, participants may have found themselves, by the time they had their hands in the cooler, possessing or not possessing the resolve to continue. Given that people are not experts on the origins of their own mental processes (Nisbett & Wilson, 1977; see Chapter 14), it is no surprise that they would be unable to tell that it was the lecture that had affected their resolve rather than the temperature of the water itself. Certainly, many psychological processes must come together for self-deception to occur, but the avoidance of threatening information is a key component.

In conclusion, self-deception is not the result of one center of intelligence hoodwinking the other. Rather, it is the result of a low-level screening process that banishes suspicious cognitions before they have the opportunity to be fully entertained by the conscious mind. (For additional commentary, and further examples of self-deception, see Gregg & Mahadevan, 2014.)

Revelation

People deceive themselves by acting so as to create signs that everything is well even when they cannot make everything well. They then deny that they have acted in this way because admitting as much would imply that those signs are bogus.

What Do You Think?

When we deceive ourselves, we find ways to convince ourselves that uncomfortable truths are false. But would life be better or worse without our capacity to engage in self-deception? What if reality really is intolerable? Would there be any value is rationally apprehending it?

Chapter Reference

Quattrone, G. A., & Tversky, A. (1980). Causal versus diagnostic reasoning: On self-deception and the voter's illusion. *Journal of Personality and Social Psychology, 46*, 237–248.

Other References

Frey, D. (1986). Recent research on selective exposure to information. In L. Berkowitz (Ed.), *Advances in experimental social psychology* (Vol. 19, pp. 41–80). New York: Academic Press.

Greenwald, A. G. (1988). Self-knowledge and self-deception. In J. S. Lockard & D. L. Paulhaus (Eds.), *Self-deception: An adaptive mechanism?* (pp. 113–131). Englewood Cliffs, NJ: Prentice Hall.

Gregg, A. P., & Mahadevan, N. (2014). Self-deception. In T. Levine (Ed.), *Encyclopedia of Deception* (pp. 836–839). London: Sage.

Jones, E. E., & Berglas, S. (1978). Control of attributions about the self through self-handicapping strategies: The appeal of alcohol and the role of underachievement. *Personality and Social Psychology Bulletin, 4*, 200–206.

Nisbett, R. E., & Wilson, T. D. (1977). Telling more than we can know: Verbal reports on mental processes. *Psychological Review, 84*, 231–259.

Taylor, S. E. (1991). Asymmetrical effects of positive and negative events: The mobilization-minimization hypothesis. *Psychological Bulletin, 110*, 67–85.

More to Explore

Varki, A., & Brower, D. (2013). *Denial: Self-deception, false beliefs, and the origins of the human mind.* New York: Twelve Books.

17 Believing Is Seeing

Partisan Perceptions of Media Bias

"As I am, so I see."

—Ralph Waldo Emerson (1803–1882), American philosopher, essayist, poet

Background

It was a brisk Saturday afternoon, late in November of 1951. Crisp autumn leaves blanketed the ground. The sun shone brightly, but the frigid breeze spoke of the approaching winter. Animated college students (sporting saddle shoes, bobby socks, and V-neck sweaters), their proud parents, and loyal alumni filled Palmer Stadium on the Princeton University campus. The *Tigers* (the home team) and the Dartmouth *Indians* battled fiercely on the gridiron in the last game of the season. The Tigers were so far undefeated, thanks in large part to All-American quarterback Dick Kazmaier, who had just appeared on the cover of *Time* magazine.

The game was brutal from the get-go. Penalty whistles blew non-stop. The second quarter saw Kazmaier taken out of the game with a crushed nose. The third quarter saw a Dartmouth player removed from the field with a broken leg. Fights between rival fans broke out on the bleachers. It was a game that will live in infamy.

Princeton won—but not without controversy and a mutual exchange of accusations afterward. The *Daily Princetonian* protested their opponent's lack of sportsmanship and savage style of play:

> This observer has never seen quite such a disgusting exhibition of so-called "sport" . . . the blame must be laid squarely on Dartmouth's doorstep. Princeton, obviously the better team, had no reason to rough up Dartmouth. Looking at the situation rationally, we don't see why the Indians should make a deliberate attempt to cripple Dick Kazmaier and other Princeton players.
>
> (Hastorf & Cantril, 1954, p. 129)

The *Princeton Alumni Weekly* echoed these sentiments:

> Into the record books will go in indelible fashion the fact that the last game of Dick Kazmaier's career was cut short by more than half when he was forced out with a broken nose and mild concussion, sustained from a tackle that came well after he had thrown a pass . . . a third quarter outbreak of roughness was climaxed when a Dartmouth player deliberately kicked Brad Glass in the ribs while the latter was on his back . . . there was undeniable evidence that the loser's tactics were an actual style of play.
>
> (Hastorf & Cantril, 1954, p. 129)

The reaction on the other side was scarcely less critical. The *Dartmouth* accused Princeton coach Charley Caldwell of maliciously convincing his squad during a half-time pep talk that the Indians had been playing dirty. The student newspaper claimed in particular that Caldwell had insinuated that Dartmouth was targeting their star player, Kazmaier:

> His talk got results. Gene Howard and Jim Miller were both injured. Both had dropped back to pass, had passed, and were standing unprotected in the backfield. Result: one bad leg and one broken.
>
> (Hastorf & Cantril, 1954, p. 129)

The next day, the *Dartmouth* went on to belittle Kazmaier's injury in light of their team's own past injuries:

> As a relatively unprotected passing and running star in a contact sport, he is quite liable to injury. Also, his particular injuries—a broken nose and slight concussion—were no more serious than is experienced almost any day in any football practice. . . . Up to the Princeton game, Dartmouth players suffered about 10 known nose fractures and face injuries, not to mention several slight concussions.
>
> (Hastorf & Cantril, 1954, p. 129)

So, which side was primarily at fault for the sorry display of unsportsmanlike conduct that fateful day? It was as if spectators and reporters alike had witnessed different games.

Enter a pair of social psychologists, seizing the chance to do some research. A week after the big game, Hastorf and Cantril (1954) administered a questionnaire to undergraduates at both universities, to gauge perceptions and opinions on each side. Later, they showed a film of the game to students at both schools, and had the students indicate, while watching it, any instances of foul play. The two groups had, indeed, perceived the game quite differently. Take the Princeton students. A full 90% of them stated that the Dartmouth players had instigated the rough and dirty play. In addition, they deemed Dartmouth players responsible for twice as many infractions as players on their own team. Finally, they saw Dartmouth players commit a greater number of flagrant infractions, whereas they saw their own side commit a greater number of mild ones. Now take the Dartmouth students. They saw Princeton students commit a greater number of flagrant infractions, but their own side commit about an equal number of flagrant and mild ones. However, they too saw a game that favored their own squad. Same game, separate loyalties, dissimilar perceptions.

Hastorf and Cantril explained what was evident in the news reports and questionnaire responses:

> The "same" sensory impingements emanating from the football field, transmitted through the visual apparatus of the brain . . . obviously gave rise to different experiences in different people . . . people don't have attitudes about "things" that exist "out there" because the "thing" is simply not the same for different people whether the "thing" is a football game, a presidential candidate, Communism, or spinach.
>
> (Hastorf & Cantril, 1954, pp. 132–133)

So there you have it: People believe certain things and this affects their experience. We each construct our own reality. Believing is seeing.

Partisan perceptions are common. Two children—with bloodied noses and tearful faces—may have a different story to tell about the same fight. Rowdy children and their sedate parents may view the same weekend keg party differently. A husband and wife may give different estimates of their respective contributions to household chores. And those for and against gun control may perceive the same address on the topic differently, and respond to it differently. In fact, staunch advocates of a particular social or political cause often see those who do not share their opinions as biased in favor of the opposite side.

The mainstream media, supposedly in the business of objectively reporting events, is often viewed as biased. Indeed, the discrepant news accounts of the Princeton-Dartmouth game may represent precisely such media bias. And perhaps this is to be expected given the loyal nature of student newspapers. However, the charge is more serious when directed at what should be non-partisan, nationally syndicated news sources. A biased medium at that level could sway political election results by drawing greater attention to particular issues or emphasizing certain arguments at the expense of others. It might even influence international relations. For instance, when reporting on events in the Middle East, the media might tendentiously portray all Israelis as oppressors, or all Arabs as terrorists.

Indeed, the average person tends to believe in mainstream media bias. For example, in 2016, Americans' trust in the mainstream media "to report the news fully, accurately and fairly" fell to an all-time low of 32%—down 20 percentage points from 1997, and 40 points from 1972 (Swift, 2016). Furthermore, in the aftermath of Donald Trump's snatching the U.S. presidency from a stunned Hillary Clinton, partisans on both sides of the aisle were vociferously accusing one another of producing "fake news." But might people regard the media as biased even when it may not be?

Why might people regard the media as biased even when it may not be? Might they see identical news items but interpret the majority of them as being hostile to their own side—just as the Dartmouth and Princeton fans saw more serious fouls committed by the opposing team? If so, this would signal interpretational prejudice. Another possibility is that they might interpret news items similarly, but then recollect them differently afterward, showing selective memory for material hostile to their own side. Or they might have selective memory for information that is consistent with their own attitudes (Goethals & Reckman, 1973; see Chapter 21). That is, they experience the same content, but recollect it differently afterward. Or, finally, they may entertain false theories of media bias, leading them to unwarranted skepticism. Perhaps they believe that the media is controlled by the liberal intellectual elite or, oppositely, by the religious far right. Regardless of the mechanism, do they indeed show a bias?

What They Did

Inspired by Hastorf and Cantril (1954), Vallone, Ross, and Lepper (1985) sought to investigate the biased perceptions of partisans, as well as the mechanisms underlying such bias. They also wanted to shed light on perceptions of media bias. In other words, their study focused on both biased perceptions and perceptions of bias.

Vallone and his colleagues capitalized on the occurrence of a tragic series of events in the Middle East in 1982. In September of that year, an Israeli invasion of the West Bank culminated in the slaughter of Palestinian refugees in camps at Sabra and Chatilla in Lebanon. Sobering developments were reported nightly on American television. How would research participants who were loyal to either the Israeli or Palestinian causes react to this news coverage? Would they view it differently? Detect media bias? Both?

One hundred and forty-four Stanford University students participated in what was described simply as a study of the media coverage of the conflict in Lebanon. The participants included students in introductory psychology classes and members of pro-Israeli and pro-Arab student organizations. To start, participants rated their factual knowledge of the Beirut Massacre and indicated their sympathies with respect to Middle East politics. For example, what historical events led up to the massacre? And how responsible were the different parties? Three groups of participants were identified, based on their answers: generally pro-Israeli, generally pro-Palestinian, or having mixed or neutral views. These groups assigned different amounts of responsibility to Israel, Lebanese officials, and the soldiers who invaded the camps. For example, whereas pro-Arab participants put 57% of the blame on Israel, pro-Israeli participants put only 22% of the blame on Israel.

The participants then watched a 36-minute video containing six segments of nationally televised news coverage of the Middle East bloodshed. They did so in small groups, each typically a mix of pro-Israeli, pro-Arab, and neutral participants. Group members were generally unaware of one another's political loyalties. Afterward, they completed a questionnaire containing items about the objectivity and fairness of the news programs, the standards applied to Israel and its adversaries, the amount of attention focused on Israel's role in the massacre, the case made for and against Israel, and the apparent personal views of the news editors. The participants were also asked to estimate the percentage of favorable, unfavorable, and neutral references to Israel in the video and how much initially neutral viewers would be likely to change to more positive or negative positions after watching it.

What They Found

Vallone and his colleagues (1985) found clear evidence for both biased perceptions and perceptions of bias. Pro-Arab participants perceived a pro-Israel bias in the news programs, whereas pro-Israeli participants perceived an anti-Israel bias. In contrast, neutral participants did not perceive any significant bias in the news programs (Figure 17). Moreover, pro-Arab participants thought the news programs neglected to adequately focus on Israel's role in the massacre, while pro-Israeli participants thought the programs concentrated too much on Israel's responsibility. Both groups inferred that the personal views of the creators of the programs were opposed to their own views.

Did the partisan groups perceive the *same* content in the news reports, and only evaluate the fairness of it differently, or did they actually perceive *different* content, due to different patterns of recollection? Some findings supported the latter conclusion. For example, Pro-Arabs thought 42% of the references to Israel were favorable, 26% unfavorable. In contrast, pro-Israelis thought

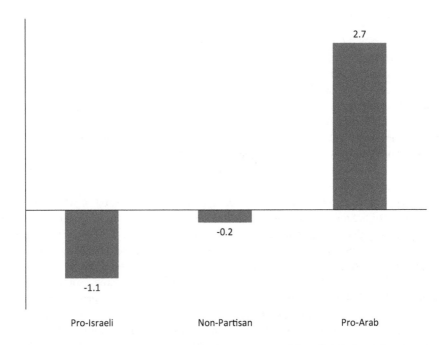

Figure 17 Perceptions of pro-Israeli bias in television coverage of the 1982 Beirut Massacre among pro-Israeli, nonpartisan, and pro-Arab participants

that 16% of the references to Israel were favorable, 57% unfavorable. Also, pro-Arabs thought that 32% of neutral viewers would be persuaded to hold a more negative view of Israel's role as a result of watching the programs, whereas pro-Israelis thought that 68% would be so persuaded. An additional analysis revealed that the pro-Israeli versus pro-Arab differences in perception of bias remained significant even when differences in perceived content were statistically held constant. Thus, both of the postulated mechanisms underlying perceptions of a hostile media seemed to operate: Partisans saw different content, and they evaluated the same content differently.

Furthermore, within both pro-Israeli and pro-Arab groups, the more knowledgeable the participants believed they were regarding Israeli-Palestinian relations and the Beirut Massacre, the more they were inclined to perceive media hostility. Arguably, they believed they had better grounds for detecting discrepancies between what was presented and what should have been presented. But then, too, participants who rated themselves as more emotionally involved in the overall issue also perceived more media bias, so it is not clear whether motivational or purely cognitive factors were the driving force behind the perceptions of bias. Conceivably, knowledge about an issue is one index of the strength of the attitudes someone holds toward it (Wood, Rhodes, & Biek, 1995). Finally, Vallone and his colleagues (1985) found evidence that both the pro-Arabs and the pro-Israelis perceived a degree of media bias that was not apparent to more neutral participants.

So What?

The present study is but one of many that reveals perceptual biases. For example, abundant research has shown how perceptions can be swayed by racial stereotypes. In an oft-cited study by Allport and Postman (1947), individual White participants looked at a drawing of a crowded New York City subway. The drawing depicted two men standing and facing each other. The one, a Black man, held up opened hands, and the other, a White man, apparently wielded a straight razor in a threatening manner. The research participants then verbally described the scene to others, who did the same in turn. It was found that, from one telling to the next, the razor often shifted from the White to the Black man's hand! In a related study, Duncan (1976) had White college students watch one of two videos of two men—one White and one Black—in a discussion. The interaction got heated and the one man pushed the other man. The Black man's shoving the White man was perceived as violent 75% of the time, and as playing around or being dramatic 6% of the time. However, the White man's shoving the Black man was perceived as playing around or being dramatic 46% of the time, and as violent 17% of the time. Such findings raise an important question: Do our perceptions reflect reality, or does reality reflect our perceptions?

Other studies have shown how perceptions can be experimentally manipulated by subtle factors outside a person's awareness (see Chapter 2). Higgins, Rholes, and Jones (1977) had participants complete word search puzzles. Participants in two groups searched for the same words, with a few exceptions. In one group, some words were synonyms for *reckless* (e.g., *careless* and *foolish*). In the other group, some words were synonyms for *adventurous* (e.g., *brave* and *spirited*). Then, in an apparently unrelated task, the participants evaluated a fictitious person, Donald, who was described as having gone white water rafting, having driven in a demolition derby, and planning to go skydiving. Participants perceived Donald relatively positively if the schema for adventurousness had been *primed* (mentally activated so as to make it subsequently more accessible). However, they perceived Donald relatively negatively if carelessness had been primed. Importantly, activating unrelated schemas, such as *neatness* or *shyness*, did not affect perceptions of Donald (because his bold behaviors had little to do with those traits).

What is perceived and subsequently remembered can also be subtly manipulated. Cohen (1981) had participants watch a film of a woman at home with her husband. It was mentioned in passing that the woman was either a waitress or a librarian. Weeks later, the participants were asked to recall the contents of the film. Which participants do you think were more likely to remember the woman wearing glasses, with a piano in the background? Which do you think were more likely to remember her eating a chocolate birthday cake, with a bowling ball in the corner of the room? The casual mention of the woman's vocation caused participants to recall details that were consistent with their stereotype. That said, sometimes stereotypes can operate on memory the other way around. People often remember *exceptions* to stereotypes better, because they stick out more (Stangor & McMillian, 1992). Thus, an African-American math whiz, or an Asian-American basketball star, can be especially memorable. Which items of information—stereotype-consistent or stereotype-inconsistent—enjoy a memory advantage depends on several factors. Stereotype-consistent items tend to be better remembered when people are mentally busy (Sherman & Frost, 2000), or where expectations are understated (Heider et al., 2006).

Perceptions can also be influenced by body language and facial expressions. Even when a news broadcaster's words are impartial, he or she may nonverbally leak personal prejudice. Mullen and ten colleagues (1986) videotaped the evening news on three major American networks (ABC, NBC, and CBS), deleted all sound, and played the tapes for an audience of judges, who rated the positive or negative nonverbal expressions of the newscasters as they were speaking about Ronald Reagan or Walter Mondale prior to the 1984 presidential election (the judges had no idea who or what the newscasters were reporting on). It was discovered that ABC's Peter Jennings (unlike Dan Rather and Tom Brokaw) smiled more and generally appeared happier when talking about Reagan than when talking about Mondale. Perhaps this was one reason why people in a random phone survey, who reported watching the most ABC newscasts, were relatively more likely to vote for Reagan.

These and many other studies show how people's perceptions are often misinformed and malleable. The impression given is that humans are very biased. Strictly speaking, this may be true. Every schema or stereotype is a simplification of reality. When people use them, they ignore some details, and may make errors as a result. That can be unfortunate for the people they judge.

But think of it from the point of view of people making the judgments. The world is complex and mental resources are limited. Hence, people must judge economically. One way to do so is to use rules of thumb—fast, frugal *heuristics*—which are good enough under the circumstances (Gigerenzer & Goldstein, 1996). Schemas and stereotypes often contain a kernel of truth (Jussim, Crawford, & Rubinstein, 2015), so they can work well as heuristics. Research shows that using stereotypes allows people to free up mental resources for other purposes (Macrae, Milne, & Bodenhausen, 1994)

Pragmatically justified or not, perceptual biases can be curtailed. In this regard, it is sometimes helpful for us to be our own devil's advocate. Lord, Lepper, and Preston (1984) had participants read about two studies, one supporting capital punishment (arguing that it deters murder and other crimes), the other against capital punishment (arguing that it has no deterrent effect, and even models violence). Participants judged the study that agreed with their own stand on the issue to be methodologically stronger. A second group of participants, however, went through the same procedure, but were informed about perceptual biases beforehand. They were taught that people see things in ways that fit their expectations or motives and were encouraged to try to counter this natural tendency: "Be as objective and unbiased as possible." This simple advice did not work. Personal biases still crept in. However, a more specific directive did reduce bias: "Ask yourself at each step whether you would have made the same high or low evaluations had exactly the same study produced results on the other side of the issue" (Lord et al., 1984, p. 1233). Participants using this strategy gauged the two studies to be equally credible and convincing. Just actively considering multiple alternative possibilities is often enough to de-bias one's judgment (Hirt & Markman, 1995).

Research finds that we can also negate the power of cultural stereotypes, although the process is effortful and error-prone. Devine (1989) showed that people are generally aware of prevailing stereotypes, even if they deny consciously endorsing them. For example, they readily report that Blacks are supposedly aggressive, athletic, and rhythmic, or that the Irish are supposedly talkative, sentimental, and fond of a pint. Devine found that when one encounters a member of a particular social category—a Native American, exotic dancer, or college professor—the relevant stereotype is automatically activated. This causes the group member's ambiguous behaviors to be interpreted stereotypically: "He's lying under the table because he's drunk—the Irish are always drunk."

However, Devine (1989) showed that it is possible to rein in such automatic responses. Indeed, people who are low in prejudice seem to be those who consciously replace stereotypic thoughts (which, like everyone, they too possess) with those that negate the stereotype. In her words: "Inhibiting stereotype-congruent or prejudice-like responses and intentionally replacing them with non-prejudiced responses can be likened to the breaking of a bad habit" (p. 15). Human perception is readily biased, but perhaps not necessarily so.

That said, biases can be difficult to escape. The main problem is that we are not aware of them. We suffer from a *bias blind spot* (Pronin, Lin, & Ross, 2002). For example, Pronin and colleagues (2002) found that most of their participants reported that they were less susceptible to biases (included the *hostile media bias* highlighted in this chapter) than other people. Ironically, in claiming to be so rational, they were thereby showing another bias: the *better-than-average* effect! (Alicke & Govorun, 2005). Worse, even when informed that this bias existed, they denied being susceptible to it also! But perhaps cognitive biases mainly affect people who are less intelligent.

Some evidence supports this suspicion (Kruger & Dunning, 1999). In particular, to the extent that people lack the mental ability to excel at humor, grammar, or logic, they also lack the mental ability to *recognize* that they fail to excel. Accordingly, such people overestimate their abilities. In contrast, people who do excel, if anything, underestimate their own abilities. To quote a line from Shakespeare's *As You Like It* (Act 5, Scene 1), "The fool doth think he is wise, but the wise man knows himself to be a fool."

On the other hand, being smarter, or even having a more reflective disposition, is no guarantee of rationality. Students with higher SAT scores, and even those who score higher on problems requiring them *not* to jump to conclusions, still believe themselves to be less prone to various cognitive biases, while continuing to exhibit those same cognitive biases to an at least equal degree (West, Meserve, & Stanovich, 2012)! Perhaps having more brains only means one can come up with better justifications for what one prefers to believe.

Afterthoughts

The studies described in this chapter highlight what most social psychologists firmly believe: Cognition plays a central role in human behavior. Indeed, a subfield of social psychology, *social cognition* devotes itself to analyzing the nuts and bolts of social thinking (Fiske & Taylor, 2017). Let's reflect a bit on the various stages of how we make sense of the social world.

To start, something grabs our attention: a person acting suspiciously, an inviting smile, a piercing scream. Or we attempt to deliberately focus our mind: on our performance before an audience, the arguments of a politician, or possible signs of suicide in a friend. Either way, our attention is *partial*. We look upon reality as if through a keyhole, attending to a mere fraction of available information. Biased attention then gives way to perception, which itself is potentially biased, as we have seen. We notice someone's body language; we decode it. Someone fails to return our phone call or e-mail; we guess why. A child spends a lot of time alone; we wonder if he or she is ostracized or merely introverted. Our perceptions—innumerable and incessant—are all-important. In fact, psychologists often claim that people do not interact with reality; rather, they interact with their *perception* of reality. That may be an exaggeration. However, we do *construe* the events and dynamics of the world in which we live. We even construe ourselves in the form of our self-concept. Our perceptions and construals feed our decisions, which influence our behaviors, which evoke responses from others that feed back to our perceptions (see Chapter 15, on *behavioral confirmation*).

Is there an objective reality out there, one that we can all agree upon? How can we know things accurately if our perceptions are so biased? If we only see what we want or expect to see, how do we ever know what is real? These are serious *epistemological* questions (i.e., having to do with how knowledge is obtained). Should we concur with the philosopher, George Berkeley, who argued that reality is a mere idea? (If a tree falls in a forest and no one is around to hear it, does it make a sound?) Should we accept the claim, made by extreme skeptics, that we can never know anything for certain? On the other hand, can the word "bias" even mean anything sensible unless there is some standard in reality against which a judgment can be measured?

Religion, philosophy, and the science of psychology rely upon different methods for knowing things. Religion relies on divine revelation and mystical insights, philosophy on reason and logic, and the science of psychology on empirical methods—observation, measurement, experimentation, and replication (although, to be sure, reason and logic also come into play). Indeed, psychologists and other scientists believe that the best way of knowing the truth about everyday things—what size dam is needed to hold back a river, how to vaccinate against a disease, and whether the two hemispheres of the brain serve different functions—is by *empirical* methods. Using such methods, psychologists are able to slice through the very biases they detect. Although psychology and other sciences are not completely free of biases, the give-and-take of scholarly criticism and the demand for replication ensure a reasonable degree of objectivity (see the Introduction to this book). Of course, even if science can provide us with reliable knowledge about ourselves and the world, it still has its limits. There may be some knowledge—such as why anything exists at all, how to best live one's life, or whether there is life after death—that science is not equipped to provide.

At any rate, perceptions will never cease being important. As we rewrite this chapter, tensions between Israelis and Palestinians remain high, with many on either side seeing no peaceful end to the cycle of violence they believe is being pedaled by their enemies. Could it be that biased perceptions and perceptions of media bias are fueling the flames of this seemingly interminable conflict?

Furthermore, Donald Trump has just been sworn in as the 45th president of the United States. Although tempted to opine on this interesting turn of events, we limit our comments to the back-and-forth allegations of media bias during the nomination and election processes. As Trump steadily eliminated the Republican field of contenders, and as Clinton staved off the tenacious challenge of Bernie Sanders, accusations of media bias were already in the wind. On the one hand, journalists were purportedly giving Trump undue and uncritical airtime, and on the other hand, they seemed to support Clinton as the inevitable Democratic front runner. During the election itself, the media was seen as promoting Trump as a colorful alternative to a mistrusted Washington insider (recall how Clinton's e-mail practices were under FBI investigation), or as promoting Clinton as the sane alternative in light of Trump's dubious antics (recall how he was caught on video bragging about fondling women). No doubt, different news outlets (*New York Times*, Fox News, *The Wall Street Journal*, *Washington Post*, and so on) did each harbor a modicum of journalistic bias. A slight bias is unavoidable, even intentional perhaps. However, it is significant that individuals on opposite ends of the political spectrum, evaluating the *same* news content, often perceived *opposite* biases. For many Democrats, the media was complicit in denying Clinton the presidency. For many Republicans, the media was the enemy that, despite its concerted efforts to get Clinton elected, was countermanded by a "silent majority" of Americans. Could it be that biased perceptions and perceptions of media bias are fueling the flames of acrimonious bipartisanship in the United States?

Revelation

Our group loyalties and preconceptions cause us to perceive events and other stimuli in a biased manner. One consequence of this is that partisans on both sides of an issue tend to overestimate bias in media reports.

What Do You Think?

The mainstream media are in decline. Younger people increasingly get their information from "social media" platforms (such as Twitter™) accessed through electronic devices. Do you think that commentators on these platforms are more or less biased than the mainstream media?

Chapter Reference

Vallone, R. P., Ross, L., & Lepper, M. R. (1985). The hostile media phenomenon: Biased perception and perceptions of media bias in coverage of the Beirut Massacre. *Journal of Personality and Social Psychology, 49*, 577–585.

Other References

Alicke, M. D., & Govorun, O. (2005). The better-than-average effect. In M. D. Alicke, D. A. Dunning, & J. I. Krueger (Eds.), *The self in social judgment: Studies in self and identity* (pp. 85–106). Hove, UK: Psychology Press.

Allport, G. W., & Postman, L. J. (1947). *The psychology of rumor*. New York: Henry Holt and Company.

Cohen, C. E. (1981). Person categories and social perception: Testing some boundaries of the processing effects of prior knowledge. *Journal of Personality and Social Psychology, 40*, 441–452.

Devine, P. G. (1989). Stereotypes and prejudice: Their automatic and controlled components. *Journal of Personality and Social Psychology, 56*, 5–18.

Duncan, B. L. (1976). Differential social perception and attribution theory of intergroup violence: Testing the lower limits of stereotyping of blacks. *Journal of Personality and Social Psychology, 34*, 590–598.

Fiske, S. T., & Taylor, S. (2017). *Social cognition: From brains to culture* (3rd ed.). London: Sage.

Gigerenzer, G., & Goldstein, D. G. (1996). Reasoning the fast and frugal way: Models of bounded rationality. *Psychological Review, 103*, 650–669.

Goethals, G. R., & Reckman, R. F. (1973). The perception of consistency in attitudes. *Journal of Experimental Social Psychology, 9*, 491–501.

Hastorf, A. H., & Cantril, H. (1954). They saw a game: A case study. *Journal of Abnormal Social Psychology, 49*, 129–134.

Heider, J. D., Scherer, C. R., Skowronski, J. J., Wood, S. E., Edlund, J. E., & Hartnett, J. L. (2006). Trait expectancies and stereotype expectancies have the same effect on person memory. *Journal of Experimental Social Psychology, 43*, 265–272.

Higgins, E. T., Rholes, W. S., & Jones, C. R. (1977). Category accessibility and impression formation. *Journal of Experimental Social Psychology, 13*, 141–154.

Hirt, E. R., & Markman, K. D. (1995). Multiple explanation: A consider-an-alternative strategy for debiasing judgments. *Journal of Personality and Social Psychology, 69*, 1069–1086.

Jussim, L., Crawford, J. T., & Rubinstein, R. S. (2015). Stereotype (in)accuracy in perceptions of groups and individuals. *Current Directions in Psychological Science, 24*, 490–497.

Kruger, J., & Dunning, D. (1999). Unskilled and unaware of it: How difficulties in recognizing one's own incompetence lead to inflated self-assessments. *Journal of Personality and Social Psychology, 77*, 1121–1134.

Lord, C. G., Lepper, M. R., & Preston, E. (1984). Considering the opposite: A corrective strategy for social judgment. *Journal of Personality and Social Psychology, 47*, 1231–1243.

Macrae, C. N., Milne, A. B., & Bodenhausen, G. V. (1994). Stereotypes as energy-saving devices: A peek inside the cognitive toolbox. *Journal of Personality and Social Psychology, 66*, 37–47.

Mullen, B., Futrell, D., Stairs, D., Tice, D. M., Baumeister, R. F., Dawson, K. E., Riordan, C. A., Radloff, C. E., Goethals, G. R., Kennedy, J. G., & Rosenfeld, P. (1986). Newscasters' facial expressions and voting behavior of viewers: Can a smile elect a president? *Journal of Personality and Social Psychology, 51,* 291–295.

Pronin, E., Lin, D. Y., & Ross, L. (2002). The bias blind spot: Perceptions of bias in self versus others. *Personality and Social Psychology Bulletin, 28,* 369–381.

Sherman, J. W., & Frost, L. A. (2000). On the encoding of stereotype-relevant information under cognitive load. *Personality and Social Psychology Bulletin, 26,* 26–34.

Stangor, C., & McMillan, D. (1992). Memory for expectancy-congruent and expectancy-incongruent information: A review of the social and social developmental literatures. *Psychological Bulletin, 111,* 42–61.

Swift, A. (2016, September 14th). *Americans' trust in mass media sinks to new low.* Retrieved from www. gallup.com/poll/195542/americans-trust-mass-media-sinks-new-low.aspx

West, R. F., Meserve, R. J., & Stanovich, K. E. (2012). Cognitive sophistication does not attenuate the bias blind spot. *Journal of Personality and Social Psychology, 103,* 506–519.

Wood, W., Rhodes, N. D., & Biek, M. (1995). Working knowledge and attitude strength: An information-processing analysis. In R. Petty & J. Krosnick (Eds.), *Attitude strength: Antecedents and consequences* (pp. 283–313). Hillsdale, NJ: Erlbaum.

More to Explore

Atkins, L. (2016). *Skewed: A critical thinker's guide to media bias.* Amherst, MA: Prometheus Books.

18 Love Thy Neighbor or Thyself?

Empathy as a Source of Altruism

"Act so as to treat humanity . . . never as a means only, but always at the same time as an end."
—Immanuel Kant (1724–1804), German philosopher

Background

Chapter 5 investigated the phenomenon of *bystander non-intervention*: the tendency of people in crowds to stand idly by while someone suffers desperately before their very eyes or within earshot. On the face of it, such passive behavior indicates an appalling lack of human sympathy. It seems to prove just how threadbare the fabric of public morality has become. However, social psychological research has established that bystanders stay put for quite another reason: the sheer ambiguity of the situation. Bystanders wonder: Whose responsibility is it to help? Is it really an emergency if no one else is doing anything? Tellingly, when bystanders do define a situation as an emergency, accept that it is up to them to intervene, and feel confident they can be of assistance, they quickly channel their concern for victims into concrete action (Latané & Darley, 1970). Hence, the underlying goodwill of people in large gatherings need not be doubted. The problem stems from without. The presence of others fosters perceptions that make the expression of goodwill less likely.

In this chapter, we delve deeper into people's *motives* for helping each other. In particular, we consider research that seeks to answer the following question: Are people's motives for performing helpful acts always, in the last analysis, *self-serving*?

Ask yourself: Do your friends give you gifts out of a genuine desire to make you happy? Or are they trying to endear themselves to you? Or are they just doing their duty, which they may privately resent? Suppose that your friends really *do* desire to make you happy. Even then, are they motivated by the anticipated pleasure of seeing you happy? Or by the pride of knowing that they were able to make you happy? How certain can you be, when it comes right down to it, that your friends were interested in fostering your happiness *for its own sake*?

The fundamental issue is whether people promote the welfare of others ever as an *ultimate* goal, or whether they do so only as an *instrumental* goal. That is: Is helping someone ever people's final selfless aim, or do they help only to satisfy some other selfish desire? Some people—perhaps because of their faith in God—tend to view humankind sympathetically. They may prefer to believe that we are capable of genuine charity. Other people—perhaps impressed by Darwinian evolution—tend to view humankind cynically. They may prefer to believe that we always have an ulterior motive. Can any objective evidence assist us in deciding who might be right?

Consider what everyday observation tells us. It is evident that coming to the aid of others often gives joy and satisfaction, whereas leaving them to suffer often induces distress and guilt. So, we have much to gain, emotionally speaking, from lending a hand, and much to lose by not doing so. Could we help, then, just to make ourselves *feel better*?

Indeed, research shows that people help in order to repair bad moods. In one study, participants were led to believe that they, or another person, had accidentally harmed a confederate (who was actually fine). In both conditions, participants were understandably dismayed, compared to participants in a control condition. They were also more likely to volunteer for a worthy cause later on. Crucially, however, if participants received, directly after the manipulation, either praise or cash, then their likelihood of volunteering dropped to the level of the control group (Cialdini, Darby, & Vincent, 1973). Evidently, it is the receipt of praise or cash, by repairing participants' bad mood, was enough to short-circuit their "concern" for the confederate—suggesting that their motive to help had been selfish all along.

The situation might thus appear unpromising for proponents of altruism. Everyday observation suggests, and some empirical research shows, that people help for selfish reasons. However, such evidence is not decisive. First, the mere fact that two phenomena are *correlated* (i.e., tend to go together) is not in itself a guarantee that one *causes* the other. For example, day and night follow each other with perfect regularity, but neither can be said to cause the other. Second, even if helping others benefits us in some way, it does not follow that we help *in order* to benefit. Any benefit we receive may conceivably be an innocent (although well-deserved) byproduct of our helping. Granted, psychological rewards can and do motivate us to help. Yet it is a far from settled question whether they always must. Thus, proponents of the *possibility of altruism* (Nagel, 1979) can cheerfully concede the existence of any number of selfish motives because they do not logically exclude the existence of selfless motives. Hence, the evidence discussed so far for *universal egoism* (as this philosophical view of human motivation is called) can only ever be circumstantial, never enough to establish it beyond reasonable doubt.

Experimentation in the social psychological laboratory would appear to offer hope of untangling the causal knot. Yet, creating a paradigm capable of yielding evidence in favor of either egoism or altruism presents quite a challenge. What would its elements be?

First, a source of altruistic motivation needs to be identified. What state of mind could be expected to prompt altruistic acts? Thinkers throughout the ages have been fairly unanimous in singling out *empathy* as the prime candidate, so social psychologists have followed their lead (Batson, 2011). Empathy can be defined as an emotional orientation that comprises feelings of sympathy and compassion for others combined with a tendency to see things from their perspective. The hypothesis that empathy prompts altruistic acts is called—no surprise here—the *empathy-altruism hypothesis*.

Second, a large number of alternative selfish reasons need to be advanced for why people who feel empathy might help. Do such *empathizers* help to improve their mood, enhance their self-regard, or alleviate their discomfort? Or any number of other plausible selfish reasons? Each alternative advanced constitutes a rival *egoistic hypothesis* to the empathy-altruism hypothesis.

The last step involves devising experimental tests to decide between the empathy-altruism hypothesis and each of its egoistic rivals. The details differ from case to case, but an attempt is always made to rule out one particular selfish reason at a time for why empathizers might provide help. Of course, given the abundance of such reasons, multiple studies are required to test the empathy-altruism hypothesis fully. Nonetheless, at any point along the way, the empathy-altruism hypothesis could be disconfirmed, and its egoistic rival supported. Hence, if the empathy-altruism hypothesis survives a succession of determined attempts to disconfirm it, and no plausible egoistic alternatives to it remain, then that should be regarded as provisional evidence in its favor. (A useful analogy may be the following. Suppose you wanted to test whether some man was the best fighter in the village. Each time someone challenged him, he might well lose. However, if he continued to beat all other men in the village who look likely contenders to beat him, then it becomes increasingly plausible that he really is the best fighter in the village.)

Later, we summarize the many experimental findings that bear on the existence of altruism. For the moment, however, we consider findings that pertain to just one alternative to the empathy-altruism hypothesis. The alternative runs as follows: Whenever we feel empathy for others, we help in order to *forestall the guilt* that would otherwise result from not helping (i.e., prevent it from occurring in advance). This alternative is interesting insofar as it is somewhat subtle.

Advocates of this particular rival hypothesis point out that decent people typically berate themselves whenever they violate private standards of conduct. They argue that people's reluctance to violate such standards stems from their natural desire to avoid painful feelings of self-censure. Now, helping other people in distress is a standard of conduct to which most people subscribe. Hence, the argument goes, empathizers help in order to make sure that they avoid painful feelings of guilt. In other words, it is a selfish concern with their own well-being that motivates them, not any altruistic concern with the well-being of the distressed.

Advocates of the empathy-altruism hypothesis disagree. They propose that empathizers help with the ultimate goal of benefitting the distressed. Any guilt they might forestall in the process is merely an unsought-after bonus. Who is right?

What They Did

Batson and his colleagues (1988) had to manufacture an experimental situation in which one outcome would occur if a desire to forestall guilt lay behind empathic helping, but another outcome would occur if it did not. Their ingenious strategy was as follows. They realized that the degree of guilt that someone anticipates for not helping is not only a function of the private standards to which they subscribe; it is also a function of the social context in which they find themselves. For example, suppose that, to help your long-suffering mother, you know you ought to wash up after dinner, but you selfishly opt not to, and later feel guilty. Suppose too that your siblings either regularly wash up or rarely wash up. You would probably feel less guilty in the latter case because you would have a credible excuse for not helping: My siblings don't wash up, so why should I? In the psychological laboratory, the social context can also be explicitly adjusted to raise or lower levels of guilt. Such adjustments provide the key to testing whether or not empathy-based helping does or does not stem from the desire to forestall guilt.

The logic goes like this. If forestalling guilt is the ultimate goal of empathizers, then the strength of their resolve to help, and the amount of help they provide, should be reduced by changes in context that provide excuses for not helping. However, if forestalling guilt is not the ultimate goal of empathizers, then neither the strength of their resolve to help, nor the amount of help they provide, should be reduced by such contextual adjustments. Thus, one pattern of results would support the egoistic guilt-forestalling hypothesis, the other contradict it.

There is one complication however. Suppose the researchers demonstrated that providing an excuse for not helping had no effect on empathic helping. Would that by itself be enough to refute the egoistic guilt-forestalling hypothesis? No. The absence of a result could be put down to some defect in the study, such as an unconvincing excuse, or an insensitive measure of helping. To meet such objections, the researchers also had to show that they *could* undermine helping with an excuse. In particular, they had to show that providing participants with an excuse when they felt little empathy for a victim would reduce their helpfulness, whereas providing participants with the same excuse when they felt much empathy for a victim would not. Such a result would indicate that empathy made participants immune, so to speak, to the help-undermining effects of excuses. It would indicate that empathizers do not help with the ultimate goal of forestalling guilt, for if they did, the availability of an excuse would have reduced the amount of help they provided.

Batson and his colleagues (1988) conducted several studies that relied on this logic. In each study, participants were provided with a different justification for not helping. We focus here on just one of these studies—where participants were led to believe that a minority, as opposed to a majority, of their peers had previously helped in a similar situation. The expectation was that participants would adjust their private standards based upon the reported conduct of their peers.

One hundred and twenty undergraduates from Kansas University took part in the study. Matters were neatly arranged so that the 60 males and 60 females were equally represented in all conditions.

Participants were told that the purpose of the study was to pilot test some new programs for a local university radio station. One of the two programs to which they listened was entitled "News from the Personal Side." It consisted of an interview with a college student named Katie Banks. (The other program, more blandly informational, was included merely to make the cover story seem plausible.) As the interview proceeded, it became clear that tragedy had recently befallen Katie. Both of her parents, and one of her sisters, had been killed in an automobile accident. Katie had since struggled to support her two younger siblings because her parents had never taken out life insurance. To make matters even worse, Katie had had to withdraw from college in her final year, because if she did not, her siblings would be put up for adoption.

Before playing the tape, the experimenter instructed participants to listen to each program in one of two ways. They were told either to "imagine how the person who is being interviewed feels about what has happened and how the events have affected her" or to "focus on the technical aspects of the broadcast." These differing instructions constituted the experimental manipulation of empathy. The former instruction encouraged participants to identify with Katie, thereby placing them in the high-empathy condition. The latter instruction encouraged participants not to identify with Katie, thereby placing them in the low-empathy condition.

When the tape had finished, the experimenter "discovered" that the questionnaires he had intended to administer to participants had been made illegible by a photocopying glitch. He explained that he would have to leave briefly in order to obtain replacements. On his way out, he handed participants two letters that allegedly the professor in charge of the study had asked him to pass on. The first letter was apparently written by the professor himself. In the letter, the professor explained how, after listening to the tape, he imagined some participants might wish to help Katie. He went on to say that he had asked Katie to write a letter of her own, to indicate how participants could help her if they so desired. The second letter was apparently Katie's. In it, she outlined a number of possible ways in which participants could be of assistance to her, for example, by baby-sitting her younger brother and sister, helping out with transportation, or assisting in fundraising efforts.

Included with these letters was a response form, on which participants could indicate whether or not, and to what extent, they wished to help Katie. Participants had the option of pledging between 0 and 10 hours of assistance. Each response form featured eight spaces, seven of which had already been filled in by previous participants, so that one space remained for the real participants to fill in. This was done so that participants would not expect their responses to be seen by other participants, an expectation that might have biased their responses.

The availability of the excuse for not helping was manipulated by adjusting how the number of previous participants had responded to Katie's request for help. In the excuse condition, only two out of these seven participants had volunteered to help, whereas in the no-excuse condition, a full five of them had. An additional control condition was included in which the response form was designed to contain only a single signature. The purpose of this condition was to allow the researchers to test whether empathizers would help more than non-empathizers when no information was available about whether other students' helped. (Note that, had the experimenter still been present at this stage, difficulties might have arisen. Participants might have been more likely to conclude that the letters were just part of the study, or may have helped Katie simply because they felt that the experimenter was around to monitor them.)

Upon the return of the experimenter, participants were asked to fill out two questionnaires. Most of the items they featured were bogus, but a few served as a check on whether the experimental manipulations had worked as intended. Two items assessed the effectiveness of the empathy manipulation. The first asked participants how much they focused on the technical aspects of the broadcast, the second, how much they focused on the feelings of the person interviewed. Another item assessed the effectiveness of the excuse manipulation. Participants were asked to what extent they believed that other students had an obligation to help Katie. (The researchers reasoned that judgments of peer obligation would closely match judgments of personal obligation, and that both would reflect the availability of the excuse for not helping.) A final item asked participants to rate how much Katie herself stood in need of assistance. After completing these paper-and-pencil measures, participants were debriefed and dismissed.

What They Found

Preliminary checks indicated that the two manipulations had worked as expected. Participants in the high-empathy condition reported focusing more on Katie's feelings than on the technical aspects of the broadcast, whereas participants in the low-empathy condition reported the opposite. (A gender difference was also noted. Women on the whole were more likely to focus on Katie's feelings than men were.) In addition, participants in the excuse condition thought it less imperative that university students help Katie than did participants in the no-excuse condition. At the same time, no differences were found across conditions in how pressing Katie's need was judged to be. Neither level of empathy, nor excuse availability, influenced this perception. This makes interpretation of the study's results more straightforward.

The researchers quantified the help that participants provided in two ways. First, they noted the percentage of participants who volunteered any help; second, they noted the number of hours that participants pledged. For statistical reasons that we need not go into, the percentage measure was deemed the primary index of helping, and the number-of-hours measure the secondary index.

So what did the researchers find? As expected, when empathy for Katie was low, participants with an excuse for not helping volunteered in far fewer numbers than participants with no excuse. This indicates that having an excuse undermined helping when empathy was low—presumably by reducing the guilt that participants anticipated for not helping. However, a different picture emerged among participants who empathized with Katie. Participants who had a good excuse for not helping helped almost as often as participants who did not. In fact, the difference was no greater than would be expected by chance. This means that having or not having an excuse did not influence whether or not these participants volunteered to help Katie (Figure 18).

The secondary measure, the number of hours participants pledged, yielded a roughly similar pattern of results. Far fewer hours were pledged by participants in the low-empathy-excuse condition than by participants in the other three conditions, who did not differ in terms of the average number of hours they pledged.

How should these results be interpreted? The effectiveness of the excuse manipulation when empathy was low, coupled with its ineffectiveness when empathy was high, suggests that while forestalling guilt is the ultimate goal of non-empathizers, it is not the ultimate goal of empathizers. The guilt-forestalling hypothesis was therefore disconfirmed, and the empathy-altruism hypothesis survived one substantial attempt at disconfirmation.

In the study we have described, the excuse for not helping involved leading participants to believe that a minority rather than a majority of undergraduate peers had provided help. In companion studies, also designed to rule out the guilt-forestalling hypothesis, the researchers provided alternative excuses for not helping, and in other types of helping scenarios. The findings of both of these studies dovetailed those of the present study. Hence, converging evidence was obtained of the falsity of the guilt-forestalling hypothesis as an explanation for why people help when moved by empathy.

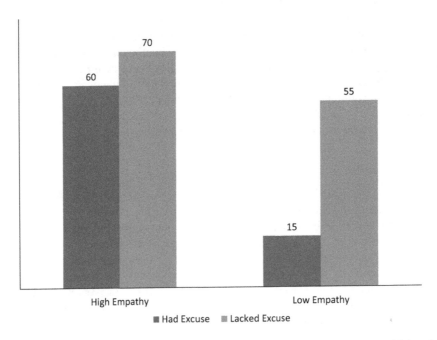

Figure 18 Percentage of participants who helped Katie, when their empathy for her was high or low, and when they had or lacked an excuse for not helping her

So What?

As mentioned previously, obtaining evidence in favor of the empathy-altruism hypothesis is a cumulative process. The present study and its two follow-ups effectively rule out only a single egoistic alternative to the empathy-altruism hypothesis. Other egoistic alternatives, of equal or greater plausibility, remain. However, many of these have themselves been convincingly ruled out in additional research.

Here is an example. In the "Background" section, we describing an experiment showing that helping can be motivated by the desire to repair one's own bad mood (Cialdini et al., 1973). Along similar lines, might people who empathize with a victim merely help them to *alleviate the personal distress* they feel on contemplating the suffering of the victim? It turns out that this explanation fits people who do *not* empathize with a victim. If they are given the opportunity to dodge the responsibility of helping—an alternative route to alleviating distress—they tend to take it, and to help the victim less. However, people who *do* empathize with the victim do *not* take advantage of this opportunity, suggesting that their goal is *not* to selfishly alleviate their own distress. Rather, their goal is genuine altruism (Batson, Duncan, Ackerman, Buckley, & Birch, 1981; Batson, O'Quinn, Fultz, Vanderplas, & Isen, 1983).

Many other studies, drawing on the same comparative logic, indicate that empathic helping is not motivated by a wide range of egoistic motives. These include enhancing self-image, taking pride in helping, and obtaining social praise (Batson et al., 1991; Dovidio, Piliavin, Gaertner, Schroder, & Clark, 1991; Fultz, Batson, Fortenbach, McCarthy, & Varney, 1986). Although the research is not completely consistent (e.g., Schaller & Cialdini, 1988), the balance of evidence suggests that the main egoistic alternatives to the empathy-altruism hypothesis have been credibly ruled out. The odds of the empathy-altruism hypothesis being true have therefore increased.

Of course, someone could always come along and identify a new egoistic motive that accounts for empathic helping. For example, it has been claimed that feeling empathy leads us to see other people as part of ourselves, so that by selflessly helping them we are in fact selfishly helping ourselves (Cialdini, Brown, Lewis, & Luce, 1997). However, both the reasoning behind this claim, and the data supporting it, have been critiqued (Batson, 1997). Interested readers are encouraged to read further and make up their own minds. Yet, with plausible egoistic motives for emphatic helping dwindling, the contention that human beings are capable of disinterested altruism no longer seems idealistic or naive. Rather, it seems empirically defensible.

The results of research on altruism are significant for two reasons. First, they provide a fresh perspective on human motivation. In particular, they suggest that *psychological hedonism*—the theory that all our behavior is governed by the experience, or the anticipated experience, of pleasure and pain—may be false. Rather, some motivations may have nothing to do with our own well-being, being focused solely on the well-being of others. (Chapters 2 and 9 likewise saw a refutation of the related theory that behavior is simply governed by rewards and punishments.) As a consequence, the results of research on altruism also tell us something deep about human beings as moral creatures. The cynical view that we are all ultimately selfish, implying that the motives of humanitarians and misanthropes are somehow on an equal footing, need not be endorsed.

Afterthoughts

It is interesting to speculate on what sources of altruism might exist in addition to empathy. Batson, Ahmad, & Stocks (2011) considers two possibilities: *collectivism*, the motivation to selflessly benefit a group with which one identifies, and *principlism*, the motivation to uphold some moral principle for its own sake. Collectivism might inspire a patriot to give up his life for the sake of his country (rather than, say, for personal glory). Principlism might keep a married man from committing adultery because he believes doing so would be wrong in itself (rather than, say, because he could not live with himself if he did). Such possibilities remain to be fully tested. However, it may be possible to modify the designs used in the present study to investigate the matter.

The question of whether other sources of altruism exist is important because empathy, for all the accolades bestowed upon it, has two serious drawbacks. We conclude by highlighting them. (For a more sustained critique of empathy, see Bloom [2014].)

First, empathy is largely *emotional*. As such, it is something that happens to us, not something we freely choose to bring about. Of course, like participants in the present study, we could deliberately try to take the perspective of another person; but this rarely happens in everyday life. Mostly, we are passively seized by tender feelings that prompt us to help others without thought of ourselves. Yet, such feelings are often created by situational factors, many of which are a matter of chance (e.g., whether the victim resembles us, or whether his plight is vividly communicated). This being the case, how much praise do we truly deserve for altruistic acts inspired by empathy? Having pure motives may not make us praiseworthy if those motives are partly the result of factors beyond our control. Altruistic acts inspired by principlism, however, could not be criticized on such grounds. Conforming to a moral principle for its own sake would require a conscious and deliberate act of will. It would not be something that just happens to us; rather, it would be the expression of our deepest character (Kant, 1785/1898). We could therefore justifiably take full credit for any and all altruistic acts we performed when inspired by principlism—unless, of course, it turns out that free will itself is merely a cognitive illusion (Wegner & Wheatley, 1999; see Chapters 22 and 29).

Another drawback of empathy is that it can inspire actions that violate the moral principle of fairness. Victims who arouse our empathic concern may not always be the ones who are objectively most in need of our help (Batson, Klein, Highberger, & Shaw, 1995; Singer, 1995). It may seem legitimate that we put the welfare of friends and family before those of strangers. More ethically worrisome is that the sentimental portrayal of the needs of the few can elicit more empathic help than the impartial description of the needs of the many. Thus, we may give more to a charity for cute mistreated animals than to a charity for emaciated starving children. The virtue of principled altruism is that it transcends parochial concerns. A passionate commitment to universal human rights might prompt one to work toward a fairer distribution of benefits across individuals. However, it may be that abstract principles, at least for most people, have less motivating force than empathy precisely because of their lack of specificity (Eisenberg, 1991). As the dictator Stalin once commented, with ironic insight into the nature of empathy: "The death of one man is a tragedy, the death of a million a statistic."

Revelation

When moved by empathy, people help not because they are motivated to avoid the guilt that would result from not helping, nor, it seems, for many other selfish reasons. Rather, they likely help with the ultimate goal of benefiting other people.

What Do You Think?

People disagree about whether or not human beings are capable of acting selflessly. Could these differences of opinion be partly due to the fact that some people are naturally capable of great empathy whereas others are not? Are our theories of human virtue linked to our own virtue?

Chapter Reference

Batson, C., Dyck, J., Brandt, J. R., Batson, J., Powell, A., McMaster, M. R., & Griffitt, C. (1988). Five studies testing two new egoistic alternatives to the empathy-altruism hypothesis. *Journal of Personality and Social Psychology*, *55*, 52–77.

Other References

Batson, C. D. (1997). Self-other merging and the empathy-altruism hypothesis: Reply to Neuberg et al. *Journal of Personality and Social Psychology*, *73*, 517–522.
Batson, C. D. (2011). *Altruism in humans*. New York: Oxford University Press.
Batson, C. D., Ahmad, N., & Stocks, E. L. (2011). Four forms of prosocial motivation: Egoism, altruism, collectivism, and principlism. In D. Dunning (Ed.), *Frontiers of social psychology: Social motivation* (pp. 103–126). New York: Psychology Press.
Batson, C. D., Batson, J. G., Slingsby, J. K., Harrell, K. L., Peekna, H. M., & Todd, R. M. (1991). Empathic joy and the empathy-altruism hypothesis. *Journal of Personality and Social Psychology*, *61*, 413–426.
Batson, C. D., Duncan, B. D., Ackerman, P., Buckley, T., & Birch, K. (1981). Is empathic emotion a source of altruistic emotion? *Journal of Personality and Social Psychology*, *40*, 290–302.
Batson, C. D., Klein, T. R., Highberger, L., & Shaw, L. (1995). Immorality from empathy-induced altruism: When compassion and justice conflict. *Journal of Personality and Social Psychology*, *68*, 1042–1054.
Batson, C. D., O'Quinn, K., Fultz, J., Vanderplas, M., & Isen, A. (1983). Influence of self-reported distress and empathy and egoistic versus altruistic motivation for helping. *Journal of Personality and Social Psychology*, *45*, 706–718.
Bloom, P. (2014). *Against empathy*. New York: Harper-Collins.
Cialdini, R. B., Brown, S. L., Lewis, B. P., & Luce, C. (1997). Reinterpreting the empathy-altruism relationship: When one into one equals oneness. *Journal of Personality and Social Psychology*, *73*, 481–494.
Cialdini, R. B., Darby, B. L., & Vincent, J. E. (1973). Transgression and altruism: A case for hedonism. *Journal of Experimental Social Psychology*, *9*, 502–516.

Darley, J. M., & Latané, B. (1968). Bystander intervention in emergencies: Diffusion of responsibility. *Journal of Personality and Social Psychology, 8*, 377–383.

Dovidio, J. F., Piliavin, J. A., Gaertner, S. L., Schroder, D. A., & Clark, R. D. III (1991). The arousal/cost-reward model and the processes of intervention: A review of the evidence. In M. S. Clark (Ed.), *Prosocial behavior* (pp. 86–118). Newbury Park, CA: Sage.

Eisenberg, N. (1991). Meta-analytic contributions to the literature on prosocial behavior. *Personality and Social Psychology Bulletin, 17*, 273–282.

Fultz, J., Batson, C. D., Fortenbach, V. A., McCarthy, P. M., & Varney, L. L. (1986). Social evaluation and the empathy-altruism hypothesis. *Journal of Personality and Social Psychology, 50*, 761–769.

Kant, I. (1898). *Kant's critique of practical reason and other works on the theory of ethics* (4th ed.; T. K. Abbott, Trans.). New York: Longman, Green, and Co. (Original work published in 1785.)

Latané, B., & Darley, J. M. (1970). *The unresponsive bystander: Why doesn't he help?* Englewood Cliffs, NJ: Prentice-Hall.

Nagel, T. (1979). *The possibility of altruism.* Princeton, NJ: Princeton University Press.

Schaller, M., & Cialdini, R. B. (1988). The economics of empathic helping: Support for a mood-management motive. *Journal of Experimental Social Psychology, 24*, 163–181.

Singer, P. (1995). *How are we to live? Ethics in an age of self-interest.* New York: Prometheus Books.

Wegner, D. M., & Wheatley, T. P. (1999). Apparent mental causation: Sources of the experience of will. *American Psychologist, 54*, 480–492.

More to Explore

Wilson, D. S. (2016). *Does altruism exist? Culture, genes, and the welfare of others.* New Haven, CT: Yale University Press.

19 When Two Become One

Expanding the Self to Include the Other

"How do I love thee? Let me count the ways."

—Elizabeth Barrett Browning (1806–1861), English poet

Background

One of the most celebrated romantic novels of all time is Erich Segal's (1970) *Love Story*. In this 20-million-copy bestseller, Oliver Barrett IV is the leading character. He has many claims to fame: Harvard student, ice-hockey jock, and heir to a fortune. Indeed, he is the great-grandson of the man after whom a colossal dormitory and several other campus buildings are named. However, Oliver is ambivalent about being the perfect preppie. And he loathes being programmed into the Barrett tradition: "It's all crap." Jenny Cavilleri, on the other hand, is a sarcastic Radcliff music major with gorgeous legs (by Oliver's account). Her mother's fatal car crash left Jenny to be raised by her big-hearted, pastry-chef father (whom she lovingly calls "Phil").

Oliver and Jenny meet in the Radcliff library. From the word go, she calls him "preppie." He calls her "snotty Radcliff bitch." A few dates later, opposites have attracted, and Oliver utters these immortal words: "I'm in love with you." She tells him he's "full of shit." Even so, the two soon get married, but predictably, without the blessing of Oliver's father, "Old Stonyface." ("Marry her now and I will not give you the time of day!" he thunders.)

At their do-it-yourself wedding, Oliver and Jenny stare blissfully into each other's eyes, as she recites a sonnet from Elizabeth Barrett Browning:

> When our two souls stand up erect and strong,
> Face to face, silent, drawing nigh and nigher,
> Until the lengthening wings break into fire . . .
> . . . a place to stand and love in for a day,
> With darkness and the death hour rounding it.

In turn, he reads aloud Walt Whitman's *Song of the Open Road*:

> . . . I give you my hand!
> I give you my love more precious than money,
> I give you myself before preaching or law;
> Will you give me yourself?
> Will you come travel with me?
> Shall we stick by each other as long as we live?

After the ceremony, they reflect on their new status as husband and wife. "Jenny, we're legally married!" he exclaims. "Yeah, now I can be a bitch," she quips.

With Oliver estranged from his imperious father, and cut off from the family fortune, the couple move into a cheap apartment and eke out a living. But despite their poverty, they are immeasurably happy. Conflicts arise ("God damn you, Jenny, why don't you get the hell out of my life!"), but their love always prevails. Jenny works to support Oliver through Harvard Law School. He finally graduates third in his class and makes the *Law Review*. "I owe you a helluva lot," he acknowledges. "Not true," she replies, "you owe me everything." Later in the story, Jenny utters her most memorable line: "Love means never having to say you're sorry."

We will not divulge the story's heartrending plot twists and final consolation. Suffice it to say that *Love Story* leaves one shaken, yet grateful, for what love is, or might be.

But have you ever wondered: What is *love*? What is the source of the poignant, often unaccountable, affinity between two people? How are we to understand the dynamics of an intimate relationship? What are the causes of satisfaction, or of conflict, in close relationships? Why do some flourish and endure, and others deteriorate and end? More generally, how do *personal relationships* (with family members, friends, and romantic partners) differ from *social relations* (with neighbors, coworkers, and strangers)? Historically, social psychology has mostly concerned itself with the latter, although a vibrant *relationship science* has emerged in the past few decades (see, for example, Lewandowski, Loving, Le, & Gleason, 2011).

Though we will attempt to address a few of the previous questions in this chapter, our main focus will be on one simple question: What *is* a close relationship? In the research literature, *behavioral* definitions stipulate that close relationships involve interdependence and mutual influence. Thus, lovers, friends, and family members typically spend considerable time together, share a diversity of activities, and reciprocate guidance and protection. But what is the *cognitive* significance of being in a close relationship?

Taking hints from William James (1890/1948) and Kurt Lewin (1948)—the so-called fathers of American psychology and social psychology, respectively—Arthur and Elaine Aron (1986) suggested that people relate to close others much as they relate to themselves. That is, they tend to view and treat loved ones as *equivalent* to their own selves. This inclusion of *other* in *self* is said to occur for (a) resources, (b) perspectives, and (c) characteristics.

To begin with, one tends in a close relationship to allocate *resources* to one's partner as if one were allocating them to oneself. One views benefits to a partner, or joint benefits, as accruing to the self. One wants to give to the other because the other is cognitively *part* of the self. Also, in a close relationship, one's *perspective* of the other's behavior is equivalent to one's perspective of one's own behavior. For example, one recognizes how much the other's behavior is influenced by the prevailing situation. This means that in loving relationships there may be less of an *actor-observer effect* (in which one attributes what one does to situational factors, but what others do to dispositional factors; Nisbett, Caputo, Legant, & Marecek, 1973; see Chapter 10). The contention that our perspective of the other is different depending on whether he or she is an intimate partner or a relative stranger is supported by a number of empirical findings. For example, whereas research participants remember their own performance on a laboratory task better than they do the performance of a stranger, they remember the performance of a friend or romantic partner nearly as well as their own (Brenner, 1973). Finally, in close relationships, a partner's *characteristics* are more easily confused with one's own. Thus, it is more difficult, and requires more time, to say that a particular trait describes oneself when a close other lacks it, and to say that a particular trait does not describe oneself when a close other possesses it.

Aron, Aron, Tudor, and Nelson (1991) sought to test the foregoing three claims—pertaining to resources, perspectives, and characteristics—in three corresponding experiments. We describe the methods and results of their first experiment in the next two sections, and then more briefly describe their second and third experiments in the "So What?" section.

What They Did

In their first experiment, Aron and his colleagues (1991) adopted a procedure pioneered by Liebrand (1984). They compared how participants would allocate money to themselves or to another, when that other was a stranger, friendly acquaintance, or best friend.

Twenty-four college students were presented, on a computer screen, with a series of choices having to do with allocating money to themselves and another person. For example, one choice was between (a) the self gaining $14.50 and the other losing $3.90 and (b) the self gaining $16.00 and the other losing $7.50. Thus, participants had to choose between outcomes that were more or less favorable to self at the expense of the other. Each choice was preceded by an instruction to imagine that the other was a stranger, friendly acquaintance, or best friend, who would or would not know the participant's allocation choice. Participants made 24 choices for each of the six possible combinations of instructions. For example, one set of 24 trials had them choose between allocation options while imagining that the other was a best friend who would not know their choices.

Following the logic of the inclusion-of-other-in-self approach, Aron and his colleagues (1991) predicted that the difference between self-allocations and other-allocations would be least when the other was their best friend, greatest when the other was a stranger, and intermediate when the other was a friendly acquaintance. They further predicted that this pattern would *not* be affected by whether participants assumed the other would or would not know about their choices. That is, they predicted that allocations would only be based on including or not including the other in the self, and be unaffected by self-presentational concerns or hopes of obtaining something in exchange for a favorable allocation. In the lingo of experimental design, they did not expect the manipulation of relationship closeness (stranger—acquaintance—friend) and the manipulation of the other's knowledge of the allocation (knowing—not knowing) to *interact* (i.e., the impact of the one manipulation would depend on the impact of the other).

The foregoing allocation task may strike the reader as a bit abstract or artificial. However, previous research had shown that hypothetical allocations are significantly correlated with real ones (Liebrand, 1984). This gave Aron and his colleagues (1991) some confidence that their findings would generalize to real-life situations (i.e., exhibit *external validity*). Nonetheless, this did not deter the researchers from conducting a follow-up experiment in which participants were led to believe that they would be allocating hard cash to real people, in some cases disclosing details of the allocation by letter. In this follow-up experiment, the friendly acquaintance condition was excluded, and more emphasis was put on the manipulation of whether or not the other would know about a participant's allocation. This experiment also included checks on whether participants understood the manipulation instructions.

Again, the researchers predicted that the difference between the amount of money participants allocated to themselves and to another person would be smaller when the other person was a best friend as opposed to a stranger.

What They Found

Aron and his colleagues (1991) analyzed their data in several ways, but always found the same pattern of results. Using allocations to self minus allocations to other as a dependent variable—an index of selfishness as opposed to selflessness in how they wanted money divided—they found the pattern of allocations they had predicted. In particular, the difference in allocations was least for self and best friend, intermediate for self and friendly acquaintance, and greatest for self and stranger. In fact, participants actually allocated *more* money to their best friend than to themselves—an altruistic gesture consistent with feeling greater empathy for close others (see Chapter 18). Importantly, they did not find any differences in allocation choices based on whether the imagined other would know about their choices. Thus, self-presentation was effectively ruled out as a factor in their allocations (Figure 19).

In the follow-up study, involving real money and people, a similar pattern of results emerged. In particular, the self-other difference in allocation was smaller for best friends than for strangers. This time, best friends, unlike strangers, were allocated almost as much money as the self. Again, these results did not hinge on whether the friend or stranger would subsequently learn about the allocations. Aron and his colleagues (1991) thus concluded: "We treat close others as if their resources were, to some extent, our own" (p. 246).

So What?

The results of this first experiment provided an important insight into the cognitive implications of being in a close relationship: Rewards to family members, friends, or romantic partners are experienced much as rewards to the self. The second and third experiments by Aron and his colleagues (1991) yielded complementary insights.

The second experiment featured a procedure first used by Lord (1980). Participants were presented with a series of concrete nouns each projected onto a screen for 10 seconds. They were instructed to form a vivid mental image of either themselves or a target person interacting with whatever each noun denoted. The target person was either their mother or Cher (a well-known and much esteemed singer and actress who had recently won an Academy Award). Participants were given 20 seconds to write down a description of their image before a new noun was presented. Once all the nouns had been presented, participants were given a surprise memory test. Specifically, they were asked to write down as many of the nouns as they could recall (in any order).

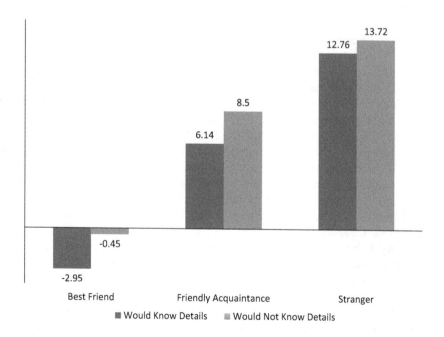

Figure 19 Extra dollars that participants allocated to themselves over three types of other person, when told each type would or would not know the details of the allocation

In previous research by Lord (1980), participants had been instructed to form (again in response to concrete nouns) mental images of themselves, their father, or Walter Cronkite (a well-known and much respected national news anchor at the time). Participants best recalled those nouns previously linked to Walter Cronkite and worst recalled those previously linked to themselves (which is surprising in that much research shows that we tend to better recall information encoded with reference to self; e.g., Rogers, Kuiper, & Kirker, 1977). Recall for nouns previously linked to their fathers fell in between. Such results are explained in terms of perspective: Socially distant others are viewed as part of the outer world (*figures* in one's *phenomenological field*), whereas one's intimately familiar self is viewed as part of the inner world (the *ground* of that field). Perhaps it is easier to form vivid images (and subsequently recall those images, and the nouns they bring to mind) of objective others than of the self. At any rate, Aron and his colleagues (1991) found precisely the same pattern of results for the self-mother-Cher manipulation. Participants remembered more nouns referring to things that were imagined to be interacting with Cher than they did nouns referring to things imagined to be interacting with their mother or themselves.

The same pattern of results was found in a follow-up experiment that involved, instead of Cher, a not-too-close female friend, or a relative of the participant's mother. Participants were also asked to rate how close they felt to their mothers. As predicted, their ratings of closeness were significantly correlated with the extent to which their memory for mother nouns was similar to their memory for self nouns, showing that inclusion-of-self-in-the-other is not an all-or-none phenomenon, but a matter of degree. These various findings all suggest that participants treated someone with whom they have a close relationship much as they would themselves.

A third experiment by Aron and his colleagues (1991) capitalized on the so-called *distinctiveness effect* (Mueller, Thompson, & Dugan, 1986), which refers to participants being slower to say that a trait applies to them the more unique it is to them. Aron and his colleagues (1991) reasoned that, because in a close relationship, the mental representation of one's partner is blended with that of one's self, there will be more confusion and slower reaction times in cases where the self and other do not share the same trait (i.e., when the trait is more distinctive).

In order to test their hypothesis, Aron and his colleagues (1991) had participants rate a series of trait adjectives for how well they described themselves, their spouse, and the comedian Bill Cosby (then famous and much-admired—before allegations of sexual misconduct destroyed his reputation decades later). Participants then engaged in a distraction task (which served to clear their minds of the previous ratings—a kind of cognitive sorbet), followed by a series of timed trials in which they classified those adjectives into the categories "Me" or "Not Me." Aron and his colleagues (1991) examined reaction times for four sets of traits: those rated as (a) true of participants and their spouses, but not of Bill Cosby; (b) not true of participants and their spouses, but true of Bill Cosby; (c) true of participants and Bill Cosby, but not of their spouses; and (d) true of their spouses and Bill Cosby, but not of participants. Aron and his colleagues (1991) predicted that participants, who they believed would mentally incorporate their spouse into their self, would experience more confusion (resulting in slower reaction times) for traits on which they differed from their spouse. Being dissimilar to Bill Cosby (a distant other), however, was not expected to slow reaction times.

The foregoing design was admittedly complicated; however, the results were clear-cut. Participants were slowest to respond to traits on which they and their spouses differed. When they and their spouses were the same, or when they or their spouses differed from Bill Cosby, they responded relatively more quickly. Furthermore, in a follow-up experiment that required participants to indicate how close they were to their spouses, perceived closeness was significantly correlated with slower reaction times for traits on which self and spouse differed. This correlation between closeness and self-other confusions was exactly what Aron and his colleagues (1991) had predicted, and resembled the results of the two experiments described earlier.

The findings of all these three experiments gel nicely. They support the contention that love is an inclusionary process: One mentally includes a loved one into his or her self. In other words, there is an overlap between the mental representations of self and the representations of close (but not distant) others. In this sense, a friend or lover is a second self! Never before had such an experimental examination of the cognitive significance of being in a close relationship been conducted.

Returning to Segal's (1970) *Love Story*, how might Aron and his colleagues' (1991) research shed light on the love between Oliver and Jenny? It does so by revealing that such closeness involves the breakdown of cognitive boundaries. The distinction between self and other, in both Jenny and Oliver's minds, became increasingly blurred as the two fell in love. Each became an extension of the other's self. Neither partner was particularly concerned about receiving a greater allocation of resources than the other—any benefit to a partner was most likely viewed as a benefit to the self. Moreover, typical differences between actors and observers, in terms of perceptions and attributions, may have all but disappeared in Jenny and Oliver's case. Rather than merely looking *at* each other, the two were each seeing each other as they saw themselves. Furthermore, they probably came to characterize themselves and their partners similarly—each other's traits becoming blended into closely overlapping *schemas* (mental structures). This would have resulted in a failure to appreciate real differences between them in personality traits.

This raises an interesting issue. What is the relation between people's *perceptions* of one another's traits and the *facts* about those traits? An early pioneer of psychology, William James, allegedly once said: "Whenever two people meet, six people meet: each person as they think they are, each person as the other person thinks they are, and each person as they are really are!" Indeed, accurate knowledge of self can be hard to come by (see Chapter 14). The same goes for accurate knowledge of others. However, to understand others, people use themselves as a base—they engage in *egocentric projection* (Dunning, 2012). One example is the *false consensus effect*: People's own willingness to perform an odd act (like wearing a sandwich board that reads "Repent!") predicts how willing they think other people would be to do so (Ross, Greene, & House, 1977). Although Aron and his colleagues did not objectively assess the traits of participants, nor of others that they imagined, it seems plausible that "including others in the self" involves thinking that others resemble the self. If so, it would also be an example of egocentric projection.

Finally, not perceiving yourself to be the same as a close other may even be a source of *cognitive dissonance* (a state of mental tension or uneasiness; see Chapters 2 and 3). Indeed, Aron and his colleagues (1991) suggested that dissimilarity between one's own and a close other's attitudes may cause dissonance in the same way that holding opposite attitudes within oneself can cause dissonance. Thus, dissonance may at times be a function of the closeness of a relationship—the degree to which the other is included in the self.

Afterthoughts

Most of the research described in this book addresses how relative strangers think about and influence one another. Even so, relationships have become a vibrant area of research. Social psychologists now investigate such topics as attraction, love, communication, resource allocation, jealousy, conflict, conflict resolution, satisfaction, and commitment in personal relationships.

One classic theory of human relationships is *social exchange theory* (Kelley & Thibaut, 1978; Thibaut & Kelley, 1959). It applies an *economic* analysis to interpersonal interactions. Relationships are said to afford various *rewards* (love, status, money, goods, services, and information) and *costs* (time, energy, money, stress, loss of identity, and loss of freedom). The underlying assumption of the theory is that people seek out and maintain relationships in which the rewards exceed the costs. Thus, one is likely to compare his or her current relationship to past relationships ("Hey, I'm not used to being treated this badly in a relationship!" or "I've never felt so loved in all my life!"). He or she is also likely to compare a current relationship to possible alternative relationships that might prove more rewarding ("Sure I'm engaged, but there's no reason I can't get friendly with that guy who keeps checking me out!").

Social exchange theory helps explain the so-called *matching principle* (Berscheid, Dion, Walster, & Walster, 1971): the tendency for people to choose partners who are similar in physical attractiveness (not to mention age, height, intelligence, education, social background, religion, attitudes, and values). People usually know their own *market value* (what their looks, personality, and social standing can buy in the marketplace of people and relationships). Someone who's drop-dead gorgeous does not get involved with someone who looks like a potato. (This might explain why Swedish actress, Alicia Vikander, never returned my emails.) Social exchange theory also helps explain the *principle of least interest*: The partner who is least interested in a relationship wields the most power (Waller, 1938). Such a person is in a position to call the shots and make demands in a relationship ("Stop drinking and get a job, or else!") because he or she is more liable to leave, perceiving more rewarding relationship opportunities elsewhere. In general, social exchange theory claims that people focus on the outcomes—the profits and losses—of a relationship. They seek relationship bargains. A relationship is a commodity bought at a price, a stock to invest in.

Yet do economic metaphors fully explain interpersonal dynamics? Might social relations (among relative strangers) operate differently than personal relationships (among family members, friends, and lovers)? Clark and Mills (1979, 1993) claimed that they do, making a key distinction between *exchange* and *communal* relationships. In an exchange relationship, it is appropriate to give a benefit in return for one of equal value. "The neighbors lent us their garden tools, so we should have them over for dinner." In a communal relationship, however, it is appropriate to give a benefit in response to the *need* for it. "Our in-laws have fallen on hard times, so we should have them over for dinner more often and help watch their kids until their situation improves." In other words, exchange relationships tend to be reciprocal or tit-for-tat, communal relationships not—at least in the short-term. In exchange relationships, each partner seeks *equity*—what each person gives to a relationship should correspond to what he or she gets out of a relationship. Thus, one person's giving a lot when the other gives only a little is not a problem so long as the first person gets proportionately more out of the relationship. However, in communal relationships one responds to a loved one's needs—for emotional and other forms of support—with a sense of genuine care and without counting the cost (again, see Chapter 18).

What are the empirical implications of this exchange—communal distinction? Clark and Mills (1979) demonstrated that, whereas strict reciprocity is welcome and increases attraction in exchange relationships, such behaviors *decrease* attraction in communal relationships. Clark, Mills, and Powell (1986; see also Clark, Mills, & Corcoran, 1989) also demonstrated that members of exchange relationships, concerned about equity, monitor their own and their partner's *inputs* into a joint task, whereas members of communal relationships are more inclined to keep track of others' *needs*. Finally, Clark and Taraban (1991) found that, whereas people in exchange relationships tend to talk about unemotional topics, people in communal relationships tend to talk about emotional ones (and problems can arise when these norms are violated; see Chapter 1). The research by Aron and his colleagues (1991) featured in this chapter is important because it was one of the first explorations of the cognitive consequences of being in a communal relationship.

It is important to recognize that, although love has been contemplated by poets and philosophers (and practically everyone else) for thousands of years, it has only been studied scientifically (let alone experimentally) for a few decades. What has been learned about love and close relationships in this relatively short time? A great deal, although we can only mention the smallest fraction of it here. One interesting line of research has focused on the *components* of love.

According to Sternberg (1986), love is shaped like a triangle, with each of its sides representing an important component of love: *passion* (an intense longing for union with the other), *intimacy* (the breadth and depth of communication with the other), and *commitment* (the determination to stick with the other). More or less emphasis can be placed on any one of these components (each side of the triangle can be a variable length), so that there are innumerable possible love triangles (not to be confused with three-way relationships!). Moreover, the various components can combine to produce different types of love—much like the primary colors of red, green, and blue combine to produce additional colors. A relationship that includes only intimacy: *liking*. One that includes only passion: *infatuation*. Only commitment: *empty love*. Then there are the combinations. Intimacy and passion, but no commitment: *romantic love*. Intimacy and commitment, but no passion: *companionate love*. Passion and commitment, but no intimacy: *fatuous* (i.e., superficial) *love*. Finally, a love that involves a good measure of all three components: *consummate love*. If you are in love with someone, you may want to read more about these types and reflect on your type. In the fictional case of Oliver and Jenny, there is evidence of all three components of love. Might their story be so appealing because it so eloquently describes the perfect synthesis? By the way, although it may be easy to *achieve* consummate love, after a short period of time, it is difficult to *maintain* it, over a long period of time. Relationship satisfaction often and perhaps typically declines as the years progress (Kurdek, 1998). That said, a third of couples who stay together long-term still report being very much in love (O'Leary, Acevedo, Aron, Huddy, & Mashek, 2012).

Another theoretical approach to love that has prompted much research and received a fair amount of empirical support is that of Lee (1973) and, later, Hendrick and Hendrick (1986). After surveying adults in Canada, the United States, and Great Britain (keep in mind the possible cultural bias here), Lee identified six distinct *styles* of love: *eros* (romantic love), *mania* (possessive love), *storge* (best-friends love), *pragma* (pragmatic love), *agape* (altruistic love), and *ludus* (game-playing love). Each person possesses a somewhat unique combination of these idealized styles. Hendrick and Hendrick (1986) viewed the styles more as attitudes that can change over time than as fixed traits. Also, different relationship partners and other situational constraints can bring out different love styles in a person. Hendrick and Hendrick's (1986) *Love Attitudes Scale* can help determine one's love style.

One can see in Oliver and Jenny the expression of all six love styles, and some differences between the two lovers. If Oliver and Jenny do exhibit different love styles, perhaps they do so in a way that fits with research findings of gender differences in this regard (Hendrick & Hendrick, 1995). Perhaps, too, their approach to love reflects the prevailing culture (America in the late 1960s).

Social psychology continues to provide many other insights into love and personal relationships. There are now entire journals and many books devoted to relationship science. But then too, there is much to discover about love and relationships from life itself!

Revelation

To love a person means, among other things, to include that person in one's self. This involves perceiving, characterizing, and, critically, allocating resources to that person in much the same way one does one's self.

What Do You Think?

Might evolution have shaped the nature of love—including by making men and women love differently? For example, why do as many women as men accept the offer of date from someone attractive, but far fewer women accept the offer of casual sex (e.g., Clark & Hatfield, 1989)?

Chapter Reference

Aron, A., Aron, E. N., Tudor, M., & Nelson, G. (1991). Close relationships as including other in the self. *Journal of Personality and Social Psychology, 60,* 241–253.

Other References

Aron, A., & Aron, E. N. (1986). *Love as the expansion of self: Understanding attraction and satisfaction.* New York: Hemisphere.

Berscheid, E., Dion, K., Walster, E., & Walster, G. W. (1971). Physical attractiveness and dating choice: A test of the matchmaking hypothesis. *Journal of Experimental Social Psychology, 7,* 173–189.

Brenner, M. (1973). The next-in-line effect. *Journal of Verbal Learning and Verbal Behavior, 12,* 320–323.

Clark, M. S., & Mills, J. (1979). Interpersonal attraction in exchange and communal relationships. *Journal of Personality and Social Psychology, 37,* 12–24.

Clark, M. S., & Mills, J. (1993). The difference between communal and exchange relationships: What is and is not. *Personality and Social Psychology Bulletin, 19,* 684–691.

Clark, M. S., & Taraban, C. (1991). Reactions to and willingness to express emotion in communal and exchange relationships. *Journal of Experimental Social Psychology, 27,* 324–336.

Clark, M. S., Mills, J., & Corcoran, D. M. (1989). Keeping track of needs and inputs of friends and strangers. *Personality and Social Psychology Bulletin, 15,* 533–542.

Clark, M. S., Mills, J., & Powell, M. C. (1986). Keeping track of needs in communal and exchange relationships. *Journal of Personality and Social Psychology, 51,* 333–338.

Clark, R. D. III, & Hatfield, E. (1989). Gender differences in receptivity to sexual offers. *Journal of Psychology & Human Sexuality, 2,* 39–53.

Dunning, D. (2012). The relation of self to social perception. In M. Leary & J. Tangney (Eds.), *Handbook of Self and Identity* (2nd ed., pp. 481–501). New York: Guilford.

Hendrick, C., & Hendrick, S. S. (1986). A theory and method of love. *Journal of Personality and Social Psychology, 50,* 392–402.

Hendrick, S. S., & Hendrick, C. (1995). Gender differences and similarities in sex and love. *Personal Relationships, 2,* 55–62.

James, W. (1948). *Psychology.* Cleveland, OH: Fine Editions Press. (Original work published 1890).

Kelley, H. H., & Thibaut, J. W. (1978). *Interpersonal relations: A theory of interdependence.* New York: Wiley-Blackwell.

Kurdek, L. A. (1998). The nature and predictors of the trajectory of change in marital quality over the first 4 years of marriage for first-married husbands and wives. *Journal of Family Psychology, 12,* 494–510.

Lee, J. A. (1973). *The colors of love.* New York: Bantam.

Lewandowski Jr., G., Loving, T. J., Le, B., & Gleason, M. E. J. (Eds.). (2011). *The science of relationships: Answers to your questions about dating, marriage and family.* Dubuque, IA: Kendall Hunt.

Lewin, K. (1948). The background of conflict in marriage. In G. Lewin (Ed.), *Resolving social conflicts: Selected papers on group dynamics* (pp. 84–102). New York: Harper.

Liebrand, W. B. G. (1984). The effect of social motives, communication and group size on behavior in an N-person, multi-stage mixed-motive game. *European Journal of Social Psychology, 14,* 239–264.

Lord, C. G. (1980). Schemas and images as memory aids: Two models of processing social information. *Journal of Personality and Social Psychology, 38,* 257–269.

Mueller, J. H., Thompson, W. B., & Dugan, K. (1986). Trait distinctiveness and accessibility in the self-schema. *Personality and Social Psychology Bulletin, 12,* 81–89.

Nisbett, R. E., Caputo, C., Legant, P., & Marecek, J. (1973). Behavior as seen by the actor and as seen by the observer. *Journal of Personality and Social Psychology, 27,* 154–164.

O'Leary, K. D., Acevedo, B. P., Aron, A., Huddy, L., & Mashek, D. (2012). Is long-term love more than a rare phenomenon? If so, what are its correlates? *Social Psychological and Personality Science, 3,* 241–249.

Rogers, T. B., Kuiper, N. A., & Kirker, W. S. (1977). Self-reference and the encoding of personal information. *Journal of Personality and Social Psychology, 35,* 677–678.

Ross, L., Greene, D., & House, P. (1977). The false consensus effect: An egocentric bias in social perception and attribution processes. *Journal of Experimental Social Psychology, 13*, 279–301.

Segal, E. (1970). *Love story*. New York: HarperCollins.

Sternberg, R. J. (1986). A triangular theory of love. *Psychological Review, 93*, 119–135.

Thibaut, J. W., & Kelley, H. H. (1959). *The social psychology of groups*. New York: Wiley-Blackwell.

Waller, W. (1938). *The family: A dynamic interpretation*. New York: Dryden Press.

More to Explore

Anderson, J., & Szuchman, P. (2011). *Spousonomics: Or how to maximise returns on the biggest investment of your life*. New York: Random House.

20 The Eye Is Quicker Than the Mind
Believing Precedes Disbelieving

"Man is a credulous animal, and must believe something; in the absence of good grounds for belief, he will be satisfied with bad ones."
—Bertrand Russell (1872–1970), British philosopher and mathematician

Background

We often find ourselves provoked by some TV or radio advertisement, research report, political speech, courtroom testimony, overheard rumor, or face-to-face comment. Someone wants to persuade or even deceive us about an idea, person, or commercial product. The assumption is that we respond to these various persuasion ploys by evaluating them, before accepting or rejecting them. But is this the case? According to Gilbert (1992), people believe everything they read or hear—whether truth, fiction, or outright lie—when they first read or hear it. It is only afterward that they may come to disbelieve it.

Gilbert (1992) was interested in the sequence by which someone comprehends a statement and assesses its *truth value* (accepts it as true or rejects it as false). The usual assumption, apparently commonsensical, is that people first comprehend the meaning of a given assertion, and then decide whether it is true or false. Gilbert traced this account back to Rene Descartes, the 17th-century mathematician and philosopher who devised the *Cartesian coordinate* system that gave rise to analytic geometry. Descartes also famously addressed the epistemological question of what (if anything) can be known for certain. Can we even be sure of our own existence? His answer was: "I think, therefore I am." (Joke: One day, Rene Descartes woke at noon with a bad hangover. His head throbbing, he went to a nearby restaurant. The waitress asked if he would like his usual decanter of wine. "I think not!" he exclaimed, and vanished.)

Gilbert was skeptical of Descartes' assumption that the truth of a statement is assessed only after that statement is comprehended. Gilbert was more sympathetic to an alternative model of belief developed by Baruch Spinoza, a Dutch philosopher and Descartes' younger contemporary. According to Spinoza, the process of comprehension cannot be separated from the process of acceptance. More specifically, we initially accept everything we hear or read. We may, however, reject some or all of it at a later time, when by one means or another we become aware of features that are suspect or false. We will heretofore refer to this surprising (if not seemingly goofy) idea as the Gilbert-On-Spinoza Hypothesis, or "GOSH" for short. Consider this: In the case of pictures (instead of verbal statements) we do not make a distinction between comprehension and acceptance. They are one and the same. We *see* things automatically, and almost always take what we see to be what is there. This accords with common sense, and is linguistically embedded in such phrases as "Seeing is believing" and "I saw it with my own eyes." Or, as famed baseball star Yogi Berra once quipped, "You can see a lot just by looking."

There is good reason to believe what we see. In confrontations with danger, it is vital to act quickly. We do not stand around weighing the evidence for and against the belief that the animal we have comprehended 100 yards away is a real—as opposed to a paper—tiger. We have a greater chance of survival if we take it to be real, and get the heck out of there. The earliest humans (and other primates) must have faced a number of life-threatening situations, and therefore the evolutionary advantage was with the development of fast, relatively uncritical perceptual systems. No physical harm results from fleeing two comedians in a tiger suit.

However, there is something of a conceptual leap from visual perception to verbal processing. The analogy alone doesn't prove that comprehension of a statement is the same thing as acceptance of the statement as true. An experiment was needed that could distinguish between the aforementioned Cartesian and Spinozan possibilities.

There are important differences in the predictions of these two models. If we spontaneously accept a statement the very moment we read or hear it in its entirety, and don't have the opportunity to scrutinize it afterward, then the statement will remain accepted. We thereby run the risk of being misled. In contrast, the commonsense Cartesian model predicts that this will not happen. We will defer accepting or rejecting a statement until after it has been understood and we have weighed any evidence for or against it. These different predictions gave Gilbert, Tafarodi, and Malone (1993) the hook they needed to tell the two models apart.

What They Did

Two things were needed: a mixture of true and false statements, and a procedure for distracting one from processing those statements. The most woodenheaded, straightforward way to assemble a set of trues and falses is to collect facts from the real world and distort some of them. For example, "Germany, Italy, and Japan were the three powers that fought against the U.S. and its allies in World War II" is true. "Madrid is the capital of Mexico" is false. The truth value of these statements is determined by information that often has been learned by rote from teachers or school books. This means, however, that the statements are not useful for testing the GOSH, which is essentially concerned with the processing of new statements or information more generally.

To avoid well-learned facts, a seemingly promising strategy is to invent facts, using made-up concepts, such as "greebles eat mung." The experimenters could then tell the participants which of these assertions were true and which false (on Planet Zorg, or in some other fictional setting where the use of strange words might be reasonable). Psychologists have used fictional stimuli in many different experiments for more than 100 years. For example, Ebbinghaus (1885/1964) used so-called nonsense syllables in his pioneering studies of memory and forgetting.

However, Gilbert and his colleagues (1993) did not like these hypothetical statements either. They wanted statements that—if accepted—would have important consequences (assertions about greebles do not, unless one happens to be a greeble). But if, for example, false testimony in a jury trial tended to be one-sidedly favorable or unfavorable to the defendant, it could alter the verdict from guilty to innocent, or vice versa. It could also affect the severity of the sentence if the defendant were found guilty. These would be consequential outcomes.

In the first of their three studies (for simplicity, the only one we will describe in detail), 71 female college students read aloud two unrelated crime reports presented as lines of text crawling across a computer monitor. One report was about a man named Tom who was accused of robbing a stranger who had given him a ride. The second report was about a man named Kevin who was charged with robbing a convenience store. Each of the reports contained both true statements (displayed in black) and false statements (displayed in red). The participants were told that the statements in red were false—details taken from unrelated police reports and mixed in with the facts, much as false testimony is often mixed in with true testimony during a trial. The participants were asked to consider the crime reports, play the role of trial court judges, and determine the prison sentences of each of the two defendants.

One clever feature of their experiment was that, half the time, the false statements were favorable to the defendant in the first trial and unfavorable to the defendant in the second trial. In other words, the false statements made the first crime seem less serious and the second more serious. The remainder of the time, it was the other way around. The false statements made the first crime seem more serious and the second less serious. This counterbalancing ensured that the results of the experiments could not be attributed to differences between the two crimes, as any results obtained would be averaged across both crimes.

A second manipulation was necessary to test the GOSH. It involved either distracting or not distracting participants from processing the statements. To this end, in one condition, participants performed a digit-search task while reading about the crimes. A string of blue digits crawled across the screen just below the text they were asked to read aloud—participants had to push a certain button every time they encountered the digit 5. In the other condition, participants did not perform a digit-search task—they could focus all of their cognitive resources on the text describing the two crimes, including the false statements printed in red. Thus, each of the two crime cases involved a *2 × 2 design*: The false statements were either favorable or unfavorable to the perpetrator of the crime, and the participants were either distracted by a digit-search task or not.

Then, after reading the two reports, participants were asked to recommend a prison sentence, between 0 and 20 years, for each of the defendants. This recommended sentence was the main dependent variable, although Gilbert and his colleagues collected additional data, such as participants' ratings of how much they liked each of the perpetrators, and how dangerous they believed each of them to be.

Gilbert and his colleagues predicted that the addition of the digit-search task would prevent participants from being able to reject false statements they had initially accepted. Participants would therefore continue to accept these statements as true, which would bias the prison sentences they recommended. Among participants who were distracted, therefore, false statements supportive of a defendant would prompt more lenient sentencing, and false statements critical of a defendant more severe sentencing. For participants who were not distracted, however, the false statements would have little, if any, impact on judgments, because those false statements would be appropriately rejected or ignored.

What They Found

This is precisely what Gilbert and his colleagues found. Distracted participants rendered more lenient prison sentences (on average, about 6 years) when the false statements made the crime seem less serious, and more severe prison sentences (on average, about 11 years) when the false statements made the crime seem more serious. (Notice that the recommended prison time was almost double in the latter condition.) However, when participants were not mentally burdened by the digit-search task, the false statements had a negligible influence on the sentence they rendered (about 6 and 7 years, respectively; Figure 20). Participants' ratings of the perpetrators' likableness and dangerousness followed the same pattern. False statements favorable to the defendant rendered him more likable and less dangerous, and false statements unfavorable to the defendant rendered him less likeable and more dangerous, but only when, crucially, participants were distracted by the digit-search task. Taken together, these results indicate that participants who were overloaded by the digit search acted as though many of the false statements were true. Evidently, they had initially believed most of those statements, but had no opportunity to disbelieve them.

At this point, the astute reader may raise a possible objection. Perhaps being interrupted by the digit-search task did not so much prevent participants from disbelieving the false statements as confuse them about which statements were true and which were false. This could have led to the pattern of results obtained. (Specifically: If the false exacerbating statements had been more

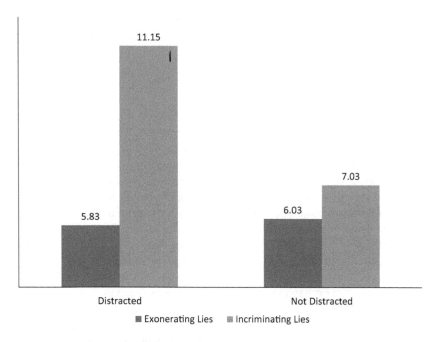

Figure 20 Years in prison that participants recommended for defendants, after reading—while being distracted or not—exonerating or incriminating lies about the defendants

negative than the true statements about the crime, then the overall impression of the defendant would have been more negative. Similarly, if the false extenuating statements had been more positive than the true statements about the crime, then the overall impression of the defendant would have been more positive.) Gilbert and his colleagues (1993) were alert to this potential alternative explanation. To test its validity, they had wisely included a recognition memory task at the end of their experiment. Participants had to indicate whether some of the statements they had previously seen were true or false. Now, if participants had simply been confused by the digit-search task, then they would have misremembered as many true statements as false as they had false statements as true. However, if the digit-search task would have made them specifically unable to disbelieve false information, then they would only have misremembered false statements as true. The pattern of recognition observed was asymmetrical in precisely this way, consistent with the GOSH.

Worth mentioning briefly are the results of the second study by Gilbert and his colleagues (1993), which focused on the durability of the effects of false statements. Recognition memory after about 20 minutes showed that 54% of interrupted false statements were recalled as true. In contrast, when not interrupted, 29% of the false statements were recalled as true. Thus, the interruption manipulation almost doubled the number of false statements miscategorization as true ones. By comparison, true statements were very rarely recalled as false—only 4% and 5% in the two conditions.

Gilbert and his colleagues (1993) had begun by revisiting an unresolved philosophical debate over the nature of belief. From there, they proceeded to formulate a tentative working hypothesis: "Acceptance . . . may be a passive and inevitable act, whereas rejection may be an active operation that undoes the initial passive acceptance" (Gilbert and others, 1993, p. 222). Then, in a series of elegant studies, they experimentally manipulated how mentally busy participants were, by having them do or not do concurrent tasks that undermined their ability to process information normally. As we have seen, this allowed them to test whether rejection is indeed an active operation, one that can be prevented. Their compelling results led them to conclude with a bold statement: "People do have the power to assent, to reject, and to suspend their judgment, but only after they have believed the information to which they have been exposed" (Gilbert and others, 1993, p. 230).

So What?

One might be tempted to pooh-pooh the debate between the Cartesian and Spinozan positions as mere intellectual posturing. However, Gilbert's data are far from trivial. We would argue that the laboratory situation, even with its fussy details and short time scale, maps well onto the real world with all its uncontrolled happenings. What is required to make this leap from the lab to life is the realization that critical incidents can take place rapidly in the real world too. A remark may be overheard just prior to having one's attention diverted by any of a number of things. Indeed, a colleague of the author's once used this device to political effect. Disliking John Lindsay, then a candidate for mayor of New York City, he arranged for like-minded students to converse with each other while standing in a subway car next to one target person after another. Just before stopping at a station, one student gossiped to the other: "Did you hear about that Lindsay scandal? One of Lindsay's men had his hand in the till. And Lindsay ain't talkin'!" There was a confusion of people going in and out after the train stopped—the distraction served to undermine capacity for doubt. Beyond that, in every domain there are people who are somewhat gullible because they don't have enough knowledge and confidence to reject an incoming claim.

In the real world the GOSH effect is nothing less than a systematic formula for getting away with telling lies, and a prescription for massive public misinformation. There are an astonishing number of wrong-headed beliefs in circulation in the United States, and elsewhere (Gilovich, 1993; Schermer, 1997). Beyond the penchant for members of the public to fall prey individually to misinformation, there is a *polluted well effect* (terminology ours). Circulating falsehoods contaminate the well of public opinion. People convey medical advice picked up from general gossip—for example, they declare the good health benefits of drinking eight glasses of water a day, even though there is absolutely no good evidence for this. Or someone sends an embellished e-mail message, tells a revealing joke at a business luncheon, or reports some hearsay to the editor of the local paper. Then a second set of media sources gets hold of what seems to be an interesting item, and passes it along, typically without attribution. Then there comes a third layer, and a fourth, and so on. Now the item is in the public domain. Almost nobody knows the original source, and after passage through several generations, it becomes too difficult to trace the source, and no one seems to care. When the item is issued in several disparate outlets, it carries much more weight than it would have deserved had the possibly biased or unreliable source been identified at the time the message was received. And if it comes from all parts of the ideological spectrum, one cannot reasonably attribute blame to the communicators' biases (unless one has a well-developed conspiracy theory about all available sources of communication). The polluted well effect is not strictly a GOSH effect. It is closely related, however, in that the message is presumed true in the absence of further specification. Consider a few vivid examples.

The Good Old Days. Apparently, problems in our schools have turned gravely worse in the last 40 years. In the 1950s, teachers listed the three most serious problems in school as running in the halls, chewing gum, and making too much noise. The three most serious problems in the 1990s, by contrast, were drugs, pregnancy, and rape. O'Neill (1999), in an investigative tour de force, located the originator of the survey of the school problems legend. You guessed it—there never was a survey yielding such comparative results over time. The conclusions were made up by a man named T. Cullen Davis of Fort Worth, Texas, a Christian fundamentalist who defended his thesis of moral decay by stating that he had talked to teachers personally, who told him how bad things were in the 90s, and who remembered how much better they had been in the 50s. (See Chapter 21 for a discussion of the pitfalls of retrospective memory.) The job of locating Mr. Davis was monumental. O'Neill likened it to peeling an onion with a million layers.

Love, Oh Love, Oh Proven Love! Did you hear about the Yale study that discovered the 12 most persuasive words in the English language: *love, beauty, proven,* etc.? At the Yale Communication and Attitude Change Project throughout the 1950s and 1960s, we would get a letter every two months or so, asking who ran this study, and whether we had the data. During this period, the results appeared in a widely read airline magazine, among many other publications. As a member of the Yale Project, I remember other members asking everybody they knew who the author of the study was. It sounded like a pretty silly thing to waste time on, but in any case, no indication was ever found that anyone connected with Yale had done such a study. We suspected that it was a Madison Avenue project. Or perhaps a research assistant who had once been a Yale undergraduate put a misleading Yale imprimatur on the story.

Your Elevator or Mine? In November of 1976, a power outage knocked out electricity from New York to Montreal. Manhattan was especially hard hit when the juice went off. Thousands of people were marooned between floors in dark elevators. Thousands more gamely staggered down many flights of stairs in the dark. Once outside, they discovered that there were no streetlights, and that, although navigating Manhattan's streets in the dark might be adventurous, crossing the Brooklyn or Queensboro bridges would be utter madness. Those who weren't stuck in elevators were often parked at the curb, waiting hours for the outage to be fixed. When things returned to normal early the next day, there was a great deal of conversation about what people had done during those lost hours. Exactly nine months later, a local reporter happened to be in a big New York hospital, where he thought he saw a great volume of activity in the maternity ward. He checked with a passing nurse, and also called other New York hospitals. He was consistently told that the number of births was clearly above average that day. His newspaper then printed his alleged proof that a substantial number of the men and women who had spent long hours in darkness the night of the blackout had done what men and women are prone to do during long hours of darkness. The story was picked up by many other papers and magazines, helped along by wire service coverage. Years later, virtually everybody who had heard of the blackout believed that one of its consequences was an increase in sexual activity.

A modicum of thought about the matter should have raised some doubts. It is unlikely that the groups trapped in the elevators would have been sympathetic to one or more couples mating on the floor in their midst. Imagine the stress the blackout victims were under: not knowing if and when they would get home, worrying about friends and family but having no way to contact them, having no dinner, and so on. Meanwhile, couples at home suddenly thrown into darkness would have been more worried about batteries, candles, and dead refrigerators than their own libidos. In fact, the data are subject to a little-known artifact: There is a weekly cycle of delivery dates (including Caesarian deliveries) with its peak on Monday, so that had the reporter sent in the figures for the day a week later or earlier, or three or seven weeks later, the result would have been the same. The human gestation period had nothing to do with the case. This example is discussed in further detail in Abelson (1995).

Afterthoughts

Not only can we be fooled by others' false claims; we can also fool ourselves. Consider the common practice of intentionally setting one's watch or clock a few minutes fast. According to strict logic, this practice is absurd: One knows that the timepiece is fast. However, the time-setter is cleverly capitalizing on the seductive nature of appearance. In glancing at one's watch, one gets the immediate impression that the false time on the watch is true, causing him or her to hurry faster to an appointment.

A similar, albeit more confusing, example is Daylight Savings Time. Clearly, time is not saved—the light hours are merely moved up along the arbitrary scale of clock time. The idea of Daylight Savings Time was to make the long days of spring and summer seem even longer. Suppose that sunset is at 7 p.m. We can lengthen the apparent evening by calling 7 p.m. 8 p.m. Now the sun sets later. All the changed clocks around the country tell us that it is really 8 p.m., even though we know that we used to call this very moment 7 p.m. The change amounts to a societal collusion to promote the fiction that the evenings are even longer than what is ordained by earth and sun.

One other example of group collusion comes from a Yale faculty group that met regularly to play table stakes poker. In this version of poker there is essentially no limit on the size of bets. The amounts won and lost in a session often ran in the $100 to $200 range, and various attempts were made to decrease these unacceptably large amounts while still maintaining the same level of excitement. Almost all the fixes we tried failed. Finally, somebody got a crazy idea, and it worked. The chips were given double values. Each player got $20 worth of chips for $10 of real money. At the end of the game, the chips were cashed, with players getting $10 for each $20 of chips. There were no other changes in the game.

Logically, this doubling-and-halving maneuver is vacuous. The players all realize that when they make a bet of $50 with the cheap money, they are really only betting $25. Why, then, should the 2-for-1 procedure make any difference? Well, when a player says, "I bet $50!" it sounds like a big, bold bet. It is really only worth $25, but his words are taken at face value, just as the GOSH would predict. The net result was that less money was won and lost by the biggest winner and loser. Everybody fumbled for an explanation for this seemingly childish self-deception. Gilbert's experiments help to clarify the matter: The value of the chips is perceived true unless further reflection reveals its inflated value. Yet the players are too involved in the game to be reminded of this on every bet. The chip inflation effect may not have been rational, but it worked.

There are many other phenomena that depend on the immediately distinctive features of a stimulus to create audience gullibility. Economists puzzle over the *money illusion* (Levin, Faraone, & McGraw, 1981), whereby the face value of the money involved in a decision-making situation is taken to be more important than other factors that can matter a great deal. The archetypal illustration of the money illusion is that a majority of workers would prefer a $100 a month raise in an era of 7% inflation to a raise of $50 a month in an era of 1% inflation. It is considered irrational to choose the first option, because the increase in real wages is only 3% net, compared to 4% for the second option. This is not a perfect case of the GOSH effect, but it broadly relates in that people tend to focus on the size of the raise, and neglect to consider the inflation factor.

We think that there is great psychological generality to the formula of doing the simplest thing in a situation unless some factor warns us away. People tend to believe what they hear or are told unless there is reason to be suspicious. They accept their first impressions in the absence of contrary information. Among computer scientists, the term for a standard response to any stimulus not otherwise categorized is the default value. We are claiming here that persons have default responses to situations, and under ordinary circumstances use these defaults. Overriding a default requires one of several active processes. This is a general statement, which includes the case at hand. Namely, that the default in reading or hearing some information is acceptance; subsequent rejection requires overriding that default.

What might allow one to reject a message that he or she would otherwise accept? One possibility is that the person is somehow predisposed to reject the message. Gilbert and his colleagues (1993) do not consider this possibility, but it certainly deserves consideration. Often people say things like: "I don't believe a word that guy says." For example, at a public meeting on school busing in New Haven, as a liberal local priest came to the microphone to speak in favor of a busing plan, a woman in the audience whispered audibly: "What does he know? He never had any children!" The most common cases of this sort of resistance are probably those arising from quarrels over territory, ideology, rights, or morality, where each party regards the other as chronically misguided or lying, and tells each other so. Both observation and experimental research suggest that in these circumstances the outcome is negative persuasion, where both sides are driven farther and farther from each other's positions (Abelson & Miller, 1967).

When resistance has been established prior to the communication, it would seem that a reject response must occur immediately, contrary to the GOSH effect. Yet this is not necessarily so. A participant primed for resistance need not exercise it immediately. There is, in fact, some experimental evidence for the phenomenon of delayed resistance. McHugo, Lanzetta, and Bush (1991) chose video clips from the more emotional passages of political speeches, and then had participants rate their own feelings at certain key moments of the tapes. The researchers found a general tendency for participants' emotions to mimic those of the speaker, particularly with regard to fear or anger. When the candidate knitted his brows or looked worried there was an immediate echo of a worried expression on audience members' faces. In general, participants' ratings during the speech of their own feelings were consistent with the facial expressions they showed. However, there was one curious exception. When former president Ronald Reagan spoke with the intention of reassuring his audience, virtually all participants' spontaneous responses showed the echo effect. They looked reassured and relaxed, and many smiled. A few seconds later, however, Democrats rated their own feelings as negative, not as relieved and reassured. It was as though they couldn't help but smile at a smiling face, no matter whose face, but then realized they were smiling at Ronald Reagan, enemy of Democrats! They must have said to themselves: "Whoa! Why am I smiling at that guy?" whereupon they gained control of themselves and reported negative feelings, as the GOSH would predict.

Revelation

Although commonsense suggests that we suspend belief or disbelief until after we have understood a message, research shows that, initially, belief accompanies understanding, and that doubt follows later only if mental resources and motivation are sufficient.

What Do You Think?

Can you think of your own examples of the GOSH effect? Have others used the effect to fool you, have you used it to fool others, or have you used it to fool yourself?

Chapter Reference

Gilbert, D. T., Tafarodi, R. W., & Malone, P. S. (1993). You can't not believe everything you read. *Journal of Personality and Social Psychology, 65,* 221–233.

Other References

Abelson, R. P. (1995). *Statistics as principled argument*. Mahwah, NJ: Lawrence Erlbaum Associates.

Abelson, R. P., & Miller, J. C. (1967). Negative persuasion via personal insult. *Journal of Experimental Social Psychology, 3,* 321–333.

Ebbinghaus, H. (1964). *Memory*. New York: Dover. (Original work published 1885.)

Gilbert, D. T. (1992). How mental systems believe. *American Psychologist, 46,* 107–119.

Gilovich, T. (1993). *How we know what isn't so: The fallibility of human reasoning in everyday life*. New York: Free Press.

Levin, I. P., Faraone, S. V., & McGraw, J. A. (1981). The effects of income and inflation on personal satisfaction: Functional measurement in economic psychology. *Journal of Economic Psychology, 1,* 303–318.

McHugo, G. J., Lanzetta, J. T., & Bush, L. K. (1991). The effect of attitudes on emotional reactions to expressive displays of political leaders. *Journal of Nonverbal Behavior*, *15*, 19–41.

O'Neill, B. (1999). *Honor, symbols, and war*. Ann Arbor: University of Michigan Press.

Schermer, M. (1997). *Why people believe weird things: Pseudoscience, superstition, and other confusions of our time*. New York: W. H. Freeman.

More to Explore

Sunstein, C. R. (2014). *On rumors: How falsehoods spread, why we believe them, and what can be done*. Princeton, NJ: Princeton University Press.

21 Mythical Memories

Reconstructing the Past in the Present

"The most faithful autobiography is less likely to mirror what a man was than what he has become."
—Fawn M. Brodie (1915–1981), American biographer

Background

To prepare yourself for this chapter, try the following autobiographical exercise. Sift through your memory until you locate an episode from your distant past. Next, attempt to recall what happened as clearly as you can, paying special attention to visual details. Spend a few moments doing so before proceeding to the next paragraph.

Ready? Now, replay the entire episode once again. Looking at it with your inner eye, what precisely do you see? Though the imagery may be faint, and the scenes disjointed, an odd fact may be apparent. Your recollections may *not* resemble the visual images that a *camera on your head* would have recorded. Rather, in accordance with cinematic convention, the remembered events may be depicted from a third-person perspective. You may picture yourself as part of the scene (Nigro & Neisser, 1983).

The existence of such impossible memories proves a surprising but important point: Not only are memories capable of being retrieved, they are also capable of being *reconstructed*. In today's hi-tech culture, people could be forgiven for thinking that human memories, once properly stored, can be retrieved from the mind as faithfully as computer files are downloaded from a disk. However, the analogy is mistaken. The memories people retrieve are often biased by the state of mind they are in. A better analogy for how human memory operates (staying within the hi-tech world) might be an eccentric word processor that keeps reinterpreting the contents of documents as it opens them.

Several factors can lead memories to be unreliably reconstructed. Consider, for example, mood. People remember information better when they learned it in a mood similar to their current one (Clore, Schwartz, & Conway, 1994). In other words, people's minds select some memories, but ignore others, based on their current emotional state. This tendency is also apparent in people suffering from depression, whose mood often varies over the course of the day. They recall more pleasant memories, and fewer unpleasant memories, when happy than when sad (Clark & Teasdale, 1982).

Memories for once-held opinions provide another vivid example of how the past is reinterpreted in terms of the present. In one experiment (Goethals & Reckman, 1973), high school students were first classified, based on their earlier responses to a questionnaire, as being either for or against the busing of poor Black kids to better-off schools. (At the time, this was a controversial proposal, aimed at achieving better racial integration in classrooms.) Several days later, in a different setting, the students were divided into discussion groups based on their pro-busing or anti-busing opinions. In each group, the discussion came to be dominated by an experimental confederate, posing as a respected senior student. The confederate presented compelling arguments *against* the opinions held by the other group members. The effect, predictably, was to induce students to revise their opinions. The critical part of the experiment, however, came 4 to 14 days later. All students were asked to fill out a repeat version of the questionnaire, and to give their original answers. To ensure that students were highly motivated to accurately recall their opinions, the experimenter claimed that he would be carefully checking the correspondence between both versions of the questionnaire. Nevertheless, students' recall of their opinions was distorted. They falsely remembered their original opinions as having been consistent with their newly acquired ones. The authors of the study interpreted these results in terms of cognitive dissonance theory (Festinger & Carlsmith, 1959; see Chapter 2), the idea being that participants, driven by the motivation to hold consistent opinions, were averse to concluding that their opinions had changed. However, a non-motivational explanation is also possible. Participants may have reconstructed their past opinions on the basis of false theories about how much their opinions were likely to have changed, using their current opinions as a benchmark (Ross, 1989). Whatever the explanation, retrospective editing of one's opinions appears to be no fluke. For example, one large study found that, over a 9-year period, people's current political attitudes were more closely related to the attitudes they *remembered* holding than to the attitudes they *actually* held (Marcus, 1986).

Such findings have an Orwellian feel to them. Yet at least the characters in George Orwell's provocative book, *1984*, knew that a vast propaganda campaign was being waged against them. In contrast, we seem to be largely unaware that our minds fabricate and revise our personal histories (Greenwald, 1980). Our ignorance of these mental dynamics should not come as a surprise to readers of Chapter 14. There, research was reviewed showing that our intuitive theories about how the mind works, and about the factors that influence its operation, can be woefully wide of the mark. We should hardly expect the experience of remembering to be accompanied by better insight into how remembering occurs, or how faithfully the past is recorded.

The challenge for the experimental social psychologist is to demonstrate that people's intuitive theories can bias recall. To meet this challenge, three things need to be assessed: (a) people's intuitive theories about the mind, (b) the events addressed by those theories, and (c) people's memories for those events. To satisfy these requirements, McFarland, Ross, and DeCourville (1993) seized upon a phenomenon that might seem a strange candidate: *menstruation*.

In Western culture, the negative impact of menstruation on well-being is taken as a given (Brooks-Gunn & Ruble, 1986). *Premenstrual syndrome* (more recently labeled *Premenstrual Dysphoric Disorder*; American Psychiatric Association, 2013) is the household name for the array of symptoms, ranging from chocolate cravings to homicidal impulses, that falling levels of the hormone progesterone are alleged to trigger toward the end of the menstrual cycle. The syndrome is popularly regarded as a scientific fact. It is often soberly discussed by media commentators, and is a staple of the self-help literature. Many readers may be surprised to learn, therefore, that evidence for the syndrome is remarkably scarce. Numerous studies have failed to substantiate any systematic change across the menstrual cycle in psychological symptoms (Klebanov & Ruble, 1994; Romans, Clarkson, Einstein, Petrovic, & Stewart, 2012). Indeed, it can be argued that premenstrual syndrome is not so much a bona fide medical disorder as a cultural myth that persists as a way of explaining women's distress in terms of their presumed emotional and biological fragility (Tavris, 1992). (Lest readers think that these claims reflect male bias, we point out that women have done much of the relevant research on the topic.)

For the purposes of demonstrating that memory is shaped by intuitive theories, menstruation was therefore an ideal choice. First, it was associated with a prevalent stereotype. Second, the reality of menstrual events could be assessed from daily self-reports of mental and physical symptoms. And third, memories for those same menstrual symptoms could be assessed from retrospective self-reports.

In the study described, the researchers also made three specific predictions. First, they predicted that participants' intuitive theories of menstrual distress, being shaped by negative cultural stereotypes, would be at odds with their actual experience of menstruation. Second, they predicted that women's intuitive theories of menstrual distress would lead them to recall their menstrual symptoms as being worse than they actually were. Finally, they predicted that the more strongly women held those theories, the more biased their recall of those menstrual symptoms would be.

What They Did

Sixty-five Canadian females, mostly college students in their late teens and early twenties, participated in the study. To assess the nature and strength of their intuitive theories of menstrual distress, the researchers had them complete a subset of items from the *Menstrual Distress Questionnaire*, or *MDQ* (Moos, 1968). These items tapped the extent to which participants believed they were susceptible to three general types of symptom over the course of their menstrual cycle: pain, water retention, and unpleasant emotion. Participants rated the severity of six specific symptoms of each general type (i.e., 18 in all) on scales that ranged from *symptom absent* to *symptom acute and disabling*. The researchers' assumption that the MDQ items would reflect intuitive theories about, rather than actual experience of, menstrual distress had been supported by two previous findings. First, MDQ scores and daily self-reports of menstrual distress tend to correlate only modestly (Ascher-Svanum, 1982; see also Hawes & Oei, 1992). Second, responses to the MDQ before the onset of menstruation resemble responses to it afterward (Clarke & Ruble, 1978). The MDQ was administered approximately 2 weeks after the rest of the study was over, in order to avoid arousing participants' suspicions.

To assess actual symptoms over the course of the menstrual cycle, the researchers had participants fill out daily questionnaires that asked, among other things, about their experiences of pain, water retention, and unpleasant emotion. The researchers, however, disguised the purpose of these daily questionnaires. Prior research had shown that people report extra symptoms if they believe that they are participating in a study on menstruation (Ruble & Brooks-Gunn, 1979). Hence, the daily questionnaires consisted mostly of bogus items, designed to back up the researchers' cover story that they were investigating the links between legal drug use, life events, psychological states, and physiological states. Only one other questionnaire item was genuine: It asked unobtrusively whether participants were currently menstruating.

Participants agreed to complete the daily questionnaires at bedtime for a period of 4 to 6 weeks. They deposited each questionnaire in a public mailbox the day after they completed it. (This was in the days before email—think how much easier this study would be to run today!) If participants ever failed to submit a questionnaire, they were immediately contacted and given a reminder. It is a tribute to the management abilities of the researchers, and to the conscientiousness of the participants, that over 99% of the questionnaires given out were returned.

Finally, some days after the daily questionnaire phase of the study had concluded, the researchers assessed participants' recall of their menstrual symptoms. Participants were asked to remember, as best they could, the responses that they had given to the daily questionnaire exactly two weeks earlier. The administration of the recall measure was scheduled so that half the participants had been in the menstrual phase of their cycles when they had filled out the original questionnaire, and half in their post-menstrual phase. (The menstrual phase was defined as the first 3 days of menstruation, and the post-menstrual phase as a subsequent 3-day period beginning 5 days later.) The researchers assumed that the former participants would use their intuitive theories of menstrual distress to inform their recollections only if made aware that they had been menstruating. So to ensure participants were in fact aware of their prior menstrual status, the experimenter let them see their responses to the first three items on the life-events section of the questionnaire, where the third item conveyed the relevant information. (This was done supposedly to help jog their memory for all their questionnaire responses). Finally, to oblige participants to rely solely on their memories of menstrual symptoms, the researchers ensured that no participants were menstruating at the time they attempted to recall their responses to the daily questionnaire.

What They Found

Participants' intuitive theories of menstrual distress, indexed by their MDQ scores, bore out cultural stereotypes. Specifically, participants believed that they had experienced more pain, retained more water, and felt worse during the menstrual and premenstrual phases of their cycle. On a 6-point scale of severity, they indicated that each type of symptom had been, on average, 1 scale point worse than at other times.

However, participants' intuitive theories of menstrual distress did *not* match their actual experience. Participants' responses to the daily questionnaires indicated that their pain and water retention levels had only been a quarter scale point worse during their menstrual and premenstrual phases. Even more strikingly, participants' levels of unpleasant emotion did not show any fluctuation across the whole of their cycle. Thus, the undergraduates in the present study seemed blessedly immune to the premenstrual blues. Statistical tests confirmed these patterns. In addition, participants not only overestimated the intensity of their symptoms during the menstrual and premenstrual phrases of their cycle, but they also underestimated them during the remainder of their cycle (Figure 21).

Such results demonstrate that participants' theories of menstrual distress did not correspond with the reality of their symptoms. But could their theories also *distort* participants' specific recollections of their menstrual distress? One way to test this would have been to check whether, for each type of symptom, the discrepancy between daily reports and subsequent memories was greater for participants scoring higher on the MDQ, but only when the reports and memories

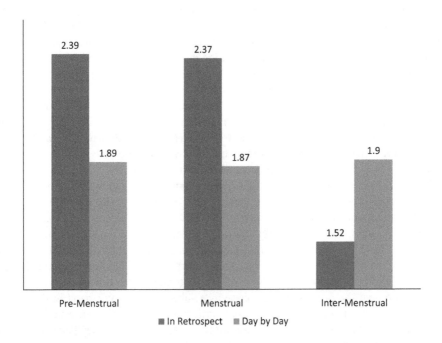

Figure 21 The levels of unpleasant emotion that participants reported across different phases of their menstrual cycle, both in retrospect and day by day

pertained to the menstrual phase of participants' cycle (as they did for half the sample). The researchers conducted a series of conceptually similar, but statistically more powerful, tests to address these questions. The predicted findings emerged. The more severe participants expected their period to be (based on their intuitive theories about menstrual symptoms), the more they retrospectively exaggerated the severity of their symptoms. However, this only happened when the period of recollection pertained to the menstrual phase of their cycle, not to other phases. The effects obtained were most pronounced for pain and unpleasant emotion.

A supplementary analysis underlined the very specific nature of the memory distortion. The MDQ items, you will recall, surveyed intuitive theories of menstrual distress for the whole of the monthly cycle, not just the menstrual phase. As expected, participants' intuitive theories about the distress they would experience during the non-menstrual phases of their cycles did not predict their recall of menstrual symptoms.

Taken altogether, these findings neatly show that intuitive theories of menstrual distress (but not of non-menstrual distress) biased participants' memory for menstrual symptoms (but not for non-menstrual symptoms). They provide strong evidence that intuitive theories about the mind—in particular, about how it is affected by bodily events—can distort recollections. In fact, it is conceivable that the results obtained even underestimated the magnitude of the distortion. Participants' daily reports of their symptoms had been equated with objective reality. However, these reports, being themselves somewhat retrospective in nature by several hours, were *also* liable to have been somewhat influenced by participants' intuitive theories of menstrual distress. The fact that positive findings were obtained nonetheless points to the potency of the longer-term memory distortion found.

One final subtle issue deserves comment. Participants' intuitive theories were assessed only *after* they had attempted to recall their symptoms. Might participants' mistaken theories have therefore been a *consequence* of the symptoms they misremembered rather than the cause of them? A final set of analyses ruled out this alternative explanation. We have not mentioned it until now, but the researchers also conducted a parallel study in which they had participants complete the MDQ immediately following the recall task, rather than two weeks later as in the main study. If participants' recollections had influenced their theories, then the correspondence between the measures would have been greater in the parallel study (no delay) than the main study (two-week delay). However, no greater correspondence was found. Hence, this alternative memories-cause-theories hypothesis was not supported.

So What?

We typically believe ourselves to be remembering events exactly as they occurred. But studies like the present one suggest that we may often be unconsciously constructing events on the basis of mistaken beliefs. So counterintuitive is this possibility that an analogy may help incredulous readers to digest the point.

The moon *looks* bigger over the horizon than it does in the center of the sky. Nonetheless, the moon always remains the same size, always subtending a constant angle of half a degree to the eye regardless of its position. This is the so-called *moon illusion*. One explanation for it is that faraway overhead objects typically do subtend a smaller angle to the eye than nearby overhead objects (e.g., airplanes get smaller as they recede into the distance). Consequently, our visual system cleverly corrects for the smaller angle to give the useful impression that faraway objects remain the same size. However, because the size of the moon remains the same, our visual system is conned into correcting for non-existing lunar shrinkage, and the perceptual distortion results (Baird, Wagner, & Fuld, 1990). The point is this: We are not aware of the underlying inferences that shape our false perception of the moon, only of the final perception itself. Similarly, we are not aware of the unconscious beliefs that shape our false recollections, only of the recollections themselves. In the first case, it takes a cognitive psychologist to highlight our errors, in the second case, a social psychologist.

Our lack of insight into how our minds work can be explained (see Chapter 14). However, what explains the *persistence* of our intuitive theories when our ongoing experience repeatedly disconfirms them? In particular, why did participants in the present study, who had menstruated for many years, not learn that menstruation was unrelated to psychological distress? Perhaps the main reason is that memories shaped by intuitive theories feel subjectively compelling, which in turn is taken as evidence that these intuitive theories are true. Another general reason why false intuitive theories may persist is that espousing them enables desirable conclusions to be reached. For example, in one study, students who enlisted in a study skills program known to be ineffective later recalled their prior studying habits as having been poorer compared to a matched control group (Conway & Ross, 1984). Wanting to believe that all the effort they invested had been justified (Aronson & Mills, 1959; see Chapter 3), they espoused the theory that the program worked, and then altered their recollections to match. A final reason why false intuitive theories persist is that the evidence bearing on them may be processed in a biased manner (Kunda, 1990; see also Chapter 17). A useful distinction can be drawn here between one-sided and two-sided events (Madey & Gilovich, 1993). Two-sided events capture our attention no matter how they turn out, whether they confirm or violate our expectations. For example, a honeymoon in Vegas is likely to prove memorable whether it turns out to be a fairytale or a fiasco. In contrast, one-sided events only capture our attention if they turn out a particular way. For example, if I guess correctly who is calling before I pick up the phone, I may marvel at my clairvoyance; but if I guess incorrectly, I may instantly switch my attention to other topics. Consequently, my "hits" will be recalled, my "misses" forgotten. Given that estimates of likelihood depend upon the ease with which material can be retrieved from memory (Kahneman & Tversky, 1973), I might then lean toward the false conclusion that I possess psychic ability. Similarly, participants in the present study may have been more impressed by, and hence have better remembered, those occasions on which their menstruation coincided with psychological distress than those on which it did not. Occasions confirming the stereotype would likely have been more dramatic (because of the emotional upset they have entailed), whereas occasions disconfirming the stereotype would likely have been less so (because they entailed no departure from normal well-being).

Afterthoughts

It is likely that many participants in the present study felt they were genuinely *recalling* their menstrual symptoms, not simply inferring or imagining them. To the extent that this was so, they were exhibiting *false memories*. This brings us neatly to our final topic of discussion.

Questions concerning the reliability of memory have attracted intense public and scientific scrutiny due to the heated controversy surrounding the alleged phenomenon of *recovered memory* (Loftus, 1994). Many clinicians believe, following Freud, that traumatic experiences in childhood, too harrowing to be consciously assimilated, get involuntarily *repressed* (split off from conscious awareness) and remain so for many years. Although the repression initially allows the trauma to be endured, it later gives rise to an array of psychological symptoms that the patient is at a loss to explain. Diagnosis of these symptoms by a clinician is followed by intensive psychotherapy aimed at enabling patients to recall their trauma, the underlying premise being that remembering is a necessary or sufficient condition for healing. Clinicians typically rely heavily on techniques such as guided hypnosis and suggestive prompting to get to the root of their patients' repression. Patients undergoing the therapy often find themselves supported and encouraged by a community of like-minded survivors.

Unfortunately, patients' alleged memories often push the limits of credibility. Impassioned crusaders urge us to accept that the abuse of children by Satanists, or the abduction of humans by aliens, is alarmingly commonplace—a silent epidemic that our society refuses to acknowledge (Bass & Davis, 1994; Mack, 1995). The impressionable would therefore do well to heed an argument first formulated by the philosopher David Hume (1990), which he hoped would "serve as an everlasting check on superstition of all kinds." Hume asked which we have better grounds for believing: that a religious miracle occurred and was accurately reported, or that it did not occur and was inaccurately reported? He concluded that, given our background knowledge of how the world works, the latter possibility is always the more likely. Consequently, there can never be adequate grounds for believing in miracles on the strength of testimony alone (not even if such miracles actually occurred). A similar argument could be brought to bear on the more extravagant claims of those who champion the cause of recovered memory.

Nonetheless, some recovered memory claims *do* fall within the bounds of credibility. In such cases, memory-based testimony cannot simply be dismissed out of hand. It seems improbable, on the face of it, that large numbers of patients would allege traumatic abuse without due foundation, or that memories for such abuse would be so vivid were they mere mental fictions. Yet are things as they seem? The stakes are high. On the one hand, every moral person rightly recoils from the prospect of dismissing a genuine case of abuse as bogus. On the other hand, accepting as genuine a false allegation of abuse risks ruining the lives and reputations of those who stand unjustly accused. In the absence of decisive physical evidence, the evidential value of memory-based testimony must be carefully determined. Scientific psychology has played a key role in this regard. As it turns out, its findings tend to justify skepticism about the validity of recovered memories.

First of all, the available laboratory evidence does not support the view that people repress unpleasant memories (Holmes, 1990). (Note: Repression differs from suppression in that it is involuntary; see Chapter 22 for more on the effects of voluntary suppression.) Indeed, one of the hallmarks of real traumatic memories, observed in people who have been through verifiable ordeals like wartime killing, is that such memories *cannot be forgotten*. They intrusively recur during both waking and sleeping (Krystal, Southwick, & Charney, 1995). Admittedly, post-traumatic amnesia does occur but when it does it is global in nature, such that all sorts of events, traumatic and non-traumatic, are forgotten (Schacter & Kilstrom, 1989). However, even if a trauma were selectively forgotten, repression would not be automatically implicated. Everyday forgetting, due to competition from other material or to the decay of memory traces, would be an equally if not more plausible explanation. True, unpleasant autobiographical memories do tend to fade faster than pleasant ones, but repression does not appear to be involved (Walker, Skowronski, & Thompson, 2003). Hence, the prima facie case for recovered memory is not compelling.

Moreover, numerous studies attest to the surprising malleability of memory. Taken as a whole, these lend credence to the view that recovered memories may be artificially induced. For example, when people read a list of related words (e.g., bedtime, yawn, pillow), most of them then recall having read, or report recognizing, other thematically related words that did not in fact appear (e.g., sleep; Roediger & McDermott, 1995). Moreover, people's confidence in the accuracy of their memories, and their feeling of remembering rather than guessing, is no higher for words previously presented than for words falsely identified. Hence, subjective judgments about the validity of memories can go astray when highly consistent mental concepts are activated.

Other research shows that post-event questioning can modify memories. In one study, for instance, a series of slides was presented in which a car came to a halt at a *stop* sign. Some participants were then asked, misleadingly, what the car did after coming to a halt at the *yield* sign. These participants were more likely to later remember having actually seen a yield sign than were those who were not asked the misleading question. Such findings have been replicated for features like speed and color, and carry obvious implications for the reliability of eyewitness testimony (Loftus, Miller, & Burns, 1987). Clearly, how questions are asked can bias the content of what is recalled.

However, can recollections be fabricated from nothing if others merely insist that fictitious events occurred? Remarkably, they can. In a study of false confessions (Kassin & Kiechel, 1996), participants performed a computer task either speedily or slowly. The experimenter warned participants at the outset not to press the ALT key accidentally, as this would later cause the computer program to crash. All heeded this warning, but later found themselves wrongfully accused of pressing the key. For some participants, the accusations were backed up by a confederate, who whispered audibly to the experimenter that he had witnessed the alleged transgression. Of those participants who performed the computer task hurriedly, and who overheard the confederate ratting them out, one-third fabricated detailed false recollections about pressing the ALT key. This study shows that, when memory for an event is vague, and others make a credible case for its having occurred, such a memory stands a reasonable chance of becoming integrated into one's mental autobiography. Indeed, a substantial minority of people remember fictitious childhood events when it is only casually suggested to them that they occurred (Ceci, 1995).

Sessions with recovered memory therapists are anything but casual however. First of all, patients are openly pressured to generate memories in order to surmount the retrieval block that repression is presumed to impose. Second, recovered memory therapists often employ hypnosis or guided imagination to facilitate patients' recall of events. Although research shows that such techniques can improve memory for real events, it also shows that they can do the same for fictitious events (Spiegel, 1995). Third, patients are liable to be steeped in the lore of the recovered memory movement, ensuring that they will possess rich intuitive theories concerning the nature of trauma, memory, and therapy. Extrapolating from the present study, we could expect such theories to spawn theory-consistent recollections. Fourth, paradoxical as it may seem, patients may be powerfully motivated to believe that they are victims of trauma. Full assimilation into a sympathetic community of fellow survivors requires that a patient exhibit the authenticating signs, and the emotional stress of the therapy itself is likely to strengthen a patient's commitment to that community (Aronson & Mills, 1959; see Chapter 3).

At the end of the day, the fact that recovered memories do assume fantastic forms is the best evidence for their potential unreliability. Devotees of recovered memory therapy, now legally compelled to admit the reality of some false memories and the devastation they can wreak (see Wright, 1994, for one harrowing example), nonetheless continue to maintain that genuine instances of repressed trauma do exist, and that these can be diagnosed by experienced clinicians with tolerable accuracy. However, it is difficult to see how such clinicians could acquire such expertise in the first place. They have rarely if ever had access to individuals who can be positively identified as abused or non-abused by any criterion independent of their own clinical judgment.

Even if genuine cases of recovered memory do exist, the therapeutic value of dredging up a traumatic past is still debatable. Modern scholarship has argued that Freud, the originator of supposed memory cures, never actually cured any of his patients, despite his extravagant claims to the contrary (Crews, 1995). Certainly, it is good to face unresolved psychological issues. Even confiding one's woes to a diary modestly benefits one's mental and physical health (Frattaroli, 2006; Pennebaker, 2000). However, becoming preoccupied with the past, and bogged down in one's own victimhood, is an unlikely recipe for triumphing over adversities past. Forging ahead courageously, finding hope in the new rather than fault with the old, is a more reliable road to recovery.

Revelation

Our intuitive theories about how things are subtly shape our memories of what has been. Thus, we unknowingly reconstruct the past in terms of the present rather than simply remembering the past in its original form.

What Do You Think?

Are you troubled by the fact that the past you remember may be partly an illusion based on your present understanding of the world? Or do you trust your mind to edit your personal history in your best interest?

Chapter Reference

McFarland, C., Ross, M., & DeCourville, N. (1993). Women's theories of menstruation and biases in recall of menstrual symptoms. *Journal of Personality and Social Psychology, 65*, 1093–1104.

Other References

American Psychiatric Association. (2013). *Diagnostic and statistical manual of mental disorders* (5th ed.). Arlington, VA: American Psychiatric Publishing.

Aronson, E., & Mills, J. (1959). The effect of severity of initiation on liking for a group. *Journal of Abnormal and Social Psychology, 59*, 177–181.

Ascher-Svanum, H. (1982). *Alcohol use and psychological distress during the menstrual cycle*. Unpublished doctoral dissertation, University of Minnesota, Twin Cities, MI.

Baird, J. C., Wagner, M. F., & Fuld, K. (1990). A simple but powerful theory of the moon illusion. *Journal of Experimental Psychology: Human Perception & Performance, 16*, 675–677.

Bass, E., & Davis, L. (1994). *The courage to heal: A guide for women survivors of sexual abuse*. New York: Harper Perennial Library.

Brooks-Gunn, J., & Ruble, D. N. (1986). Men's and women's attitudes and beliefs about the menstrual cycle. *Sex Roles, 14*, 287–299.

Ceci, S. J. (1995). False beliefs: Some developmental and clinical considerations. In D. L. Schacter (Ed.), *Memory distortion: How minds, brains, and societies reconstruct the past* (pp. 91–128). Cambridge, MA: Harvard University Press.

Clark, D. M., & Teasdale, J. D. (1982). Diurnal variation in clinical depression and accessibility of memories of positive and negative experiences. *Journal of Abnormal Psychology, 91*, 87–95.

Clarke, A., & Ruble, D. N. (1978). Young adolescents' beliefs concerning menstruation. *Child Development, 49*, 201–234.

Clore, G. L., Schwartz, N., & Conway, M. (1994). Cognitive causes and consequences of emotion. In R. S. Wyer & T. K. Srull (Eds.), *Handbook of social cognition* (2nd ed., Vol. 1, pp. 323–418). Hillsdale, NJ: Lawrence Erlbaum Associates.

Conway, M., & Ross, M. (1984). Getting what you want by revising what you had. *Journal of Personality and Social Psychology, 47*, 738–748.

Crews, F. (1995). *The memory wars: Freud's legacy in dispute*. New York: The New York Review of Books.

Festinger, L., & Carlsmith, J. (1959). Cognitive consequences of forced compliance. *Journal of Abnormal and Social Psychology, 58*, 203–210.

Frattaroli, J. (2006). Experimental disclosure and its moderators: A meta-analysis. *Psychological Bulletin, 132*, 823–865. Retrieved from http://dx.doi.org/10.1037/0033-2909.132.6.823

Goethals, G. R., & Reckman, R. F. (1973). The perception of consistency in attitudes. *Journal of Experimental Social Psychology, 9*, 491–501.

Greenwald, A. G. (1980). The totalitarian ego: Fabrication and revision of personal history. *American Psychologist, 35*, 603–618.

Hawes, E., & Oei, T. P. S. (1992). The menstrual distress questionnaire: Are the critics right? *Current Psychology, 11*, 264–281. doi:10.1007/BF02686846

Holmes, D. S. (1990). The evidence for repression: An examination of sixty years of research. In J. L. Singer (Ed.), *Repression and dissociation: Implications for personality theory, psychopathology, and health* (pp. 85–102). Chicago, IL: University of Chicago Press.

Hume, D. (1990). *Principal writings on religion including dialogues concerning natural religion and the natural history of religion*. New York: Oxford University Press.

Kahneman, D., & Tversky, A. (1973). On the psychology of prediction. *Psychological Review, 80*, 237–251.

Kassin, S., & Kiechel, K. L. (1996). The social psychology of false confessions: Compliance, internalization, and confabulation. *Psychological Science, 7*, 125–128.

Klebanov, P. K., & Ruble, D. N. (1994). Toward an understanding of women's experience of menstrual cycle symptoms. In V. J. Adesso & D. M. Reddy (Eds.), *Psychological perspectives on women's health* (pp. 183–221). Philadelphia: Taylor & Francis.

Krystal, J. H., Southwick, S. M., & Charney, D. S. (1995). Post-traumatic stress disorder: Psychobiological mechanisms of traumatic remembrance. In D. L. Schacter (Ed.), *Memory distortion: How minds, brains, and societies reconstruct the past* (pp. 150–172). Cambridge, MA: Harvard University Press.

Kunda, Z. (1990). The case for motivated reasoning. *Psychological Bulletin, 108*, 480–498.

Loftus, E. F. (1994). *The myth of repressed memory*. New York: St. Martin's Press.

Loftus, E. F., Miller, D. G., & Burns, H. J. (1987). Semantic integration of verbal information into a visual memory. In L. S. Wrightsman & C. E. Willis (Eds.), *On the witness stand: Controversies in the courtroom* (pp. 157–177). Newbury Park, CA: Sage.

Mack, J. E. (1995). *Abduction: Human encounters with aliens*. New York: Ballantine.

Madey, S. F., & Gilovich, T. (1993). Effect of temporal focus on the recall of expectancy-consistent and expectancy-inconsistent information. *Journal of Personality and Social Psychology, 65*, 458–468.

Marcus, G. B. (1986). Stability and change in political attitudes: Observe, recall, and "Explain". *Political Behavior, 8*, 21–44.

Moos, R. H. (1968). The development of a menstrual distress questionnaire. *Psychosomatic Medicine, 30*, 853–867.

Nigro, G., & Neisser, U. (1983). Point of view in personal memories. *Cognitive Psychology, 15*, 467–482.

Pennebaker, J. W. (2000). The effect of traumatic disclosure on physical and mental health: The values of writing and talking about upsetting events. In J. M. Violanti & D. Paton (Eds.), *Posttraumatic stress intervention: Challenges, issues, and perspectives* (pp. 97–114). Springfield, IL: Charles C. Thomas.

Roediger, H. L., & McDermott, K. B. (1995). Creating false memories: Remembering words not presented in lists. *Journal of Experimental Psychology: Learning, Memory, & Cognition, 21*, 803–814.

Romans, S., Clarkson, R., Einstein, G., Petrovic, M., & Stewart, D. (2012). Mood and the menstrual cycle: A review of prospective data studies. *Gender Medicine, 9*, 361–384.

Ross, M. (1989). Relation of implicit theories to the construction of personal histories. *Psychological Review, 96*, 341–357.

Ruble, D. N., & Brooks-Gunn, J. (1979). Menstrual symptoms: A social cognition analysis. *Journal of Behavioral Medicine, 2*, 171–194.

Schacter, D. L., & Kilstrom, J. F. (1989). Functional amnesia. In F. Boller & J. Grafman (Eds.), *Handbook of neuropsychology* (Vol. 3, pp. 209–231). Amsterdam, The Netherlands: Elsevier.

Spiegel, D. (1995). Hypnosis and suggestion. In D. L. Schacter (Ed.), *Memory distortions: How minds, brains, and societies reconstruct the past* (pp. 129–149). Cambridge, MA: Harvard University Press.

Tavris, C. (1992). *The mismeasure of woman*. New York: Simon & Schuster.

Walker, W. R., Skowronski, J. J., & Thompson, C. P (2003). Life is pleasant—and memory helps to keep it that way! *Review of General Psychology, 7*, 203–210.

Wright, L. (1994). *Remembering Satan*. New York: Knopf.

More to Explore

Shaw, J. (2016). *The memory illusion: Remembering, forgetting, and the science of false memory*. London: Random House.

22 Pitfalls of Purpose

Ironic Processes in Mood Control

"The best-laid schemes of mice and men/Often go astray/And leave us nought but grief and pain/ For promised joy!"

—Robert Burns (1759–1796), Scottish poet

Background

As the classic hit movie *Ghostbusters* (1984) careers toward its conclusion, its four reluctant heroes—Spengler, Venkman, Stantz, and Zeddemore—find themselves facing off against an evil demigod. In a rasping voice, the demigod addresses them:

> *Subcreatures! Gozer the Gozerian, Gozer the Destructor, Volguus Zildrohar, the Traveler, has come! Choose and perish!*

The Ghostbusters wonder what these ominous words might mean. Spengler is the first to catch on. He explains to the others that Gozer is about to bring about a calamity of cosmic proportions. However, the precise form this calamity will take depends on whatever they are currently thinking about. Frantically, the Ghostbusters yell at one another not to think of anything. A moment later, however, Gozer declares:

> *The choice is made! The Traveler has come!*

With matters going from bad to worse, Venkman angrily demands to know who thought of something. Both Spengler and Zeddemore protest their innocence. All eyes turn slowly to Stantz. He whimpers in self-defense:

> *I couldn't help it! It just popped in there!*

In the background, booming footsteps can be heard, growing louder with each passing moment. Then, out of the metropolitan night, the dreaded Agent of Destruction emerges. A terrifying colossus, he towers above the city streets. Yet there is something distinctly odd about him. His entire body is white and pudgy. He sports a dinky sailor's hat and a smart blue scarf. The Agent of Destruction is—no, it can't be!—*Stay Puft*, the Marshmallow Man!

Contemplating this 300-foot mass of malevolent goo, the deadpan Venkman remarks:

> *Good job, Ray!*

The preceding is a salutary (if reassuringly fictional) reminder of how our mental control can break down under precisely those circumstances where it is most crucial to maintain it. You will probably recall times when your own attempts to master your mind failed. You tried to forget your cares and fall asleep but stayed awake all night worrying. You tried to study for an exam but could not help daydreaming about your lover. But equally, you may recall times when your attempt to master your mind succeeded. You were irked by a casual insult but still managed to stay cool. You lost a large sum of money but did not let that spoil your evening. Such varied outcomes raise an interesting question. Why do some of our attempts at mental control succeed but others fail?

A partial answer to the question comes from research on *willpower*. Consider how a muscle works. When vigorously exercised, it loses strength; but when allowed to relax, its strength returns. Some research suggests that the human will operates in a similar way. The expenditure of willpower through use is technically known as *ego depletion*.

In one memorable study (Baumeister, Bratslaysky, Muraven, & Tice, 1998) participants were seated in front of two plates. One was filled with scrumptious freshly baked cookies, the other with unappetizing raw radishes. The experimenter instructed participants to consume items from one plate only—either cookies or radishes in different conditions. He then left them alone for a few minutes. When he returned, he had them complete a problem-solving task that required them to copy two geometrical figures, without lifting pen from paper. Unbeknownst to participants, the task was impossible to complete. The point, however, was to measure how long they persisted in the face of certain frustration. Participants permitted only to eat the radishes (i.e., barred from eating the cookies) gave up sooner than participants who had eaten the cookies. Thus, resisting temptation seemed to use up some willpower so that less of it was available for use on subsequent tasks. Additional studies reported found that willpower could also be depleted by bottling up feelings or by repeatedly. Is it any wonder, then, that we sometimes blow our top after a succession of small annoyances, or that we are as exhausted by a shopping expedition as by a vigorous hike? The idea is that willpower is a *limited resource*: Mental control succeeds when it is available but fails when it is not. (That said, subsequent research has not readily replicated the results of earlier studies, so some caution is warranted in drawing conclusions here; Hagger & Chatzisarantis, 2016.)

Failures of mental control can come about for others reasons too. It turns out that our minds also have a built-in kink that can confound even a will of iron. This kink comes to light when attempts at mental control not only fail but *backfire*. Familiar examples include becoming more wakeful while trying to fall asleep, or collapsing in a fit of giggles when trying to keep a straight face. How can such obviously unintended outcomes be explained? According to Wegner (1994), they are best understood as the outcome of an interaction between two psychological processes.

The first of these is the *intentional operating* process—or *intender* for short. It consists of the conscious, deliberate, and effortful attempt to seek out mental contents that match some desired mental state. For example, to improve our mood, the intender steers our attention toward cheery thoughts and diverts it away from gloomy ones.

Although the intender is in charge of exerting mental control, it often acts on information gathered by its undercover accomplice, the *ironic monitoring process*—or *monitor* for short. Behind the scenes, invisible yet all seeing, the monitor checks that no unwanted intruders have penetrated the psychological fortress. If they have, it dispatches the intender to deal with them. Cloak-and-dagger metaphors aside, the monitor's role is to signal failures of mental control to the intender so it can act upon them.

Matters work in reverse too. The intender can also trigger the monitor. In particular, whenever the intender attempts to realize a particular mental state, the monitor looks for specific failures to realize it. For example, if your intender sought not to think of Stay Puft, your monitor would be on guard specifically for thoughts of Stay Puft. (As an exercise, try not to think of Stay Puft for the rest of this chapter. Will you succeed where Stantz failed? You may find your monitor reminding you! The same thing happens when people try not to think of any particular thing—most commonly, a white bear; Wegner & Schneider, 2003.)

A key feature of the monitor is that it operates covertly. If news of every little mental mishap reached consciousness, the resulting brouhaha would bamboozle the conscious mind, making self-control quite impossible. In that sense, the monitor really does resemble a spy. If its cover is blown, it cannot do its job.

How does all of this help to explain why mental control sometimes backfires? The key point is that the intender and monitor place different demands upon the mind. The first—being conscious and effortful—makes heavier use of available mental resources; the second, being automatic and efficient—makes lighter use of them. So, if mental resources are taxed by some secondary task—thereby imposing a *cognitive load*—the functioning of the intender will be impaired relative to the functioning of the monitor. However, although distractions undermine the capacity of the intender to control mental content, they do not undermine the capacity of the intender to trigger the monitor. The mere intention to exert control is enough. Taken together, these two facts set the stage for the occurrence of ironic reversals under cognitive load.

Suppose Síobhan is studying for her upcoming statistics exam. Her conscious mind is therefore keenly focused on thoughts of means, medians, and modes. However, somewhere at the fringes of her consciousness, a worrisome thought intrudes: her period is late. Her monitor dutifully signals to her intender that this unwanted thought is lurking. However, because she is already devoting most of her available mental resources to studying, her intender lacks the usual where-withal to banish the worrisome thought. Its repeatedly attempts to banish it only prompt further vigilance on the part of the monitor, which now signals with greater insistence that this unwanted thought is still present. In desperation, the intender redoubles its resolve to suppress the thought. Unfortunately, this merely initiates a self-reinforcing loop, in which evermore effortful attempts at mental control result in ever more frustrating failures to achieve it. Soon, Síobhan's consciousness is preoccupied with the very thought that her intender sought to banish, thanks to all the attention that her monitor has drawn to it. Her keen focus on means, medians, and modes gives way to a resigned preoccupation with potential pregnancy. Note that these dynamics may *not* have occurred if sufficient mental resources had been available—if Síobhan had, for example, been relaxing on her study break. In that case, the intender would have stood a fighting chance of successfully suppressing the unwanted thought.

Ironic process theory, which we have been describing, applies across a wide range of psychological phenomena, from physical movements (Wegner, Ansfield, & Pilloff, 1998) to dream contents (Wegner, Wenzlaff, & Kozak, 2004). In this chapter, however, we focus on how it applies to a single phenomenon: *mood*. Wegner, Erber, and Zanakos (1993) predicted that attempts to deliberately alter mood, though normally successful, would backfire when people were placed under cognitive load. Furthermore, they predicted that this would occur both when people tried to improve their negative moods and when they tried to worsen their positive ones. Admittedly, trying to worsen a positive mood is a rather perverse undertaking. However, it made good sense as an experimental goal because it allowed a surprising implication of ironic process theory to be tested, namely, that deliberately trying to feel worse, under cognitive load, makes you feel better.

What They Did

Mood control can obviously only be attempted when people are actually *in* a mood. So the first step for Wegner and his colleagues (1993) was to induce moods in their experimental participants. To this end, they asked 184 female and 105 male undergraduates to think back to a significant event in their life and to recall the concrete details of that event as vividly as they could ("picture the event happening to you," "think of what was going through your mind at the time"). Some participants were told to recall a happy event, others a sad one.

The experimenter then said aloud one of several phrases with a view to manipulating what participants did with their self-induced moods. Some participants in the happy memory condition were told to relive the happiness associated with the remembered event, others to avoid reliving it. Similarly, some participants in the sad memory condition were told to relive their sadness, others to avoid doing so. In addition, to provide a baseline against which the effects of the mood-control instructions could be evaluated, the experimenter did not give any mood-control instructions to another control group, whose members included participants from both the happy and sad memory groups.

Note that trying to feel happy, and not to feel sad, both represent attempts to improve mood, whereas trying to feel sad, and not to feel happy, both represent attempts to worsen mood. The reason that the researchers included both kinds of instruction was to test a subtle secondary hypothesis, namely, that deliberate attempts to induce a mood under cognitive load would produce weaker ironic effects than deliberate attempts to suppress it. The researchers' reasoning was as follows. When mental *suppression*—trying *not* to think or feel something—backfires under cognitive load, the ironic result will be specific, that is, consciousness will be flooded with precisely that mental content that the intender is trying to eliminate (e.g., happy for sad, sad for happy). However, when mental *induction*—trying *to* think or feel something—backfires, the result will be non-specific, that is, a mix of contents will flood consciousness (happy and neutral for sad, sad and neutral for happy). So, if you tried not to feel sad under cognitive load you would end up more ironically sad than if you simply tried to feel happy. Similarly, if you tried not to feel happy under cognitive load you would feel more ironically happy than if you simply tried to feel sad.

Returning to the details of the procedure, the researchers also imposed a cognitive load on some but not on other participants. Those on whom a load was imposed were required to remember until the end of the study a non-repeating 9-digit number (e.g., 175263948). The remaining participants were free of this requirement.

To summarize the experimental design: All participants were asked to recall memories that either put them in a happy or a sad mood. While recalling these memories, some participants were instructed to try to worsen their mood (by trying to be sad if recalling happy memories, or trying not to be happy if recalling sad memories), while others tried to improve their mood (by trying to be happy if recalling sad memories, or trying not to be sad if recalling happy memories). Still other participants were not instructed try to change their mood at all. In each of these three conditions, half the participants were saddled with a cognitive load, the other half not.

After 7 minutes of reminiscence, participants reported their final mood. This was the main dependent variable on which ironic effects were predicted to emerge. Participants rated how happy or sad they felt along a series of scales. Extra scales assessing levels of tension or relaxation were also included to verify that the experimental manipulations had affected feelings of happiness and sadness in particular, rather than unrelated aspects of mood.

Participants were also asked to write down whatever thoughts came to mind while recalling happy or sad events from their lives. During the period in which they did so, the experimenter absented himself so as to avoid potentially biasing their reports. The written protocols that participants produced were then given to two trained assistants to code for mood-relevant content.

One final detail is worth noting. The study had been advertised as an investigation into how doing one mental task affects performance on another. In keeping with this cover story, the researchers had participants engage in a period of free writing prior to beginning the study proper. The purpose of including this initial phase was to encourage participants to draw the erroneous inference that the purpose of the study was to assess how free writing influenced subsequent measures and manipulations. Throwing participants off the scent ensured that the experimental hypotheses would not be inadvertently confirmed or refuted by savvy participants trying to please or peeve the experimenter.

What They Found

The first noteworthy finding of the study was that the mood control instructions had no *overall* impact on mood. That is to say, participants told to improve their mood (by trying to be happy or not to be sad) were no happier on average than participants told to worsen their mood (by trying to be sad or not to be happy). The mood of participants in either condition was equal to that of participants who were given no mood control instructions. Does this imply that the mood control manipulation was ineffective?

A closer look at the data reveals not. Participants' attempts at mood control produced *diametrically opposite* results depending on whether or not they were under cognitive load. When participants had no digits to remember, they successfully improved or worsened their mood, just as they intended. However, when they did have digits to remember, their attempts at mood control backfired. Trying to improve their mood only made their mood worse, while trying to worsen their mood only made their mood better. This is a clear confirmation of the predictions of ironic process theory. The contrary trends obtained, in the presence and absence of cognitive load, were about equal in magnitude. The mood control manipulation had no overall effect only because the intended and ironic effects, both substantial, canceled one another out (Figure 22).

The researchers also obtained some evidence that attempting to suppress a mood produced stronger ironic effects than attempting to induce a mood. Participants under cognitive load who tried to suppress a mood failed miserably in the attempt, whereas participants who tried to cultivate a mood did not fail quite so miserably. However, the differential failure rate was not particularly large. One reason might have been that, in the absence of strict warnings to the contrary, participants instructed to cultivate a mood might sometimes have tried to suppress its opposite, while participants instructed to suppress a mood might sometimes have tried to cultivate its opposite. This would have undermined the difference between the suppression and cultivation conditions.

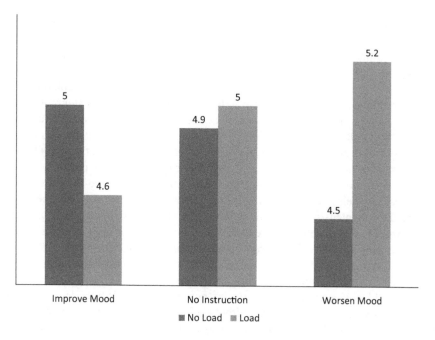

Figure 22 Happiness of participants instructed to improve their mood, worsen their mood, or do neither, when they were under, or not under, cognitive load

The researchers also analyzed participants' thought-listings for positive or negative content. It was expected that the results here would mimic those for self-reported mood. Sure enough, in the absence of cognitive load, participants instructed to improve their mood wrote down more positive thoughts than participants instructed to worsen their mood (with participants given no mood-control instructions falling in between). However, under cognitive load, ironic reversals did not emerge: There was no significant difference in the positivity of participants' listed thoughts across the three conditions. Only when mental control succeeded did participants' thoughts match their eventual mood, not when mental control backfired.

What accounts for the curious discrepancy? One possibility is that the requirement of remembering a 9-digit number may have interfered with participants' ability to write down meaningful thoughts capable of taking on a positive or negative character. Instead, participants may have limited themselves to expressing brief, scattered thoughts, and noting them down dryly.

However, an additional study by Wegner and his colleagues (1993) again found clear-cut ironic effects. In that study, the index of interest was the *mental accessibility* of positive and negative thoughts—or the degree to which those thoughts were active in participants' mind. Such accessibility can be measured, among other things, by how distracted people are by words related to the thoughts in question—something revealed by how much slower they are name the colors in which the words appear. Results showed that suppressing mood, although it normally reduced the accessibility of mood-related thoughts, ironically increased them when participants were placed under cognitive load.

So What?

The present study demonstrated that deliberate attempts to control mood backfire when mental resources are scarce. This may help to explain the origin and persistence of some forms of depression and anxiety. Due to external demands, or poor multi-tasking skills, some people may find themselves continually under cognitive load. As a result, their best efforts to cheer up or calm down may only make their symptoms worse.

On the bright side, however, the present study also suggests three strategies that people might use to improve psychological performance. First, take steps to minimize ongoing cognitive load so that mental resources are freed up. Second, stop trying to obsessively control your mind, as Eastern religions like Buddhism and Taoism have long recommended (Smullyan, 1992). (Note that both of these strategies would also protect against the effects of ego depletion, mentioned in the Background section.) Third, deliberately try to induce unwanted symptoms in order to take ironic advantage of the cognitive load, and thereby alleviate those symptoms.

The idea that the deliberate cultivation of unwanted psychological states could be psychologically beneficial is not new. In particular, the existential psychologist Frankl (1963) recommended the use of *paradoxical intention* as a therapeutic technique. Take people who suffer from *alektorophobia*—a morbid dread of chickens. Frankl would have recommended that, instead of trying to escape their fear, by mentally tuning out every time chickens are mentioned, they should instead try to intensify it, by deliberately calling to mind flapping wings and squawking beaks. This would force patients to face their fear and allow them to reclaim their psychological autonomy. More seriously, Frankl recommended his technique for clients with such conditions as failing to orgasm and sweating too much (i.e., they should try not to orgasm, but try to make themselves sweat). The technique was also just one feature of a more general therapeutic approach, termed *logotherapy*, aimed at restoring purpose to people's lives. However, the idea of combining paradoxical intention with cognitive load is unique to ironic process theory. Indeed, without that cognitive load, there is a danger that paradoxically intending an unwanted mental outcome might actually bring it about!

In this regard, consider a symptom that plagues many of us from time to time: *insomnia*. As we settle down to sleep, worries can no longer be drowned out by external distractions. As a consequence, we must rely on purely internal means of keeping worries at bay. This can be difficult, especially if our mind is already tired. The very worries that monopolize our attention can impose their own cognitive load. Is it any wonder, then, that our determined attempts to fall asleep sometimes result in persistent wakefulness?

In a test of whether insomnia could be ironically engineered or eliminated, participants were told either to fall asleep or to stay awake while they were or were not under cognitive load (Ansfield, Wegner, & Bowser, 1996). As it would have been unethical to burden participants with real worries, the researchers manipulated cognitive load in another way. They had half the participants listen to upbeat attention-grabbing music (John Philip Sousa marches) and the other half listen to soothing background music (New Age vibes). In the soothing condition, where cognitive load was low, participants who tried to fall asleep predictably nodded off more quickly than participants who tried to stay awake. However, in the upbeat condition, where cognitive load was high, the reverse occurred. Participants who tried to stay awake actually nodded off more quickly than participants who tried to fall asleep. The practical implication is clear: If your noisy neighbors are throwing a party late at night, you should struggle to stay awake.

The significance of ironic process theory extends beyond explaining psychiatric symptoms. Have you ever found yourself, to your great embarrassment, saying exactly the opposite of what you intended to say? Freud (1914) famously drew attention to such slips of the tongue. He argued that they reflected unconscious impulses erupting into everyday speech. However, more mundane explanations are possible. Verbal slips may reflect a combination of syntactic mix-ups and situational priming—as when a male traveler mistakenly asks a busty ticket clerk for "a picket to Titsburgh." Nonetheless, given that slips of the tongue are certainly unintended acts, it would be surprising if ironic process theory did not throw some light on them.

Ironic process theory predicts that slips of the tongue will occur when people try hard to avoid saying something. Take, for example, sexist language. Closet chauvinists must watch their words and intentionally avoid making potentially insulting remarks about the, ahem, strength-impaired sex. Could being mentally busy interfere with their efforts at self-censorship? In a test of this hypothesis (Wegner, 1994), student participants were asked to read aloud a number of sentence fragments that could be completed in either a sexist or non-sexist manner (e.g., "Women who go out with a lot of men are . . . [sluts]/[popular]"). Given no special instructions, participants made slightly fewer sexist completions when mentally busy than when not. However, when explicitly instructed to avoid being sexist, participants made far more sexist completions when mentally busy than when not. Interestingly, the tendency to show this effect was unrelated to participants' attitudes toward women. These findings imply that a genuine feminist trying hard not to be sexist would be as prone to stereotypical slips as a chauvinist pig trying to please his liberal audience. In other words, slips of the tongue are evidence, not of unconscious sentiments, but of conscious attempts at mental control.

Ironic process theory nicely explains and correctly predicts a range of paradoxical intentional phenomena. It is proof that scientific psychology can address the same puzzling quirks of motivation that Freudian psychoanalysis did and provide more plausible and empirically grounded accounts of them. Nonetheless, it still leaves a number of important questions unanswered. For example, even in the absence of mental load, suppressed thoughts rebound back into consciousness (Wegner, Schneider, Carter, & White, 1987). This suggests that mental control is intrinsically imperfect. One intriguing study found that participants who spent time suppressing a negative stereotype of skinheads later sat further away from a chair that had recently been vacated by a skinhead, who would shortly return (Macrae, Bodenhausen, Milne, & Jetten, 1994). Apparently, compressing our mental springs only makes them decompress with greater force when we release them. In addition, although mental state and cognitive load can be distinguished in the laboratory, they tend to get mixed up in everyday life. Suppose you have a persistent worry that you wish to control. Does that worry, by preoccupying your thoughts, not impose a cognitive load by itself? Complications like this muddy the waters a bit.

Afterthoughts

Ironic process theory is mainly concerned with explaining why attempts at mental self-control fail. True, the theory can also be used to deduce a surprising tactic for achieving mental self-control—striving to bring about the unwanted state while under cognitive load. However, this tactic may be of limited utility in practice. For example, can one always arrange for a suitable distraction to be present? In addition, ironic process theory only deals with intentional attempts to alter one's immediate state of mind. Does social psychology offer any suggestions for how people might succeed in realizing their longer-term goals? In this regard, self-help books often offer to share with readers the secret of self-motivation. Is there any handy technique (or as click-bait might put it, is there "one weird trick") that can turn your unreliable intentions into effective actions? The answer may be "yes."

One can identity two different types of intentions. The first type—a simple intention—you will already be familiar with. It takes the general form: "I intend to reach goal X!" The second type, however, takes this general form: "In situation Y, I intend to do Z, as a means of reaching goal X"! This is called an *implementation intention* (Gollwitzer, 1999).

To illustrate, consider the writing of this book—a long-term goal for its authors. Each of us has the simple intention "I intend to complete *Experiments With People*." However, along the way, we have implementation intentions too. For example, the present author has one today: "In my office, at 4 p.m., I intend to write the *Afterthoughts* section of *Pitfalls of Purpose*, as a means of completing *Experiments With People*."

Two features distinguish implementation intentions from simple intentions. First, whereas simple intentions are *general*—often merely vague types of aspiration—implementation intentions are *specific*—referring to a concrete action in a definite setting. In the above example, place and time are specified. Second, whereas simple intentions are *unconditional*—one can complete them whenever—implementation intentions are *conditional*—they take an "if-then" form. Another way of writing the above example would be as follows: "*If* I am in my office at 4 p.m., *then* I will write the *Afterthoughts* section." The content of an implementation intention has the feel of a rule, triggered under such-and-such circumstances.

Now, even simple intentions are reasonably well-linked to behavior. Consider, in this connection, the *theory of planned behavior* (Ajzen, 1991). It proposes that two factors shape most of human behavior. First, *personal attitudes*—defined as beliefs about outcomes alongside how much those outcomes are desired. Second, *subjective norms*—defined as beliefs about what others want alongside one's motivation to comply with them. According to the theory, both personal attitudes and subjective norms affect behavior *via* intentions to perform behavior. This makes sense. Suppose you like the idea of going to college. Suppose your parents approve too. The stage is set: You can now form the intention to go. Next, you start planning, and acting on those plans. But it seems silly to suppose that you would ever start planning or acting without forming the intention. Unsurprisingly, much research shows that personal attitudes and subjective norms strongly predict intentions, and that intentions in turn strongly predict behavior. This is the case, for example, for intentions to use condoms (Albarracin, Johnson, Fishbein, & Muellerleile, 2001) or to quit smoking (Topa & Moriano, 2010). (The theory of planned behavior has been used a lot in health-promotion contexts; see also Chapter 24.)

However, this is not the whole story. Although the prediction describe above is strong, it is far from perfect. Additional factors are known to be involved—such as one's *perceived control* over the behavior in question. When perceived control is low, intentions are less predictive;

and perceived control can even predict behavior independently of intentions. Such eventualities likely reflect the influence of "irrational" factors, such as habit and impulse.

Indeed, consider all the ways in which good intentions to achieve a goal can go astray. One may fail to get started, due to forgetfulness or lack of resolve; or one may get knocked off track, by distractions or temptations; or one may simply run out of the energy required to keep going. No wonder intentions often fail. Yet, it is in precisely such cases that implementation intentions assist people in attaining goals (Gollwitzer & Sheeran, 2006).

Consider a study by Sheeran and Orbell (2000). Here, the goal was to assist ladies in keeping an important medical appointment—a smear test to check for early signs of cervical cancer. In addition to receiving the standard reminder by mail, participants also received a questionnaire. It asked questions relevant to the theory of planned behavior. At the end of the questionnaire came the key experimental manipulation. Half the participants read the following words, directing them to form an implementation intention: "You are more likely to go for a cervical smear if you decide when and where you will go. Please write in below when, where, and how you will make an appointment." As it turned out, the usual suspects (e.g., personal attitudes, subjective norms, perceived control, and simple intentions) did predict keeping the medical appointment. However, the implementation intentions predicted above and beyond them. In fact, whereas only a reasonable 69% of participants kept the appointment in the control condition, a full 92% kept it in the experimental condition.

Consider another example. One reason that dieting is hard (most diets fail: Mann et al., 2007) is that tasty treats tempt us to abandon the long-term goal of being slim and healthy to realize the incompatible short-term goal of being gluttonous and full. When the craving strikes, our willpower wilts. But here, one can get clever with implementation intentions. What if one were to use the *craving itself* as the if-then trigger for adhering to one's diet? This is what Van Koningsbruggen, Stroebe, Papies, & Aarts (2011) tried. Half their participants read the instruction: "Please tell yourself: 'The next time that I am tempted to eat [food item], then I will think of dieting!' When you have said the line to yourself, tick this box." Those participants who had previously been unsuccessful chronic dieters specifically benefitted from this instruction. In general, implementation intentions shrink waistlines, and may be especially effective in promoting the consumption of healthy food (Adriaanse, Vinkers, De Ridder, Hox, & De Wit, 2011).

This brings us to the question of *why* implementation intentions work. What is the underlying mental mechanism that mediates the effects? Gollwitzer (2014) provides a concise overview of relevant research. It is not simply a matter of breaking down goals into smaller components, nor of merely enhancing one's commitment to a goal (for more on the latter, see Chapter 3). Rather, two particular things seem to be going on. First, the cue that triggers the implementation intention becomes more mentally accessible. People notice it more, and it serves as a reminder. Second, the link between the cue and the behavior to be performed becomes stronger. Moreover, it seems to have an automatic character to it: Once the cue goes "click," the behavior goes "whirr." This is what may explain their capacity to compete with habit and impulse, which also tend to produce "automated" behavior. In support of this view, implementation intentions have been shown to speed up responding (Brandstätter, Lengfelder, & Gollwitzer, 2001). Presumably, they make it unnecessary for people to form a new intention from scratch in the moment. Indeed, one can perhaps understand implementation intentions as bespoke intentions that were generated in advance—a bit like TV cooks preparing ingredients beforehand to speed up the completion of their recipes. But beware: Simplicity appears to be the key. The more implementation intentions one uses, the less effective they become (Dalton & Spiller, 2012).

In conclusion, the capacity for self-control is a beneficial characteristic (Tangney, Baumeister, & Boone, 2004). Children who can wait to consume two marshmallows, rather than eating one marshmallow immediately, show better life outcomes years later—including having less body fat (Schlam, Wilson, Shoda, Mischel, & Ayduk, 2013). Does the scary Mr. Stay Puft have a deeper symbolic meaning, we wonder? Hopefully, after learning about some of the social psychological literature on the topic, readers will come away with a sharper sense of why their intentions sometimes fail or backfire, and how they might be made more effective.

Revelation

Attempts to bring about a desired mental state tend to backfire if people are distracted or preoccupied. Under such circumstances, they would be well advised to abandon the attempt, or, even better, to try not to bring about that mental state, as this will ironically tend to bring it about.

What Do You Think?

Suppose you stopped trying to exert any control whatsoever over your mental processes, and simply let them occur. What would happen? Would you succumb to horrible moods, be extremely distractible, and never get out of bed? Or would you simply do what you needed to do naturally, without any effort?

Chapter Reference

Wegner, D., Erber, R., & Zanakos, S. (1993). Ironic processes in the mental control of mood and mood-related thought. *Journal of Personality and Social Psychology, 65*, 1093–1104.

Other References

Adriaanse, M. A., Vinkers. C. D. W., De Ridder, D. T. D., Hox, J. J., & De Wit, J. B. F. (2011). Do implementation intentions help to eat a healthy diet? A systematic review and meta-analysis of the empirical evidence. *Appetite, 56*, 183–193.

Ajzen, I. (1991). The theory of planned behavior. *Organizational Behavior and Human Decision Processes, 50*, 179–211.

Albarracin, D., Johnson, B. T., Fishbein, M., & Muellerleile, P. A. (2001). Theories of reasoned action and planned behavior as models of common use: A meta-analysis. *Psychological Bulletin, 127*, 142–161.

Ansfield, M. E., Wegner, D. M., & Bowser, R. (1996). Ironic effects of sleep urgency. *Behaviour Research and Therapy, 34*, 523–531.

Baumeister, R. F., Bratslaysky, E., Muraven, M., & Tice, D. M. (1998). Ego depletion: Is the active self a limited resource? *Journal of Personality and Social Psychology, 74*, 1252–1265.

Brandstätter, V., Lengfelder, A., & Gollwitzer, P. M. (2001). Implementation intentions and efficient action initiation. *Journal of Personality and Social Psychology, 81*, 946–960.

Dalton, A. N., & Spiller, S. A. (2012). Too much of a good thing: The benefits of implementation intentions depend on the number of goals. *Journal of Consumer Research, 39*, 600–614.

Daniel, M. W., & Schneider, D. J. (2003). The white bear story. *Psychological Inquiry, 14*, 326–329.

Frankl, V. E. (1963). *Man's search for meaning.* New York: Pocket Books.

Freud, S. (1914). *The psychopathology of everyday life.* New York: Palgrave Macmillan.

Gollwitzer, P. M. (1999). Implementation intentions: Strong effects of simple plans. *American Psychologist, 54*, 493–503.

Gollwitzer, P. M. (2014). Weakness of the will: Is a quick fix possible? *Motivation and Emotion, 38*, 305–322.

Gollwitzer, P. M., & Sheeran, P. (2006). Implementation intentions and goal achievement: A meta-analysis of effects and processes. *Advances in Experimental Social Psychology, 38*, 69–119.

Hagger, M. S., & Chatzisarantis, N. L. D. (2016). A multilab preregistered replication of the ego-depletion effect. *Perspectives on Psychological Science, 11*, 546–573. doi:10.1177/1745691616652873

Macrae, C. N., Bodenhausen, G. V., Milne, A. B., & Jetten, J. (1994). Out of mind but back in sight: Stereotypes on the rebound. *Journal of Personality and Social Psychology, 67*, 808–817.

Mann, T., Tomiyama, A. J., Westling, E., Lew, A. M., Samuels, B., & Chatman, J. (2007). Medicare's search for effective obesity treatments: Diets are not the answer. *American Psychologist, 62*, 220–233.

Schlam, T. R., Wilson, N. L., Shoda, Y., Mischel, W., & Ayduk, O. (2013). Preschoolers' delay of gratification predicts their body mass 30 years later. *The Journal of Pediatrics, 162*, 90–93.

Sheeran, P., & Orbell, S. (2000). Self-schemas and the theory of planned behaviour. *European Journal of Social Psychology, 30*, 533–550.

Smullyan, R. M. (1992). *The Tao is silent.* New York: Harper.

Tangney, J. P., Baumeister, R. F., & Boone, A. L. (2004). High self-control predicts good adjustment, less pathology, better grades, and interpersonal success. *Journal of Personality, 72*, 271–324.

Topa, G., & Moriano, J. A. (2010). Theory of planned behavior and smoking: Meta-analysis and SEM model. *Substance Abuse Rehabilitation, 1*, 23–33.

Van Koningsbruggen, G. M., Stroebe, W., Papies, E. K., & Aarts, H. (2011). Implementation intentions as goal primes: Boosting self-control in tempting environments. *European Journal of Social Psychology, 41*, 551–557.

Wegner, D. M. (1994). Ironic processes of mental control. *Psychological Review, 101*, 34–52.

Wegner, D. M., Ansfield, M., & Pilloff, D. (1998). The putt and the pendulum: Ironic effects of the mental control of action. *Psychological Science, 9*, 196–199.

Wegner, D. M., & Schneider, D. J. (2003). The white bear story. *Psychological Inquiry, 14*, 326–329.

Wegner, D. M., Schneider, D. J., Carter, S., & White, T. (1987). Paradoxical effects of thought suppression. *Journal of Personality and Social Psychology, 53*, 5–13.

Wegner, D. M., Wenzlaff, R. M., & Kozak, M. (2004). Dream rebound: The return of suppressed thoughts in dreams. *Psychological Science, 15*, 232–236.

More to Explore

Leaf, C. (2009). *Who switched off my brain: Controlling toxic thoughts and emotions.* Nashville, TN: Thomas Nelson.

23 Digital Diagnosis

Technical Tools for Unearthing the Unconscious

"He who has eyes to see and ears to hear can convince himself that no mortal can keep a secret. If his lips are silent, he chatters with his fingertips; betrayal oozes out of every pore."
—Sigmund Freud (1865–1939), Austrian pioneer of psychoanalysis

Background

When we—the authors of this book—mention to laypeople that we are (social) psychologists, we almost always get one of two replies. The first reply: "That must be *so* interesting, right?" Well, yes and no. We think to ourselves: "Sure, the hypotheses are profound, the experiments are clever, and the results are revealing. But man, the database management sure is a bummer." The second reply: "I'd better watch out—you might start *analyzing* me!" To this, we have two reactions. First, we are wryly amused that laypeople think that this is how we spend our spare time. Second, we are slightly frustrated that they misunderstand the way we do science. We find ourselves on the back foot, having to gently refute some widely held misconceptions.

In particular, laypeople often fear that (social) psychologists like us can figure them out just by making a few shrewd observations. In this regard, we are likened to Sherlock Holmes—the famous sleuth who drew astounding inferences from clues that lesser mortals overlooked. A speck of dust here, a muddy footprint there, and Holmes could deduce that Moriarty had murdered Sir Percy Wigglebottom. Similarly, a nervous gesture here, a slip of the tongue there, and we can supposedly deduce the dark secrets of a person's psyche.

Sherlock Holmes was, of course, a fictional character, whose investigative methods would likely have come to grief in the real world. Indeed, many of his so-called deductions were really speculative guesses based on slender evidence. Holmes's creator, Conan Doyle, made sure his hero always triumphed; but flesh-and-blood detectives cannot count on Conan Doyle for assistance. Instead, everyday detective work is more mundane and methodical. Specialized techniques and tools are used to gather evidence (e.g., profiling, forensics, surveillance), and teams of individuals pool their expertise to crack a case. It is not just a matter of some lone genius turning up one day and single-handedly solving crimes that left the rest of the criminal justice system perplexed.

The stereotypical psychologist who sizes people up at a glance turns out to be as fictional as Sherlock Holmes. Take the pioneer of psychoanalysis himself, Sigmund Freud. Although he clearly regarded himself as a brilliant diagnostician, his case histories, when looked at objectively, tell a very different story. Freud boldly assumed that an accurate analysis would lead to the remission of neurotic symptoms. However, his claims to have cured any patient have since largely been discredited, calling into question the soundness of his original interpretations (Crews, 1995). Ultimately, it is not clear whether his ingenious interpretations—often sexually perverse—were real patterns that he detected within people's dreams and reveries, or imaginary patterns that he projected onto them.

Indeed, *nobody* may be able to wield the diagnostic powers claimed by Freud. People's intuitive understanding of others is known to be systematically compromised. For example, we often invalidly infer the existence of personality traits from isolated behaviors (see Chapter 10), and fail to grasp how such behaviors can be influenced by the social context (Chapters 8 and 15). But perhaps the most clear-cut sign of our mind-reading limitations is our near inability to detect lying. The accumulated results of hundreds of studies show that laymen and professionals alike distinguish lying from truth-telling at little more than chance levels (Bond & DePaulo, 2006, 2008). This is for two primary reasons (Vrij, 2008). First, people do not recognize, or are unable to keep track of, the telltale cues to deceit (e.g., a shrill voice). Second, those cues are only weakly predictive of lying anyhow (i.e., there is no "Pinocchio's nose").

To discover how the human mind works, then, what is needed is not so much an individual with superior insight, but rather a community of scientists who put forward theories and then test them. Indeed, you can think of social psychologists (and their colleagues in related fields) as a squad of hard-working detectives, each of whom is trying to solve a piece of an incredibly complex case. Like detectives, social psychologists depend, not on unaided intuition, but on specialized techniques and tools. Their preferred technique is *experimentation* because it clarifies what causes what (see the book's Introduction). However, they also use an array of *measurement* tools to assess people's mental states and underlying dispositions.

Much of the time, the tool choice is the humble *questionnaire*, given its versatility and convenience. Note, however, that questionnaires must be carefully assembled and validated prior to use. It is not merely a matter of cobbling together a bunch of items that look right; rather, it is a matter of proving in advance that they measure what they are intended to measure (Bradburn, Sudman, & Wansink, 2004). A questionnaire must contain items that are clearly worded, go together statistically, and distinguish among respondents. In addition, the questionnaire as a whole must yield results that replicate over time, and predict established outcomes that make theoretical sense. These virtues are what distinguish the questionnaires that social psychologists employ from those that appear in popular magazines.

Yet, even the best-validated questionnaires can only shed so much light on what people are like. This is so for three reasons (Gregg & Klymowsky, 2013). First, people sometimes do not wish to reveal to others what they really think and feel about sensitive topics. For example, a closet male chauvinist will be reluctant to reveal his true sexist attitudes, even with anonymity guaranteed. Second, people may not wish to admit to themselves how they really think and feel. For example, a liberal White may refuse to acknowledge, much less express, his or her underlying racial prejudice. Third, people may simply not know what they really think or feel. For example, someone may discover, to their own surprise, that they have a stronger attraction to someone than they initially reckoned.

Is there any way, then, of accessing the deeper recesses of the mind, without relying on everyday perception or psychoanalytic interpretation, both known to be compromised by biases of one sort or another? Might there be, indeed, a *technical* solution to this age-old problem? It turns out there might.

In the 1970s, cognitive psychologists—who focus more on the nuts and bolts of human mental processing—made a methodological breakthrough. They discovered how to identify and quantify, in an objective way, the *mental associations* that people hold between one concept and another. They did so using the *sequential priming paradigm* (Chartrand & Bargh, 2000). Shortly thereafter, social psychologists adapted the paradigm to look at mental associations of greatest interest to them, namely, those that pertained to the social world.

The way this paradigm works is best illustrated by an actual experiment (Banaji & Hardin, 1996). Imagine that you are seated in front of a computer. Your task is easy enough: to sort *target* words that appear on the screen one after the other. Each of these words is either a male pronoun (e.g., *he*) or a female pronoun (e.g., *she*). To classify pronouns as *MALE*, you press a key on the left; to classify pronouns as *FEMALE*, you press a key on the right. You must go as quickly as you can without making errors.

Now comes the twist. On each trial, a *prime* word is flashed up briefly a moment before each target word appears. You are told to ignore all these primes. This prime is either the name of a traditionally male job (e.g., *doctor*) or the name of a traditionally female job (e.g., *nurse*). This means that, in terms of gender stereotypes, some of the prime-target pairs match (*doctor* = *he*, *nurse* = *she*) whereas others mismatch (*nurse* = *he*, *doctor* = *she*).

If you are like most people, then which primes precede which targets will affect your *response speed*. In particular, you will respond more rapidly on trial with matching rather than mismatching pairs. From prior research in cognitive psychology, we know that such patterns of *facilitation* and *inhibition* signify the existence of automatic associations between concepts. Here, the automatic associations can be interpreted as *implicit stereotypes*. Note that, by featuring categories such as *GOOD* and *BAD*, the sequential priming paradigm can also be adapted to assess *implicit prejudices*—which involve evaluative rather than semantic associations (Fazio, Jackson, Dunton, & Williams, 1995).

What is interesting is that the correlation between people's *explicit* stereotypes and prejudices (i.e., those they subjectively report) and their implicit stereotypes and prejudices (i.e., those that they objectively show) is often low (Nosek, 2007), with levels of the latter also coming out higher. For example, people's responses to a questionnaire assessing attitudes toward women might not predict how they would perform in the experiment above; however, the results of the experiment above would be more suggestive of sexism (Rudman & Kilianski, 2000). What *explicit-implicit dissociations* of this sort mean is debatable. However, one leading interpretation, popular in the left-leaning corridors of academia, is that many liberal-minded Westerners, despite their consciously egalitarian outlook, still harbor *unconscious biases* toward various social groups (Dovidio & Gaertner, 2004).

Yet the sequential priming paradigm has a drawback. It can quantify the average levels of automatic associations that are present. However, it is not sensitive enough to reliably quantify automatic associations at an individual level. Hence, social psychologists sought to develop a new paradigm that could. Enter the *Implicit Association Test* (*IAT*; Greenwald, McGhee, & Schwartz, 1998; Nosek, Greenwald, & Banaji, 2007). This has been the tool that social psychologists have most frequently used to probe what might be called the *social unconscious* (Bargh, 2007).

The IAT's modus operandi is a little more complicated than the sequential priming paradigm—so stay with us. Once again, you sort items into categories as quickly and as accurately as you can, by pressing either one key or another. This time, however, you press one key if an item belongs to one *pair* of categories, and another key if an item belongs to a different pair. For example, suppose a researcher had wanted, in the run-up to the 2016 U.S. presidential election, to measure your automatic associations toward the two rival candidates. In one block of the IAT, she would have you follow these two rules: (a) press "Q" if a word belongs to the categories *HILLARY* or *GOOD*; and (b) press "P" if a word belongs to the categories *TRUMP* or *BAD*. In the other block, she would have you follow these two rules: (c) press "Q" if a word belongs to the categories *HILLARY* or *BAD*; and (d) press "P" if a word belongs to the categories *TRUMP* or *GOOD*. The researcher would then measure your average speed across the first block, and your average speed across the second block, and compare the two. If you went more quickly in Block 1 than Block 2, that would suggest an implicit preference for Hillary over Trump; and if you went more quickly in Block 2 than Block 1, that would suggest an implicit preference for Trump over Hillary.

Because the IAT is difficult to grasp when described verbally, we include a low-tech, paper-and-pencil version of it at the end of this chapter. The two blocks are represented on adjacent pages. Follow the simple instructions, and see which one feels easier or harder to complete, even after repeated attempts.

The IAT has proven highly controversial. There is as yet no consensus as to whether it truly measures implicit biases, or whether the large effects it produces are merely misleading artifacts (see Gregg & Klymowsky, 2013, for a review). However, if it transpired that the IAT *could* consistently predict important outcomes—especially ones that self-report could *not* predict—then that would provide compelling evidence for its validity in principle and its utility in practice. Accordingly, we here focus on how well the IAT can predict one important outcome of obvious social relevance: *voting behavior*.

One curiosity is that, in the domain of political attitudes, the correlations between self-report measures and the IAT scores are among the highest obtained (Nosek, 2007). Hence, both might here be expected to tell a similar story, and to overlap in what they predict. Nonetheless, the IAT might still prove especially informative with respect to one group of potential voters—those who are as yet *undecided*. Such individuals are openly declaring that they do not themselves know whom they will vote for. This raises an interesting question: If they do not know, could anyone else? Well, if the IAT taps into unconscious biases, and those unconscious biases guide behavior, then IAT scores might predict whom undecided voters would vote for, even if those voters cannot. Success here would be a ringing endorsement for the IAT as a technical tool.

Galdi, Arcuri, and Gawronski (2008) reported an initial result along these lines in the prestigious journal *Science*. The issue on which participants would shortly vote was the proposed expansion of a U.S. military base in Vicenza, Italy—a prospect that had left the local residents sharply divided. First, the researchers assessed participants' conscious beliefs toward the base, using a short survey about the expected consequences of its enlargement. Second, they assessed participants' automatic associations, using a version of the IAT that permitted associations toward a single target to be assessed (Karpinski & Steinman, 2006). Third, they assessed participants' voting intentions—by asking whether they had decided to vote for or against the proposed expansion, or whether they remained as yet undecided. The researchers conducted all three of these assessments on two occasions (Time 1, Time 2).

The results were striking. Among decided voters at Time 1, only their conscious (self-reported) beliefs predicted their voting intentions at Time 2. In contrast, among undecided voters at Time 1, only their automatic (IAT-assessed) associations predicted their voting intentions at Time 2. Apparently, the IAT "knew" which way undecided voters were intending to vote before they did.

However, the study had a major shortcoming: It only measured *intentions* to vote, not actual *voting* itself. Furthermore, a single day off does not make a vacation. Additional studies—to be reviewed later—had already called this finding into question. This led Raccuia (2016) to conduct further research into the matter, to help sort out what the IAT could or could not predict as regards voting.

What He Did

Raccuia conducted three large online studies, all based in Switzerland. This setting was ideal, because the Swiss are unique in holding regular referendums, on issues of national concern, where the votes of the citizens themselves decide the outcome (i.e., *direct democracy*). This means that, when participants vote in these referendums, their behavior can be presumed to map on precisely to their attitudes toward the issue. In contrast, citizens in other democracies rarely hold referendums, instead nearly always electing politicians to act on their behalf (i.e., *representative democracy*). In doing so, their behavior in the voting booth is liable to reflect a more complex mix of attitudes—toward parties, politicians, and policies.

In the first two studies, Raccuia laid the groundwork for a third and most telling study. A key goal along the way was to figure out the optimal way to administer the IAT.

Study 1 dealt with two Swiss referendums, having to do with a minimum wage initiative (soundly rejected) and the purchase of expensive fighter jets (narrowly rejected). Here, to assess implicit attitudes, the researcher used a computer-based single-target IAT, but one featuring both words and pictures. To assess explicit attitudes, he used a standard self-report measure of left-right political orientation. Unlike Galdi and colleagues (2008), he assessed both voting intentions and actual voting—depending on whether voters had not yet, or already had, voted. (The voting period in Swiss referendums extends over several weeks.) To keep things simple at this stage, he excluded undecided voters from his analysis.

Study 2 dealt with a referendum to replace the existing system of competing healthcare insurers with an alternative system featuring a single healthcare insurer (broadly rejected). In this study, Raccuia tried out a different, and in some ways more straightforward, single-target IAT. The reason was logistical. In Study 1, the necessity of obtaining a web browser plug-in to run the previous IAT online had deterred nearly 95% of potential participants from taking it, for fear of acquiring a computer virus. (Such are the unexpected obstacles researchers face!) To solve this problem, he ran an online version of a paper-and-pencil IAT, which required no web browser plug-in. (It was similar in form to the IAT featured in the Appendix—except that participants had to check as many boxes as they could in 20 seconds, and only one target category appeared.) He also used the same self-report measure of left-right political orientation as in Study 1, as well as similar measures of voting intention and actual voting. Undecided voters were again excluded.

Study 3 was Raccuia's key study. Here, the referendum pertained to a proposal—made by an organization called *Ecology and Population*—to limit annual immigration to Switzerland to a mere one-fifth of 1 percent of the population, on the grounds that immigration led to the environmental degradation of Switzerland (soundly rejected). This time, the explicit attitude mapped more precisely onto the referendum issue, which hinged, not only on the environmental impact of immigration, but also on whether restricting immigration would harm the Swiss economy, and imply it had a xenophobic culture. Accordingly, respondents self-reported their beliefs about the impact of immigration on the Swiss environment, economy, and culture. The single-target IAT—the variant used in Study 2—featured the names of parties ad politicians supporting the proposal. Furthermore, and going beyond the first two studies, Raccuia now drew a distinction between decided and undecided voters. In particular, he assessed participants on two occasions, both well in advance of the referendum, and then once the referendum was over. As such, he was able to compare his results precisely to those of Galdi and colleagues (2008), and with a substantially larger sample.

What He Found

In Study 1, self-reported political orientation, on its own, predicted both voting intentions and actual voting in both referendums. IAT scores, on their own, did the same. Such findings show that the IAT *can* predict voting behavior, thereby implying that it measures *something* real. Nonetheless, in all cases, self-reported political orientation emerged as a *stronger* predictor. This raises the question: Why not rely only on self-report, and forget about the IAT? One reason might be that the IAT, even if it is overall a weaker predictor, could still predict *above and beyond* self-report. Did it? Here, the results differed by referendum. In the case of the case of the minimum wage initiative, all the predictiveness of the IAT was accounted for by self-report. However, in the case of the fighter jet purchase, the IAT showed some independent predictive power, albeit modest. This latter result testified to the IAT having the capacity to tap into something that self-report could not. (That said, the self-report measure, pertaining to generic left-right political preferences, mapped on less precisely than the IAT to the referendum issues; so perhaps the IAT had an "unfair advantage" in terms of correspondence with the outcome predicted.)

In Study 2, the initial results resembled those of Study 1. On its own, self-reported political orientation predicted both voting intention and behavior; and so did IAT scores on their own, but once again, to a lesser extent. This time, however, the evidence for the independent predictive power of the IAT was weaker, falling short of statistical significance in some cases.

In Study 3, Raccuia broke down his findings by whether voters were decided or undecided. Recall that, if the IAT is indeed a window on the unconscious mind, then one might expect—as Galdi and colleagues (2008) had found—that it would particularly predict voting among undecided voters. However, that is *not* what Raccuia found. Instead, he found, if anything, the *opposite*. For decided voters, a pattern emerged similar to that obtained in Study 1 with respect to the fighter jet purchase. To reiterate: Both self-report and the IAT, on their own, predicted actual voting; self-report was nevertheless the stronger predictor; yet the IAT still showed a small degree of independent predictive power. For undecided voters, the same pattern emerged; but it was *less* pronounced when it should have been more pronounced. Thus, Raccuia did not replicate the striking findings of Galdi and colleagues (2008). The IAT's unique value as a predictor, whatever it was, was greater for decided voters than for undecided voters.

So What?

Compared to other chapters, the findings here do not bear out theoretical expectation. Instead, they cast serious doubt on a hypothesis about a particular social process. It is important that readers realize that this is neither alarming nor unusual; on the contrary, it is part and parcel of how science works. Every active researcher in social psychology regularly has the experience of empirical reality not playing ball. Sir Thomas Huxley, cousin of Charles Darwin, once remarked that the slaying of a beautiful hypothesis by an ugly fact was the great tragedy of science. However, he meant this ironically. For a scientist, a slain hypothesis is a step in the right direction, a welcome encounter with the truth. It is disappointing, certainly, to be wrong; but the alternative—blindly or dogmatically persisting in one's errors—is idiotic. Moreover, when a result comes out "the wrong way," it at least shows that one's hypothesis was *testable*—that it was specific enough to be consistent or inconsistent with the data obtained. Some hypotheses are so vague and flexible as to not even meet this standard.

Other researchers (e.g., Roccato & Zogmaister, 2010; Friese, Smith, Plischke, Bluemke, & Nosek, 2012) had also checked to see whether they could replicate the striking effects originally obtained by Galdi and colleagues (2008). Their findings were largely in line with those of Raccuia (see Gawronski, Galdi, & Arcuri, 2015, for a review). In particular, these researchers found some evidence that the IAT could predict voting intentions and behavior above and beyond some typical self-report measures. Nonetheless, two important caveats applied. First, the predictive advantage was statistically small and practically trivial. Second, the theoretical expectation—that the IAT should be especially predictive for undecided voters—was also contradicted. Hence, the empirical picture is currently complicated. The IAT goes beyond self-report, but only slightly; and when it does so, it predicts what it shouldn't. Perhaps the theoretical takeaway is that what the IAT assesses is not so necessarily unconscious after all (Gawronski, Hofmann, & Wilbur, 2006).

Consider also the bigger picture. The IAT's predictive validity has been assessed in other domains. One is *consumer behavior*. Here, much the same story has emerged (Maison & Gregg, 2016). In particular, the IAT sometimes, but not always, uniquely assists in the prediction of consumer behavior; however, the consumer behavior predicted is not what you might theoretically expect (e.g., not *only* the spontaneous choice of consumer products). Another domain is *discriminatory behavior*. Here, people—owing to the pressure of political correctness—might conceal their social stereotypes and prejudices from others, or even deny it to themselves. Hence, one might theoretically expect the IAT to tell a "truer" story. Findings across a wide range of studies seem to be consistent with this expectation (Greenwald, Poehlman, Uhlmann, & Banaji, 2009). However, even this conclusion has been challenged. Some critics charge that the relevant findings are highly variable and have been overestimated (Oswald, Mitchell, Blanton, Jaccard, & Tetlock, 2013), others that many of the studies cited did not assess behavioral discrimination properly (Carlsson & Agerström, 2016).

If you are feeling a little confused and overwhelmed, well, you should be! Empirical findings are piling on thick and fast. Claims and counter-claims abound. The devil is in the details—and its hell to sort through them all. Alas, as Oscar Wilde once remarked, truth is rarely pure and never simple. Nonetheless, we hope to have given you an authentic insight into how complex the state of play in social psychology can be. Check out for yourself one or more of the relevant papers we cite. You will see how sophisticated discussions can get, and how intelligent research-ers can disagree.

For now, let us draw a provisional conclusion. In our view, the IAT can definitely detect some-thing special about people's attitudes. However, exactly what that is remains to be clarified. Nonetheless, take a step back for a moment. Isn't it remarkable that a humble sorting task can even compete with self-reported attitudes in forecasting how people will behave? From the sheer speed of people's digital reactions much can be diagnosed.

Afterthoughts

The IAT was designed as a technical tool to detect beliefs and feelings that people might not be aware of. But what about those beliefs and feelings that people are fully aware of but still wish to misreport? We noted earlier that people are very poor at intuitively detecting deception. Is there any technical tool that can do better? You likely have heard of one already, commonly called the *lie detector* or *polygraph*. We conclude by examining its pros and cons, and consider some alternatives.

Two main types of polygraphic lie detector exist. The first—the one most people are familiar with—is called the *Control Question Test* or *CQT* (Krapohl & Shaw, 2015). Suspects to a crime are asked a series of questions. Their physiological reactions while replying are then continu-ously recorded on a graph. These include their heart rate, pulse rate, respiration rate, and perspi-ration rate—hence, the "poly-" in "polygraph." Suspects are asked, often repeatedly, three sets of questions: those having to do with the crime itself (*relevant*); those that have nothing to do with the crime (*irrelevant*); and those that, while having nothing to do with the crime, are nonetheless designed to upset innocent suspects more than the relevant questions (*control*). If all goes accord-ing to plan, guilty suspects should react more strongly to relevant than to control questions, whereas innocent suspects should show either the reverse pattern or no difference. Regardless of guilt, irrelevant questions should elicit the weakest reactions of all.

The main problem with the CQT is that circumstantial factors can conspire to make innocent suspects exhibit a guilty profile (Lykken, 1998). For example, a genuine rape victim accused of making up charges against her assailant may react most strongly to relevant questions simply because any reference to her rape evokes traumatic memories. Alternatively, a man mistakenly accused of rape may react in the same way because relevant questions evoke legitimate anxi-ety over false prosecution. In such cases, control questions—which are typically broad in scope and concerned with misdemeanors past—simply cannot compete impact-wise with relevant ques-tions. Nor can CQT administrators always be trusted to accurately judge the effects of relevant and control questions on innocent suspects. Hence, the CQT is in principle fallible (National Research Council, 2003). Accordingly, literature reviews (e.g., Vrij, 2008, p. 391, Table 15.1) report that, when the CQT is applied in the field, it is very poor at clearing suspects who are innocent (only 53% to 75% of the time), even if it is much better at identifying suspects who are guilty (a full 83% to 89% of the time). Such a tool is arguably unsuitable for making legal decisions about the guilt or innocence of individuals. For that reason, most countries apart from the U.S. ban the use of the CQT in court.

A more accurate way of distinguishing the guilty from the innocent is to probe them for knowl-edge of a crime. In the *Guilty Knowledge Test*, or *GKT* (Lykken, 1959; Ben-Shakhar & Elaad, 2003)—also known as the *Concealed Information Test* or *CIT*—suspects are asked a series of questions about a crime that only a guilty party could be expected to know. After each question is asked, a number of multiple-choice answers are stated aloud. Only one of these answers is correct. However, all are designed to strike an innocent suspect, unaware of the details of the crime, as equally plausible. Suspects' physiological reactions to each answer are then recorded. If the information conveyed by an answer is recognized, then a stronger physiological reaction results. Hence, guilty suspects will yield a pattern of reactions that reflects knowledge of the crime, whereas innocent suspects will show a largely random pattern. With enough questions and answers, an increasingly clear-cut discrimination can be made.

Note that, precisely because there is no reason for the right answers to stand out for innocent suspects, false positives are unlikely. Accordingly, literature reviews, like those cited previously, report that, when the GKT is applied in the field, it is very good at clearing innocent suspects (a full 94% to 98% of the time), even if it is considerably worse at identifying suspects who are guilty (only 42% to 76% of the time). However, given the "innocent until proven guilty" rule, this presents less of an ethical problem. One limitation of the GKT, relative to the CQT, is that suitable questions can be difficult to construct if the details of the crime have been widely publicized, or if innocent suspects have also witnessed the crime. Even still, the GKT is not as widely employed in the criminal justice system as it perhaps should be.

Recent years have seen an outpouring of research on alternative lie detection tools (Meijer, Verschuere, Gamer, Merckelbach, & Ben-Shakhar, 2016). Many, like the IAT, rely on response speed (Verschuere, Suchotzki, & Debey, 2015). Indeed, it has been reliably observed that, because lying is a more mentally complex activity than truth-telling, it slows people down (Suchotzki, Verschuere, Van Bockstaele, Ben-Shakhar, & Crombez, 2017). However, other tools aim, not merely to capitalize on this difference, but to amplify it. One of them—a brainchild of one of the authors (APG)—is called the *Timed Antagonistic Response Alethiometer*, mercifully abbreviated to *TARA*. Like the IAT, it is a sorting task. Unlike the IAT, participants classify statements— two sets of them—into the categories *TRUE* and *FALSE*. We won't detain you here with the details. We merely note that the TARA has achieved accuracy rates of up to 80% in the laboratory (Gregg, 2007; Gregg, Mahadevan, Edwards, & Klymowsky, 2014), and is one of many new and promising methods being developed at the time of writing.

In conclusion, clever technologies can help us peel away the superficial layers of the mind when our native powers of discernment fail us. However, we must remain mindful of their shortcomings. If there is any royal road to the unconscious mind—a claim Freud made of dreams—it is strewn with obstacles that need to be carefully negotiated.

Revelation

Social psychologists use technical tools, such as the Implicit Association Test, to tell more about people than they are willing or able to say about themselves. The use of such tools can assist in the prediction of behavior.

What Do You Think?

To what extent do you think that your mind contains thoughts and feelings that you are unaware of? To what extent to you think other people's minds do? Do your answers to these two questions differ? If so, why might this be? What evidence do you use to decide in each case?

Chapter Reference

Raccuia, L. (2016) Single-Target Implicit Association Tests (ST-IAT) predict voting behavior of decided and undecided voters in Swiss referendums. *PLoS ONE, 11*, e0163872.

Other References

Banaji, M. R., & Hardin, C. D. (1996). Automatic stereotyping. *Psychological Science, 7*, 136–141.

Bargh, J. A. (Ed.). (2007). *Social psychology and the unconscious: The automaticity of higher mental processes* (pp. 265–292). New York: Psychology Press.

Ben-Shakhar, G., & Elaad, E. (2003). The validity of psychophysiological detection of information with the guilty knowledge test: A meta-analytic review. *Journal of Applied Psychology, 88*, 131–151.

Bond, C. F., Jr., & DePaulo, B. M. (2006). Accuracy of deception judgements. *Personality and Social Psychology Review, 10*, 214–234.

Bond, C. F., Jr., & DePaulo, B. M. (2008). Individual differences in judging deception: Accuracy and bias. *Psychological Bulletin, 134*, 477–492.

Bradburn, N. M., Sudman, S., & Wansink, B. (2004). *Asking questions: The definitive guide to questionnaire design—for market research, political polls, and social and health questionnaires* (Rev. ed.). San Francisco, CA: Jossey-Bass.

Carlsson, R., & Agerström, J. (2016). A closer look at the discrimination outcomes in the IAT literature. *Scandinavian Journal of Psychology, 57*, 278–287.

Chartrand, T. L., & Bargh, J. A. (2000). Studying the mind in the middle: A practical guide to priming and automaticity research. In H. Reis & C. Judd (Eds.), *Handbook of research methods in social psychology* (pp. 253–285). New York: Cambridge University Press.

Crews, F. (1995). *The memory wars: Freud's legacy in dispute*. New York: A New York Review book.

Dovidio, J. F., & Gaertner, S. L. (2004). Aversive racism. *Advances in Experimental Social Psychology, 36*, 1–52.

Fazio, R. H., Jackson, J. R., Dunton, B. C., & Williams, C. J. (1995). Variability in automatic activation as an unobtrusive measure of racial attitudes: A bona fide pipeline? *Journal of Personality and Social Psychology, 69*, 1013–1027.

Friese, M., Smith, C. T., Plischke, T., Bluemke, M., & Nosek, B. A. (2012). Do implicit attitudes predict voting behavior particularly for undecided voters? *PLoS ONE, 7*, e85680.

Galdi, S., Arcuri, L., & Gawronski, B. (2008). Automatic mental associations predict future choices of undecided decision-makers. *Science, 321*, 1100–1102.

Gawronski, B., Galdi, S., & Arcuri, L. (2015). What can political psychology learn from implicit measures? Empirical evidence and new directions. *Political Psychology, 36*, 1–17.

Gawronski, B., Hofmann, W., & Wilbur, C. (2006). Are "Implicit" attitudes unconscious? *Consciousness and Cognition, 15*, 485–499.

Greenwald, A. G., McGhee, D. E., & Schwartz, J. K. L. (1998). Measuring individual differences in implicit cognition: The Implicit Association Test. *Journal of Personality and Social Psychology, 74*, 1464–1480.

Greenwald, A. G., Poehlman, T. A., Uhlmann, E. L., & Banaji, M. R. (2009). Understanding and using the Implicit Association Test: III. Meta-analysis of predictive validity. *Journal of Personality and Social Psychology, 97*, 17–41.

Gregg, A. P. (2007). When vying reveals lying: The timed antagonistic response Alethiometer. *Applied Cognitive Psychology, 21*, 621–647.

Gregg, A. P., & Klymowsky, J. (2013). The implicit association test in market research: Potentials and pitfalls. *Psychology & Marketing, 30*, 588–601.

Gregg, A. P., Mahadevan, N., Edwards, S. E., & Klymowsky, J. (2014). Detecting lies about consumer attitudes using the timed antagonistic response alethiometer. *Behavior Research Methods, 46*, 758–771.

Karpinski, A., & Steinman, R. B. (2006). The single category implicit association test as a measure of implicit social cognition. *Journal of Personality and Social Psychology, 91*, 16–32.

Krapohl, D., & Shaw, P. (2015). *Fundamentals of polygraph practice*. San Diego, CA: Academic Press.

Lykken, D. (1959). The GSR in the detection of guilt. *Journal of Applied Psychology, 43*, 385–388.

Lykken, D. (1998). *A tremor in the blood: The uses and abuses of the lie detector*. Reading, MA: Perseus Books.

Maison, D., & Gregg, A. P. (2016). Capturing the consumer' unconscious: Applying the IAT in consumer research. In C. Jansson-Boyd & M. Zawisza (Eds.), *International handbook of consumer psychology* (pp. 143–153). London: Routledge.

Meijer, E. H., Verschuere, B., Gamer, M., Merckelbach, H., & Ben-Shakhar, G. (2016). Deception detection with behavioral, autonomic, and neural measures: Conceptual and methodological considerations that warrant modesty. *Psychophysiology*, *5*, 593–604.

National Research Council. (2003). *The polygraph and lie detection.* Washington, DC: The National Academies Press.

Nosek, B. A. (2007). Implicit-explicit relations. *Current Directions in Psychological Science*, *16*, 65–69.

Nosek, B. A., Greenwald, A. G., & Banaji, M. R. (2007). The implicit association test at age 7: A methodological and conceptual review. In J. A. Bargh (Ed.), *Social psychology and the unconscious: The automaticity of higher mental processes* (pp. 265–292). New York: Psychology Press.

Oswald, F. L., Mitchell, G., Blanton, H., Jaccard, J., & Tetlock, P. E. (2013). Predicting ethnic and racial discrimination: A meta-analysis of IAT criterion studies. *Journal of Personality and Social Psychology*, *105*, 171–192.

Raccuia, L. (2016). Single-Target Implicit Association Tests (ST-IAT) predict voting behavior of decided and undecided voters in Swiss referendums. *PLoS ONE*, *11*, e0163872.

Roccato, M., & Zogmaister, C. (2010). Predicting the vote through implicit and explicit attitudes: A field research. *Political Psychology*, *31*, 249–274.

Rudman, L. A., & Kilianski, S. E. (2000). Implicit and explicit attitudes toward female authority. *Personality and Social Psychology Bulletin*, *26*, 1315–1328.

Suchotzki, K., Verschuere, B., Van Bockstaele, B., Ben-Shakhar, G., & Crombez, G. (2017). Lying takes time: A meta-analysis on reaction time measures of deception. *Psychological Bulletin*, *143*, 428–453.

Verschuere, B., Suchotzki, K., & Debey, E. (2015). Detecting deception through reaction times. In P. A. Granhag, A. Vrij, & B. Verschuere (Eds.), *Deception detection: Current challenges and new approaches.* Chichester, UK: John Wiley & Sons, Ltd.

Vrij, A. (2008). *Detecting lies and deceit* (2nd ed.). New York: Wiley-Blackwell.

More to Explore

Banaji, M. R., & Greenwald, A. G. (2013). *Blindspot: Hidden biases of good people.* New York: Delacorte Press.

Sample Implicit Association Test (IAT)

Donald J. Trump vs. Hillary R. Clinton

Instructions

On each of the two pages that follow, you have a central column of words.

These words fall into four different categories.

Trump, Donald, DJT	=	**TRUMP**
Clinton, Hillary, HRC	=	**HILLARY**
Horrible, Nasty, Awful	=	BAD
Lovely, Nice, Great	=	GOOD

Your job is to sort the words into their categories.

Do this as quickly as you can without making errors.

On the left and right of each word, there is a box.

One box, on the left, is below two category labels, also on the left.

The other box, on the right, is below two category labels, also on the right.

To sort a word into a category, check the box below the corresponding category label.

(*Note*: To save the book, make a photocopy of the pages, or use the blunt end of a pen or pencil instead.)

To start, put your pen or pencil in the extra box above the column of words. Then work your way down, word by word, checking the correct box each time.

Just before you begin, note the time on your watch. And just after you finish, note the time again. Then compute how long it took you, to the nearest second.

Do the same on both pages, which feature different IAT blocks.

Finally, compare how long it took you to complete each.

Did you notice a difference? Did it fit with your conscious attitudes toward Trump and Clinton? (*Note*: If trying the exercise for a second time, sort words from the bottom to the top instead, to reduce practice effects.)

BLOCK 1

	TRUMP BAD		HILLARY GOOD	
		❏		
1	❏	**Hillary**	❏	1
2	❏	Horrible	❏	2
3	❏	**Trump**	❏	3
4	❏	Nice	❏	4
5	❏	**DJT**	❏	5
6	❏	Nasty	❏	6
7	❏	**HRC**	❏	7
8	❏	Great	❏	8
9	❏	**Donald**	❏	9
10	❏	Awful	❏	10
11	❏	**Clinton**	❏	11
12	❏	Lovely	❏	12
13	❏	**Hillary**	❏	13
14	❏	Nasty	❏	14
15	❏	**Trump**	❏	15
16	❏	Lovely	❏	16
17	❏	**Clinton**	❏	17
18	❏	Awful	❏	18
19	❏	**HRC**	❏	19
20	❏	Nice	❏	20
21	❏	**Donald**	❏	21
22	❏	Horrible	❏	22
23	❏	**DJT**	❏	23
24	❏	Great	❏	24
25	❏	**Trump**	❏	25
26	❏	Nasty	❏	26
27	❏	**Hillary**	❏	27
28	❏	Lovely	❏	28
29	❏	**Clinton**	❏	29
30	❏	Awful	❏	30
31	❏	**Donald**	❏	31
32	❏	Great	❏	32
33	❏	**HRC**	❏	33
34	❏	Nasty	❏	34
35	❏	**DJT**	❏	35
36	❏	Nice	❏	36
37	❏	**Trump**	❏	37
38	❏	Horrible	❏	38
39	❏	**Hillary**	❏	39
40	❏	Great	❏	40
41	❏	**DJT**	❏	41
42	❏	Horrible	❏	42
43	❏	**Donald**	❏	43
44	❏	Nice	❏	44
45	❏	**HRC**	❏	45
46	❏	Awful	❏	46
47	❏	**Clinton**	❏	47
48	❏	Lovely	❏	48

TIME TAKEN IN SECONDS = [   ]

BLOCK 2

	TRUMP GOOD		HILLARY BAD	
		❑		
1	❑	Lovely	❑	1
2	❑	**Clinton**	❑	2
3	❑	Awful	❑	3
4	❑	**HRC**	❑	4
5	❑	Nice	❑	5
6	❑	**Donald**	❑	6
7	❑	Horrible	❑	7
8	❑	**DJT**	❑	8
9	❑	Great	❑	9
10	❑	**Hillary**	❑	10
11	❑	Horrible	❑	11
12	❑	**Trump**	❑	12
13	❑	Nice	❑	13
14	❑	**DJT**	❑	14
15	❑	Nasty	❑	15
16	❑	**HRC**	❑	16
17	❑	Great	❑	17
18	❑	**Donald**	❑	18
19	❑	Awful	❑	19
20	❑	**Clinton**	❑	20
21	❑	Lovely	❑	21
22	❑	**Hillary**	❑	22
23	❑	Nasty	❑	23
24	❑	**Trump**	❑	24
25	❑	Great	❑	25
26	❑	**DJT**	❑	26
27	❑	Horrible	❑	27
28	❑	**Donald**	❑	28
29	❑	Nice	❑	29
30	❑	**HRC**	❑	30
31	❑	Awful	❑	31
32	❑	**Clinton**	❑	32
33	❑	Lovely	❑	33
34	❑	**Trump**	❑	34
35	❑	Nasty	❑	35
36	❑	**Hillary**	❑	36
37	❑	Lovely	❑	37
38	❑	**Clinton**	❑	38
39	❑	Awful	❑	39
40	❑	**Donald**	❑	40
41	❑	Great	❑	41
42	❑	**HRC**	❑	42
43	❑	Nasty	❑	43
44	❑	**DJT**	❑	44
45	❑	Nice	❑	45
46	❑	**Trump**	❑	46
47	❑	Horrible	❑	47
48	❑	**Hillary**	❑	48

TIME TAKEN IN SECONDS = [   ]

24 Frames of Mind
Taking Risks or Playing Safe?

"The optimist believes that this is the best of all possible worlds. The pessimist fears that this may be true."

—Robert Oppenheimer (1904–1967), American father of the atomic bomb

Background

If ever you feel bored, try this neat experiment. Take three glasses. Fill the first with ice water, the second with hot water, and the third with lukewarm water. Now place your left hand in the first glass and your right hand in the second. Wait for about a minute. Finally, transfer both of your hands to the third glass. The result: The same water will feel, at the same time, warm to your left hand but cool to your right hand! What does this weird experience indicate? It indicates that perceptions of intensity do not depend only on the *absolute* intensity of a stimulus but also upon its *relative* intensity. Otherwise stated, perceptual experience is influenced by its comparative context. In this chapter, we review research showing that what is true of our perceptual experience is also true of our judgments and decisions more generally.

Suppose someone made you the following offer—call it offer X. You must choose between either (a) receiving $15,000 for certain or (b) having an equal chance of receiving $10,000 or $20,000. What would you do? It turns out that most people prefer option (a)—the "safe" one. However, one might argue that it should make no difference how someone chooses. The *expected value* of each alternative is the same.

The expected value of an alternative is the *likelihood* that it will happen multiplied by the *desirability* of its happening. Likelihood is represented by a value between 0 (impossible) and 1 (inevitable), desirability by some quantity measured in numerical units (typically monetary ones). In the previous example, the likelihood of the first alternative is 1, and its desirability is $15,000. Multiplying, this yields an expected value of $15,000. The likelihood of the second alternative is the sum of its two possible outcomes: a likelihood of 0.5 times a desirability of $10,000, plus a likelihood of 0.5 times a desirability of $20,000. This also yields an expected value of ($10,000 $\times$ 0.5) + ($20,000 $\times$ 0.5) = $15,000.

Suppose now a different offer were on the table—call it offer Y. After receiving a handsome $20,000, you must choose between either (a) definitely returning $5,000 or (b) taking an equal chance of having to return either $10,000 or $0. How would you choose this time? Here, more people prefer option (b)—the "risky" one.

Reflection reveals that offers X and Y are in fact equivalent, just differently stated. Returning $5,000 after receiving $20,000 (offer Y) is the same as receiving $15,000 outright (offer X). And receiving $20,000 and then risking having to return either $10,000 or $0 (offer Y) is the same as receiving either $10,000 or $20,000 outright (offer X). Yet the manner in which these equivalent offers are *framed* makes people plumb for different options. Why?

Prospect theory (Kahneman & Tversky, 1981) provides an answer. It proposes that we see gains or losses as, respectively, beneficial or costly departures from the status quo. The size and direction of these perceived departures depends on how the human mind transforms expected values into subjective impressions. Prospect theory states that the transformation obeys four psychological laws. We describe three now, and the fourth later in the "So What?" section.

The first law of prospect theory is this: As gains increase, the perceived benefit of each new unit gain will decrease. For example, if you only earn $10,000 a year, then getting a raise of $1,000 will be cause for celebration. However, if you already earn $1,000,000 a year, then the same raise may barely cheer you up.

The second law is the mirror image of the first: As losses increase, the perceived cost of each new unit loss will decrease. For example, a loss of $1,000 at roulette will distress you if you have only lost $10,000 so far. However, if you have already lost $1,000,000, then the same loss may hardly faze you.

The third law of prospect theory is the one most pertinent to the present study: People's preferences will *reverse* depending on whether they are envisioning potential losses or gains. Specifically, when a potential gain beckons, people will be more likely to avoid risk, but when a potential loss looms, they will be more likely to court risk.

Prospect theory thus clarifies why people typically prefer $15,000 up front to an equal chance of receiving either $10,000 or $20,000. With the payoff being framed in terms of gains, the certain outcome is preferred. The theory also clarifies why, after the initial receipt of $20,000, people typically prefer an equal chance of losing either $10,000 or $0 to a guaranteed loss of $5000. With the payoff now being framed in terms of losses, the uncertain outcome is preferred.

The fact that framing a choice in terms of losses or gains can influence how people choose has implications for, among other things, how persuasive a message is. Traditionally, one major branch of social psychology has concerned itself with establishing what causes or prevents a change in someone's attitude (Petty & Wegener, 1998; see Chapter 20). It turns out that prospect theory can be usefully extended to suggest how to enhance the persuasiveness of messages—in particular, messages that advocate the adoption of healthful behaviors.

Just as financial choices can be framed as gains or losses, so too can healthful behaviors. They can be framed in terms of the probable gains that will result from performing them, or the probable losses that will result from failing to perform them. For example, the statement "If you quit smoking, your health will benefit" is *gain-framed* because it praises the virtues of kicking the habit. In contrast, the statement "If you keep smoking, your health will suffer" is *loss-framed* because it decries the vice of continuing to indulge.

It is further possible to distinguish two distinct categories of healthful behaviors: those that involve the *detection* of physical disease (e.g., brain scans) and those that involve the *prevention* of physical disease (e.g., exercise). These categories of behavior tend to be perceived in distinct ways. Disease-detecting behaviors, because they sometimes reveal the presence of disease, are typically seen as risky to perform. Thus, a brain scan may be dreaded for fear an inoperable tumor may be discovered. Disease-preventing behaviors, on the other hand, because their goal is to maintain health, are typically seen as safe to perform. Thus, exercise is mentally linked to keeping you fit and trim, not to uncovering your ailments.

What has all this got to do with prospect theory? It could be argued that the safe—risky distinction closely corresponds to the certain—uncertain distinction. In everyday parlance, safety and certainty go together (sure things, safe bets), as do risk and uncertainty (dicey deals, iffy prospects). Consequently, the predictions of prospect theory for outcomes varying in certainty—uncertainty may also hold for outcomes varying in safety—risk.

On the basis of this reasoning, Rothman, Martino, Bedell, Detweiler, and Salovey (1999) derived the following hypothesis: Disease-preventing behaviors, being linked to safe and certain outcomes, ought to be more influenced by gain-framed messages, whereas disease-detecting behaviors, being linked to risky and uncertain outcomes, ought to be more influenced by loss-framed messages. In other words, the effectiveness of adopting one framing strategy over another should depend upon the type of healthful behavior being advocated.

Prior research had already yielded findings broadly consistent with this hypothesis. For example, loss-framed messages had proven superior to gain-framed ones in convincing women to undertake mammograms—a disease-detecting behavior (Banks et al., 1995), whereas gain-framed messages had proven superior to loss-framed ones in promoting the use of sunscreen—a disease-preventing behavior (Detweiler, Bedell, Salovey, Pronin, & Rothman, 1999). However, it is not clear whether the results of the two studies were attributable to their use of different framing manipulations or to different healthful behaviors. The researchers needed to track down a single behavior that could be convincingly described in terms of either disease-prevention or disease-detection. They settled on a promising (if unglamorous) candidate: dental rinsing.

Two types of dental rinse exist: antibacterial rinse, which prevents plaque accumulation, and disclosing rinse, which reveals the presence of plaque. Both types of rinse are similarly deployed. The use of antibacterial rinse is clearly a disease-preventing behavior, the use of disclosing rinse, a disease-detecting behavior. Rothman and his colleagues (1999) predicted that, in accordance with prospect theory, messages highlighting gains would be better at convincing participants to use an antibacterial rinse, whereas messages highlighting losses would be better at convincing them to use a disclosing rinse.

What They Did

One hundred twenty undergraduates from the University of Minnesota, mostly female, served as participants. On arriving at the lab, they were told that the purpose of the study was to evaluate the effectiveness of pamphlets aimed at promoting dental hygiene. The precise hypothesis under investigation was concealed to avoid biasing participants' responses. Participants were then handed a professional-looking pamphlet four pages in length. It contained much general information about dental health that did not differ across different experimental conditions. However, the pamphlet did differ in two critical respects: in terms of *which* dental hygiene measure was recommended, and in terms of *how* it was framed. Specifically, half the 120 participants read a message recommending the use of antibacterial rinse, half a message recommending the use of disclosing rinse. In addition, for half the participants in each of these groups, the messages were gain-framed, for the other half, loss-framed. Thus, there were four experimental conditions in all, each featuring 30 participants, arranged into what is called a 2 × 2 between-groups design.

For participants encouraged to use the antibacterial rinse, the gain-framed recommendation read, "People who use an antibacterial rinse are taking advantage of a safe and effective way to reduce plaque accumulation," whereas the loss-framed recommendation read, "People who use an antibacterial rinse are failing to take advantage of a safe and effective way to reduce plaque accumulation." For participants encouraged to use a disclosing rinse, the gain-framed recommendation read, "Using a disclosing rinse before brushing enhances your ability to detect areas of plaque accumulation," whereas the loss-framed recommendation read, "Failing to use a disclosing rinse before brushing limits your ability to detect plaque accumulation." Such differences in wording may seem trivial. However, prospect theory predicts that they will have an impact on the persuasiveness of the recommendations.

The researchers were primarily interested in the impact of the pamphlets on participants' *behavior*. Thus, at the very end of the study, participants were given a stamped postcard that they could later mail in to receive a free sample of either antibacterial or disclosing rinse (depending on the condition to which they had been assigned). The researchers predicted that, in the days that followed, more participants would request samples of antibacterial rinse when the benefits of using it had been emphasized, whereas more participants would request samples of disclosing rinse when the costs of not using it had been emphasized.

For thoroughness, self-report measures of the pamphlets' persuasiveness were also administered (prior to the distribution of postcards). Participants were asked to indicate (a) their attitude toward using the rinses (by rating their effectiveness, benefit, importance, and desirability), (b) their intentions to buy and use the rinses, and (c) how much they would be willing to pay for the rinses. The researchers also assessed how interesting, involving, and informative participants found the pamphlets to be overall (though no difference between conditions was expected).

Participants also filled out several additional self-report measures. Prior to reading the pamphlet, they provided background details about themselves and their dental history, so that the researchers could make sure that these details had no bearing on the effect of the framing manipulation. Then, after reading the pamphlet, participants completed two further measures designed to reveal how they had reacted to and processed the information contained in the pamphlet. The idea was to get a handle on some of the psychological mechanisms that might have *mediated* (been instrumental in bringing about) any effects of the message framing. Participants were instructed to indicate the feelings they had experienced, and the thoughts that had occurred to them, while reading the pamphlet.

Participants also rated—both before and after reading the pamphlet—how likely they thought they were to develop gum disease given their current dental practices, as well as how severe a problem gum disease would be for them if they ever developed it. By taking these ratings both beforehand and afterward the researchers were able to estimate how each participant's perceptions of the risk and severity of gum disease changed as a result of reading the pamphlet.

Finally, a brief check on their framing manipulation was included. Participants were asked to rate the overall tone of the pamphlet and whether the pamphlet emphasized the benefits of rinsing or the costs of not rinsing.

What They Found

Based on an extension of prospect theory, the researchers predicted that persuasion would be greater when messages recommending a disease-preventing behavior were framed in terms of potential gains and when messages recommending a disease-detecting behavior were framed in terms of potential losses. The pattern in which participants mailed in postcards to obtain a dental rinse clearly supported this hypothesis. Of those participants who read pamphlets advocating the use of antibacterial rinse (to prevent plaque accumulation and gum disease), a greater number mailed in postcards when a gain frame was employed. However, of those participants who read pamphlets advocating the use of disclosing rinse (to detect plaque accumulation and gum disease), a greater number mailed in postcards when a loss frame was employed. A comparable crisscross pattern emerged with respect to participants' intentions to purchase and use dental rinses (Figure 24).

Confidence in the validity of these findings was bolstered by two additional findings. First, manipulation checks suggested that the messages had been framed appropriately: Gain-framed messages were reported as emphasizing benefits and as being positive in tone, whereas loss-framed messages were reported as emphasizing costs and as being negative in tone. Second, none of the background variables measured, such as dental history, affected the results to any significant degree.

Having obtained a clear confirmation of their main hypothesis, the researchers went on to investigate the question of psychological mediation. What changes in participants' mental states lay behind the impact of the framing manipulation? Rather than exhaustively review the findings for each of the measures, we outline one interesting account of how the framing manipulation might have worked, and then assess the evidence obtained for mediation in general.

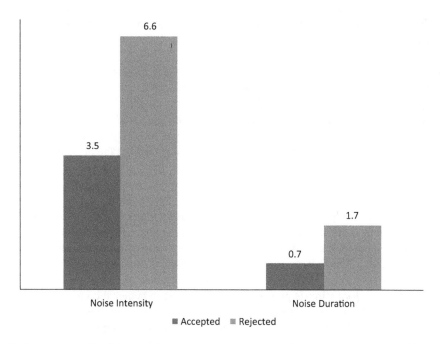

Figure 24 Percentage of participants who used antibacterial or disclosing rinse after reading loss-framed or gain-framed health messages

The more readily an event comes to mind the more likely its occurrence is judged to be (Tversky & Kahneman, 1973). Hence, people overestimate the probability of graphic or newsworthy causes of death, such as plane hijackings, and underestimate the probability of hidden and banal causes of death, such as blood clots (Coombs & Slovic, 1979). This *availability bias* may have also played a role in the present study. Specifically, messages advocating the use of disclosing rinse may have mainly brought to mind thoughts about the disadvantages of not rinsing (gum disease), thereby increasing the perceived likelihood of those disadvantages. If so, then loss-framed messages, by capitalizing on participants' aversion to those disadvantages, would have had the persuasive edge over gain-framed messages. Conversely, messages advocating the use of antibacterial rinse may have mainly brought to mind thoughts about the advantages of rinsing (healthy gums), thereby increasing the perceived likelihood of those advantages. If so, then gain-framed messages, by capitalizing on the appeal of those advantages, would have had the persuasive edge over loss-framed messages.

If this account were true, then perceived likelihood of gum disease, and expressed worries about dental health, should both have been greater in the disease-detecting conditions than in the disease-preventing conditions. However, no evidence of this pattern emerged, thereby casting doubt on the account put forward previously. In fact, no overall connection was found between participants' attitudes toward dental rinsing and their postcard-mailing propensities.

There are several possible explanations for this odd disjunction between attitudes and behaviors. First of all, the appropriate mediators may not have been sought. For example, participants were not asked to rate the likelihood of their contracting or avoiding gum disease given their use or nonuse of dental rinse, only the likelihood of their contracting or avoiding gum disease in general. A more specific inquiry may have worked better. Second, participants' self-reports may have been compromised by response biases. For example, their attitudes toward dental rinsing may have reflected whether they felt they should rinse rather than whether they felt inclined to rinse. Finally, it may have been that the psychological causes of participants' behavior were simply not available to self-report. Often the causes of our behaviors elude identification through introspection (Nisbett & Wilson, 1977; see Chapter 14).

Despite the failure to locate mediating variables (not everything works out smoothly in social psychological research), the present study nonetheless offered clear evidence that message frame and content could be manipulated to enhance the efficacy of health-promoting messages. It is also worth noting that Rothman and his colleagues (1999) ran an additional study in which participants read a message, again either gain- or loss-framed, advocating the detection or prevention of a hypothetical viral infection. Its findings dovetailed those of the present study.

So What?

If we wish to act rationally, we ought to make decisions by weighing the probability and desirability of the various outcomes that would result from deciding one way or the other. The manner in which those outcomes are portrayed should make no difference. The water in a glass that is described as half-full or half-empty will quench our thirst to an equal degree. However, the human mind turns out to be significantly swayed by how potential outcomes are portrayed. The way in which that information is presented—in particular, whether the emphasis is placed on losses or gains—influences the decision-making process. Hence, we seem to make judgments about things in the world, not as they are in themselves, but as they are relative to other things.

There are many other examples of how the framing of alternatives can influence our decisions. One is our use of *psychic budgets* (Thaler, 1980). Our readiness to part with our money often depends on how we categorize our forthcoming expenditure. For example, when buying a new house, we might be prepared to spend more on extras like garden gnomes than we would if the house were already ours. The reason is that, before the house is bought, the cost of the gnomes falls under the generous budget for the entire house, and so seems comparatively trivial. However, after the house is bought, the cost of the gnomes falls under the tighter budget of everyday expenses, and so seems comparatively extravagant. Needless to add, sales professionals are happy to exploit our budgeting biases, craftily inflating the asking price for accessories to a major purchase.

Another example of framing effects involves presenting alternative options as either maintaining the status quo or as altering it. Suppose you have a zero chance of developing a fatal disease. How much would you now pay to avoid having a 1 in 1,000 chance of developing it? Most people say that they would be prepared to pay several thousand dollars. However, now suppose that you already have a 1 in a 1,000 chance of developing that disease. How much would you now pay to reduce that risk to zero? Inconsistently, most people say that they would be prepared to pay only a few hundred dollars. Why is this?

An answer is provided by the fourth and final law of prospect theory: The loss of a benefit is considered more costly than the gain of that benefit is considered beneficial. One implication of this postulate is that, to induce people to accept a gamble involving an equal chance of winning or losing, it is necessary to award them more for winning than to penalize them for losing. For example, only a third of people accept an equal chance of winning $200 or losing $100, even though the expected value of the gamble is positive: $(0.5 \times \$200) - (0.5 \times \$100) = \$50$ (Tversky & Shafir, 1992). Findings like this strongly suggest that people have a bias toward maintaining the status quo, at the expense of foregoing likely benefits. This *status quo bias* manifests itself in many ways. For example, the price at which people are prepared to sell some article tends to be higher than the price at which they are prepared to buy it (Kahneman, Knetsch, & Thaler, 1991). This suggests that the potential "loss" of the article to a buyer is deemed more unpleasant than the potential "gain" of the same article is considered pleasant. Indeed, everything else equal, arrangements that currently exist, and have been around for some time, seem to be preferred to arrangements that potentially might exist (Eidelmann & Crandall, 2012).

The existence of this bias in favor of the status quo can explain why people pay more to avoid potential risks than they do to eliminate preexisting ones. Potential risks strike people as disrupting the status quo. Hence, running them seems costly, not running them just par for the course. In contrast, preexisting risks strike people as reflecting the status quo. Hence, running them seems par for the course, not running them beneficial.

But why do costs psychologically outweigh benefits? Perhaps it is just a brute fact that our potential for experiencing suffering exceeds our potential for experiencing joy. Bad experiences appear to have a more powerful effect on us than good experiences (Baumeister, Bratslaysky, Finkenhauer, & Vohs, 2001). Hence, prudence may serve us better than pluckiness overall. Another possibility is that the tendency to weigh costs more heavily than gains may have evolved over time because it conferred a survival benefit on our forefathers. Our hazardous ancestral environment may have happened to suit risk-averse cave-dwellers better than risk-seeking ones, so that the former reproduced in greater numbers, thereby making us what we are today. This is not to deny that people vary considerably in their penchant for risk-taking. For example, people with high self-esteem take more risks on average than people with low self-esteem (Baumeister, Tice, & Hutton, 1989). It is merely to affirm that risk-aversion is, on the whole, characteristic of the human race.

At this point, an astute reader may be wondering: If prospect theory is true, then why is gambling such a popular pastime? Why do people commonly throw caution to the wind in defiance of the objective odds? One answer is that most amounts gambled are psychologically trivial. If only very large bets (relative to one's income) could be laid, gambling would disappear overnight. Prospect theory properly applies only when significant amounts of money are involved.

Afterthoughts

Once we understand how the framing of a particular problem undermines the rationality of our judgments we may find ourselves in a curiously divided mental state. On the one hand, we can see how our judgments ought to remain unaffected. On the other hand, we can still feel our judgments being swayed one way or the other. It is as if two distinct levels of understanding coexist, or at least alternate in quick succession: a smart one that grasps the irrationality, and a dumb one that falls for it hook, line, and sinker (Kahneman, 2011).

This kind of mental duality also emerges when people are alerted to other cognitive biases, in particular those that involve probability judgments. Consider a lottery in which the winning 6 numbers are to be chosen at random from a pool of 36 numbers. There are two tickets for sale. One features the numbers "1,2,3,4,5,6," and the other, "2,18,17,29,4,35." Which ticket would you buy, given the choice? You probably feel an instinctive preference for the second ticket. The odds of a ticket with haphazard numbers winning certainly *seem* better than the odds of a ticket with consecutive numbers winning. Of course, a little reflection reveals that a preference for one ticket over another is irrational, because any set of six numbers, regardless of its composition, is equally likely to be chosen in a truly random lottery. The mistake is to think that, because, as a class, haphazard combinations are more likely to occur than consecutive combinations, any single haphazard combination is more likely to occur than any single consecutive combination. This is one example of the *representativeness bias* in operation. The ticket featuring the haphazard numbers is chosen on the basis of its similarity to past winning tickets, not on the basis of correct statistical logic (Kahneman & Tversky, 1972). Nonetheless, despite finding this explanation rationally convincing, you may still find that your preference for tickets featuring nonconsecutive numbers remains.

How can we make sense of the fact that half our mind can understand something while the other half cannot? One way to view the matter is by analogy with perceptual illusions (Piattelli-Palmarini,

1996). Have you ever been gazing out of the window of a train, only to notice, when it comes to a halt, the train nonetheless appears to be moving in reverse? You can prove that the train is in fact stationary by aligning any point on the window with a point on the platform and confirming the absence of relative motion. Nevertheless, despite this conclusive visual test, the train still appears to be moving backward. Perceptual illusions of this sort cannot be eliminated from consciousness because our brains are physiologically hard-wired to produce them (Bruce, Green, & Georgeson, 1996). No amount of effort can reason them out of existence. Their illusory quality can only be abstractly pondered. The same may be true of many of our cognitive biases.

Revelation

People avoid risks when they stand to gain, but take risks when they stand to lose. Consequently, how a choice is framed, in terms of loss or gain, can influence how people choose, over and above the objective consequences of choosing one way or the other.

What Do You Think?

To live at all is to expose oneself to some level of risk. But some risks we consider acceptable and others unacceptable. How well does our aversion to different risks map on to their objective probabilities? Should we fear traffic accidents, gunshots, religious terrorism, or heart disease?

Chapter Reference

Rothman, A. J., Martino, S. C., Bedell, B. T., Detweiler, J. B., & Salovey, P. (1999). The systematic influ-ence of gain- and loss-framed messages on interest in and use of different types of health behavior. *Personality and Social Psychology Bulletin, 25*, 1355–1369.

Other References

Banks, S. M., Salovey, P., Greener, S., Rothman, A. J., Moyer, A., Beauvais, J., & Epel, E. (1995). The effects of message framing on mammography utilization. *Health Psychology, 14*, 178–184.

Baumeister, R. F., Bratslaysky, E., Finkenauer, C., & Vohs, K. D. (2001). Bad is stronger than good. *Review of General Psychology, 5*, 323–370.

Baumeister, R. F., Tice, D. M., & Hutton, D. G. (1989). Self-presentational motivations and personality dif-ferences in self-esteem. *Journal of Personality, 57*, 547–579.

Bruce, V., Green, P. R., & Georgeson, M. (1996). *Visual perception: Physiology, psychology and ecology* (3rd ed.). New York: Psychology Press.

Coombs, B., & Slovic, O. (1979). Newspaper coverage of causes of death. *Journalism Quarterly, 56*, 837–843.

Detweiler, J. B., Bedell, B. T., Salovey, P., Pronin, E., & Rothman, A. J. (1999). Message framing and sun-screen use: Gain-framed messages motivate beach-goers. *Health Psychology, 18*, 189–196.

Eidelmann, S., & Crandall, C. C. (2012). Bias in favor of the status quo. *Social and Personality Psychology Compass, 6*, 270–281.

Kahneman, D. (2011). *Thinking fast and slow*. New York: Farrar, Strauss, Giroux.

Kahneman, D., Knetsch, J. L., & Thaler, R. H. (1991). Anomalies: The endowment effect, loss aversion, and status quo bias. *Journal of Economic Perspectives, 5*, 193–206.

Kahneman, D., & Tversky, A. (1972). Subjective probability: A judgment of representativeness. *Cognitive Psychology, 3*, 430–454.

Kahneman, D., & Tversky, A. (1981). The framing of decisions and the rationality of choice. *Science, 221*, 453–458.

Nisbett, R. E., & Wilson, T. D. (1977). Telling more than we can know: Verbal reports on mental processes. *Psychological Review, 84*, 231–259.

Petty, R. E., & Wegener, D. T. (1998). Attitude change: Multiple roles for persuasion variables. In D. Gilbert, S. Fiske, & G. Lindzey (Eds.), *The handbook of social psychology* (4th ed., pp. 323–390). New York: McGraw-Hill.

Piattelli-Palmarini, M. (1996). *Inevitable illusions: How mistakes of reason rule our minds*. New York: Wiley-Blackwell.

Thaler, R. (1980). Towards a positive theory of consumer choice. *Journal of Economic Behavior and Organization, 1*, 39–60.

Tversky, A., & Kahneman, D. (1973). Availability: A heuristic for judging frequency and probability. *Cognitive Psychology, 5*, 207–232.

Tversky, A., & Shafir, E. (1992). The disjunction effect in choice under uncertainty. *Psychological Science, 3*, 305–309.

More to Explore

Sukel, K. (2016). *The art of risk: The new science of courage, caution, and chance*. New York: National Geographic.

25 The Wrath of the Rejected

Being Shut Out Makes One Lash Out

"No man is an island, entire of itself; every man is a piece of the continent, a part of the main."
—John Donne (1572–1631), English metaphysical poet

Background

One sunny morning in April of 2000, two students, Eric Harris and Dylan Klebold, arrived at their high school a little later than usual. Their goal that fateful day was to murder as many of their classmates and teachers as possible. Dressed in black trench coats, and carrying two duffel bags stuffed with firearms and explosives, they methodically embarked on a killing spree. Within 15 minutes, they had slaughtered 13 people, and wounded a further 21. Had all their explosives detonated as intended, the death toll would have been several times greater. Half an hour later, cornered by police, and knee-deep in human carnage, Harris and Klebold turned their guns on themselves.

Whenever something bad, unexpected, or out-of-the-ordinary happens, people want to know why (Pyszczynski & Greenberg, 1981). The massacre at Columbine High School is a case in point. In the days and weeks following the tragedy, the question on everybody's lips was: Why? Why did two students try to wipe out an entire school? What made them believe that such ghastly acts were worth committing? What fanned the flames of their hatred, and led them to express it in such an indiscriminate way?

All sorts of explanations were offered. Perhaps Harris and Klebold were natural-born killers acting on their instincts for destruction. Perhaps they were corrupted by sinister influences in their environment: the North American gun lobby, the glamour of movie violence, the pessimism of Goth subculture. Or perhaps it was all their parents' fault. They had not shown their sons enough love, brought them up to respect others, or cared enough to notice what monsters they were turning into.

As with many unique events, there may be no simple explanation for the Columbine killings. Several factors likely conspired to prompt Harris and Klebold to act as they did. Singling out any one as *the* cause does not solve the mystery, even if it does bring a sense of closure to the bereaved. All that can be done is to critically survey the set of possible causes, and hope to piece together a provisional understanding of what turns small-town teenagers into big-time killers.

What sorts of insights do social psychologists have to contribute? Some start from the assumption that the power of the situation is often underestimated (see especially Chapters 4, 8, and 10). They wonder: What *social* influences, perhaps not immediately apparent, might have driven Harris and Klebold over the edge?

A few of the usual suspects can be dismissed at once. For example, there was no pressure on Harris and Klebold either to conform to social norms (Chapter 1) or to obey authority figures (Chapter 4); nobody had been around to set a bad example or to issue a hostile order. In fact, what the duo did was an act of brazen self-assertion. They brutally defied the dictates of civil society.

If any social influence did act on them, it must have operated *distally* (far removed in space and time) rather than *proximally* (in the immediate context) and must have gradually rather than suddenly tainted their outlook. Extracts from Harris's diary indicate that he had been contemplating a massacre for a year.

What sorts of distal social influences could have made Harris and Klebold run amok? One possibility is *social exclusion*. The boys had lived for some time on the fringes of their teenage community. They had been denied access to the dominant cliques that would have accorded them the popularity and status teenagers typically crave. Their diaries indicate how alienated they felt, and how much they resented their peers for rejecting them. Klebold, for example, wrote, "I swear—like I'm an outcast, and everyone is conspiring against me." The official police report noted: "Harris and Klebold both wrote of not fitting in, not being accepted . . . They plotted against all those persons who they found offensive—jocks, girls that said no, other outcasts, or anybody they thought did not accept them."

In keeping with this possibility, several lines of research document an association between social exclusion and antisocial behavior. For example, most violent crimes are committed by young men who lack strong interpersonal ties (Garbarino, 1999). In addition, children who are rejected by their peers are more likely on average to intimidate and attack other children (Newcomb, Burowski, & Pattee, 1993). Perhaps being excluded simply makes people more hostile toward those who seem to have been unfairly included. Or perhaps it makes other challenges they face seem less solvable without violence, because they have fewer people to constructively talk to.

Such correlations are consistent with the thesis that social exclusion prompts antisocial behavior. However, they are equally consistent with the mirror-image thesis, namely, that antisocial behavior prompts social exclusion. Violent people tend to make disagreeable company. A person who, without good reason, insults or assaults the other members of his social group, is liable to be shunned—at least in a well-organized, civil society.

It is not clear, therefore, whether social exclusion triggers antisocial behavior or vice versa. On the one hand, being excluded certainly thwarts one of the strongest drives in human nature: the *need to belong* (Baumeister & Leary, 1995). One might therefore expect that the failure to form harmonious relationships with others would cause mental disturbance, possibly spilling over into antisocial behavior. On the other hand, if the need to belong is so pressing, might not socially excluded individuals try even harder to be liked than their socially included peers? Would they not be expected to redouble their efforts to be friendly, cooperative, and generous?

Thus, the case for social exclusion being a cause of antisocial behavior is suggestive but not compelling. To make it compelling, the best approach would be to run an experiment. This allows social exclusion to be isolated from everything else with which it tends to be naturally confounded (e.g., a nasty disposition) and permits its unique impact on antisocial behavior to be assessed. Twenge, Baumeister, Tice, and Stucke (2001) adopted precisely this approach.

What They Did

Twenge and her colleagues (2001) reported a total of five studies in their paper. We begin by focusing on just one of them, and later comment briefly on the remaining four.

Thirty undergraduates, 17 males and 13 females, served as participants. The study kicked off with a manipulation of social exclusion, which involved giving some participants the proverbial cold shoulder. The study was run in same-gender groups of four to six members. Participants engaged in an exercise ostensibly designed to acquaint them with one another. During this exercise, they memorized each other's names, and took turns sharing thoughts and feelings. Fifteen minutes later, they were transferred to private cubicles. There, they were asked to write down on a sheet of paper which two participants they would most like to collaborate with on an upcoming task. The experimenter then took the sheet away, promising to return shortly with information about the composition of the new groups. During the experimenter's temporary absence, participants passed the time writing an essay in which they expressed their opinions about abortion. (The purpose of this essay will be made clear in a moment.) When the experimenter returned, she told them one of two things. In the *acceptance* condition, she told them: "I have good news for you—everyone chose you as someone they'd like to work with." In the *rejection* condition, she told them: "I hate to tell you this, but no one chose you as someone they wanted to work with."

Twenge and her colleagues (2001) were interested in how participants felt after being rejected or accepted. They hypothesized that rejection would create feelings of sadness or anxiety. After all, the fear of social exclusion is a prominent correlate of mental distress (Baumeister & Leary, 1995). To check how participants felt, the researchers had them fill out a self-report measure of mood. It assessed both their positive and negative feelings.

While participants were busy reporting their mood, the experimenter took their essay on abortion and allegedly gave it to another participant to evaluate. This participant—supposedly in a different room—was described as being the same gender as the real participants, but not part of the original groups. However, this "participant" was purely fictitious—invented so that the experimenters could provide the real participants with credible but hurtful feedback, as well as assess their subsequent levels of reactive aggression.

Soon after participants had finished filling out the mood measure, they received feedback from the "participant" on the quality of their essay. This feedback was severely critical. The summary comment on the feedback sheet blatantly stated: "One of the worst essays I have ever read!" Various aspects of the essay (e.g., organization, style) were given correspondingly miserable ratings. One can imagine how many people's natural response to such undeservedly harsh feedback would have been wounded indignation. Just who did this other "participant" think they were, to be insulting their efforts and intelligence?

Participants now began a computer game. Fittingly, they were led to believe that they would be competing against the very "participant" who had so tactlessly bruised their egos. The game was allegedly a test of who could press a computer key more rapidly in response to a prompt. On each trial, the person who was slower was supposed to receive an unpleasant blast of white noise through a pair of headphones. The entire game, however, was made up. The computer merely delivered the occasional blast of noise to participants to maintain the cover story. The important feature of the setup was that participants had some control over the unpleasantness of the blast they gave. In particular, they could set the intensity of the blast prior to each trial (its level ranged from 0 to 10) and vary its duration during each trial by holding down the mouse button for a longer or shorter period. Participants' level of aggression was indexed by the intensity and duration of the blast that they administered on the first trial (on which their fellow participant conveniently went slower). Previous research had shown this to be the most sensitive measure of aggression.

Participants were then carefully debriefed. Twenge and her colleagues (2001) were mindful of the fact that the manipulations they had employed were somewhat stressful. Telling participants that no one wanted to work with them, or that they had written a hopeless essay, or both, would hardly have cheered them up! Consequently, the experimenter did not permit participants to leave until they fully understood that they had not really been rejected, nor their essays really evaluated. The experimenter reassured participants in the rejection condition that other participants had chosen to work with them, as was almost invariably the case. The experimenter also apologized for any discomfort participants might have experienced as a result of being deceived.

We leave it to the reader to decide whether the scientific value of the study justified its methods. Note, however, that temporarily being left out or harshly evaluated are not uncommon events in most people's lives, and most of us get over them quickly. Chapters 4 and 10 provide a fuller discussion of the ethics of experimenting on human participants.

What They Found

The key question was whether the experience of social exclusion would increase participants' aggression toward a person who had (apparently) harshly criticized them. It did. Participants who had previously been rejected were substantially more aggressive toward the participant than those who had previously been accepted. They chose to deliver more intense blasts of noise for a longer period of time. Feeling that they had been cut off from other people made them retaliate with greater venom (Figure 25).

The results of some of the other studies reported by Twenge and her colleagues (2001) reinforced this finding. In these studies, social exclusion was manipulated in a more abstract way: Participants were told, on the basis of a bogus personality profile, that one of two contrasting futures lay in store for them. In the exclusion-feedback condition, they were told that they would likely spend their later years in solitude. Although they might currently be enjoying satisfying social relationships, over time these relationships would weaken and disintegrate. In the inclusion-feedback condition, they were told that they would likely spend their later years in the convivial company of many other people. Their network of social affiliations would remain reassuringly intact.

Aggression was also measured in a different way. Participants were told that the person who had earlier denounced their essay was applying to become a research assistant in the Department of Psychology. The experimenter claimed that the Department was interested in knowing what those who had taken part in the study thought of the person. Participants responded to a questionnaire that featured such items as "If I were in charge of hiring research assistants, I would hire this applicant." In this and further studies, participants were consistently more hostile following social exclusion. The value of using various manipulations and measures is that research findings are less likely to be an artifact of any one research methodology. This builds confidence that the

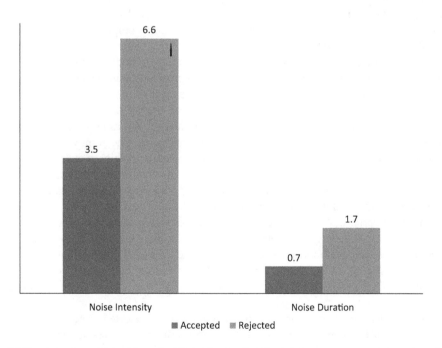

Figure 25 The intensity and duration of a blast of noise that participants gave to someone who criticized them, after they had been accepted or rejected by peers

effects observed are reliable and related to what the researchers are conceptually interested in. (For a further review, see Williams, 2007.)

Some studies also featured a third condition, in which participants were told that they would be accident-prone later in life, even if they currently showed no sign of being that way (*misfortune* feedback). The purpose of including this condition was to allow the researchers to separate out the effects of anticipating social exclusion from the effects of anticipating an unpleasant but non-social eventuality. As predicted, only the receipt of social exclusion feedback made participants act more aggressively.

But why does social exclusion make people act more aggressively? One possibility is that it puts people in a bad mood, and that their bad mood then induces them to go on the offensive. To their surprise, however, Twenge and her colleagues (2001) did *not* find that being sidelined by peers (the present study) or expecting to end up alone (the other studies) made participants feel any worse. The effects of social exclusion on aggression did not seem to depend on the positivity or negativity of their feelings. Hence, although social exclusion prompted aggressive behavior, it did not seem to do so by making people feel bad.

So What?

Prior to the research conducted by Twenge and her colleagues (2001), it was not clear whether social exclusion could in principle amplify aggression. Now we know that it can, particularly by way of retaliation for criticism. That makes it more probable that social exclusion is one variable in the equation of why troubled people like Harris and Klebold embark on their campaigns of terror.

That equation can take on complex forms. For instance, the situational impact of social exclusion, and the dispositional impact of a problematic personality, can combine to reinforce each other. Take the case of Ted Kaczynski, the notorious Unabomber. Over a 20-year period, this former mathematics professor mailed deadly explosives to (mostly) computer specialists, in protest against what he regarded as the evils of modern technology. As a child, Kaczynski had been painfully shy and socially awkward. His difficulties were only compounded by his intelligence, which led him to skip grades in school (where the older boys bullied him) and to enter Harvard at the tender age of 16 (where he became more isolated still). Finding himself unable to relate to others, Kaczynski entered into a pattern of ever-increasing reclusiveness, culminating in a decision to live alone in the Montana wilderness. At each step of the way, his avoidance of other people would have only further impaired his ability to relate to them. Denied the consolation of friendship, he was eventually led to view technological society as hopelessly corrupt, and to kill those in favor of it as a way of publicly airing his grievance. The point we wish to bring out here is that Kaczynski's preexisting propensity for introversion led him to make life choices that placed him in situations liable to exacerbate his feelings of social exclusion. It is not implausible that, over time, such acute feelings could have nurtured his aggression, eventually transforming him from a diffident whizz-kid into a heartless assassin.

Laboratory research has shown that social exclusion fosters a variety of antisocial tendencies (Tice, Twenge, & Schmeichel, 2001). For example, undergraduates led to believe that they would end up alone in adulthood are more likely to cheat on a test (by exceeding a time limit), to behave antagonistically (in a tit-for-tat game), and to refrain from helping others (by not donating money). Ironically, being cut adrift from the mainland of social life tends to make people less fit to live there.

Still one wonders: What is going on inside the mind of the rejected? Recall that Twenge and her colleagues (2001) found little evidence that positive or negative emotions were responsible for aggression. If anything, socially excluded participants reported not feeling much of anything, a sort of emotional numbness. Some other mental process must therefore provide the missing internal link.

One possibility is that, after being socially excluded, people attempt to suppress their growing sense of isolation. Their attempt is largely successful, and they manage to cultivate a more-or-less neutral emotional state. However, the effort they exert doing so may induce a state of ego-depletion in which reserves of willpower become temporarily scarce (Baumeister, Bratslavsky, Muraven, & Tice, 1998; see Chapter 22). As a consequence, the socially excluded may act on urges that they might otherwise resist. Several studies support this line of reasoning (Baumeister, Twenge, & Ciarocco, 2002). For example, when offered the choice between a high-fat candy bar and a healthy food snack, socially excluded participants chose the former option—the impulsive and imprudent one—more often than other participants did.

Perhaps individuals who are chronically cut off from others are mentally worn down much of the time, with the result that they lose interest in long-term constructive goals, and opt instead for more harmful short-term alternatives. Or perhaps, unaccustomed to fulfilling the duties and obligations of social life, their ability to restrain their antisocial inclinations diminishes (Baumeister & Exline, 1999). Either way, the socially excluded can be prone to lash out at enemies they perceive to be around them.

To an outsider, the targets of their aggression often appear arbitrary. Take Harris and Klebold again. The media made much of the fact that, prior to their shooting spree, they had drawn up a hit list of hated schoolmates. However, only one of their eventual victims was actually on that list. As witnesses testified, the killing was haphazard and capricious. This fact squares with another finding by Twenge and her colleagues (2001): Socially excluded participants behaved more aggressively, not only toward a person who had given them offense, but *also* toward a person whom they had never met before. Their vengeance appears to have a generalized quality, directed not only at the guilty but also at the innocent.

One of the tragedies of social exclusion is that it thwarts not only the need to belong, but other fundamental needs. According to *self-determination theory* (Deci & Ryan, 2000), people have three needs that must be satisfied if their minds are to keep running smoothly: relatedness, efficacy, and autonomy. Obviously, being socially excluded makes it difficult to relate to others (and hence to satisfy one's need to belong). But it also makes it difficult to be effective in completing tasks (e.g., by convincing people to lend you practical assistance) or to assert oneself individually (e.g., by forging professional links to facilitate a business venture). Perhaps the terrible deeds that alienated people sometimes carry out represent a drastic way of satisfying their frustrated needs: to become infamous in the eyes of others (relatedness), to accomplish something important (efficacy), or to take control of their destiny (autonomy).

Given that social exclusion produces such damaging effects, what can be done about it? A final study by Twenge and her colleagues (2001) suggested one possible answer. It found that, although socially excluded people behaved more aggressively toward both someone who offended them earlier and a stranger, they did *not* behave more aggressively toward someone who had earlier praised them (commended their essay). It follows that a kind word may negate the antisocial tendencies that social exclusion breeds. Perhaps if Klebold and Harris had received a genuine compliment now and again from their classmates they would never have elected to murder them. Social exclusion combined with insulting derision—calling a loner a loser—may be a toxic cocktail. Indeed, social exclusion is found to be *physically* painful (Eisenberg, Lieberman, & Williams, 2003; MacDonald & Leary, 2005), which may account for its capacity to provoke aggression.

Of course, the most direct way of undoing the damage caused by social exclusion is to bring the shy, lonely, and alienated back into the embrace of society. Unfortunately, such people tend to be regarded as undesirable interaction partners by those with greater social skills. This is because they are objectively less rewarding to spend time with and because associating with them carries with it a social stigma. What is necessary, therefore, are policies to ensure that social cohesion is maintained within various social institutions, and in society at large. Small-scale programs to get lonely schoolchildren more involved can work exceedingly well (Bagley & Pritchard, 1998). However, finding ways to reverse the increasingly individualistic trend in Western societies is a much taller order. Yet, if we value our collective well-being, we should do something about it. A lack of social integration goes hand in hand with a host of other social pathologies (Twenge, 2000).

Afterthoughts

As mentioned previously, social exclusion is merely one factor among many that disposes people to commit violent acts. In itself, social exclusion is not *sufficient* for violence. Most solitary individuals are inoffensive and law-abiding. Neither is social exclusion *necessary* for violence. Most violence is committed, not by isolated malcontents, but by organized collectives of individuals who have long-standing political grievances (such as governments; Rummel, 1994). Indeed, the causes of antisocial behavior are manifold, and differ from situation to situation. We close this chapter by discussing a factor that has, nonetheless, been widely invoked as an explanation for antisocial behavior (and for a variety of personal and societal ills): *self-esteem*.

Should you care to browse through the many books located in the self-help section of your local bookshop, you will repeatedly encounter the view, asserted or assumed, that human misery is predominantly a product of low self-esteem. If only we could all learn to see ourselves in glowing terms, the argument runs, a golden new age would be ushered in. People would become spiritually fulfilled and financially prosperous; individuals and groups would resolve their long-standing enmities and live forever in peace and harmony. If you suspect that this view may be a little simplistic, you are right. The benefits of self-esteem are modest, and are mostly of a personal nature. People with high self-esteem feel happier, are surer of who they are and what they like, and persist longer in the face of adversity (Baumeister, Campbell, Krueger, & Vohs, 2003). Although there may be some truth to the idea that high self-esteem goes together with happiness, because it likely fosters, good social adjustment (Donnellan, Trzesniewski, Robins, Moffitt, & Caspi, 2005), this truth has commonly been overstated.

The notion that high self-esteem has substantial interpersonal benefits is reflected in the oft-quoted proposition that unless one first loves oneself one cannot love other people. One merit of this proposition (widely regarded as a truism by non-psychologists) is that it can be tested. Simply divide people into those with high and low self-esteem and then examine their relative propensities to engage in antisocial behavior. If the received wisdom is correct, then people with high self-esteem ought to be more peaceful and well-behaved, whereas those with low self-esteem ought to be more belligerent and ill-mannered.

In two laboratory studies (Bushman & Baumeister, 2002), participants went through a procedure similar to that of the present study. All began by writing an essay expressing their views on abortion; the essay was then favorably or unfavorably evaluated by another participant; and an opportunity to punish the participant was provided (he or she could be blasted with aversive noise). It turned out that self-esteem was irrelevant to how aggressively participants behaved. Those whose self-esteem was low were no more likely to retaliate against the participant than those whose self-esteem was high.

These studies did turn up one significant finding, however. Participants who were high in *narcissism*—the tendency to entertain an unduly inflated, grandiose view of oneself—were more likely to retaliate than those who were low in it. This suggests that it is not so much an inferiority complex that predisposes people to aggression but rather a superiority complex. When narcissists encounter a threat to their cherished view of self, they react more harshly against it than a humbler person would.

Data from everyday life corroborates the results of these experiments. Perpetrators of serious violence everywhere—murderers, wife-beaters, gang members, dictators—all tend to be rather fond of themselves (Baumeister, Smart, & Boden, 1996). They are not the sort of people who are uncertain of themselves or who fret over their own unworthiness. When someone disses them, they have the self-assurance to strike back. If their self-esteem were low, this is not how they would react. Instead, they would go on the defensive, internalizing the pain and attempting to escape.

Research suggests, however, that people with high self-esteem are something of a mixed bag. For example, one study categorized participants both on the basis of their self-esteem being high or low and on the basis of it being stable or unstable (that is, staying the same over time or fluctuating). Results showed that participants whose self-esteem was both high and stable showed the least hostility, whereas those whose self-esteem was both high and unstable showed the greatest hostility (Kernis, Grannemann, & Barclay, 1989). It seems that some people with high self-esteem are quietly self-confident, and relatively impervious to social irritations, whereas others are vainly puffed up, and acutely sensitive to criticism.

How does the psychology of these two groups differ? One suggestion is that some people's sense of self-worth is more *contingent* than that of others. That is, it depends on certain conditions being met—on gaining popularity, achieving coveted goals, or fulfilling prescribed duties. In contrast, people whose self-worth is non-contingent see themselves positively regardless. They are not unduly perturbed when someone criticizes them, or when they mess up. They accept themselves, warts and all. Studies confirm that having non-contingent self-esteem is associated with equanimity in the face of threats to one's self-esteem (Kernis, 2003).

Looking back on the Columbine killings, we can probably characterize Harris and Klebold as individuals who had high self-esteem overall. They did not respond to their marginalization with despair and self-pity; rather, they responded with brutality and disdain. Their self-esteem, however, appears to have been unstable, highly contingent upon the respect and admiration of their peers. Unable to accept the fact that their peers would never hold them in as much esteem as they held themselves, they exacted a terrible revenge. Those who glibly advocate raising self-esteem levels as a panacea for social problems should take note.

Revelation

Social exclusion causes aggression. People ostracized by others are more likely to hurt those who offend them, and even those who do not.

What Do You Think?

Some people get socially excluded. But it is always other people who are responsible? Could people be responsible for their own exclusion (e.g., criminals)? Could trying to include unsuitable people sometimes cause more problems than it solves?

Chapter Reference

Twenge, J. M., Baumeister, R. F., Tice, D. M., & Stucke, T. S. (2001). If you can't join them, beat them: The effects of social exclusion on aggressive behavior. *Journal of Personality and Social Psychology*, *81*, 1058–1069.

Other References

Bagley, C., & Pritchard, C. (1998). The reduction of problem behaviors and school exclusion in at-risk youth: An experimental study of school social work with cost-benefit analyses. *Child and Family Social Work, 3*, 219–226.

Baumeister, R. F., Bratslavsky, E., Muraven, M., & Tice, D. M. (1998). Ego depletion: Is the active self a limited resource? *Journal of Personality and Social Psychology, 74*, 1252–1265.

Baumeister, R. F., Campbell, J. D., Krueger, J. I., & Vohs, K. D. (2003). Does high self-esteem cause better performance, interpersonal success, or healthier lifestyles? *Psychological Science in the Public Interest, 4*, 1–44.

Baumeister, R. F., & Exline, J. J. (1999). Virtue, personality, and social relations: Self-control as a moral muscle. *Journal of Personality, 67*, 1165–1194.

Baumeister, R. F., & Leary, M. R. (1995). The need to belong: Desire for interpersonal attachments as a fundamental human motivation. *Psychological Bulletin, 117*, 497–529.

Baumeister, R. F., Smart, L., & Boden, J. M. (1996). Relation of threatened egotism to violence and aggression: The dark side of high self-esteem. *Psychological Review, 103*, 5–33.

Baumeister, R. F., Twenge, J. M., & Ciarocco, N. (2002). The inner world of rejection: Effects of social exclusion on cognition, emotion, and self-regulation. In J. Forgas & K. Williams (Eds.), *The social self: Cognitive, interpersonal, and intergroup perspectives* (pp. 161–174). New York: Psychology Press.

Bushman, B. J., & Baumeister, R. F. (2002). Does self-love or self-hate lead to violence? *Journal of Research in Personality, 36*, 543–545.

Deci, E. L., & Ryan, R. M. (2000). The "What" and "Why" of goal pursuits: Human needs and the self-determination of behavior. *Psychological Inquiry, 11*, 227–268.

Donnellan, M. B., Trzesniewski, K. H., Robins, R. W., Moffitt, T. E., & Caspi, A. (2005). Low self-esteem is related to aggression, antisocial behavior, and delinquency. *Psychological Science, 16*, 328–335.

Eisenberg, N. I., Lieberman, M. D., & Williams, K. D. (2003). Does rejection hurt? An fMRI study of social exclusion. *Science, 302*, 290–292.

Garbarino, J. (1999). *Lost boys: Why our sons turn violent and how we can save them.* San Francisco: Jossey-Bass.

Kernis, M. H. (2003). Towards a conceptualization of optimal self-esteem. *Psychological Inquiry, 14*, 1–26.

Kernis, M. H., Grannemann, B. D., & Barclay, L. C. (1989). Stability and level of self-esteem as predictors of anger arousal and hostility. *Journal of Personality and Social Psychology, 56*, 1013–1022.

MacDonald, G., & Leary, M. R. (2005). Why does social exclusion hurt? The relationship between social and physical pain. *Psychological Bulletin, 131*, 202–223.

Newcomb, A. F., Burowski, W. M., & Pattee, L. (1993). Children's peer relations: A meta-analytic review of popular, rejected, neglected, controversial, and average sociometric status. *Psychological Bulletin, 113*, 99–128.

Pyszczynski, T. A., & Greenberg, J. (1981). Role of disconfirmed expectancies in the instigation of attributional processing. *Journal of Personality and Social Psychology, 40*, 31–38.

Rummell, R. J. (1994). *Death by government.* New Brunswick, NJ: Transaction Publishers.

Tice, D. M., Twenge, J. M., & Schmeichel, B. J. (2001). Social exclusion and prosocial and antisocial behavior. In J. P Forgas & K. D. Williams (Eds.), *The social self: Cognitive, interpersonal, and intergroup perspectives* (pp. 175–187). Philadelphia: Psychology Press.

Twenge, J. M. (2000). The age of anxiety? The birth cohort change in anxiety and neuroticism, 1952–1993. *Journal of Personality and Social Psychology, 79*, 1007–1021.

Williams, K. D. (2007). Ostracism. *Annual Review of Psychology, 58*, 425–452.

More to Explore

Williams, K. D., Forgas, J. P., & Hippel, W. V. (2015). *The social outcast: Ostracism, social exclusion, rejection, and bullying.* New York: Psychology Press.

26 Prosocial Scuttlebutt

Sharing the Bad to Promote the Good

"Every man is surrounded by a neighborhood of voluntary spies."
—Jane Austin (1775–1817), English romantic novelist

Background

A Yiddish tale (there are several versions) tells of a man who was a flagrant gossip. Much of his gossip was about a local rabbi. The man eventually felt ashamed and went to the rabbi, asking for forgiveness and seeking to make amends. The rabbi told him to go into the marketplace with a knife and two pillows, cut the pillows open, and shake them vigorously in the air. The man went and did exactly as he was told, and then returned to the rabbi to ask if there was anything else he should do. The rabbi told him to go back and collect all the feathers that were now fluttering about the marketplace. Obviously, this was impossible. The man came to realize how much harm gossip does and how difficult it is to undo.

Gossip (one of many terms coined by Shakespeare) is synonymous with idle talk, rumormongering, spreading dirt, and scuttlebutt. It typically occurs at the office water cooler, over the backyard fence, during family get-togethers, on the school playground, or via social media. While gossip might be considered a lighthearted way of passing along juicy news, it is more commonly known for its malicious intent and harmful effects. Gossip often serves to malign and marginalize particular individuals. *Whisperers* and *backbiters* are said to have an evil tongue. Gossip is considered by some to be an egregious sin, apparently one of the six sins God hates the most (see Proverbs 6:16–19). One is advised to avoid it at all costs.

But might some gossip serve a vital social function? While it is easy to imagine gossip that is cruel and harmful, it is also possible to imagine gossip that is compassionate and constructive. Ben-Ze'ev (1994) made a case for such *good gossip*. Dunbar (1996, 2004) claimed that analysis of human communication reveals that two-thirds of it is devoted to social topics, much of which takes the form of gossip. Because gossip is ubiquitous throughout history and across cultures, it is most likely an evolved human tendency, one that provides individual and collective benefits. Arguably, gossip originated in prehistoric societies to help create social bonds and to protect vulnerable individuals and group-level interests. As early groups increased in size, it was necessary to develop a communication system that would allow one to keep tabs on as many people in the group as possible. One could then avoid or at least be wary of others who were reputed to have bad character and selfish ways. Thus, gossip serves as an early-warning communication system among like-minded people as a means of thwarting antisocial behavior. It fosters cohesion, cooperation, and solidarity in groups. Rather than being malevolent and destructive, gossip can be well-intentioned and beneficial.

Feinberg, Willer, Stellar, and Keltner (2012) developed a theoretical model to explain the functions of gossip more precisely. According to their model, witnessing an unjust or dubious act causes one to experience negative emotions (which can be self-reported or physiologically measured). These emotions, along with prosocial motives that seek cooperation and fairness, lead one to engage in prosocial gossip. Engaging in this gossip provides cathartic relief: It permits people to get those negative emotions out of their system. Individuals may engage in prosocial gossip without material or social incentives to do so, and even at their own expense. The threat of prosocial gossip also serves to deter antisocial behaviors, because the person who might be gossiped about does not want to earn a negative reputation that would cause him or her to be marginalized or ostracized. People who hear prosocial gossip about another person can take precautions against that person. Thus, prosocial gossip protects vulnerable individuals and promotes the greater good.

Feinberg and his colleagues' also stipulated that one's degree of *prosocial orientation* (how unselfish, cooperative, and fair one is) influences both the motivation to prosocially gossip and the impact of such gossip. Those who are more prosocially oriented will experience more negative emotions upon witnessing unfairness, be more likely to engage in prosocial gossip, and experience more emotional relief after gossiping. In contrast, those who are less prosocially oriented will be more affected by the threat of prosocial gossip. They will worry that others will gossip about them and thus be reluctant to carry out noticeably antisocial acts.

Feinberg and his colleagues set out to experimentally test various elements of this model. They sought answers to two related questions: What *motivates* people to engage in prosocial gossip, and what *functions* does prosocial gossip serve? They tested four hypotheses. Their *frustration* hypothesis stated that witnessing antisocial behavior causes one to feel bad, and the more one feels bad, the more one will engage in prosocial gossip. Their *prosocial* hypothesis stated that the main motive of prosocial gossip is a genuine desire to help and protect others, without material or social incentives. Their *relief* hypothesis stated that prosocial gossip reduces negative feelings. Finally, their *deterrence* hypothesis stated that prosocial gossip curtails selfish behaviors. Feinberg and his colleagues had a full research agenda.

What They Did

Feinberg and his colleagues (2012) conducted four studies. We describe their first study in considerable detail here, and then briefly describe their second, third, and fourth studies in the "So What?" section.

Study 1 involved 52 college students who each thought they were participating in a group study as one of four members. Upon arriving at the lab, two participants—actually *confederates* (research accomplices)—were already present. The three individuals (the actual participant and the two other presumed participants) were told that they were waiting for one more participant to arrive (to complete the foursome), but that they would go ahead and get started anyway. One of the confederates and the actual participant were escorted to an adjacent room and directed to sit down at opposite computers, separated by a cloth divider that prevented them from seeing each other. The two were told not to communicate unless prompted via computer to do so. They were each connected (on the left and right sides of their abdomens) to a heart rate monitor. They then completed some background surveys before engaging in a *trust* game.

The game involved two people—an Investor and a Trustee. The Investor would initially receive 10 points. He could send any number of his points to the Trustee. The amount of points the Investor sent to the Trustee would automatically be tripled. The Trustee would then have the opportunity to send any number of the tripled points back to the Investor. For example, the Investor might send 5 points to the Trustee, these would triple to 15 points, and then the Trustee might send 10 points back to the Investor, leaving them both with a profit. Participants were told that they could exchange the points for money at the end of the study.

Participants were told that there would be four game roles: Investor A, Investor B, Trustee, and Observer. The Investors would each play a round of the game with the Trustee. The Observer would be told how many points the Investor sent to the Trustee and how many points the Trustee sent back to the Investor in each round of play. The participant and confederate who had been taken to the adjacent room then drew envelopes that would indicate their assigned roles. In fact, the envelopes were rigged: They both contained a slip of paper indicating "Observer." The actual participant correctly announced that he was the Observer, while the confederate deceptively announced that he was Investor B, who would be playing the trust game with the Trustee in the second round.

The participant (the Observer) and the confederate (Investor B) then waited while Investor A and the Trustee supposedly played the first round. After an appropriate delay, the experimenter brought the Observer (but not Investor B) a sheet of paper that revealed the action of the first game. The Observer was informed that Investor A had given *all 10* of his points to the Trustee, the points automatically tripled in value, and the Trustee chose to give *nothing* back to Investor A. No doubt, the Observer would take due note of this exploitative behavior ("That despicable S.O.B.!").

The experimenter then provided the participant with an envelope labeled, "Do not open this packet until the computer instructs you to do so." Importantly, the experimenter was unaware of who the confederate was and who the actual participant was, and was also unaware of the study's hypotheses. This *double-blind* arrangement (the experimenters, as well as the participants, were unaware of the experimental manipulations) prevented the experimenters' expectations from biasing the results of the study.

Before opening the envelopes, participants responded to computer questions pertaining to negative emotions (see below). They then opened their packets, which contained one of two instructions, allocated at random, representing the experimental versus control conditions. In the experimental condition, a given participant was reminded that Investor B (sitting at the computer opposite him) would be playing with the Trustee in the next round and told that, if the participant wanted, he could pass a one- or two-sentence handwritten note to Investor B (without the Trustee's knowledge). It was explicitly emphasized that any such note was optional. (Participants were also told that Investor B had already been informed that he or she might be given a note, without saying what the note would be about. This information about possibly receiving a note was designed to reassure the participant that sending a note would not be out of the ordinary.) The instructions also informed the participant that, after the second game, all participants would leave separately and most likely never meet again. This information served to prevent participants from expecting some type of reward for their note. In the control condition, participants were also reminded that Investor B would be playing with the Trustee in the next round, but were instructed to copy a particular nonsensical sentence onto a note and pass it to Investor B, who they were told was expecting it.

After forwarding (or not forwarding) a note, participants responded to a second set of questions about any negative emotions they might be experiencing (again, see below). They then answered two more questions: "How relieved do you feel after writing the note?" and "Overall, how much better do you feel after writing the note?" These two questions served as a measure of emotional *relief*. Participants then observed (via the computer) a staged trust game between Investor B and the Trustee, and then completed a short survey designed to probe for any suspicions about the study. They were then disconnected from the heart rate monitors and *debriefed* (the experimenter discussed the true nature of the study with them, including the study's hypotheses and the need for the use of deception).

A few final points should be noted. First, on two occasions—just before and just after they were given the opportunity to pass a note to Investor B—participants reported how frustrated, annoyed, and irritated they felt, from *0* (not at all) to *100* (very much). Second, although the heart-rate monitor was active during the entire experiment, data were only collected for two 1.5-second intervals, during which participants provided self-reports of negative emotions. The heart rate data served as an additional check on the intensity of the emotions participants had been feeling (heart rates were expected to increase as negative emotions increased). Third, the notes passed by participants were independently analyzed by two judges. The judges determined whether a particular note qualified as prosocial gossip by Feinberg and his colleagues' (2012) definition: "sharing evaluative information about a target in a way that protects others from anti-social or exploitative behaviors" (p. 1019). Feinberg and his colleagues provided several examples of actual gossip notes sent by participants: "Trustee didn't send anything back last round. I'd advise not sending anything," "Try to keep all the money you can, because the trustee will not give you much in return," and "Your trustee is not reliable, he/she is playing for their own selfish interest. Try being careful with your investment."

What They Found

Twenty-seven participants in the experimental (gossip) condition sent notes to Investor B (whom they were unaware was a research accomplice and whom they assumed would be playing the next round of the trust game with the exploitative Trustee). Of these notes, 26 qualified as proso-cial gossip. Importantly, negative emotions decreased significantly from before to after writing gossip notes but did not do so in the control condition, in which participants instead copied and sent nonsensical notes. Evidently, participants tended to respond with negative emotions to what they were led to believe was selfish, exploitative behavior on the part of the Trustee in the first game. However, only those who delivered prosocial gossip notes to Investor B experienced a subsequent decrease in negative emotions. Copying a nonsensical statement and passing it to Investor B had no such effect. Furthermore, significantly more relief was reported in the gossip condition than in the control condition. Finally, it was found that heart rates rose from before to after copying the gibberish statement and passing it to the confederate in the control condition, whereas heart rates did not significantly change in the gossip condition. Presumably, while heart rates increased in both the experimental and control conditions upon witnessing antisocial behav-ior, only prosocial gossip served to return it to normal levels.

So What?

The results of Study 1 confirmed that, when faced with another person's antisocial behavior, par-ticipants typically chose to engage in prosocial gossip (all but one person given the opportunity did so). They chose to share judgmental information about a greedy Trustee in order to protect an Investor from victimization, even though they would get no material or social reward for doing so. Self-report and heart rate data mirrored each other and indicated that witnessing exploitative behavior increased negative emotions, whereas prosocial gossip relieved those negative emo-tions. Thus, in Study 1, Feinberg and his colleagues (2012) garnered support for their *prosocial*, *frustration*, and *relief* hypotheses.

While Feinberg and his colleagues' second, third, and fourth studies each employed different methods, they too were clear-cut in their results. Study 2 found, first, that the more prosocially oriented participants were, the more likely they were to engage in prosocial gossip. Second, self-report responses indicated that participants sent the note because they wanted to help the vulnerable Investor, not because they wanted to punish the stingy Trustee. Third, participants who experienced relatively more negative emotions after witnessing the Trustee's exploitive behavior were more inclined to send a gossip note. Fourth, participants who knew their written notes would be delivered to the Investor experienced more relief from negative emotions than did participants who were told that their written notes would not be delivered. Evidently, it was the *sending* of the note—and the knowledge that it would reach and benefit its intended recipient—and not just the *writing* of the note that was cathartic. Fifth, participants who scored higher on the prosocial orientation measure reported greater frustration after witnessing the Trustee's self-ish behavior, and they also reported greater relief following their prosocial gossip. And sixth, the more participants believed their gossip would help the Investor, the more their emotional state was improved.

In Study 3, Feinberg and his colleagues found that 34 of the 45 participants were willing to pay to send a note, offering an average of $1.19 to do so. Thus, a majority of the participants were willing to endure a personal cost to be able to prosocially gossip (see Chapter 18 for more about altruistic behavior). Moreover, the higher they scored on prosocial orientation, the more they were willing to pay. Also, the more frustrated they felt after witnessing exploitation, the more they were willing to pay to prosocially gossip, and the more they paid to gossip, the more relieved they felt immediately afterwards. Finally, altering the nature of the game (this time by using a so-called *dictator* game, where the Investor is a donor, and can receive nothing back) made it possible to conclude that the participants were not out to punish the transgressor; rather, they were out to help the would-be victim.

Whereas the first three of Feinberg and his colleagues' studies examined participants' motives for prosocial gossip, Study 4 examined the functions of such gossip. Specifically, Study 4 sought to determine whether prosocial gossip can actually deter selfishness and foster cooperation. This was accomplished by having participants play the role of Trustee in one of three conditions: They were told either that (a) the Observer would have an opportunity to gossip to an Investor about the Trustee's behavior in earlier rounds (gossip condition), (b) their behavior would be observed but the Observer would not have an opportunity to gossip about it (observer condition), or (c) their behavior would not be observed and there would be no one to gossip about it (control condition). Feinberg and his colleagues found that the Trustee in the gossip condition sent back significantly more points, originally given to him by the Investor, than he or she did in the observer or control conditions—direct support for their *deterrence* hypothesis. Furthermore, those who scored low on prosocial orientation (relatively selfish participants) sent back more points in the gossip condition than did those who scored high on prosocial orientation in that condition. Apparently, they restrained their relative selfishness and returned more points to an Investor in order to avoid earning a negative reputation (Figure 26).

The upshot of these four studies is that gossip is not all bad. Yes, it can on occasion be petty, exploitative, hurtful, even cruel, but it can also be good in the sense that it can protect particular individuals and groups, and the greater good. Such good gossip may be more common than bad gossip, even if it receives less attention. However, Feinberg and his colleagues (2012) did more than simply reiterate this. They experimentally demonstrated the motivational impetus for such gossip and the preventative functions it serves, while also exploring a personality difference—how prosocially oriented one is—that moderates these motives and functions. To be sure, Feinberg and his colleagues' research is not without potential problems (no research is air-tight). It relies mostly on self-report data (along with some heart rate data), which may suffer from a lack of insight (see Chapter 14) or honesty. Also, it may have been biased by *demand characteristics* (suspicions about what the study was really about; see Chapter 13). And, finally, its methods and results may not mirror the complexity of gossip in the so-called real world. (Feinberg and his colleagues acknowledged all of these possible shortcomings.) Nonetheless, their study is a veritable blockbuster.

Afterthoughts

It is painfully obvious that people often behave selfishly—they always have and probably always will. Exploitative and harmful behaviors have been a major problem in practically every society throughout history. Individuals readily use and abuse each other for personal gain. Some individuals ignore other's bothersome needs, malign others to appear superior, lie and cheat to obtain

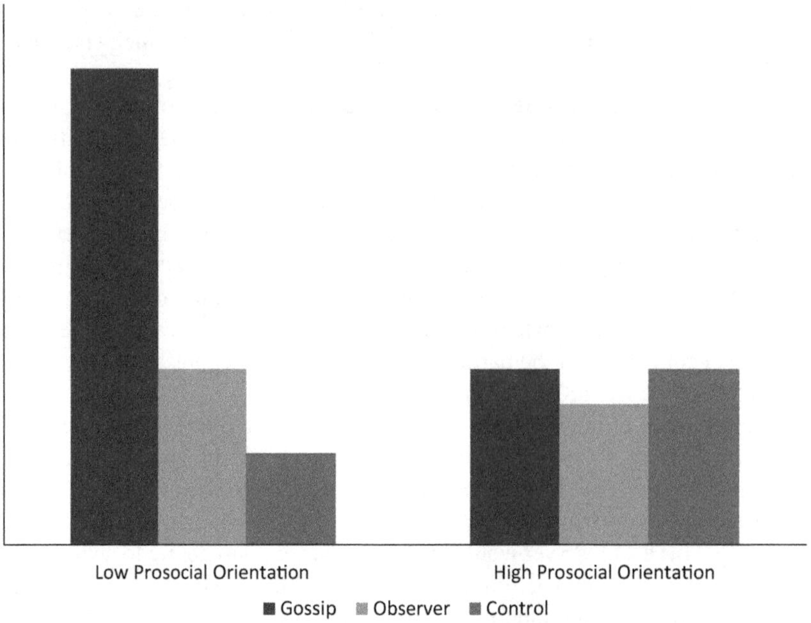

Figure 26 Number of points returned by a Trustee, who had a low or high prosocial orientation, to an Investor when the Trustee was told that (a) an Observer would have an opportunity to gossip about
the Trustee, (b) an Observer would not have an opportunity to gossip, or (c) there would be no
Observer. (*Note*: The figure is schematic because mean scores were not provided in the orginal
article.)

some objective, assault and steal from others, and even murder others if it is personally convenient and profitable. In groups, individuals free-ride, hide from responsibility, and attempt to
benefit from their membership, whenever they believe that doing so will go undetected or unpun-
ished. No doubt, there are often incentives, or at least perceived incentives, to behave selfishly at
the expense of others. Antisocial behavior can seem rational from a purely gain-loss perspective.
Cooperation and support of the greater good can seem foolish. Thus, there are myriad examples
of individuals acting selfishly, without regard to the loss and pain they inflict on others. Additionally, there are *social dilemmas*, wherein individual interests are pitted against group interests
(Dawes, 1980). Why make a donation to public radio when not doing so won't prevent one from
listening to public radio? Why conserve water during a drought when one's water use will have
but a trivial effect on the water table?

There are three ways of dealing with antisocial behavior. The first involves sanctioning those
who perpetrate such behavior. In *peer sanctioning*, members of a social network punish the guilty
person. The punishment takes numerous forms: unfriendly nicknames, ridicule, denial of privileges, physical retaliation, ostracism, and so on. In *formal sanctioning*, some central authority or
agency does the punishing. For example, law enforcement personnel arrest and juries and judges
sentence individuals for criminal offenses.

Education is a second way of dealing with antisocial behavior. Both secular education and
religious education attempt to cultivate good character and promote cooperation and service
to others. We are taught not to lie, steal, cheat, or murder, and to treat others fairly, kindly, and
compassionately. Education also attempts to solve social dilemmas: When individual and collective interests collide, individuals are encouraged to yield to the greater good. In the mid-1970s, a

public service announcement (PSA) aired on TV, showing a Native American paddling a canoe down a stream, wearing handmade clothing, long braids, and a small crop of feathers on his head. As he paddled, he encountered trash floating in the water on both sides of his canoe. The polluted stream carried him into an oily bay surrounded by smoky factories. He pulled his canoe up onto a littered shore and walked toward a highway, where someone in a passing car tossed a bag of garbage out the window (the bag exploded at his feet). The Native American maintained his majestic posture and solemn expression as he stared at the refuse strewn along the highway, while a pregnant tear ran down his cheek. (Anyone watching TV in the early 1970s will remember this poignant scenario.) What purpose did this PSA serve? Clearly, the purpose was to educationally reign in selfish behavior and curtail runaway pollution.

A third means of curbing antisocial behavior is that of sharing reputational information. When people talk with each other, they often talk about third parties, especially anyone with bad character, selfish motives, and a track record of exploitation, someone who should be watched carefully, if not avoided. Feinberg and his colleagues (2012) research reminds us not to overlook this important and common form of communication. Indeed, prosocial gossip has most likely existed since it originated in the earliest human groups, and seems to have been embraced by every society since.

Revelation

Though gossip is often condemned, it frequently serves a cathartic and prosocial function. Prosocial gossip relieves negative emotions that result from witnessing an antisocial act and protects others from victimization. It also functions to deter selfish, exploitative behaviors.

What Do You Think?

Gossip is stereotypically associated with women. Do you think that there is something to this stereotype? Or do you think that both men and women gossip equally? Is the way in which men and women gossip differently, or do they gossip about different topics? Also, have you ever engaged in gossip or been the target of gossip—what motivated the gossip and how was it helpful or hurtful?

Chapter Reference

Feinberg, M., Willer, R., Stellar, J., & Keltner, D. (2012). The virtues of gossip: Reputational information sharing as prosocial behavior. *Journal of Personality and Social Psychology, 102*, 1015–1030.

Other References

Ben-Ze'ev, A. (1994). The vindication of gossip. In R. F. Goodman & A. Ben-Ze'ev (Eds.), *Good gossip* (pp. 11–24). Lawrence, KS: University Press of Kansas.

Dawes, R. M. (1980). Social dilemmas. *Annual Review of Psychology, 31*, 169–193.

Dunbar, R. I. M. (1996). *Grooming, gossip, and the evolution of language*. Cambridge, MA: Harvard University Press.

Dunbar, R. I. M. (2004). Gossip in evolutionary perspective. *Review of General Psychology, 8*, 100–110.

More to Explore

Westacott, E. (2011). *The virtues of our vices: A modest defense of gossip, rudeness, and other bad habits*. Princeton, NJ: Princeton University Press.

27 Loving Regards

Antidote to Existential Terror

"Men have died from time to time, and worms have eaten them, but not for love."
—Roselind, in English dramatist William Shakespeare's (1564–1616) *As You Like It*

Background

Let's get morbid for a moment. How old do you imagine you will be when you die? What will be the cause of your death? Where will you die? Who will be with you at the moment of your expiry? What will be the last thing you say before dying? What will be your final facial expression? Will you be cremated? What will your coffin look like? Where will your body be buried? Who will miss you after you die?

One more question: How do the above questions make you *feel*? You hardly enjoy thinking about death. At most, you find it intriguing to speculate on what it might involve, or what might or might not come after. Perhaps the above questions make you anxious or unnerved. That wouldn't surprise me. I have several times taught on the topic of *thanatology* (the study of death) and required students to write their obituary and epitaph. Many of them balked at this assignment. It gave them the "creeps."

Of course, the truth is that everyone eventually dies. You will die, all your family members and friends will die, and everyone else will die. To die means to no longer exist physically. While misfortune and tragedy take many forms in life, death ranks high on the list of bad outcomes. As Ernest Becker (1997) pointed out, all of us go "back into the ground a few feet in order blindly and dumbly to rot and disappear forever." We ultimately become "food for worms." Good news for worms perhaps, but not so good for us.

How do we reconcile ourselves with this hard truth? What makes us think about death, and what enables us to not think about it? In general, how do we manage the potentially paralyzing terror prompted by thoughts of our unpreventable demise? Enter *terror management theory* (TMT; Greenberg, Solomon, & Arndt, 2008; Solomon, Greenberg, & Pyszczynski, 1991). According to TMT, the terror associated with death is a primary human motive (Greenberg et al., 2008). Much of a person's activity is driven by his or her fear of death. We avoid thinking about death. We are likely to belong to a culture that sweeps death under the rug. We never personally deal with dead bodies or dig graves. And we adopt protective euphemisms, such as "passed away" or "is no longer with us." However, thoughts of death are often unavoidable and influence us in various ways. Research finds that reminders of death—or making *mortality salient* in TMT jargon—motivate us to exercise, have children, go to war, punish moral transgressors, adhere to social norms, dissociate ourselves from failure, accept undue credit for personal success, believe that humans are unique and superior to animals, prefer clear-cut information and well-structured physical environments, and believe in life-after-death and the supernatural (Arndt, Schimel, & Goldberg, 2003; Dechesne et al., 2003; Gailliot, Stillman, Schmeichel, Maner, & Plant, 2014; Landau et al., 2004; Wisman & Goldenberg, 2005).

According to TMT, we attempt to manage the terror of death in a number of ways. To start, our culture provides sources of personal meaning and significance. We adopt, adhere to, take pride in, and defend philosophies of life and worldviews (religious or otherwise) that provide us with a sense of value. These meanings and values displace terrifying thoughts of death. We also bolster our sense of self by harboring prejudice and discriminating against those who do not hold our beliefs (Strachman & Schimel, 2006). (Recall the tendency to favor ingroups discussed in Chapter 7.) In general, we look for boosts to our self-esteem (Harmon-Jones et al., 1997). High self-esteem enables us to cope with the stark reality of death; low self-esteem undermines our ability to face it.

Another buffer against the terror of death awareness is one's relationships with family members, friends, and romantic partners (Florian, Mikulincer, & Hirschberger, 2002; Kosloff, Greenberg, Sullivan, & Weiss, 2010; Mikulincer, Florian, Birnbaum, & Malishevich, 2002; Mikulincer, Florian, & Hirshberger, 2003). Such attachments give us comfort and support. Reminders of death have been found to promote a sense of closeness, love, and commitment in relationships (Cox et al., 2008; Mikulincer et al., 2003). But why is it that close relationships allay our existential concerns? One possible answer is that close relationships involve mutual feelings of positive regard. Positive regard enhances feelings of self-worth and security (Pyszczynski, Greenberg, Solomon, Arndt, & Schimel, 2004). Over a century ago, Cooley (1902) proposed the *looking glass self*, the idea that we see ourselves through the eyes of others: "Each to each a looking glass, reflects the other that doth pass" (p. 152). We often regard ourselves the way we think significant others regard us, and this perceived regard is perhaps a key element of close relationships that enables us to cope with our fear of death. In our relentless progression toward death, we are soothed by the affection of loved ones.

In order to explore this theme, Cox and Arndt (2012) conducted no fewer than seven experiments. For the sake of brevity, we only deal here with the first four. Experiment 1 examined whether reminders of death cause people to exaggerate how positively their romantic partners view them (perceived regard). Experiment 2 examined whether the exaggeration of perceived regard following mortality salience would occur with any person, not only a romantic partner. Experiment 3 examined whether the perceived regard of a romantic partner is a causal link between reminders of death and commitment to that partner. Finally, Experiment 4 measured the *accessibility* of a person's death-related thoughts (how uppermost they were in their mind) following a mortality salience manipulation and instructions to think about an occasion when a romantic partner either did or did not regard them positively.

What They Did

Experiment 1 involved 15 male and 28 female college students. The students began by completing a series of questionnaires designed to disguise the purpose of the experiment. The next step was to manipulate mortality salience. A random half of the participants answered two question about death: "Briefly describe the emotions that the thought of death arouse in you" and "Jot down, as specifically as you can, what you think will happen to you as you physically die and once you are physically dead." The other random half of the participants answered similar questions about experiencing an unexpected event that was unrelated to death. Then, for approximately 5 minutes, participants completed a word search puzzle in which neutral words, such as *movie* and *book*, were hidden in a 10×10 matrix of letters. This word search task was included because previous research had demonstrated that mortality salience effects are strongest after a delay (see Greenberg, Pyszczynski, Solomon, Simon, & Breus, 1994). Participants then completed a 23-item measure of perceived regard. Following the precedent of previous research, participants were presented with positive and negative adjectives, such as *kind, affectionate, lazy,* and *controlling,* and rated the extent to which they believed their partner evaluated them on each trait, using a 9-point scale from *not at all characteristic* to *completely characteristic*. Participants also responded to the same 23 adjectives in terms of how they perceived themselves (the order of the two sets of ratings was randomized, to ensure that the order in which they were presented made no overall difference to the results). For both sets of ratings, negative items were reverse-scored to arrive at an overall measure of perceived partner regard, and of self-regard, respectively. Cox and Arndt's hypothesis: Stirring up death-related thoughts via the mortality salience manipulation would produce exaggerated perceptions of being favorably regarded by a close partner, but have no effect on self-regard.

Experiment 2 involved 20 male and 17 female college students. The students completed the same mortality salience task and underwent the same five-minute delay as in Experiment 1. However, whereas in Experiment 1 the control topic was an unexpected event unrelated to death, in Experiment 2 the control topic was intense physical pain. (Notice how these control topics, like death, refer to unpleasant and unpredictable subjects. They permit the inference that death itself, and not just some feature of it shared with many other events, is responsible for the effect.) Participants then responded to the same 23 adjectives, using the same 9-point scale, as in Experiment 1, but this time ratings pertained to how an average person regarded them, along with how a close partner regarded them and how they regarded themselves (the order of these sets of ratings was also randomized). Cox and Arndt's hypothesis: The exaggeration of perceived regard following the mortality salience manipulation would be specific to close partners; it would not occur with the perceived regard of an average person or self-regard.

Experiment 3 involved 29 male and 19 female college students, all of whom had been involved in a romantic relationship for between one month and four years. Participants responded to the same two questions about death as in Experiments 1 and 2 or, in a control condition, two questions about dental pain. The participants then went through the same delay exercise as in Experiments 1 and 2. They then responded to the same 23 adjective traits pertaining to perceived partner regard. Finally, they were given 15 items that assessed their commitment (attraction, trust, and love) toward their relationship partner—for example, "I'm completely devoted to my partner"— using a 9-point scale from *not at all* to *very much*. They were instructed to think about their relationship partner as they made these ratings. The items were averaged together to yield an overall commitment score. Cox and Arndt's hypothesis: Death reminders would cause participants to exaggerate their commitment to their partners, and this connection would be due to—or *mediated by* in technical jargon—intervening perceptions of their partner's regard for them. In other words, death reminders would cause exaggerated perceptions of partner regard, which in turn would cause greater relationship commitment.

Experiment 4 involved 16 male and 42 female college students who, as in Experiment 3, had been in romantic relationships for between one month and four years. Participants randomly assigned to the mortality salience condition completed a *Fear of Death Scale*, which contained items such as, "I am very much afraid to die" (*true* or *false*). Those randomly assigned to the control condition were given a similar questionnaire pertaining to dental pain, which contained items such as, "I am very much afraid of dental pain" (*true* or *false*). (Note that the main goal here was not to measure fear of death or dentistry, but to arouse it.) All participants were then asked to think of a time when their dating partner either held a positive view of them or did not hold a positive view of them ("Please write about a time when your dating/romantic partner made you feel good about yourself" versus ". . . did not make you feel good about yourself"). Participants in both conditions were instructed to visualize being in the presence of their partner and to write for the length of a full page. Thus, the two independent variables in this experiment were mortality salience versus dental pain and positive regard versus no positive regard. The dependent measure was a *word stem completion task* designed to assess death-thought accessibility. Participants were presented with 25 word fragments, five of which could be completed with either neutral or death-related words. For example, the participants could fill in the blanks of a stem like DE_ _ to make a mortality-relevant word like DEAD or a mortality-irrelevant word like DEED. Similarly, they could fill out COFF_ _ as either COFFIN or COFFEE. The other critical word fragments were GRA_ _, SK_ _ L, and KI_ _ED (what words would you, the reader, most spontaneously come up with?). Participants' death accessibility scores were their total number of death-related word completions (ranging from 0 to 5). Cox and Arndt's hypothesis: In the mortality salience condition, visualizing a partner making them feel good (compared to not making them feel good) would reduce the accessibility of death-related thoughts. (Note how this final study gets at the *mental mechanisms* postulated by TMT. Note too how it assesses them *indirectly*. Even if participants were consciously suppressing explicit thoughts of death, the word-stem completion task would still reflect an implicit preoccupation with them.)

What They Found

In Experiment 1, the manipulation (where participants were reminded either of death or of a different unexpected event) impacted the two dependent variables differently. Specifically, perceived partner regard was higher in the death salience condition than in the other unexpected event condition, whereas self-regard was not significantly different between the two conditions. Thus, participants were more likely to exaggerate how positively their partners regarded them following mortality salience, as Cox and Arndt had predicted. In Experiment 2, a similar pattern was found: There were significantly higher ratings of perceived regard from romantic partners in the death salience condition than in the physical pain condition, but this was not the case for the perceived regard of an average person or for self-regard, as Cox and Arndt also had predicted: Only the mortality salience manipulation made thoughts of death accessible (Figure 27).

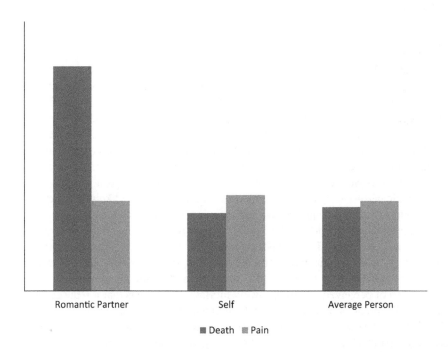

Figure 27 Perceived positive regard from a romantic partner, positive self-regard, and perceived positive regard from an average person, when either death or intense physical pain was made salient. (*Note*: The figure is schematic because mean scores were not provided in the orginal article.)

Experiment 3 involved a *mediation analysis*. It addresses the following general situation. Suppose you have (independent variable) X and (dependent variable) Y. You know, from doing an experiment, that X causes Y. However, you think this might be because X causes M, which in turn causes Y. How can you find evidence for this without manipulating M? Well, one quick way is *statistical*. You can measure M and see whether the link between X and Y statistically depends on M—in other words, whether M *mediates* the two. Now apply this idea to the main question of Experiment 3: If mortality salience caused greater partner commitment, was this due to the mediation of perceived partner regard? As predicted, there was an effect of mortality salience on commitment (but not of dental pain). There was also, as in the first two experiments, a significant relationship between mortality salience and perceived partner regard. Furthermore, there was a significant relationship between perceived regard and relationship commitment in the mortality salience condition. However, when Cox and Arndt statistically *controlled* (held constant) perceived partner regard, the effect of mortality salience on relationship commitment was no longer significant. This is exactly what one would expect if perceived regard is a causal link between mortality salience and relationship commitment (see Baron & Kenny, 1986). Evidently, people are more committed to romantic partners after reminders of death to the extent that their partners are a perceived source of positive regard. That said, it is important to note that the experiment did not feature any independent and specific manipulation of partner regard, making inferences about its causal role plausible but not watertight.

In Experiment 4, participants who imagined receiving positive regard from their partners reported fewer death-related thoughts than did participants who imagined not receiving positive regard from their partner, as Cox and Arndt predicted. This main effect was qualified by an interaction effect: When participants visualized not receiving positive regard from their relationship partners, they reported a higher number of death-related thoughts after mortality salience than after dental pain, but this difference did not occur for participants who visualized receiving positive regard from their partners. This interaction is precisely what Cox and Arndt predicted.

So What?

Cox and Arndt's (2012) first four experiments pack quite a punch. First, they demonstrated that people exaggerate perceived regard from their romantic partners, but do not exaggerate self-regard, following reminders of mortality. Evidently, following reminders of mortality, perceptions of partner regard are more malleable than self-perceptions in that only perceived partner regard is exaggerated after mortality salience. Cox and Arndt then demonstrated that exaggerations of perceived regard occur for a romantic partner but not for just anyone. Apparently, an average person's regard does not serve the same function as a romantic partner's regard. An average person does not know us as well, or have the same emotional significance, as a romantic partner does. Thus, a romantic partner's regard is more meaningful, desirable, and likely to offset reminders of death. Cox and Arndt then demonstrated that the capacity for relationships to serve as a source of existential protection depends on the amount of positive regard they perceive from those partners. That is, positive regard is a demonstrated mediator of the link between mortality salience and commitment to a romantic partner. (Note, however, that perceived regard is *a* mediator, not necessarily *the* one and only mediator.) Finally, Cox and Arndt found support for their claim that the function of perceived regard following mortality salience is that it reduces death-thought accessibility. When one is reminded of death and then imagines a time when a romantic partner regarded them positively, they end up thinking less about death, compared to when they imagine not receiving a partner's positive regard. The love, trust, and commitment of others serve to distract and protect us from the terror of death.

Granted, people pursue close relationships for various reasons. Relationships provide emotional, informational, and practical support. They also provide meaning and value. Furthermore, they provide an opportunity to love and nurture. In general, close and romantic relationships contribute to our physical and psychological health. Cox and Arndt's study makes clear yet another benefit provided by relationships: When they are a source of perceived positive regard, they offer protection against death terror.

Additionally, TMT serves as a personality theory as well as a social psychological theory. Individuals vary in terms of their *attachment styles*, which have been found to *moderate* (increase or decrease the size of) the link between mortality salience and relationship seeking (Cox & Arndt, 2012, Experiment 7; Taubman-Ben-Ari, Findler, & Mikulincer, 2002). Individuals also vary in terms of how much they base their *self-esteem* on close relationships (Cox & Arndt, 2012, Experiments 5 and 6), which might explain varying effects of close relationships on terror management. Personality may also come into play in terms of how each person uniquely responds to the threat of death. In this regard, Niemiec et al. (2010) found that individuals who were more *mindful* wrote about their death for a longer period of time and were less likely to suppress death-related thoughts than individuals who were less mindful. Also, Kesebir (2014) found that *humility* (accepting oneself and one's life without illusions) can buffer death anxiety. Less humble people tend to respond to reminders of death with increased fear. Also, *priming* humility (making it more mentally accessible) reduces death anxiety relative to priming pride. These and several related findings led Kesebir (2014) to conclude that, "the dark side of death anxiety is brought about by a noisy ego only and not by a quiet ego, revealing self-transcendence as a sturdier, healthier anxiety buffer than self-enhancement" (p. 610). Finally, certain profound experiences may also buffer death anxiety. For example, *near-death experiences* can also counteract death anxiety (Pyszczynski, Greenberg, Solomon, Arndt, & Schimel, 2003).

Afterthoughts

Contemplating death may not be all bad, despite the anxiety, even terror, it may arouse. Arguably, giving conscious attention to death can be constructive and healthy. For example, recognizing that one's days are numbered can promote a more deliberate lifestyle. It can also provoke one to reflect more deeply on the meaning of life. Moreover, acknowledging one's fleeting existence can put daily inconveniences and problems into perspective. In general, reflecting on death can enhance gratitude—it can remind one to appreciate life as a limited resource (Frias, Watkins, Webber, & Froh, 2011).

This is a macabre chapter, given how frequently "death" has been mentioned in it. Indeed, this chapter is an unintended mortality salience manipulation, one that is potentially disturbing. As such, it may prompt a host of coping mechanisms: embracing reassuring worldviews, favoring ingroups and derogating outgroups, seeking to bolster one's self-esteem, and finding refuge in loving relationships. To lighten the mood, we dare to introduce a bit of gallows humor. Like almost anything, death can be funny. It often feels good to cathartically release pent up death anxiety in playful and socially acceptable ways. (Sigmund Freud, in his *Jokes and their Relation to the Unconscious* [1960], made this claim with regard to sexual and aggressive impulses.) In fact, death jokes are plentiful. Here are a few:

"'What's the death rate around here?' 'Same as everywhere else—one per person.'"

"When I die, I'm leaving my body to science fiction."

"The biggest downside of sudden unexpected death is being unable to delete your Internet search history."

"A doctor pulls the bed sheet over the face of one of his patients. He turns to the nurse and says, 'Well look on the bright side. At least he's stable.'"

"A son is discussing funeral arrangements with his dying mother. 'Would you like to be buried or cremated?' asks the son. The mother replies, 'I don't know. Surprise me.'"

"A man came home forlorn from his doctor's visit. His wife asked why. He replied, 'The doc told me I'd have to take a tablet every day for the rest of my life!' She consoled him, 'That's not so bad, is it?' He countered, 'He only gave me five tablets!'"

And finally, from celebrated American actor and director, Woody Allen: "I'm not afraid to die. I just don't want to be there when it happens."

Revelation

The certainty of death is a major source of terror in life. While this terror can be moderated by one's personality (attachment style, self-esteem, worldview, mindfulness, humility, and more), it is lessened by the positive regard of loved ones.

What Do You Think?

Some people claim that death threatens to make life meaningless. However, could it be the other way around? If we lived forever, and everything was permanent, could anything become precious to us? Would eternity make us infinitely complacent? Also, how you and others close to you view death and cope with the inevitability of death?

Chapter Reference

Cox, C. R., & Arndt, J. (2012). How sweet it is to be loved by you: The role of perceived regard in the terror management of close relationships. *Journal of Personality and Social Psychology*, *102*, 616–632.

Other References

Arndt, J., Schimel, J., & Goldberg, J. L. (2003). Death can be good for your health: Fitness intentions as a proximal and distal defense against mortality salience. *Journal of Applied Social Psychology*, *33*, 1726–1746.

Baron, R. M., & Kenny, D. A. (1986). The moderator/mediator variable distinction in social psychological research: Conceptual, strategic, and statistical considerations. *Journal of Personality and Social Psychology*, *51*, 1173–1182.

Becker, E. (1997). *The denial of death*. New York: Free Press.

Cooley, C. H. (1902). *Human nature and the social order*. New York: Scribners.

Cox, C. R., Arndt, J., Pyszczynski, T., Greenberg, J., Abdollahi, A., & Solomon, S. (2008). Terror management and adult's attachment to their parents. *Journal of Personality and Social Psychology*, *94*, 696–717.

Dechesne, M., Pyszczynski, T., Arndt, J., Ranson, S., Sheldon, K. M., van Knippenberg, A., & Janssen, J. (2003). Literal and symbolic immortality: The effect of evidence of literal immortality on self-esteem striving in response to mortality salience. *Journal of Personality and Social Psychology*, *84*, 722–737.

Florian, V., Mikulincer, M., & Hirschberger, G. (2002). The anxiety-buffering function of close relationships: Evidence that relationship commitment acts as a terror management mechanism. *Journal of Personality and Social Psychology*, *82*, 527–542.

Freud, S. (1960). *Jokes and their relation to the unconscious* (J. Strachey, Trans.). New York: W. W. Norton. (Original work published 1905.)

Frias, A., Watkins, P. C., Webber, A. C., & Froh, J. J. (2011). Death and gratitude: Death reflection enhances gratitude. *Journal of Positive Psychology*, *6*, 154–162.

Gailliot, M., Stillman, T. F., Schmeichel, B. J., Maner, J. K., & Plant, E. A. (2014). Mortality salience increases adherence to salient norms and values. *Personality and Social Psychology Bulletin*, *40*, 289–300.

Greenberg, J., Pyszczynski, T., Solomon, S., Simon, L., & Breus, M. (1994). Role of consciousness and accessibility of death-related thoughts in mortality salience effects. *Journal of Personality and Social Psychology*, *67*, 627–637.

Greenberg, J., Solomon, S., & Arndt, J. (2008). A basic but uniquely human motivation: Terror management. In J. Shah (Ed.), *Handbook of motivation science* (pp. 114–134). New York: Guilford Press.

Harmon-Jones, E., Simon, L., Greenberg, J., Pyszczynski, T., Solomon, S., & McGregor, H. (1997). Terror management theory and self-esteem: Evidence that increased self-esteem reduces mortality salience effects. *Journal of Personality and Social Psychology, 72*, 24–26.

Kesebir, P. (2014). A quiet ego quiets death anxiety: Humility as an existential buffer. *Journal of Personality and Social Psychology, 106*, 610–623.

Kosloff, S., Greenberg, J., Sullivan, D., & Weiss, D. (2010). Of trophies and pillars: Exploring the terror management functions of short-term and long-term relationship partners. *Personality and Social Psychology Bulletin, 36*, 1037–1051.

Landau, M. J., Solomon, S., Greenberg, J., Cohen, F., Pyszczynski, T., Arndt, J., Miller, C. H., Ogilvie, D. M., & Cook, A. (2004). Deliver us from evil: The effects of mortality salience and reminders of 9/11 on support for President George W. Bush. *Personality and Social Psychology Bulletin, 30*, 1136–1150.

Mikulincer, M., Florian, V., Birnbaum, G., & Malishevich, S. (2002). The death-anxiety buffering function of close relationships: Exploring the effects of separation reminders on death-thought accessibility. *Personality and Social Psychology Bulletin, 28*, 287–299.

Mikulincer, M., Florian, V., & Hirshberger, G. (2003). The existential function of close relationships: Introducing death into the science of love. *Personality and Social Psychology Bulletin, 28*, 287–299.

Niemiec, C. P., Brown, K. W., Kashdan, T. B., Cozzolino, P. J., Breen W. E., Levesque-Bristol, C., & Ryan, R. M. (2010). Being present in the face of existential threat: The role of trait mindfulness in reducing defensive responses to mortality salience. *Journal of Personality and Social Psychology, 99*, 344–365.

Pyszczynski, T. A., Greenberg, J., Solomon, S., Arndt, J., & Schimel, J. (2003). *In the wake of 911: The psychology of terror.* New York: American Psychological Association.

Pyszczynski, T. A., Greenberg, J., Solomon, S., Arndt, J., & Schimel, J. (2004). Why do people need self-esteem? A theoretical and empirical review. *Psychological Bulletin, 130*, 435–468.

Solomon, S., Greenberg, J., & Pyszczynski, T. (1991). Terror management theory of self-esteem. In C. R. Snyder & D. Forsyth (Eds.), *Handbook of social and clinical psychology: The health perspective* (pp. 21–40). New York: Pergamon Press.

Strachman, A., & Schimel, J. (2006). Terror management and close relationships: Evidence that mortality salience reduces commitment among partners with different worldviews. *Journal of Social and Personal Relationships, 23*, 965–978.

Taubman-Ben-Ari, O., Findler, L., & Mikulincer, M. (2002). The effects of mortality salience on relationship strivings and beliefs: The moderating role of attachment style. *British Journal of Social Psychology, 41*, 419–441.

Wisman, A., & Goldenberg, J. L. (2005). From the grave to the cradle: Evidence that mortality salience engenders a desire for offspring. *Journal of Personality and Social Psychology, 89*, 46–61.

More to Explore

Solomon, S., Greenberg, J., & Pyszczynski, T. (2015). *The worm at the core: On the role of death in life.* New York: Random House.

28 Punishing Perpetrators
Motivated Belief in Free Will

"The conundrum of free will and destiny has always kept me dangling."
—William Shatner (1931–), Canadian actor, a.k.a. Captain James T. Kirk

Background

An annoying commercial comes on the radio. So you turn it off. Simple enough, right? But probe deeper: Was your action freely chosen, or was it just an automatic reaction to the radio chatter? Or a friend sends you a text message. But you're busy and don't feel like texting back. So you leave him hanging. Could you ever have acted any differently, under exactly the same set of circumstances? Or, as a college sophomore, you haven't yet declared a major and are unsure of your future career. Then, while taking a psychology course, you have an epiphany: to major in psychology, attend graduate school, and become an experimental social psychologist! What role has *free will* played in this life-changing decision? Maybe it played *no* role—it was simply your destiny. A final scenario: At 90 years of age, you reflect on your extensive past. It is full of twists and turns—some fortunate, others regrettable. You consider some of the highlights: who you married, your midlife career change, your donation of a windfall to charity. Did you freely steer yourself through life, or was everything that happened pre-determined and inevitable? If you're not sure, join the club. The issue of *free will* versus *determinism* perplexes many people (including Captain Kirk) and has been hotly debated by philosophers for thousands of years without resolution.

Whatever the truth is, most people believe in free will (Nahmias, Morris, Nadelhoffer, & Turner, 2005). That is, most of us believe that we consciously control our more important decisions and behaviors. We feel that we choose our actions, whatever has happened before. We are, in our minds, the shapers of our own destiny. And we have the same impression when we look at others. For example, the perception that behavior is unconstrained prompts people to infer that free will exists (Nichols, 2004). A criminal, while locked up, commits no crime; once released, however, he reoffends. A simple observation suggests that he commits crimes of his own free will—that he is the sole author of his actions. Indeed, the entire criminal justice system, which metes out punishments to offenders, arguably presumes free will. The bottom line: Whether we look inward or outward, free will seems like commonsense.

But reflection tells a different story. Suppose *nothing* caused what we do. Wouldn't our behavior then be completely chaotic and unpredictable? However, free will doesn't mean that our behavior is without rhyme or reason: It only means that we somehow sidestep the past when we act in the present. Being "free" does not mean being "crazy": It means being at liberty to make rational choices. The difficulty, however, is coming up with a coherent account of free will that can explain how our behavior is, at the same time, not a product of the past, yet not a completely chaotic affair. For many, there are only two options: *determinism* or *randomness*.

Determinism says that everything that happens in the world is the necessary result of preexisting circumstances, in a manner described by universal laws and principles. Every event—chemical, physical, biological, psychological, social—has one or more causes. Such causes *explain* the event. There is always only one way things can turn out, even if we can imagine possible alternatives (given that what we imagine is itself determined). Moreover, if we could fully understand all preexisting occurrences—from the microscopic to the cosmic—then we could accurately predict all subsequent occurrences. According to determinism, then, all events in the universe, including human events, are nestled within an infinitely complex web of cause-and-effect relationships. Science, including social psychology, seeks to identify those relationships. (True, physics posits the existence of randomness on a quantum scale. However, this still cancels on an everyday scale. So, scientists still concern themselves with causes.) Determinism holds that free will is an illusion; acts only seem freely chosen due to ignorance about their causes.

It may be possible to strike a compromise by claiming that all actions are determined only in the sense that they are *influenced* (made more or less likely) by other events. One action may be more likely than another action, but both are still possible. True, most human thoughts and behaviors are the result of a confluence of both internal and external factors. Psychology seeks to identify as many of those factors as possible. But even if an act is heavily determined, there still may be some enclave of free will in a person that is inviolable. There may be some psychological space from which one simply chooses, even overriding a host of potent forces. On this view, when an act is caused by physical force, whether physiological or environmental, it is determined; but when it is caused by one's choice, it is free. However, this may all be wishful thinking, taking advantage of our ignorance of subtle causes.

What do learned philosophers say? Well, they take every possible position on this issue! Existentialists view freedom of will as a core feature of human nature. Sartre (1946/2007), for example, asserts that the essence of a person lies in the free choices that he or she makes. Free will not only exists, but it is unavoidable: "Man is condemned to be free" (p. 29). Sartre championed the idea that we are free to create ourselves in whatever way we wish, and must accept the responsibility, burden, and anguish of doing so. At the opposite extreme are the many philosophers—perhaps the majority today—who side with determinism. But even they express different shades of opinion. For example, philosophers still disagree over whether a deterministic universe rules out free will. The stubborn *incompatibilists* (or "hard" determinists) say yes; the flexible *compatiblists* (or "soft" determinists) say no. A compatibilist (e.g., Harris, 2012) might assert, for example, that as long as you are *not being forced* to do something against your will, you can still exercise free will, even if all your behavior is ultimately caused. However, the incompatibilist (e.g., Honderich, 2002) sees such subtlety as a sell-out. We are really not free, and that means abandoning some of our deepest intuitions and hopes about life.

Whether or not free will exists seems to have profound consequences for whether people should be blamed or punished for committing crimes. Think about it: If a particular criminal act is not freely chosen, then the person who performs it arguably cannot be responsible for it. And if they cannot be responsible for it, then it makes little sense to punish him or her, at least by way of retribution. Free will is almost always viewed as a prerequisite for moral responsibility and for righteous punishment. If someone is temporarily insane, cognitively challenged, or too young to know better, we tend not to morally condemn him or her. We are inclined to punish someone if we believe that he or she *should* have acted otherwise, because, more fundamentally, we believe that he or she *could* have acted otherwise. Thus, *attributions* of free will are relevant to our view of others' behaviors, especially their antisocial behaviors. Belief in moral agency and responsibility, predicated on the existence of free will, helps to justify punishment. (One could argue—as a compatibilist might—that society needs protection from criminals *regardless* of whether they possess or lack free will. If so, then *holding* criminals responsible, whether deservedly or undeservedly, might be justified solely on the grounds of deterrence. On this view, the criminal justice system serves as a kind of fancy obedience training school.)

Forgive us if we're leading you on a wild goose chase! The present chapter is not about research that resolves this controversial issue of free will versus determinism. Instead, it explores some of the potential causes of *belief* in free will. In particular, Clark et al. (2014) tested the interesting claim that the widespread belief in free will is *motivated*. People believe in it, at least partly, because they *want* to. Why? Clark and his colleagues wondered whether a specific social psychological factor might be responsible: the desire to see immoral or criminal behavior punished. This tendency, they also speculated, might have evolved as a way of inducing people to protect society, by nixing the ne'er-do-wells. Clark and his colleagues took their cue from the philosopher Nietzsche (1889/1954), a strict determinist: "Today we no longer have pity for the concept of 'free will': we know only too well what it is—the foulest of all theologians' artifices, aimed at making mankind 'responsible' in their sense . . . Whenever responsibilities are sought, it is usually *the instinct of wanting to judge and punish* which is at work" (cited in Clark and others, 2014, p. 499 [italics added]). Thus, Clark and his colleagues sought to investigate whether belief in free will might be both motivated and functional, rather than being based solely on personal introspection or logical arguments.

What They Did/What They Found

Clark and his colleagues (2014) conducted five studies: four experiments and one *archival* study (in which data is collected from an existing database). All five studies tested the hypothesis that belief in free will stems, at least in part, from a desire to hold people morally responsible for their wrongdoings. Because we will present the main details of all five studies, we will depart from our format of separating methods and results into two sections.

In the first study, 171 participants were told that the study was concerned with *memory* (a *cover story* designed to disguise its true purpose). Participants were randomly assigned to read either (a) a newspaper article about a corrupt judge, who was caught jailing children in order to receive kickbacks from a private juvenile detention center, or (b) an article about a search for a new school superintendent (both news articles were based on real events). After reading either article, participants responded to a number of personality scales, including the *Free-Will and Determinism Scale* (Paulus & Carey, 2011) containing statements such as "people have complete free will" and "strength of mind can always overcome the body's desires." Clark and his colleagues sought to determine whether participants would report greater belief in free will after exposure to an immoral act than after exposure to a morally neutral act. They did: Participants who read about the scandalous judge reported significantly higher levels of belief in free will than did participants who read about the prosaic job search. Keep in mind that participants were randomly assigned to the two conditions. Simply reading one or the other article affected self-reported belief in free will (Figure 28).

Study 2 also examined whether prior exposure to an immoral behavior would amplify belief in free will. Ninety-five participants were randomly assigned to read a hypothetical account in which a man robs a home and sells the goods on eBay (an immoral behavior) or in which a man removes aluminum cans from a recycling bin and sells them to a recycling company (a morally neutral behavior). After reading either scenario, participants rated whether the behavior was freely chosen, whether the perpetrator could have made other choices, whether the perpetrator exercised his own free will, and how much he should be punished. Participants also rated their own beliefs about free will on the *Free-Will and Determinism Scale* used in the first study. Clark and his colleagues found that participants who read about the robber expressed greater belief in free will than did participants who read about the aluminum can forager. The same difference was found for specific ratings: The robber was seen as possessing more free will, and as having more options, than was the forager. Also, ratings of wanting to punish the robber were predictably higher than ratings of wanting to punish the forager. Finally, Clark and his colleagues showed

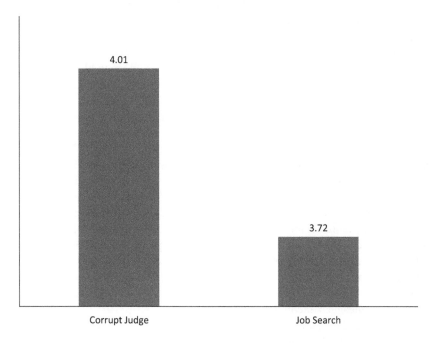

Figure 28 Self-reported belief in free will after reading about a corrupt judge or a job search

that participants' desire to punish the perpetrator likely *mediated* (was a bridge between) the effect of immoral behavior on belief in free will. (See Chapter 27 for more details on the logic of mediation.) Clark and his colleagues were beginning to build a case for their theoretical model of motivated belief in free will.

Study 3 was conducted outside of the laboratory. Two days after taking a midterm exam, 277 undergraduates received one of three emails from their professor. The one email stated that a cheat sheet was found in the classroom after the exam but that the cheater had not been identified. The second email stated that a cheat sheet was found and the cheater had already been identified and duly punished. The third email stated that recipients would be engaging in an activity in the next class (this was the *control* condition). In all three conditions, participants were asked to complete an attached survey that would supposedly facilitate a discussion in the next class. The survey included the same measure of belief in free will that was included in the first two studies, along with a question about how severely any student found using a cheat sheet should be punished (from *not at all* to *very severely* on a 5-point scale) and a question about the appropriate punishment for someone caught using a cheat sheet on an exam (from *no punishment* to *fail the class and be put on academic suspension from the University* on a 6-point scale). Participants in the two cheater conditions gave higher punishment ratings than did participants in the control condition (differences between the two cheater groups were not significant). Also, participants in the two cheater conditions reported believing in free will more than did participants in the control condition (again, differences between the two cheater conditions were not significant). Finally, as in Study 2, a desire to punish apparently mediated the influence of the experimental manipulations on belief in free will. Thus, in a natural setting, participants who learned that a fellow classmate had engaged in cheating (whether the classmate was identified and punished or not) reported believing more in free will than did participants who were simply notified about an upcoming class exercise. And, as found previously, an increased desire to punish linked exposure to an immoral behavior to an increased belief in free will. Support for Clark and his colleagues' theoretical model continued to grow.

In the first three studies, belief in free will was measured directly via Paulus and Carey's (2011) *Free-Will and Determinism Scale*. However, social psychologists like to vary how they measure a particular variable in order to ensure that their findings are not due to the idiosyncrasies of a single measure (see the Introduction to this book). Thus, in Study 4, Clark and his colleagues used an indirect measure of belief in free will that involved having participants state their degree of agreement with a passage that called free will into question on the basis of recent neuroscientific findings. In this study, 213 participants read about a man who robbed a home or about a man who removed items from an outside recycle bin, as in Study 2. After being told that the issue of the existence of free will was currently up for debate in psychology, participants were exposed to an anti-free will passage and asked to evaluate its merits. For example, how convinced were they by the passage? Or, did they think that the research cited should receive more funding? Ratings ranged from *not at all* to *extremely* on a 9-point scale. As predicted, participants rated the anti-free will passage more negatively after they had read about the home robbery than after they had read about the aluminum can forage. Thus, participants were more inclined to defend the idea of free will after considering an immoral act than after considering a morally neutral act. Being reminded of immoral behavior aroused a greater desire to punish the perpetrator, and such punishment makes more sense if one believes in free will. Study 4 thus provided further evidence for Clark and his colleagues' theoretical model.

In Study 5, Clark and his colleagues sought a much broader demonstration of the link between witnessing others' wrongful actions and belief in free will. For each of 74 countries, they obtained per capita homicide rates (from the United Nations Office on Drug and Crimes, 2011) and data on belief in free will (from the World Values Survey Association, 2009). They found that countries with higher homicide rates showed stronger average belief in free will. An index of other crimes—robbery, rape, kidnapping, assault, theft, child sexual assault, burglary, auto theft, and human trafficking—showed the same pattern of results. Also, this link between prevailing crime rates and belief in free will occurred even after *controlling* for (statistically adjusting the links in view of their overlap with) such variables as gross national product per capita, government type, degree of political freedom, and level of education. Such real-world findings, although not quite as conclusive as experimental research, are nonetheless consistent with Clark and his colleagues' claim that "belief in free will is stimulated in part by exposure to others' harmful behaviors and the associated impulse to punish" (p. 508).

So What?

Clark and his colleagues' (2014) studies build nicely upon one another. They first established a basic link: People believe more in free will after considering another person's immoral behavior. They then demonstrated that this greater belief in free will is motivated by the desire to punish. They then replicated this effect (and its mediation by the desire to punish) in a field experiment, in which participants received an email from their professor regarding either an episode of academic cheating or an upcoming classroom activity. They then again replicated this effect using an indirect measure of belief in free will, namely, how much one disagrees with an anti-free will passage. Finally, they found that, across 74 nations, higher rates of criminal offenses are associated with stronger belief in free will (the flip side is that citizens of countries with lower crime rates tend to believe less in free will).

Consider for a moment the comprehensiveness, and indeed sophistication, of the research conducted by Clark and his colleagues. Their studies included instances of corruption, robbery, and academic cheating, not just a single type of behavior. Free will beliefs were manipulated via hypothetical as well as real misdeeds, and in the laboratory as well as in the field. Experimental manipulations were found to affect beliefs about free will with regard to a specific person as well as people in general. Exposure to someone's misconduct not only increased belief in free will but also aroused skepticism toward anti-free will research. Also, a correlation between crime and belief in free will was found at a national level. Furthermore, mediation analyses in two separate studies suggested that the link between moral misdeeds and belief in free will was due to a motivation to punish. Taken together, Clark and his colleagues' studies employed the best of social psychological research techniques. The sheer *convergence* of findings makes it unlikely that they are collectively the accidental result of special features of this or that study. Rather the findings look general. Superb research!

Clark and his colleagues (2014) thus garnered strong empirical evidence for their claim that "exposure to immoral acts evokes a heightened sense that behaviors are freely chosen and thus subject to moral evaluation" (p. 508). Not only would free will, if it exists, *justify* the condemnation and punishment of wrongdoers, but the desire to condemn and punish wrongdoers, in itself, evidently *prompts* greater belief in free will. Clark and his colleagues thereby demonstrated that belief in free will derives from more than just intuitive insight, or a dispassionate appraisal of the philosophical pros and cons. It is not completely rational. In their words: "The core of our argument is that this subjective experience of free will gains motivational reinforcement by facilitating the assignment of moral responsibility, which in turn supports our crucial social task of punishing individuals who act in ways that are detrimental to cohesive group functioning" (p. 509). Clark and his colleagues were able to provide perhaps the first scientific demonstration that belief in free will is *malleable*: It can be influenced by both situational factors (others' immoral behaviors) and psychological motives (the desire to punish such behaviors). Moreover, their research fits with an impressive body of other research on how beliefs can be psychologically motivated (see, e.g., Chapters 2, 15, 16, 17, and 21).

Afterthoughts

Clark and his colleagues' (2014) research neither proves nor disproves the existence of free will. But it does provide insights into the psychology of belief in free will. These insights are set against a backdrop of progress in allied areas of psychology. We briefly consider three such areas: theories of personality, the neuroscience of free will, and research on vicarious agency.

Some of the earliest psychologists—many of them personality theorists—addressed the issue of free will versus determinism, often siding strongly with one or the other. Freud (1920) championed *psychic determinism*, the idea that thoughts and behaviors arise from preexisting unconscious mental states. Everything from neurotic symptoms and baffling dreams to career choices and artistic masterpieces is just the result of underlying instincts, anxieties, and wishes—and often of an exceedingly naughty nature. Ideas don't just pop into a person's head willy-nilly (no pun intended!). There is always a cause at work, however hard it may be to discover. Fromm (1941)—a neo-Freudian who emphasized unconscious existential and economic motives— begged to differ. Echoing Sartre, he claimed that we do possess free will, but that we tend to flee from the freedom it offers, not wanting to brave challenging implications. Erikson (1968) claimed that free will develops over the life span, but especially during the *terrible twos* (when toddlers begin to assert their will through temper tantrums) and adolescence (when teenagers rebel against parents and authority figures). In contrast, Watson (1930)—perhaps emboldened by his success in conditioning fear in an infant (you may be familiar with his infamous "Little Albert" study)—made *environmental determinism* a key feature of his *behaviorism*. Skinner (1971)—a no less radical behaviorist, and staunch proponent of *behavior modification* (manipulating the environment to control behavior)—claimed that the entrenched belief in free will hinders scientific efforts to build a more functional and happier society. Wilson (1978)—a renowned sociobiologist, famous for his work with ants, another high social species—argued that behavior can be largely understood as the product of natural selection over eons of time (no mention of free will). In contrast, Maslow (1943) and Rogers (1951)—two well-known humanistic psychologists—balked at both Freudian psychoanalysis and behaviorism, and emphasized instead the vital role of free will in a person's quest for self-actualization. One common problem of many of these approaches, however, is that they are often difficult to translate into hypotheses that can be empirically tested.

Neuroscientists (e.g., Harris, 2012) tend to claim that the brain determines behavior and that free will is nothing more than an illusion. Mind, consciousness, and the sense of personal free will are nothing but an *epiphenomenon* (incidental by-product) of biochemical brain processes—just as heartbeats are nothing but epiphenomena of the heart's pumping blood. The mind is simply what the brain does, and exerts no causal effects of its own. All of our presumed decisions are triggered by neural activity occurring outside of conscious awareness. The brain is not free; there is nothing in the brain that chooses. The brain is no more free that any other organ of the body. According to Harris (2011), intention does not initiate action: "Thoughts simply arise in the brain" (p. 112).

Is this just idle opinion? Perhaps not. In the mid-1980s, Libet (1985) conducted a series of subtle experiments, the implications of which are still being debated. The upshot is that distinct patterns of brain activation—a so-called "readiness potential"—seems to precede the self-reported intention to perform a simple bodily movement, such as flexing one's wrist. Thus, the brain seems to "initiate" a movement first, with the person only becoming consciously aware of the "decision" a few hundred milliseconds later (or, accordingly to Soon, Brass, Heinze, and Haynes, 2008, as much as 10 seconds later!). Nonetheless, once aware of the brain's action, the conscious mind may still have time to veto the imminent movement. (Libet himself believed this, and rather cleverly called it "free won't"!). That is, a thought or behavior occurs in two stages, the first being determined, and the second being freely chosen. Still, many neuroscientists contend that such experiments present a serious empirical challenge to claims that free will exists. One counterargument would be that the decision to flex one's wrist is inconsequential, not being based on reasons; instead, people rely on an arbitrary fleeting impulse to perform it, which unsurprisingly has a physiological basis. (See Mele, 2014, for further criticisms.)

In a clever study about what people *believe* about such experiments, Nahmias, Shepard, and Reuter (2014) told participants about a new wearable brain imaging cap that allows neuroscientists to predict all of a person's decisions (no such cap, as yet, actually exists). Participants read about a woman who wore the cap for a month, supposedly allowing others to predict all of her decisions. Eighty percent of the participants reported that such technology is plausible but that it does not necessarily disprove free will. However, participants reported that, if such a brain cap could be used to *manipulate* a person's decisions, then, yes, belief in the existence of free will would suffer a convincing blow. (On the plus side, it would open up a new world of research in experimental social psychology!)

If free will is an illusion, then it amounts to mistaken *judgment* about what causes one's actions. Those actions get falsely *attributed* to oneself rather than to the real cause, which ultimately lies either in the brain or in the environment. If so, then psychologists might conceivably study that process of judgment and attribution, and build a testable model of it. According to Wegner (2002), the illusion of conscious agency derives from the fact that, when we act, we typically have a thought that (a) precedes the act, (b) corresponds to the act, and (c) seems sufficient to typically explain the act, given that no obvious alternative explanations are available. For example, when I intend to make a cup of coffee, (a) I think "Now I'll make a cup of coffee" *before* I do so, (b) the thought *matches* the action I subsequently perform, and (c) no other *factor* is present to explain why the coffee gets made. However, if I had the thought only after I made the coffee, or if I had the non-corresponding thought "Now I'll make some tea," or if a robot was guiding my hands while I made coffee, I might conclude that I was *not* making coffee of my own free will. A virtue of this account is that it is testable: One might succeed in getting people to deny performing an action they did physically perform, or in claiming they performed actions they did not physically perform, by subtly manipulating their judgments and attributions.

Wegner and colleagues (Wegner 2003; Wegner, Sparrow, & Winerman, 2004; Wegner & Wheatley, 1999; see also Pronin, Wegner, McCarthy, & Rodriguez, 2006) have conducted a number of fascinating studies to do just this. In one study (Wegner et al., 2004), participants watched someone else shooting basketballs. However, if they visualized the peer's success in shooting a hoop beforehand, then the participants were more likely to believe that they had caused it. Thus, Wegner was able to demonstrate a false sense of *vicarious agency*—in which one believes that he or she can influence events that are performed by someone else. In another study in the same vein (Wegner, 2003), participants watched themselves in a mirror while another person—behind them and hidden from view—extended his hands forward on each side where the participant's hands would normally appear. The hands then performed various movements. When participants could hear instructions that preceded and matched each movement, they reported the sense that they were controlling the hands. Thus, people mistaken judged that they had a hand in actions others had in fact physically performed. In addition, other empirical evidence shows that the opposite can also occur: People can mistakenly judge that they do *not* have a hand in the action that they physically perform (Wegner, 2002). This makes "spooky" phenomena—like the planchette on a Ouija board spelling out words under the apparent influence of some alien spirit—easier to understand. The individual is actually spelling out the words, but failing to attribute the action to him or herself, in an ambiguous situation.

Could psychology ever garner sufficient empirical support for the existence of free will or determinism? Just as the theory of evolution has increasingly become a scientific fact, we may one day see the emergence of either free will or strict determinism as a scientific fact. For now, however, we are excited by progress in our understanding of the social psychological aspects of belief in free will. Why is belief in free will so pervasive and often so vigorously defended? Clark and his colleagues (2014) have provided at least one important answer: Belief in free will is psychologically and socially functional; it justifies our desire and efforts to punish those who disturb the social order with their immoral or criminal behaviors.

Revelation

Whether or not free will exists, *belief* in free will serves two important functions: It allows society to hold others morally responsible and to justify punishing criminals.

What Do You Think?

Suppose scientists discovered incontrovertible evidence that free will does *not* exist. Would it affect how society operates? For example, would criminals receive sentences that were more lenient, stricter, or the same? And how would you personally feel about being metaphysically *unfree*?

Chapter Reference

Clark, C. J., Luguri, J. B., Ditto, P. H., Knobe, J., Shariff, A. F., & Baumeister, R. F. (2014). Free to punish: A motivated account of free will belief. *Journal of Personality and Social Psychology, 106*, 501–513.

Other References

Erikson, E. (1968). *Identity: Youth and crisis*. New York: W. W. Norton Company.

Freud, S. (1920). *A general introduction to psychoanalysis* (G. Stanley Hall, Trans.). New York: Boni and Liveright.

Fromm, E. (1941). *Escape from freedom*. New York: Holt, Rinehart and Winston.

Harris, S. (2011). *The moral landscape*. New York: Free Press.

Harris, S. (2012). *Free will*. New York: Free Press.

Honderich, T. (2002). *How free are you? The determinism problem* (2nd ed.). Oxford: Oxford University Press.

Libet, B. (1985). Unconscious cerebral initiation and the role of conscious will in voluntary action. *The Behavioral and Brain Sciences*, *8*, 529–566.

Maslow, A. H. (1943). A theory of human motivation. *Psychological Review*, *50*, 370–396.

Mele, A. R. (2014). *Free: Why science hasn't disproved free will*. Oxford: Oxford University Press.

Nahmias, E., Morris, S., Nadelhoffer, T., & Turner, J. (2005). Surveying freedom: Folk intuitions about free will and moral responsibility. *Philosophical Psychology*, *18*, 561–584.

Nahmias, E., Shepard, J., & Reuter, S. (2014). It's OK if "my brain made me do it": People's intuitions about free will and neuroscientific prediction. *Cognition*, *133*, 502–516.

Nichols, S. (2004). The folk psychology of free will: Fits and starts. *Mind and Language*, *19*, 473–502.

Nietzsche, F. (1954). *Twilight of the idols* (W. Kauffman, Trans.). New York: Penguin Books. (Original work published 1889).

Paulus, D. L., & Carey, J. M. (2011). The FAD-Plus: Measuring lay beliefs regarding free will and related constructs. *Journal of Personality Assessment*, *93*, 96–104.

Pronin, E., Wegner, D. M., McCarthy, K., & Rodriguez, S. (2006). Everyday magical powers: The role of apparent mental causation in the over-estimation of personal influence. *Journal of Personality and Social Psychology*, *91*, 218–231.

Rogers, C. (1951). *Client-centered therapy: Its current practice, implications and theory*. London: Constable.

Sartre, J. P. (2007). *Existentialism is a humanism* (C. Macomber, Trans.). New Haven, CT: Yale University Press. (Original work published in 1946).

Skinner, B. F. (1971). *Beyond freedom and dignity*. New York: Alfred A. Knopf, Inc.

Soon, C. S., Brass, M., Heinze, H. J., & Haynes, J. D. (2008). Unconscious determinants of free decisions in the human brain. *Nature Neuroscience*, *11*, 543–545.

United Nations Office on Drugs and Crime. (2011). *Crime and criminal justice statistics*. Retrieved by Clark et al. (2014) from www.unodc.org/unodc/en//data-and-analysis/statistics/crime.html

Watson, J. B. (1930). *Behaviorism* (rev. ed.). Chicago, IL: University of Chicago Press.

Wegner, D. (2002). *The illusion of conscious will*. Cambridge, MA: MIT Press.

Wegner, D. M. (2003). The mind's best trick: How we experience conscious will. *Trends in Cognitive Sciences*, *7*, 65–69.

Wegner, D. M., Sparrow, B., & Winerman, L. (2004). Vicarious agency: Experiencing control over the movement of others. *Journal of Personality and Social Psychology*, *86*, 838–848.

Wegner, D. M., & Wheatley, T. (1999). Apparent mental causation: Sources of the experience of free will. *American Psychologist*, *54*, 480–492.

Wilson, E. O. (1978). *On human nature*. Cambridge, MA: Harvard University Press.

World Values Survey Association. (2009). *World values survey*. Retrieved by Clark et al. (2014) from www.worldvauessurvey.org/

More to Explore

Sternberg, E. J. (2010). *My brain made me do it: The rise of neuroscience and the threat to moral responsibility*. Amherst, NY: Prometheus Books.

Revelations

Ubiquitous and irresistible norms govern social life. Groups exert tremendous normative influence over their members that only a few brave souls can defy.

If you wish to change somebody's opinion, subtly induce him or her to act at odds with it. This tactic works because people readily rationalize objectionable actions for which they feel responsible by adjusting their attitudes to match them.

When people voluntarily undergo an unpleasant experience to achieve something, they come to value that something more, not less. This helps explain why people become committed members of groups even when membership entails considerable initial sacrifice and offers scant subsequent reward.

The power of the situation can incline people to willingly obey authority figures, with the result that they sometimes commit the most heinous of acts.

The more witnesses there are to an emergency, the less likely it is that any one of them will help. This is because individuals are often not privy to others' reactions, or because they do not feel uniquely responsible for preventing tragic outcomes.

The mere presence of others enhances performance on simple tasks but impairs performance on complex tasks. This can occur even in the absence of complex mediating cognitions.

People readily categorize themselves into ingroups and outgroups. To bolster their self-esteem, they favor their ingroup, even when categorizations are based on contrived and trivial experimental manipulations.

Small, subtle, seemingly trivial situational variables often have a greater impact on behavior than do the personality variables that we more readily, but often mistakenly, regard as influential. Something as simple as time pressure can impact something as vital as compassionate behavior.

Receiving a reward for doing something makes people want to do it more. However, when the reward is withdrawn, people want to do it even less than they did before receiving the reward.

Our explanations of behaviors are often biased. We tend to attribute our positive behaviors to dispositional causes and our negative behaviors to situational causes, whereas we tend to make the opposite attributions when observing others' behaviors.

Groups and institutions we are socially connected to are part of our identity and impact our self-esteem. We personalize their successes and failures, trumpeting the former and dissociating ourselves from the latter.

Being immersed in a group can lead to heightened arousal, a sense of anonymity, reduced self-awareness, and the automatic modeling of others' behaviors. Such a state of deindividuation can result in unrestrained—often aggressive and destructive—behavior.

 How we feel about a person (or any other stimulus) is influenced by a host of factors, but most basically, it is governed by mere exposure. We tend to like people more the more often we encounter them.

 The fact that we are aware of our own beliefs, feelings, and desires does not automatically make us experts on where they come from. Introspection is an unreliable guide to how the mind works, reflecting cultural truisms rather than providing infallible insights.

 Although our expectations of people are based on their behavior, it is likewise true that their behavior is the result of our expectations. Simply believing that someone is attractive may lead to their actually being attractive.

 People deceive themselves by acting so as to create signs that everything is well even when they cannot make everything well. They then deny that they have acted in this way because admitting as much would imply that those signs are bogus.

 Our group loyalties and preconceptions cause us to perceive events and other stimuli in a biased manner. One consequence of this is that partisans on both sides of an issue tend to overestimate bias in media reports.

 When moved by empathy, people help not because they are motivated to avoid the guilt that would result from not helping, nor, it seems, for many other selfish reasons. Rather, they likely help with the ultimate goal of benefiting other people.

 To love a person means, among other things, to include that person in one's self. This involves perceiving, characterizing, and, critically, allocating resources to that person in much the same way one does one's self.

 Although commonsense suggests that we suspend belief or disbelief until after we have understood a message, research shows that, initially, belief accompanies understanding, and that doubt follows later only if mental resources and motivation are sufficient.

 Our intuitive theories about how things are subtly shape our memories of what has been. Thus, we unknowingly reconstruct the past in terms of the present rather than simply remembering the past in its original form.

 Attempts to bring about a desired mental state tend to backfire if people are distracted or preoccupied. Under such circumstances, they would be well advised to abandon the attempt, or, even better, to try not to bring about that mental state, as this will ironically tend to bring it about.

 Social psychologists use technical tools, such as the Implicit Association Test, to tell more about people than they are willing or able to say about themselves. The use of such tools can assist in the prediction of behavior.

 People avoid risks when they stand to gain, but take risks when they stand to lose. Consequently, how a choice is framed, in terms of loss or gain, can influence how people choose, over and above the objective consequences of choosing one way or the other.

 Social exclusion causes aggression. People ostracized by others are more likely to hurt those who offend them, and even those who do not.

- Although gossip is often condemned, it frequently serves a cathartic and prosocial function. Prosocial gossip relieves negative emotions that result from witnessing an antisocial act and protects others from victimization. It also functions to deter selfish, exploitative behaviors.

- The certainty of death is a major source of terror in life. While this terror can be moderated by one's personality (attachment style, self-esteem, worldview, mindfulness, humility, and more), it is lessened by the positive regard of loved ones.

- Whether or not free will exists, *belief* in free will serves two important functions: It allows society to hold others morally responsible and to justify punishing criminals.

Index